Microsoft®

UNDERSTANDING
IPv6

D1314750

Joseph Davies

PUBLISHED BY
Microsoft Press
A Division of Microsoft Corporation
One Microsoft Way
Redmond, Washington 98052-6399

Library of Congress Cataloging-in-Publication Data
Davies, Joseph.
       Understanding IPv6 / Joseph Davies.
           p. cm.
       Includes index.
       ISBN 0-7356-1245-5
       1. TCP/IP (Computer network protocol)   2. Internet.   I. Title.

   TK5105.585 .D38   2002
   004.62--dc21   2002029525

Printed and bound in the United States of America.

2 3 4 5 6 7 8 9   QWE   8 7 6 5 4 3

Distributed in Canada by H.B. Fenn and Company Ltd.

A CIP catalogue record for this book is available from the British Library.

Microsoft Press books are available through booksellers and distributors worldwide. For further informa-tion about international editions, contact your local Microsoft Corporation office or contact Microsoft Press International directly at fax (425) 936-7329. Visit our Web site at www.microsoft.com/mspress. Send comments to *mspinput@microsoft.com.*

Acquisitions Editors: Juliana Aldous Atkinson, Jeff Koch
Project Editor: Maureen Williams Zimmerman
Technical Editor: Jim Johnson

Body Part No. X08-04478

For Kara:

Domina mea, amata mea, vita mea.

Contents at a Glance

Table of Contents

Chapters

Appendixes

List of Figures

List of Tables

Preface

This book began in the spring of 1999, when I developed a set of slides and presented an "Introduction to IPv6" course at Bellevue Community College in Bellevue, Washington, to four students. Although the turnout was not what I expected, the time spent learning IPv6, creating the slide presentation, and presenting IPv6 technology to these curious students proved to be an invaluable experience and laid down a firm foundation for future endeavors.

The next steps in the evolution of this book came in the spring of 2000, when the Windows product team was adapting the Microsoft Research IPv6 protocol stack to a developer-preview version for Microsoft Windows XP. At the time, I was writing the product documentation for TCP/IP and insisted upon also writing the product documentation for IPv6. Along the way, I also wrote the "Introduction to IP version 6" white paper that is published on the Microsoft Windows IPv6 Web site (http://www.microsoft.com/ipv6), managed the documentation for Microsoft Windows 2000 IPv6 Technology Preview, wrote the initial drafts of the *Microsoft Windows .NET Server 2003 Resource Kit* chapters about IPv6, and generally inserted myself in any documentation task associated with IPv6.

During the Windows XP product cycle, it became clear that many in the Windows Networking group and beyond knew little about IPv6 and would need to be educated before they began to adapt their applications and components to use it. I took it upon myself as a special project to develop and deliver an "IPv6 Overview" internal course, with help on Windows Sockets from Tom Fout. This one-day course was taught to Microsoft software design engineers, software test engineers, program managers, and technical writers beginning in October of 2000.

My transition to a program manager for technical content development and my previous endeavors as co-author of *Microsoft Windows 2000 TCP/IP Protocols and Services Technical Reference* (Microsoft Press, ISBN 0-7356-0556-4) afforded me the time, focus, and experience to turn the "IPv6 Overview" courseware and numerous other white papers and articles about IPv6 into this book.

It has been a long road, filled with the normal triumphs and frustrations of writing any book about networking technology that is rapidly changing. It is my fervent hope that the work that I started in the spring of 1999 has culminated into a well-organized and readable text from which you can *learn and understand* the concepts, principles, and processes of IPv6.

—Joseph Davies

Acknowledgments

Writing a book such as this is never a solitary activity. I would like to thank David Clark and Juliana Aldous at Microsoft Press for initially agreeing to publish this book. I would also like to thank Maureen Zimmerman (senior editor at Microsoft Press), for providing firm yet flexible guidance and management of the manuscript creation process, Jim Johnson (technical editor), for doing a great job of finding the holes and inconsistencies, and Catherine Albano (copy editor), for smoothing the rough edges of my technical prose. On the production team, I would like to thank Brittney Corrigan-McElroy (senior project manager), Lucie Haskins (indexer), and Jason McAlexander and his team of illustrators.

Many people on the Windows Networking and Communications team were involved in verifying the technical accuracy of this book, including the following: Balash Akbari, Richard Draves, Sandeep Prabhu, Aaron Schrader, Art Shelest, Mohit Talwar, and Stewart Tansley. I would like to thank Laura Sheppard and David Mills, my managers when I was an online help writer, for the flexibility to create and deliver the courseware on which this book is based. I would also like to thank Tom Fout, my current manager, for the content in Appendix B and for making the completion of this book a priority among all my deliverables, nurturing it to its final conclusion.

There are three individuals to whom I would like to extend special thanks and recognition:

- **Dave Thaler**

  Dave is the development lead for the IPv6 protocol on the Windows Networking and Communications team and a walking encyclopedia of TCP/IP and IPv6 knowledge. I first met Dave when writing documentation for the Windows 2000 Routing and Remote Access service and, unlike many other developers, Dave actually took the time to review what I had written for technical accuracy, clarity, flow, and relevance. I have been fortunate to continue working with Dave all through the evolution of the IPv6 protocol for Windows XP and the Windows .NET Server 2003 family. I greatly value Dave's technical expertise and documentation insight.

- **Brian Zill**

  Brian is a software development engineer and a vital resource for developing the Microsoft implementation of IPv6. Richard Draves and Brian developed the original IPv6 protocol for Microsoft Research. I first began working with Brian when the Microsoft Research IPv6 stack was being ported to Windows XP. He has been an invaluable resource for in-depth technical information and as a reviewer of this book. I don't feel good about a chapter unless Brian has reviewed it. I greatly value Brian's technical expertise, ability to explain complicated concepts, and sense of humor.

■ **Chris Clements**

Chris is an editing lead for the Windows User Assistance team responsible for Help content in the Windows .NET Server 2003 family. Chris was my editor when I was a technical writer developing online help for Windows XP and the Windows .NET Server 2003 family. Many times Chris went above and beyond in editing not only the sizable volumes of help text I produced but also white papers, courseware, Web site text, and TechNet Cable Guy articles. Chris was the editor for the original "Introduction to IP Version 6" white paper and "IPv6 Overview" internal Microsoft training course on which this book is based. In short, Chris was my partner in the crusade to document IPv6 for Microsoft; the level of writing quality achieved in this book is a direct result of his efforts. I greatly value Chris's acute editorial expertise and friendship.

These gentlemen are three of Microsoft's finest. They epitomize and exemplify the highest standards of intelligence, dedication, and commitment to quality that make working at Microsoft such a rewarding experience. I consider it an honor and a privilege to have worked with them and hope to continue working with them in the future.

And lastly, I would like to express my thanks and appreciation to my wife, Kara, and daughter, Katie. Although not directly involved in the creation of this book, they make it all worthwhile.

Introduction

This book is a straightforward discussion of the concepts, principles, and processes of Internet Protocol version 6 (IPv6) and how IPv6 is supported by the Microsoft Windows .NET Server 2003 family of operating systems. It is primarily a discussion of protocols and processes rather than a discussion of planning, configuration, deployment, and management. It is also mostly about IPv6 rather than the specifics of the implementation for the Windows .NET Server 2003 family. Therefore, this book does not contain in-depth implementation details of the IPv6 protocol for the Windows .NET Server 2003 family, such as structures, tables, buffers, or coding logic. These details are highly guarded Microsoft intellectual property that is of interest only to a relative handful of software developers.

The purpose of this book is to provide an educational vehicle that will enable one to learn IPv6 to a fair technical depth—the terms, the addresses, the protocols, and the processes. This is not intended to be a breezy marketing overview of IPv6 and how it "provides integrated and interoperable technologies to enable exciting new scenarios for personal and enterprise computing." I will leave that type of documentation to those who are much better at it than I am. The bottom line is that I am a protocols and processes person. My main concern and interest is how the protocols work and what one sees on the wire (what packets are exchanged), and these topics comprise the bulk of this book.

NOTE:
The contents of this book reflect the Internet standards for IPv6 and the feature set of the IPv6 protocol for the Windows .NET Server 2003 family as of Release Candidate 1 (RC1) of the Windows .NET Server 2003 family. For updates to the information in this book that describe changes in Internet standards and the IPv6 protocol for the Windows .NET Server 2003 family past Windows .NET Server 2003 family RC1, see the Microsoft Windows IPv6 Web site at http://www.microsoft.com/ipv6.

WHO SHOULD READ THIS BOOK

This book is intended for the following audiences:

- **Microsoft Windows XP and Windows .NET Server 2003 networking consultants and planners:** This includes anyone who will be planning for an eventual IPv6 migration with Windows XP and the Windows .NET Server 2003 family of operating systems.

- **Microsoft Windows network administrators:** This includes anyone who manages an IPv4-based network and wants to gain technical knowledge about IPv6 and the Windows .NET Server 2003 family implementation.

- **Microsoft Certified Systems Engineers (MCSEs) and Microsoft Certified Trainers (MCTs):** Regardless of the eventual IPv6 content for Microsoft Official Curriculum (MOC) courseware for the Windows .NET Server 2003 family, this book can be a standard reference for MCSEs and MCTs for IPv6 technology.

- **General technical staff:** Because this book is mostly about IPv6 protocols and processes, independent of its implementation in the Windows .NET Server 2003 family, general technical staff can use this book as an in-depth primer on IPv6 technologies.

- **Information technology students:** This book originated as courseware for internal Microsoft software developers, testers, and program managers, and retains its capability to be a textbook for IPv6 courses taught at an organization or educational institution.

WHAT YOU SHOULD KNOW BEFORE READING THIS BOOK

This book assumes a foundation of networking knowledge that includes basic networking concepts, widely used networking technologies, and sound knowledge of the TCP/IP suite. Wherever possible, I try to facilitate the reader's transition to IPv6 by comparing it with the corresponding feature, behavior, or component of IPv4. For basic networking concepts and technologies, consult a resource such as *MCSE Training Kit: Networking Essentials Plus, Third Edition* (Microsoft Press, ISBN 1-57231-902-X). For a firm foundation of knowledge of the TCP/IP protocol suite, I cannot recommend a better resource as a prerequisite for this book than either *Microsoft® Windows® 2000 TCP/IP Protocols and Services Technical Reference* (Microsoft Press, ISBN 0-7356-0556-4) or *Microsoft®*

Windows® .NET Server 2003 TCP/IP Protocols and Services Technical Reference (Microsoft Press, ISBN 0-7356-1291-9). Like this book, these two references are mostly about implementation-independent protocols and processes.

As coauthor of both of these references, I may be a bit biased. However, this book was written with them in mind. In fact, I consider this book to be a companion volume to the *Microsoft Windows® .NET Server 2003 TCP/IP Protocols and Services Technical Reference.* I recommend that this companion reference book be part of your standard reference library, whether you use Microsoft software or not.

ORGANIZATION OF THIS BOOK

Because IPv6 is a replacement for the Internet layer of the widely used TCP/IP protocol suite, there were no convenient sublayers with which to organize the material. Instead, I have ordered the chapters so that they build upon each other in a logical fashion. For example, it is difficult to understand Neighbor Discovery processes without first understanding IPv6 addressing, the IPv6 header, and ICMPv6, and almost impossible to understand IPv6/IPv4 coexistence technologies without first understanding IPv6 addressing, Neighbor Discovery processes, and routing.

APPENDICES OF THIS BOOK

This book contains the following appendices:

- **Appendix A: Link-Layer Support for IPv6**—A discussion of link-layer encapsulation of IPv6 packets for typical local area network (LAN) and wide area network (WAN) technologies. This is a subject I find fascinating, but for most people it is a yawning festival. Therefore, it is an appendix, rather than a chapter.

- **Appendix B: Windows Sockets Changes for IPv6**—A description of the enhancements to Windows Sockets to support both IPv6 and IPv4 at the same time.

- **Appendix C: IPv6 RFC Index**—A listing of the RFCs and Internet drafts for IPv6 that are the most relevant to the IPv6 implementation in the Windows .NET Server 2003 family at the time of this book's publication. This is not designed to be an exhaustive list and will certainly be obsolete at some level by the time this book is printed.

- **Appendix D: Testing for Understanding Answers**—At the end of each chapter is a "Testing for Understanding" section with a series of review questions pertaining to the material in the chapter. This appendix provides answers to those review questions.

- **Appendix E: Setting Up an IPv6 Test Lab**—This appendix answers the question "How do I get it going so that I can play with it?" By using the instructions in this appendix, you can take five computers and create an IPv6 test lab to test address autoconfiguration, routing, and name resolution. At the end, you are left with a working IPv4 and IPv6 network with which you can experiment on your own.

- **Appendix F: IPv6 Reference Tables**—A reprinting of the most relevant IPv6 tables of IPv6 protocol field values and other parameters.

ABOUT THE COMPANION CD-ROM

The companion CD-ROM included with this book contains the following:

- **Electronic version of this book (eBook)**—An HTML Help version of the book allows you to view it online and perform text searches. HTML Help is the same format that is used for online Help in Windows 2000, Windows XP, and the Windows .NET Server 2003 family.

- **Internet Explorer 6**—Microsoft Internet Explorer version 6 is included to ensure that you can view the electronic version of this book.

- **Network Monitor captures**—Throughout the book, packet structure and protocol processes are illustrated with actual IPv6 packets displayed using Microsoft Network Monitor, a frame capturing and viewing program (also known as a network sniffer) provided with Microsoft Systems Management Server 2.0 and the Windows .NET Server 2003 family. The Network Monitor capture files for all the captures mentioned in the book are included, as well as text (*.txt) versions if you do not have access to Network Monitor. Only those versions of Network Monitor that are supplied with Microsoft Systems Management Server 2.0 and the Windows .NET Server 2003 family are capable of parsing IPv6 traffic. The Network Monitor captures printed in the book were prepared using various versions of Network Monitor that were available internally within the Microsoft Corporation during the writing of this book. The .txt versions of the files on the companion CD-ROM were prepared using the version of Network Monitor provided with Release Candidate 1 of the Windows .NET Server 2003 family. The display of the frames within the capture files on the companion CD-ROM depends on the version of Network Monitor you are using. For these reasons there might be differences in the display of frame structure for the text in the book, when the capture file is displayed with Network Monitor, and the .txt version of the capture file.

■ **IPv6 RFCs and Internet drafts**—The IETF RFCs and Internet drafts for IPv6 that are most relevant to the book content and the IPv6 implementation in the Windows .NET Server 2003 family as of the publication of this book are stored in the \RFCs_and_Drafts folder. Due to the timing of the book content and CD-ROM production, the CD-ROM contains additional RFCs and Internet drafts that are not referenced in this book.

■ **Microsoft IPv6 white papers**—The set of white papers posted on the Microsoft Windows IPv6 Web site (http://www.microsoft.com/ipv6) at the time of this book's publication in both Microsoft Word and Adobe Acrobat format. After reading this book, you may find the content of some of these white papers very familiar. That is because I wrote them and leveraged them as a foundation for the chapters of this book. Does that mean that this book is just a bound version of the white papers that are already publicly available? No. This book is a superset of information found in the white papers and, in my humble opinion, has much better content. Consider the white papers as first drafts of the refined content you now hold in your hands.

■ **Checkv4.exe utility**—The Checkv4.exe tool scans software code for IPv4-specific Windows Sockets function calls, identifies potential problems or highlights code that could benefit from IPv6-capable functions or structures, and makes recommendations. With the Checkv4.exe utility, the task of porting your application from IPv4 to supporting both IPv4 and IPv6 becomes much easier. For more information about modifying your applications to support both IPv4 and IPv6, see "IPv6 Guide for Windows Sockets Applications"at http://msdn.microsoft.com/library/default.asp?url=/library/en-us/winsock/winsock/ipv6_guide_for_windows_sockets_applications_2.asp. For more information about Checkv4.exe, see "Using the Checkv4.exe Utility" at http://msdn.microsoft.com/library/default.asp?url=/library/en-us/winsock/winsock/using_the_checkv4_exe_utility_2.asp.

■ **Training slides**—A set of Microsoft PowerPoint files that can be used to teach IPv6 using this book. For more information, see "A Special Note to Teachers and Instructors."

SYSTEM REQUIREMENTS

To view the eBook form of this book, you need any system that is capable of running Microsoft Internet Explorer version 5.01 or later. To view the capture files (*.cap), you must have a version of Microsoft Network Monitor that is provided with Microsoft Systems Management Server 2.0 or the Windows .NET Server 2003 family. For more detailed information about system requirements, refer to the System Requirements page in the back of the book.

IPV6 PROTOCOL AND WINDOWS PRODUCT VERSIONS

There are different versions of the Microsoft IPv6 protocol for Windows. In this book I have chosen to confine the discussion to the versions of IPv6 that are designed and supported for production use—the ones supplied with the Windows .NET Server 2003 family and Windows XP Service Pack 1 (and later). These two versions of the IPv6 protocol are not identical.

The features included for the IPv6 protocol for the Windows .NET Server 2003 family that are not included in the IPv6 protocol for the Windows XP Service Pack 1 are the following:

■ Support for sending DNS traffic over IPv6

■ Support for file and print sharing over IPv6

■ Support for Web server

■ Support for Windows Media Services

The IPv6 protocol for the Windows XP Service Pack 1 contains the Ipv6.exe configuration tool and the Ping6.exe and Tracert6.exe diagnostics tools. These tools are not included in the IPv6 protocol for the Windows .NET Server 2003 family and will eventually be removed in future versions of Windows XP. Their use is discouraged in favor of commands in the **netsh interface ipv6** context in place of Ipv6.exe, the IPv6-enabled Ping.exe in place of Ping6.exe, and the IPv6-enabled Tracert.exe in place of Tracert6.exe.

A SPECIAL NOTE TO TEACHERS AND INSTRUCTORS

This book originated from courseware and retains many of the attributes of courseware, including the following:

- Objectives at the beginning of each chapter

- Review questions at the end of each chapter

- Training slides for each chapter on the companion CD-ROM

If you are a teacher or instructor tasked with inculcating an understanding of IPv6 protocols and processes in others, I strongly urge you to consider using this book and its slides as a basis for your own IPv6 course.

The slides are included to provide a foundation for your own slide presentation. The included slides contain either bulleted text or drawings that are synchronized with their chapter content. Because the slides were completed after the final book pages were done, there are some minor differences between the slides and the chapter content. These changes were made to enhance the ability to teach an IPv6 course based on the book.

The template I have chosen for the included slides is intentionally simple so that there are minimal issues with text and drawing color translations when you switch to a different template. Please feel free to customize the slides as you see fit.

If you are designing an implementation-independent IPv6 technology course, then I suggest that you skip Chapter 2, "The IPv6 Protocol for the Windows .NET Server 2003 Family," and cover Appendix A, "Link-Layer Support for IPv6," after Chapter 4, "The IPv6 Header."

As a fellow instructor, I wish you success in your efforts to teach this interesting and important new technology to others.

DISCLAIMERS AND SUPPORT

In the technological development of the Internet, the only constant is change. This book represents a best-effort snapshot of information for the Internet standards for IPv6 and its implementation in the Windows .NET Server 2003 family as of Release Candidate 1 of the Windows .NET Server 2003 family. There are legions of computer technology professionals who are working hard to make the information in this book obsolete (although perhaps not intentionally).

Internet draft authors are writing Internet drafts that update or enhance existing IPv6 concepts and functionality. Software developers across Microsoft are updating software code to revise the capabilities of the IPv6 protocol or enable their applications to run over either IPv4 or IPv6.

To obtain the latest information about IPv6 IETF standards, see the IP Version 6 Working Group Web site at http://www.ietf.org/html.charters/ipv6-charter.html.

To obtain the latest information about IPv6 transition technologies, see the Next Generation Transition Working Group Web site at http://www.ietf.org/html.charters/ngtrans-charter.html.

To obtain the latest information about IPv6 in the Windows family of operating systems and updates to the information in this book, see the Microsoft Windows IPv6 Web site at http://www.microsoft.com/ipv6.

If you have a question about this book or the companion CD-ROM, please visit the Microsoft Press Support Site at http://www.microsoft.com/mspress/support/. To find the Microsoft Knowledge Base article containing technical errors or changes to URLs noted in the book, visit http://www.microsoft.com/mspress/support/search.asp, type **0-7356-1245-5** in the search box, and then click **Go**.

Chapter 1

Introduction to IPv6

At the end of this chapter, you should be able to:

- Describe the shortcomings of IPv4 and the modern day Internet, and how IPv6 addresses these shortcomings.

- Describe how the address depletion problem of IPv4 leads to the use of Network Address Translators (NATs) and problems with end-to-end communication.

- List and describe the features of IPv6.

- List and describe the key differences between IPv4 and IPv6.

- State the reasons for deploying IPv6.

LIMITATIONS OF IPV4

The current version of IP (known as version 4 or IPv4) has not changed substantially since RFC 791, which was published in 1981. IPv4 has proven to be robust, and easily implemented and interoperable. It has stood up to the test of scaling an internetwork to a global utility the size of today's Internet. This is a tribute to its initial design.

However, the initial design of IPv4 did not anticipate:

- **The recent exponential growth of the Internet and the impending exhaustion of the IPv4 address space**

  Although the 32-bit address space of IPv4 allows for 4,294,967,296 addresses, previous and current allocation practices limit the number of public IP addresses to a few hundred million. As a result, IPv4 addresses have become relatively scarce, forcing some organizations to use a Network Address Translator (NAT) to map a single public IP address to multiple private IP addresses. Although NATs promote reuse of the private address space, they create performance and application bottlenecks.

Additionally, the rising prominence of Internet-connected devices and appliances ensures that the public IPv4 address space will eventually be depleted.

■ **The growth of the Internet and the ability of Internet backbone routers to maintain large routing tables**
Because of the way that IPv4 network IDs have been (and are currently) allocated, there are routinely over 85,000 routes in the routing tables of Internet backbone routers today. The current IPv4 Internet routing infrastructure is a combination of both flat and hierarchical routing.

■ **The need for simpler configuration**
Most current IPv4 implementations must be either manually configured or use a stateful address configuration protocol such as Dynamic Host Configuration Protocol (DHCP). With more computers and devices using IP, there is a need for a simpler and more automatic configuration of addresses and other configuration settings that do not rely on the administration of a DHCP infrastructure.

■ **The requirement for security at the IP level**
Private communication over a public medium like the Internet requires cryptographic services that protect the data being sent from being viewed or modified in transit. Although a standard now exists for providing security for IPv4 packets (known as Internet Protocol Security, or IPSec), this standard is optional for IPv4 and proprietary security solutions are prevalent.

■ **The need for better support for real-time delivery of data—also called quality of service (QoS)**
Although standards for QoS exist for IPv4, real-time traffic support relies on the 8 bits of the historical IPv4 Type of Service (TOS) field and the identification of the payload, typically using a User Datagram Protocol (UDP) or Transmission Control Protocol (TCP) port. Unfortunately, the IPv4 TOS field has limited functionality and, over time, has been redefined and locally interpreted. Additionally, payload identification that uses a TCP or UDP port is not possible when the IPv4 packet payload is encrypted.

To address these and other concerns, the Internet Engineering Task Force (IETF) has developed a suite of protocols and standards known as IP version 6 (IPv6). This new version, previously called IP-The Next Generation (IPng), incorporates the concepts of many proposed methods for updating the IPv4 protocol. IPv6 is designed intentionally to have minimal impact on upper- and lower-layer protocols and avoids the random addition of new features.

Consequences of the Limited IPv4 Address Space

Due to the relative scarcity of public IPv4 addresses, NATs are being deployed to reuse the IPv4 private address space. In areas of the world where public IP addresses are scarce, there are multiple levels of NATs between the client computer and the Internet. Although NATs do allow more clients to connect to the Internet, they also act as traffic bottlenecks and barriers to some types of communications. Let's examine the operation of a NAT to illustrate why network address translation is a non-scalable, stopgap solution that impairs end-to-end communication.

For example, a small business uses the 192.168.0.0/24 IPv4 private network ID for its intranet and has been granted the public address of 131.107.47.119 by its Internet service provider (ISP). The NAT deployed at the edge of this network maps all private addresses on 192.168.0.0/24 to the public address of 131.107.47.119. To distinguish one intranet location from another, the NAT uses dynamically chosen TCP and UDP ports. Figure 1-1 shows this example configuration.

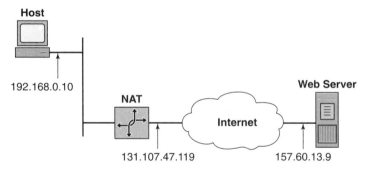

Figure 1-1. *A NAT example*

If a private host using the private IPv4 address 192.168.0.10 uses a Web browser to connect to the Web server at 157.60.13.9, the private host creates an IPv4 packet with the following:

- Destination address: 157.60.13.9

- Source address: 192.168.0.10

- Destination TCP port: 80

- Source TCP port: 1025

This IPv4 packet is then forwarded to the NAT, which translates the source address and source TCP port of the outgoing packet to the following:

■ Destination address: 157.60.13.9

■ **Source address: 131.107.47.119**

■ Destination TCP port: 80

■ **Source TCP port: 5000**

The NAT keeps the mapping of {192.168.0.10, TCP 1025} to {131.107.47.119, TCP 5000} in a local translation table for future reference.

The translated IPv4 packet is sent over the Internet. The response is sent back by the Web server and received by the NAT. When received, the packet contains the following:

■ Destination address: 131.107.47.119

■ Source address: 157.60.13.9

■ Destination TCP port: 5000

■ Source TCP port: 80

The NAT checks its translation table, translates the destination address and destination TCP port and forwards the packet to the host at 192.168.0.10. The forwarded packet contains the following:

■ **Destination address: 192.168.0.10**

■ Source address: 157.60.13.9

■ **Destination TCP port: 1025**

■ Source TCP port: 80

For outgoing packets from the NAT, the source IPv4 address (a private address) is mapped to the ISP-allocated address (a public address), and the source TCP/UDP port numbers are mapped to a different TCP/UDP port number. For incoming packets to the NAT, the destination IPv4 address (a public address) is mapped to the original intranet address (a private address), and the destination TCP/UDP port numbers are mapped back to their original TCP/UDP port numbers.

Normal network address translation relies on the following:

■ **Address translation**
Translation of the IPv4 addresses in the IPv4 header.

■ **Port translation**

Translation of the TCP port numbers in the TCP header or of the UDP port numbers in the UDP header.

Address and port translation lowers the forwarding performance of the NAT due to the additional operations that must be performed on each packet. As a result, NATs are typically not deployed in large-scale environments.

To make modifications to the IPv4 packet beyond address or port translation requires additional processing and software components on the NAT called *NAT editors*. HyperText Transfer Protocol (HTTP) traffic on the World Wide Web does not require a NAT editor because all HTTP traffic requires only address and TCP port translation. However, NAT editors are required in the following situations:

■ **An IPv4 address, TCP port, or UDP port is stored elsewhere in the payload.**

For example, File Transfer Protocol (FTP) stores the dotted decimal representation of IPv4 addresses in the FTP header for the FTP PORT command. If the NAT does not properly translate the IPv4 address within the FTP header for the FTP PORT command and adjust the TCP sequence numbers in the data stream, connectivity and data transfer problems will occur.

■ **TCP or UDP is not used to identify the data stream.**

For example, Point-to-Point Tunneling Protocol (PPTP) tunneled data does not use a TCP or UDP header. Instead, a Generic Routing Encapsulation (GRE) header is used and the Call ID field of the GRE header identifies the data stream. If the NAT does not properly translate the Call ID field within the GRE header, connectivity problems will occur.

Most traffic can traverse a NAT because either the packets require only address or port translation, or a NAT editor is present to modify the payload appropriately. However, some traffic cannot traverse a NAT. If the data requiring translation is in an encrypted part of the packet, translation is not possible. For IPSec packets, address and port translation invalidates the packet's integrity.

An additional problem with NATs is their effect on peer-to-peer applications. In the peer-to-peer communication model, peers can act as either the client or the server and communicate by sending packets directly to each other. If a peer is behind a NAT, there are two addresses associated with it, one of which is known to the peer behind the NAT (the private address) and one of which is known in front of the NAT (the public address). Let's examine a simple configuration in which NATs can cause problems for peer-to-peer applications. Figure 1-2 shows an intranet with a NAT at its edge.

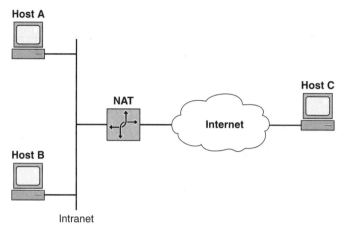

Figure 1-2. *NATs and peer-to-peer applications*

For a peer-to-peer application running on all hosts, Host A can initiate a session with Host B (directly reachable on its link) and with Host C. However, Host A cannot inform Host C of the public address of Host B because Host A does not know it. Also, Host C cannot initiate a session with either Host A or Host B without manual configuration of the NAT with a static translation table entry to translate the inbound connection request packets to Host A's private address and port. Even with the static entry, Host C cannot initiate a session with both Host A and Host B because both hosts are known by·the same public IPv4 address and application port number.

To make matters worse, it is a more common situation to have each Internet peer behind a NAT. To solve these problems, the peer-to-peer or multiple-party applications must be modified to be NAT-aware, resulting in additional complexity on the NAT and the application.

NATs are a makeshift measure to extend the life of the IPv4 public address space, and are not a solution to the IPv4 public address space problem. NATs work best for reusing the private address space for client computers. Most server computers still need unambiguous public addresses. A server can be placed behind a NAT; however, the NAT must be configured manually with a static translation table entry to translate the inbound connection request packets to the server's private address and port. In peer-to-peer communications, each end acts as both client and server and, therefore, peers separated by NATs might not operate correctly and must be modified for NAT awareness.

FEATURES OF IPv6

The following list summarizes the features of the IPv6 protocol:

- New header format

- Large address space

- Efficient and hierarchical addressing and routing infrastructure

- Stateless and stateful address configuration

- Built-in security

- Better support for QoS

- New protocol for neighboring node interaction

- Extensibility

New Header Format

The IPv6 header has a new format that is designed to minimize header overhead. This is achieved by moving both nonessential and optional fields to extension headers that are placed after the IPv6 header. The streamlined IPv6 header is more efficiently processed at intermediate routers.

IPv4 headers and IPv6 headers are not interoperable. IPv6 is not a superset of functionality that is backward compatible with IPv4. A host or router must use an implementation of both IPv4 and IPv6 to recognize and process both header formats. The new IPv6 header is only twice the size of the IPv4 header, even though the number of bits in IPv6 addresses is four times larger than IPv4 addresses.

Large Address Space

IPv6 has 128-bit (16-byte) source and destination addresses. Although 128 bits can express over 3.4×10^{38} possible combinations, the large address space of IPv6 has been designed to allow for multiple levels of subnetting and address allocation, from the Internet backbone to the individual subnets within an organization.

Even with all of the addresses currently allocated for use by hosts, there are plenty of addresses available for future use. With a much larger number of available addresses, address-conservation techniques, such as the deployment of NATs, are no longer necessary.

Efficient and Hierarchical Addressing and Routing Infrastructure

IPv6 global addresses used on the IPv6 portion of the Internet are designed to create an efficient, hierarchical, and summarizable routing infrastructure that is based on the common occurrence of multiple levels of ISPs. On the IPv6 Internet, backbone routers have much smaller routing tables, corresponding to the routing infrastructure of global ISPs. For more information, see "Aggregatable Global Unicast Addresses" in Chapter 3, "IPv6 Addressing."

Stateless and Stateful Address Configuration

To simplify host configuration, IPv6 supports both stateful address configuration (such as address configuration in the presence of a DHCPv6 server) and stateless address configuration (such as address configuration in the absence of a DHCPv6 server). With stateless address configuration, hosts on a link automatically configure themselves with IPv6 addresses for the link (called link-local addresses), addresses for IPv4 and IPv6 coexistence, and with addresses derived from prefixes advertised by local routers. Even in the absence of a router, hosts on the same link can automatically configure themselves with link-local addresses and communicate without manual configuration. Link-local addresses are autoconfigured within one second and communication with neighboring nodes on the link is possible immediately. In comparison, an IPv4 host using DHCP must wait a full minute before abandoning DHCP configuration and self-configuring an IPv4 address.

Built-in Security

Support for IPSec is an IPv6 protocol suite requirement. This requirement provides a standards-based solution for network security needs and promotes interoperability between different IPv6 implementations. IPSec consists of two types of extension headers and a protocol to negotiate security settings. The Authentication header (AH) provides data integrity, data authentication, and replay protection for the entire IPv6 packet (excluding fields in the IPv6 header that must change in transit). The Encapsulating Security Payload (ESP) header and trailer provide data integrity, data authentication, data confidentiality, and replay protection for the ESP-encapsulated payload. The protocol typically used to negotiate IPSec security settings for unicast communication is the Internet Key Exchange (IKE) protocol.

Better Support for QoS

New fields in the IPv6 header define how traffic is handled and identified. Traffic is prioritized using a Traffic Class field. A Flow Label field in the IPv6 header allows routers to identify and provide special handling for packets that belong to a flow (a series of packets between a source and destination). Because the traffic is identified in the IPv6 header, support for QoS can be achieved even when the packet payload is encrypted with IPSec and ESP.

New Protocol for Neighboring Node Interaction

The Neighbor Discovery protocol for IPv6 is a series of Internet Control Message Protocol for IPv6 (ICMPv6) messages that manages the interaction of neighboring nodes (nodes on the same link). Neighbor Discovery replaces the Address Resolution Protocol (ARP) (broadcast-based), ICMPv4 Router Discovery, and ICMPv4 Redirect messages with efficient multicast and unicast Neighbor Discovery messages.

Extensibility

IPv6 can easily be extended for new features by adding extension headers after the IPv6 header. Unlike options in the IPv4 header, which can support only 40 bytes of options, the size of IPv6 extension headers is constrained only by the size of the IPv6 packet.

COMPARISON OF IPV4 AND IPV6

Table 1-1 highlights some of the key differences between IPv4 and IPv6.

Table 1-1. DIFFERENCES BETWEEN IPv4 AND IPv6

IPv4	IPv6
Source and destination addresses are 32 bits (4 bytes) in length.	Source and destination addresses are 128 bits (16 bytes) in length. For more information, see Chapter 3, "IPv6 Addressing."
IPSec support is optional.	IPSec support is required. For more information, see Chapter 4, "The IPv6 Header."

continued

Table 1-1 *continued*

IPv4	IPv6
No identification of packet flow for QoS handling by routers is present within the IPv4 header.	Packet flow identification for QoS handling by routers is present within the IPv6 header using the Flow Label field. For more information, see Chapter 4, "The IPv6 Header."
Fragmentation is performed by the sending host and at routers, slowing router performance.	Fragmentation is performed only by the sending host. For more information, see Chapter 4, "The IPv6 Header."
Has no link-layer packet size requirements and must be able to reassemble a 576-byte packet.	Link layer must support a 1,280-byte packet and must be able to reassemble a 1,500-byte packet. For more information, see Chapter 4, "The IPv6 Header."
Header includes a checksum.	Header does not include a checksum. For more information, see Chapter 4, "The IPv6 Header."
Header includes options.	All optional data is moved to IPv6 extension headers. For more information, see Chapter 4, "The IPv6 Header."
ARP uses broadcast ARP Request frames to resolve an IPv4 address to a link-layer address.	ARP Request frames are replaced with multicast Neighbor Solicitation messages. For more information, see Chapter 6, "Neighbor Discovery."
Internet Group Management Protocol (IGMP) is used to manage local subnet group membership.	IGMP is replaced with Multicast Listener Discovery (MLD) messages. For more information, see Chapter 7, "Multicast Listener Discovery."
ICMP Router Discovery is used to determine the IPv4 address of the best default gateway and is optional.	ICMPv4 Router Discovery is replaced with ICMPv6 Router Solicitation and Router Advertisement messages and is required. For more information, see Chapter 6, "Neighbor Discovery."
Broadcast addresses are used to send traffic to all nodes on a subnet.	There are no IPv6 broadcast addresses. Instead, a link-local scope all-nodes multicast address is used. For more information, see "Multicast IPv6 Addresses" in Chapter 3, "IPv6 Addressing."
Must be configured either manually or through DHCP for IPv4.	Does not require manual configuration or DHCP for IPv6. For more information, see Chapter 8, "Address Autoconfiguration."

continued

Table 1-1 *continued*

IPv4	IPv6
Uses host address (A) resource records in the Domain Name System (DNS) to map host names to IPv4 addresses.	Uses AAAA records in the DNS to map host names to IPv6 addresses. For more information, see Chapter 9, "IPv6 and Name Resolution."
Uses pointer (PTR) resource records in the IN-ADDR.ARPA DNS domain to map IPv4 addresses to host names.	Uses pointer (PTR) resource records in the IP6.INT DNS domains to map IPv6 addresses to host names. For more information, see Chapter 9, "IPv6 and Name Resolution."

IPv6 TERMINOLOGY

The following list of common terms for network elements and concepts provides a foundation for subsequent chapters. Figure 1-3 shows an IPv6 network.

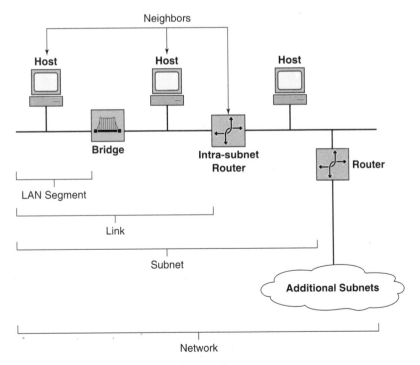

Figure 1-3. *Elements of an IPv6 network*

IPv6 common terms and concepts are defined as follows:

■ **Node**

Any device that runs an implementation of IPv6. This includes routers and hosts.

■ **Router**

A node that can forward IPv6 packets not explicitly addressed to itself. On an IPv6 network, a router also typically advertises its presence and host configuration information.

■ **Host**

A node that cannot forward IPv6 packets not explicitly addressed to itself (a non-router). A host is typically the source and a destination of IPv6 traffic, and silently discards traffic received that is not explicitly addressed to itself.

■ **Upper-layer protocol**

A protocol above IPv6 that uses IPv6 as its transport. Examples include Internet layer protocols such as ICMPv6 and Transport layer protocols such as TCP and UDP (but not Application layer protocols such as FTP and DNS, which use TCP and UDP as their transport).

■ **Local area network (LAN) segment**

A portion of an IPv6 link consisting of a single medium that is bounded by bridges or Layer 2 switches.

■ **Link**

One or more LAN segments that are bounded by routers. Many link-layer technologies are already defined for IPv6, including typical LAN technologies (such as Ethernet, Token Ring, and Fiber Distributed Data Interface [FDDI]) and wide area network (WAN) technologies (such as the Point-to-Point Protocol [PPP], Frame Relay, and Asynchronous Transfer Mode [ATM]). Additionally, IPv6 packets can be sent over logical links representing an IPv4 or IPv6 network, by encapsulating the IPv6 packet within an IPv4 or IPv6 header. For more information about LAN and WAN media support for IPv6, see Appendix A, "Link-Layer Support for IPv6."

■ **Subnet**

One or more links that use the same 64-bit IPv6 address prefix. Another term for subnet is network segment. A subnet can be divided by an intra-subnet router, which is a router providing forwarding and configuration functions for individual links of a subnet. If intra-subnet routers are not present, a subnet is equivalent to a link.

■ **Network**

Two or more subnets connected by routers. Another term for network is internetwork.

■ **Neighbors**

Nodes connected to the same link. Neighbors in IPv6 have special significance because of IPv6 Neighbor Discovery, which has facilities to resolve neighbor link-layer addresses and detect and monitor neighbor reachability.

■ **Interface**

The representation of a physical or logical attachment of a node to a link. An example of a physical interface is a network adapter. An example of a logical interface is a "tunnel" interface that is used to send IPv6 packets across an IPv4 network by encapsulating the IPv6 packet inside an IPv4 header.

■ **Address**

An identifier that can be used as the source or destination of IPv6 packets that is assigned at the IPv6 layer to an interface or set of interfaces.

■ **Packet**

The protocol data unit (PDU) that exists at the IPv6 layer and is composed of an IPv6 header and payload.

■ **Link MTU**

The maximum transmission unit (MTU)—the number of bytes in the largest IPv6 packet—that can be sent on a link. Because the maximum frame size includes the link-layer medium headers and trailers, the link MTU is not the same as the maximum frame size of the link. The link MTU is the same as the maximum payload size of the link-layer technology. For example, for Ethernet using Ethernet II encapsulation, the maximum Ethernet frame payload size is 1,500 bytes. Therefore, the link MTU is 1,500. For a link with multiple link-layer technologies (for example, a bridged link), the link MTU is the smallest link MTU of all the link-layer technologies present on the link.

■ **Path MTU**

The maximum-sized IPv6 packet that can be sent without performing host fragmentation between a source and destination over a path in an IPv6 network. The path MTU is the smallest link MTU of all the links in the path.

THE CASE FOR IPV6 DEPLOYMENT

Although the IPv6 protocol offers a host of technological advances and innovations, its use must still be deployed by information technology (IT) staff in end-user organizations and ISPs. The deployment of IPv6 involves the planning and design of coexistence and migration strategies and the installation and maintenance of hardware and software. The resulting combination of IT staff, hardware and software resources, and time required for the transition makes the decision to deploy IPv6 a significant one, especially in light of other technology initiatives that may have higher visibility or better short-term benefits.

One must consider, however, that the Internet, once a pseudo-private network connecting educational institutions and United States government agencies, has become an indispensable worldwide communications medium that is an integral part of the increased efficiency and productivity for commercial organizations and individuals, and a major component of the world's economic engine. *Its growth must continue.*

To continue the growth of the Internet, IPv4 must eventually be replaced. The sooner IPv4 is replaced, the sooner the benefits of its replacement protocol are realized. The following sections present the key evidence in the case to deploy IPv6.

IPv6 Solves the Address Depletion Problem

First, and most visibly, IPv6 solves the IPv4 public address depletion problem by providing an address space to last well into the 21st century and, probably, beyond. By moving to IPv6, mobile cell phones, personal data assistants (PDAs), automobiles, appliances, and even people can be assigned multiple public addresses. The growth of the devices connected to the Internet can proceed without restraint.

IPv6 Solves the International Address Allocation Problem

The Internet was principally a creation of educational institutions and government agencies of the United States of America. In the early days of the Internet, connected sites in the United States received IP network IDs without regard to summarizability or need. The historical result of this address allocation practice is that the United States has a disproportionate number of public IP addresses. For example, there are educational institutions in the United States that have more address space than the entire nation of the People's Republic of China.

With IPv6, public address prefixes are assigned to regional Internet registries, which, in turn, assign address prefixes to other ISPs and organizations based on justified need. This new address allocation practice ensures that addresses will be distributed globally based on regional connectivity needs, rather than historical origin. This makes the Internet more of a truly global resource, rather than a United States-centric one.

IPv6 Restores End-to-End Communication

With IPv6, NATs are no longer necessary to conserve public address space and the problems associated with mapping addresses and ports disappears for developers of applications and gateways. More importantly, end-to-end communication is restored between hosts on the Internet by using addresses that do not change in transit. This functional restoration has immense value when one considers the emergence of peer-to-peer telephony, video, and other real-time collaboration technologies for personal communications, and that the next wave of devices that are connected to the Internet include many types of peer-to-peer devices, such as mobile phones.

IPv6 Uses Scoped Addresses and Address Selection

Unlike IPv4 addresses, IPv6 addresses have a scope, or a defined area of the network over which they are unique and relevant. For example, IPv6 has a global address that is equivalent to the IPv4 public address and a site-local address that is equivalent to the IPv4 private address. Typical IPv4 routers do not distinguish a public address from a private address and will forward a privately addressed packet on the Internet. An IPv6 router, on the other hand, is aware of the scope of IPv6 addresses and will never forward a packet over an interface that does not have the correct scope.

There are many types of IPv6 addresses with different scopes. When multiple IPv6 addresses are returned in a DNS name query, the sending node must be able to distinguish their types and, when initiating communication, use a pair (source address and destination address) that is matched in scope and that is the most appropriate pair to use. For example, for a source and a destination that have been assigned both global (public) and site-local (private) addresses, a sending IPv6 host would never use a global destination with a site-local source. IPv6 sending hosts include the address selection logic that is needed to decide which pair of addresses to use in communication. Moreover, the address selection rules are configurable. This allows you to configure multiple addressing infrastructures within an organization. Regardless of how many types of addressing infrastructures are in place, the sending host always chooses the "best" set of addresses. In comparison, IPv4 nodes have no awareness of address types and can send traffic to a public address from a private address.

IPv6 has More Efficient Forwarding

IPv6 is a streamlined version of IPv4. Excluding non-default QoS traffic, IPv6 has fewer fields to process and fewer decisions to make in forwarding an IPv6 packet. Additionally, the hierarchical and summarizable addressing structure of IPv6 global addresses means that there are many fewer routes to analyze in the routing table of organization and Internet backbone routers. The outcome is traffic that can be forwarded at higher data rates, resulting in higher performance for tomorrow's high bandwidth applications that utilize multiple data types.

IPv6 has Built-in Security and Mobility

IPv6 has been designed to support security and mobility as built-in features. Although one could argue that these features are available for IPv4, they are available on IPv4 as extensions, and therefore have architectural or connectivity limitations that might not have been present if they had been part of the original IPv4 design. It is always better to build features in rather than bolt them on.

The result of building in security and mobility to IPv6 is an implementation that is a defined standard, has fewer limitations, and is more robust and scalable to handle the current and future communication needs of the Internet.

TESTING FOR UNDERSTANDING

To test your understanding of IPv6, answer the following questions. See Appendix D, "Testing for Understanding Answers," to check your answers.

1. What are the problems with IPv4 on today's Internet?

2. How does IPv6 solve these problems?

3. How does IPv6 provide better QoS support?

4. Describe at least three ways in which IPv6 is more efficient than IPv4.

5. Explain how NATs prevent peer-to-peer applications from working properly.

6. What are the key benefits of deploying IPv6 now?

Chapter 2

IPv6 Protocol
for the Windows .NET
Server 2003 Family

At the end of this chapter, you should be able to:

- Discuss the architecture of the IPv6 protocol for the Windows .NET Server 2003 family.

- List and describe the features of the IPv6 protocol for the Windows .NET Server 2003 family.

- List and describe the applications provided with the Windows .NET Server 2003 family that are IPv6-enabled.

- List and describe the application programming interfaces (APIs) in the Windows .NET Server 2003 family that are IPv6-enabled.

- List and describe the IPv6-enabled common utilities provided with the Windows .NET Server 2003 family.

- List and describe IPv6 command-line utilities provided with the Windows .NET Server 2003 family.

ARCHITECTURE OF THE IPv6 PROTOCOL FOR THE WINDOWS .NET SERVER 2003 FAMILY

For the Windows .NET Server 2003 family, the IPv6 protocol stack is a separate protocol that contains its own implementation of TCP and UDP. When used alongside the IPv4 implementation, this is known as a dual stack implementation.

Figure 2-1 shows the architecture of the TCP/IP protocols for the Windows .NET Server 2003 family.

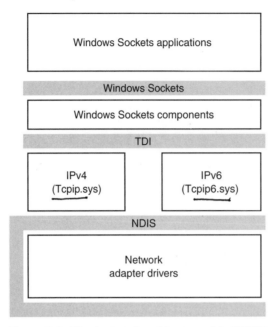

Figure 2-1. *The dual stack architecture of the TCP/IP protocols for the Windows .NET Server 2003 family*

The **Microsoft TCP/IP version 6** protocol, as it is named in the list of protocols from the properties of a LAN connection in the Network Connections folder, is contained in the file named Tcpip6.sys. The IPv4 protocol, named **Internet Protocol (TCP/IP)** in the Network Connections folder, is contained in the file Tcpip.sys. The Tcpip6.sys protocol driver, like all other protocols in Windows, is added to the system between the Transport Driver Interface (TDI) and the Network Device Interface Specification (NDIS) layers in the Windows network architecture. Tcpip6.sys is available to TDI clients, such as the Windows Sockets components, as a TDI provider that interfaces with network adapters through NDIS. The IPv6 protocol for the Windows .NET Server 2003 family works only over network adapters whose NDIS driver represents itself as an Ethernet or FDDI interface. The IPv6 protocol for the Windows .NET Server 2003 family does not support Token Ring or PPP-based interfaces.

Tcpip6.sys contains separate implementations of TCP and UDP that are functionally equivalent to the TCP and UDP provided with Windows NT 4.0 and contain all the latest security updates. TCP performance enhancements that were added to the Windows platform in Windows 2000 are not present in the TCP implementation for the Microsoft TCP/IP version 6 protocol. These performance enhancements include selective acknowledgements, TCP timestamps, better roundtrip time estimation, large TCP windows, and fast retransmit and recovery. However, the TCP implementation in the IPv6 protocol for the Windows .NET Server 2003 family does include partial synchronize (SYN) attack protection.

The ideal configuration to support both IPv4 and IPv6 is known as a dual IP layer, where only a single implementation of TCP and UDP operates over both IPv4 and IPv6. Microsoft is planning to provide a dual IP layer implementation in a future version of the Windows operating system.

FEATURES OF THE IPv6 PROTOCOL FOR THE WINDOWS .NET SERVER 2003 FAMILY

The IPv6 protocol for the Windows .NET Server 2003 family includes the following features:

- Basic stack support
- 6to4
- ISATAP
- 6over4
- PortProxy
- Temporary addresses
- DNS support
- IPSec support
- Static router support
- Address selection
- Site prefixes in router advertisements

Basic Stack Support

The IPv6 protocol for the Windows .NET Server 2003 family supports standard IPv6 protocol stack functionality, including support for:

- Unicast, multicast, and anycast addressing
- The ICMPv6, Neighbor Discovery (ND), and MLD protocols
- Stateless address autoconfiguration
- Correspondent node support for IPv6 mobility

6to4

6to4 is a component of the IPv6 protocol for the Windows .NET Server 2003 family that allows automatic tunneling and IPv6 connectivity between IPv6/IPv4 hosts across the IPv4 Internet. 6to4 hosts use IPv6 addresses derived from IPv4 public addresses. With 6to4, IPv6 sites and hosts can use 6to4-based addresses and the IPv4 Internet to communicate without having to obtain an IPv6 global address prefix from an Internet service provider (ISP), and then having to connect to the IPv6 Internet. For more information about 6to4, see Chapter 11, "Coexistence and Migration."

ISATAP

Intra-Site Automatic Tunnel Addressing Protocol (ISATAP) is an address assignment and automatic tunneling mechanism. It allows IPv6/IPv4 nodes within an IPv4 infrastructure of a site to use IPv6 to communicate with each other and with nodes on an IPv6-enabled network, either within the site or the IPv6 Internet. For more information about ISATAP, see Chapter 11, "Coexistence and Migration."

6over4

6over4, also known as IPv4 multicast tunneling, is an automatic tunneling mechanism that allows IPv6/IPv4 nodes to communicate over an IPv4 multicast-enabled infrastructure with each other and with nodes on an IPv6-enabled network, either within the site or the IPv6 Internet. 6over4 uses the IPv4 infrastructure as a multicast-capable logical link. For more information about 6over4, see Chapter 11, "Coexistence and Migration."

PortProxy

PortProxy is a component of the IPv6 protocol for the Windows .NET Server 2003 family that functions as a TCP proxy to facilitate the communication between nodes or applications that cannot connect using a common Internet layer protocol (IPv4 or IPv6). By using PortProxy, IPv6-only nodes or applications can communicate with IPv4-only nodes or applications and vice versa. For more information about PortProxy, see Chapter 11, "Coexistence and Migration."

Temporary Addresses

To provide a level of anonymity when accessing Internet resources, the IPv6 protocol for the Windows .NET Server 2003 family creates temporary addresses containing randomly derived interface identifiers. Temporary addresses change over time, making it difficult to track someone's Internet usage based on their IPv6 address. For more information about temporary addresses, see Chapter 3, "IPv6 Addressing."

DNS Support

DNS support for IPv6 in the Windows .NET Server 2003 family consists of the following:

- The querying and processing of IPv6 host (AAAA) records in the DNS.

- The sending of DNS traffic over IPv6. DNS queries by default are sent using the well-known site-local IPv6 addresses of FEC0:0:0:FFFF::1, FEC0:0:0:FFFF::2, and FEC0:0:0:FFFF::3. You can also manually configure the IPv6 addresses of your IPv6-enabled DNS server by using the **netsh interface ipv6 add dns** command.

- The dynamic registration of IPv6 host (AAAA) records in the DNS over either IPv4 or IPv6.

The DNS Server service in the Windows .NET Server 2003 family supports the storage and dynamic registration of IPv6 AAAA records over both IPv4 and IPv6.

For more information about DNS support for IPv6, see Chapter 9, "IPv6 and Name Resolution."

IPSec Support

The IPv6 protocol for the Windows .NET Server 2003 family supports processing the AH by using the Message Digest 5 (MD5) hash, and the ESP by using the NULL ESP header and the MD5 hash. There is no support for ESP data encryption. IPSec in the IPv6 protocol for the Windows .NET Server 2003 family is separate from—and not interoperable with—IPSec for the IPv4 protocol. IPSec policies that are configured with the IP Security Policies or Group Policy snap-ins have no effect on IPv6 traffic.

IPSec in the IPv6 protocol for the Windows .NET Server 2003 family does not support the use of IKE to negotiate security associations (SAs). IPSec policies and SAs must be configured manually by using the Ipsec6.exe utility, as described in the section entitled "Ipsec6.exe" later in this chapter.

Static Router Support

A computer running a member of the Windows .NET Server 2003 family can act as a static IPv6 router that performs the following:

- **Forwards IPv6 packets between interfaces based on the contents of the IPv6 routing table**

    To enable an interface for forwarding, you must use the **netsh interface ipv6 set interface** *InterfaceNameorIndex* **forwarding= enabled** command. You can configure static routes with the **netsh interface ipv6 add | set route** commands. The Windows .NET Server 2003 family does not provide support for IPv6 routing protocols.

- **Sends router advertisements**

    The contents of router advertisements are derived automatically from routes in the routing table. To enable the sending of router advertisements on an interface, you must use the **netsh interface ipv6 set interface interface=***InterfaceNameorIndex* **advertise=enabled** command.

Router advertisements always contain a source link-layer address option and an MTU option. The value for the MTU option is taken from the sending interface's current link MTU. You can change this value with the **netsh interface ipv6 set interface interface=***InterfaceNameorIndex* **mtu=***Integer* command.

A computer running a member of the Windows .NET Server 2003 family advertises itself as a default router (by using a router advertisement with a router lifetime other than zero) only if there is a default route that is configured to be published. To add a default route and publish it, you must use the **netsh interface ipv6 add route ::/0 interface=***InterfaceNameorIndex* **nexthop=***Ipv6Address* **metric=***Integer* **publish=yes** command. For an example of how to configure a computer running a member of the Windows .NET Server 2003 family as a default router, see Appendix E, "Setting Up an IPv6 Test Lab."

Address Selection

In a DNS environment that contains both host address (A) and IPv6 host address (AAAA) records, the result of a name query for a DNS name might be multiple addresses: zero or more IPv6 addresses and zero or more IPv4 addresses. Based on the configuration of the querying host, address selection rules determine which pair of addresses to use for the subsequent communication. The initiating host must determine which type of address (IPv4 vs. IPv6), and then the scope of the address (public vs. private for IPv4, and link-local vs. site-local vs. global vs. coexistence for IPv6).

You can view the default address selection rules for the IPv6 protocol for the Windows .NET Server 2003 family by using the **netsh interface ipv6 show prefixpolicy** command to display the prefix policy table. You can modify the prefix policy table by using the **netsh interface ipv6 add | set | delete prefixpolicy** commands. By default, IPv6 addresses in DNS query responses are preferred over IPv4 addresses.

For more information about address selection, see Chapter 11, "Coexistence and Migration."

Site Prefixes in Router Advertisements

Published on-link prefixes can be configured with a site prefix length. You can use the **netsh interface ipv6 add | set route** command to include a site prefix length with the address prefix. You can also use the **netsh interface ipv6 set route interface=***InterfaceNameorIndex* **siteprefixlength=***Integer* command to configure a site prefix length (the default length is 48). When a prefix information option in a router advertisement with a site prefix length is received, an entry is created in the site prefix table, which can be viewed by using the **netsh interface ipv6 show siteprefixes** command.

APPLICATION SUPPORT

The Windows .NET Server 2003 family includes the following IPv6-enabled components and applications:

- Internet Explorer
- Telnet client
- FTP client
- Internet Information Services, version 6
- File and print sharing
- Windows Media Services
- Network Monitor
- SNMP MIB support

Internet Explorer

The new Windows Internet Extensions dynamic link library, Wininet.dll, enables Web browsers to access IPv6-enabled Web servers. For example, Wininet.dll is used by Microsoft Internet Explorer to make connections with a Web server to view Web pages. Internet Explorer uses IPv6 to download Web pages when the DNS query for the name of the Web server in the URL returns an IPv6 address.

URLs that use the format for literal IPv6 addresses described in RFC 2732, "Format for Literal IPv6 Addresses in URLs," are not supported by the version of Internet Explorer provided with the Windows .NET Server 2003 family.

Telnet Client

The Telnet client, Telnet.exe, can be used to establish Telnet sessions with both IPv4 and IPv6 Telnet servers. There are no special command line options for IPv6 support. Telnet.exe attempts to connect to the Telnet server based on either the address specified on the Telnet.exe command line or an address obtained from DNS name resolution. If the address typed at the command line or the address returned from DNS name resolution is an IPv6 address, Telnet.exe attempts a session with an IPv6-enabled Telnet server.

The Windows .NET Server 2003 family does not include support for an IPv6-enabled Telnet server. However, PortProxy can be used to proxy IPv6 Telnet traffic from Telnet.exe to the IPv4-only Telnet server component provided with the Windows .NET Server 2003 family. For more information about PortProxy, see the section entitled "PortProxy" in Chapter 11, "Coexistence and Migration."

FTP Client

The FTP client, Ftp.exe, can be used to establish FTP sessions with IPv4 and IPv6 FTP servers. Like the Telnet client, there are no special Ftp.exe command line options for IPv6 support. Ftp.exe attempts to connect to the FTP server based on either the address specified on the Ftp.exe command line or an address obtained from DNS name resolution. If the address typed at the command line or the address returned from DNS name resolution is an IPv6 address, Ftp.exe attempts an FTP session with an IPv6-enabled FTP server.

The Windows .NET Server 2003 family does not include an IPv6-enabled FTP server, and because the FTP protocol uses embedded IPv4 addresses within FTP messages, the PortProxy component cannot be used to proxy IPv6 FTP traffic from Ftp.exe to the IPv4-only FTP server component of Internet Information Services (IIS) provided with the Windows .NET Server 2003 family.

Web Server

IIS provided with the Windows .NET Server 2003 family includes an IPv6-enabled HTTP server, also known as a Web server. IIS in the Windows .NET Server 2003 family will accept HTTP-based Web requests sent over IPv6 from any IPv6-enabled HTTP client, such as Microsoft Internet Explorer.

File and Print Sharing

The Windows .NET Server 2003 family includes support for file and print sharing using the Microsoft Common Internet File System (CIFS), also known as the Server Message Block (SMB) protocol. File- and printer-sharing connections made from the Windows Explorer, Printers within Control Panel, or from the command line by using the Net.exe utility use IPv6 when the server name within the Universal Naming Convention (UNC) name of the file or printer share is resolved to an IPv6 address. All file- and printer-sharing connections over IPv6 use TCP port 445.

To provide security for file and print resources, file- and-printer-sharing resources are available only within the site.

Windows Media Services

Windows Media Services is a digital media platform that allows you to deliver Advanced Streaming Format (ASF) content in a variety of different ways, based on your own needs and the capabilities or limitations of your network. Content can be delivered either live or pre-recorded, and either multicast or unicast. Windows Media Services in the Windows .NET Server 2003 family is IPv6-enabled, allowing you to stream ASF content over IPv6.

Network Monitor

The versions of Network Monitor provided with the Windows .NET Server 2003 family, Systems Management Server 2.0, and Windows 2000 support the parsing of IPv6 traffic.

SNMP MIB Support

The Windows .NET Server 2003 family includes Simple Network Management Protocol (SNMP) support for the following IPv6 management information bases (MIBs):

■   The MIB defined in RFC 2465, titled "Management Information Base for IP Version 6: Textual Conventions and General Group."

■   The MIB defined in RFC 2466, titled "Management Information Base for IP Version 6: ICMPv6 Group."

■   The ICMPv6 portions of the MIB defined in the Internet draft titled "Management Information Base for the Internet Protocol (IP)" (the file named draft-ietf-ipngwg-rfc2011-update-00.txt included in the \RFCs_and_Drafts folder of the companion CD-ROM). This Internet draft is an update to RFC 2011.

■ The MIB defined in the Internet draft titled "Management Information Base for the Transmission Control Protocol (TCP)" (the file named draft-ietf-ipngwg-rfc2012-update-01.txt included in the \RFCs_and_ Drafts folder of the companion CD-ROM). This Internet draft is an update to RFC 2012.

■ The MIB defined in the Internet draft titled "Management Information Base for the User Datagram Protocol (UDP)" (the file named draft-ietf-ipngwg-rfc2013-update-01.txt included in the \RFCs_and_Drafts folder of the companion CD-ROM). This Internet draft is an update to RFC 2013.

Although the MIBs included in the Windows .NET Server 2003 family support IPv6 elements, SNMP traffic is supported only over IPv4.

APPLICATION PROGRAMMING INTERFACES

The IPv6 protocol in the Windows .NET Server 2003 family includes IPv6 support for the following application programming interfaces (APIs):

■ Windows Sockets

■ Remote Procedure Call

■ Internet Protocol Helper

■ Win32 Internet Extensions

■ .NET Framework

Windows Sockets

Windows Sockets (Winsock) is an API-based on the familiar "socket" interface from the University of California at Berkeley. It includes a set of extensions designed to take advantage of the message-driven nature of Microsoft Windows. Version 1.1 of the Windows Sockets specification was released in January 1993, and version 2.2.0 was published in May of 1996.

The Microsoft Windows implementation of sockets, Winsock, is designed to run efficiently on Windows operating systems while maintaining compatibility with the Berkeley Software Distribution (BSD) standard, known as Berkeley Sockets. With Winsock, programmers can create advanced Internet, intranet, and other network-capable applications to transmit application-data across the wire, independent of the network protocol being used.

Winsock for the Windows .NET Server 2003 family has been enhanced to include IPv6 support as specified in RFC 2553, "Basic Socket Interface Extensions for IPv6" (with some exceptions), and portions of RFC 2292, "Advanced Sockets API for IPv6." For the details of Windows Sockets support for IPv6, see Appendix B, "Windows Sockets Changes for IPv6."

Remote Procedure Call

Remote Procedure Call (RPC) is an API that is used for creating distributed client/server programs. The RPC run-time stubs and libraries manage most of the details relating to network protocols and communication. RPC functions are used to forward application function calls to a remote system across the network. The RPC components in the Windows .NET Server 2003 family are IPv6-enabled. The RPC components have been modified to use the updated Windows Sockets, which allows RPC to work over both IPv4 and IPv6. To enable RPC over IPv6, you must restart the computer after IPv6 has been installed.

IP Helper

Internet Protocol Helper (IP Helper) is an API that assists in the administration of the network configuration of the local computer. You can use IP Helper to programmatically retrieve information about the network configuration of the local computer, and to modify that configuration. IP Helper also provides notification mechanisms to ensure that an application is notified when certain aspects of the network configuration change on the local computer.

IP Helper in the Windows .NET Server 2003 family has been extended to allow management and configuration of IPv6 and its components. Some of the areas that are IPv6-enabled are the following:

- Retrieving information about network configuration, network adapters, interfaces, addresses, IPv6, ICMPv6, routing, TCP, and UDP
- Receiving notification of network events

Win32 Internet Extensions

The Win32 Internet Extensions (WinInet) is an API used for creating an Internet client application. An Internet client application is a program that accesses information from a network data source (server) using Internet protocols such as gopher, FTP, or HTTP. An Internet client application might access a server to retrieve data such as weather maps, stock prices, or newspaper headlines. The Internet client can access the server through an external network (the Internet) or an internal network (an intranet).

WinInet in the Windows .NET Server 2003 family has been extended to support IPv6. This allows Microsoft Internet Explorer to use WinInet to access IPv6-enabled Web sites.

.NET Framework

The .NET Framework is the programming model of the .NET platform for building, deploying, and running Extensible Markup Language (XML) Web services and applications. It manages much of the plumbing, enabling developers to focus on writing the business logic code for their applications. The .NET Framework provided with the Windows .NET Server 2003 family is IPv6-enabled, allowing .NET Framework applications to operate over either IPv6 or IPv4.

INSTALLING AND CONFIGURING THE IPV6 PROTOCOL

There are two ways to install the IPv6 protocol for the Windows .NET Server 2003 family:

■ Install the **Microsoft TCP/IP version 6** protocol when configuring the properties of a LAN connection in the Network Connections folder.

■ Execute **netsh interface ipv6 install** at a command prompt.

IPv6 is designed to be auto-configuring. By default, the IPv6 protocol for the Windows .NET Server 2003 family automatically configures link-local addresses. If there is an IPv6 router on the node's subnet or an ISATAP router, the node uses received router advertisements to automatically configure additional addresses, a default router, and other configuration parameters.

There are no property pages for the **Microsoft TCP/IP version 6** protocol in the Network Connections folder. To manually configure addresses, routes, or other parameters, use the Netsh utility and commands in the **netsh interface ipv6** context. For more information, see "Netsh.exe" in this chapter.

IPV6-ENABLED UTILITIES

The Windows .NET Server 2003 family includes the following IPv6-enabled command line utilities:

■ Ipconfig

■ Route

- ■ Ping
- ■ Tracert
- ■ Pathping
- ■ Netstat

Ipconfig

The Ipconfig utility is used to display all current TCP/IP network configuration values and to perform maintenance tasks such as refreshing DHCP and DNS settings. In the Windows .NET Server 2003 family, Ipconfig used without parameters displays IPv4 and IPv6 configuration for all physical adapters and tunnel interfaces that have addresses.

The following is an example display of the Ipconfig utility on a computer running a member of the Windows .NET Server 2003 family with the IPv6 protocol installed:

```
F:\>ipconfig
Windows IP Configuration
Ethernet adapter Local Area Connection:
    Connection-specific DNS Suffix  . : example.microsoft.com
    IP Address. . . . . . . . . . . : 157.60.137.151
    Subnet Mask . . . . . . . . . . : 255.255.252.0
    IP Address. . . . . . . . . . . : fec0::f282:204:5aff:fe56:1006%1
    IP Address. . . . . . . . . . . : 3ffe:2900:d005:f282:b8df:3ec8:8a61:a06b
    IP Address. . . . . . . . . . . : 3ffe:2900:d005:f282:204:5aff:fe56:1006
    IP Address. . . . . . . . . . . : fe80::204:5aff:fe56:1006%3
    Default Gateway . . . . . . . . : 157.60.136.1
                                      fe80::210:ffff:fed6:58c0%3

Tunnel adapter Automatic Tunneling Pseudo-Interface:

    Connection-specific DNS Suffix  . : example.microsoft.com
    IP Address. . . . . . . . . . . : fe80::5efe:157.60.137.151%2
    Default Gateway . . . . . . . . :
```

For more information about Ipconfig command line options, search for "ipconfig" in the Windows .NET Server Help and Support Center.

Route

The Route utility displays and modifies the entries in the local routing tables. The Route utility has been enhanced in the Windows .NET Server 2003 family to display both the IPv4 and IPv6 routing table when you execute the **route print** command.

The following is an example display of the **route print** command on a computer running a member of the Windows .NET Server 2003 family with the IPv6 protocol installed:

```
F:\>route print
IPv4 Route Table
===========================================================================
Interface List
0x1 ........................ MS TCP Loopback interface
0x10003 ...00 04 5a 56 10 06 ...... Linksys LNE100TX Fast Ethernet Adapter(LNE100TX v4)
===========================================================================
===========================================================================
Active Routes:
Network Destination        Netmask          Gateway       Interface  Metric
          0.0.0.0          0.0.0.0      157.60.136.1  157.60.137.151      20
        127.0.0.0        255.0.0.0        127.0.0.1       127.0.0.1       1
    157.60.136.0    255.255.252.0   157.60.137.151  157.60.137.151      20
  157.60.137.151  255.255.255.255        127.0.0.1       127.0.0.1      20
  157.60.255.255  255.255.255.255   157.60.137.151  157.60.137.151      20
        224.0.0.0        240.0.0.0   157.60.137.151  157.60.137.151      20
  255.255.255.255  255.255.255.255   157.60.137.151  157.60.137.151       1
Default Gateway:      157.60.136.1
===========================================================================
Persistent Routes:
  None


IPv6 Route Table
===========================================================================
Interface List
  3 ...00 04 5a 56 10 06 ...... Linksys LNE100TX Fast Ethernet Adapter(LNE100TX v4)
  2 ...9d 3b 89 97 ............ Automatic Tunneling Pseudo-Interface
  1 ........................ Loopback Pseudo-Interface
===========================================================================
===========================================================================
Active Routes:
 If Metric Network Destination      Gateway
  2      5 fe80::5efe:157.60.137.151/128
                             fe80::5efe:157.60.137.151
```

```
3      4 fec0::f282:204:5aff:fe56:1006/128
                                 fec0::f282:204:5aff:fe56:1006
3      8 fec0:0:0:f282::/64      On-link
3      4 3ffe:2900:d005:f282:b8df:3ec8:8a61:a06b/128
                                 3ffe:2900:d005:f282:b8df:3ec8:8a61:a06b
3      4 3ffe:2900:d005:f282:204:5aff:fe56:1006/128
                                 3ffe:2900:d005:f282:204:5aff:fe56:1006
3      8 3ffe:2900:d005:f282::/64 On-link
3    256 ::/0                    fe80::210:ffff:fed6:58c0
3      8 ff00::/8                On-link
3      4 fe80::204:5aff:fe56:1006/128
                                 fe80::204:5aff:fe56:1006
1      4 ::1/128                 ::1
1      8 ff00::/8                On-link
1      4 fe80::1/128             fe80::1
===========================================================================
Persistent Routes:
  None
```

For more information about Route command line options, search for "route" in the Windows .NET Server Help and Support Center.

Ping

In previous versions of Windows, the Ping utility verified IPv4-level connectivity to another TCP/IP computer by sending Internet Control Message Protocol (ICMP) Echo messages. The receipt of corresponding Echo Reply messages is displayed, along with round-trip times. Ping is the primary TCP/IP utility used to troubleshoot reachability and name resolution.

The Ping utility in the Windows .NET Server 2003 family has been enhanced to support IPv6 in the following ways:

- Ping uses either ICMPv4 Echo or ICMPv6 Echo Request messages to verify IP-connectivity.

- Ping can parse both IPv4 and IPv6 address formats.

- If you specify a target host by name, the addresses returned by using Windows name resolution techniques can contain both IPv4 and IPv6 addresses, in which case, by default, an IPv6 address is used first.

The following is an example display of the Ping utility on a computer running a member of the Windows .NET Server 2003 family with the IPv6 protocol installed:

```
F:\>ping fec0::f282:2b0:d0ff:fee9:4143%1

Pinging fec0::f282:2b0:d0ff:fee9:4143%1 from fec0::f282:204:5aff:fe56:1006%1 with
32 bytes of data:

Reply from fec0::f282:2b0:d0ff:fee9:4143: time<1ms
Reply from fec0::f282:2b0:d0ff:fee9:4143: time<1ms
Reply from fec0::f282:2b0:d0ff:fee9:4143: time<1ms
Reply from fec0::f282:2b0:d0ff:fee9:4143: time<1ms

Ping statistics for fec0::f282:2b0:d0ff:fee9:4143:
    Packets: Sent = 4, Received = 4, Lost = 0 (0% loss),
Approximate round trip times in milli-seconds:
    Minimum = 0ms, Maximum = 0ms, Average = 0ms
```

The following command line options support IPv6:

- **-i** *HopLimit*
  Sets the value of the Hop Limit field in the IPv6 header. The default value is 128. The **-i** option is also used to set the value of the TTL field in the IPv4 header.

- **-R**
  Forces Ping to trace the round-trip path by sending the ICMPv6 Echo Request message to the destination and include an IPv6 Routing extension header with the sending node as the next destination.

- **-S** *SourceAddr*
  Forces Ping to use a specified IPv6 source address.

- **-4**
  Forces Ping to use an IPv4 address when the DNS name query for a host name returns both IPv4 and IPv6 addresses.

- **-6**
  Forces Ping to use an IPv6 address when the DNS name query for a host name returns both IPv4 and IPv6 addresses.

NOTE:
The Ping **-f**, **-v** *TOS*, **-r** *count*, **-s** *count*, **-j** *host-list*, and **-k** *host-list* command line options are not supported for IPv6.

When you specify a destination IPv6 address for a Ping, Tracert, or Pathping command, you might have to specify a zone ID as part of the address. The zone ID specifies the zone of the destination for Echo Request messages. The syntax for specifying a zone ID is: *IPv6Address%ZoneID*, in which *ZoneID* is an integer value. For typical link-local addresses, *ZoneID* is equal to the interface index, as displayed by the output of the **netsh interface ipv6 show interface** command. For site-local addresses, *ZoneID* is equal to the site number, as displayed in the output of the **netsh interface ipv6 show interface level=verbose** command (the "Zone ID for Site" property). If multiple sites are not being used, a zone ID for site-local addresses is not required. The *ZoneID* parameter is not required when the destination is a global address.

For more information about Ping command line options, search for "ping" in the Windows .NET Server Help and Support Center.

Tracert

The Tracert utility determines the path taken to a destination. For IPv4, Tracert sends ICMPv4 Echo messages to the destination with incrementally increasing Time-to-Live (TTL) field values. For IPv6, Tracert sends ICMPv6 Echo Request messages to the destination with incrementally increasing Hop Limit field values. The path displayed is the list of nearside router interfaces of the routers in the path between a source host and a destination node.

The Tracert utility in the Windows .NET Server 2003 family has been enhanced to support IPv6 in the following ways:

■ Tracert can parse both IPv4 and IPv6 address formats.

■ If you specify a target host by name, the addresses returned using Windows name resolution techniques can contain both IPv4 and IPv6 addresses, in which case, by default, an IPv6 address is used first.

The following is an example display of the Tracert utility on a computer running a member of the Windows .NET Server 2003 family with the IPv6 protocol installed:

```
F:\>tracert fec0::f282:2b0:d0ff:fee9:4143%1


Tracing route to fec0::f282:2b0:d0ff:fee9:4143%1 over a maximum of 30 hops


  1    <1 ms    <1 ms    <1 ms  fec0::f241:2b0:d0ff:fea4:243d
  2    <1 ms    <1 ms    <1 ms  fec0::f2ac:2b0:d0ff:fea5:d347
  3    <1 ms    <1 ms    <1 ms  fec0::f282:2b0:d0ff:fee9:4143


Trace complete.
```

The following Tracert command line options support IPv6:

- **-R**

  Forces Tracert to trace the round-trip path by sending the ICMPv6 Echo Request message to the destination, including an IPv6 Routing extension header with the sending node as the next destination.

- **-S** *SourceAddr*

  Forces Tracert to use a specified IPv6 source address.

- **-4**

  Forces Tracert to use an IPv4 address when the DNS name query for a host name returns both IPv4 and IPv6 addresses.

- **-6**

  Forces Tracert to use an IPv6 address when the DNS name query for a host name returns both IPv4 and IPv6 addresses.

NOTE:

The Tracert **-j** *host-list* command line option is not supported for IPv6.

For more information about Tracert command line options, search for "tracert" in the Windows .NET Server Help and Support Center.

Pathping

The Pathping utility provides information about network latency and network loss at intermediate hops between a source and destination. For IPv4, Pathping sends multiple ICMPv4 Echo messages to each router between a source and destination over a period of time, and then computes results based on the packets returned from each router. For IPv6, Pathping sends ICMPv6 Echo Request messages. Because Pathping displays the degree of packet loss at any given router or link, you can determine which routers or subnets might be having network problems. Pathping performs the equivalent of the Tracert utility by identifying which routers are in the path, and then sends messages periodically to all of the routers over a specified time period and computes statistics based on the number returned from each.

The Pathping utility in the Windows .NET Server 2003 family has been enhanced to support IPv6 in the following ways:

- Pathping can parse both IPv4 and IPv6 address formats.

- If you specify a target host by name, the addresses returned using Windows name resolution techniques can contain both IPv4 and IPv6 addresses, in which case, by default, an IPv6 address is used first.

The following is an example display of the Pathping utility on a computer running a member of the Windows .NET Server 2003 family with the IPv6 protocol installed:

```
F:\>pathping fec0::f282:2b0:d0ff:fee9:4143%1

Tracing route to fec0::f282:2b0:d0ff:fee9:4143%1 over a maximum of 30 hops

  0  server1.example.microsoft.com [fec0::f282:204:5aff:fe56:1006%1]
  1  fec0::f282:2b0:d0ff:fee9:4143

Computing statistics for 25 seconds...
            Source to Here    This Node/Link
Hop  RTT    Lost/Sent = Pct   Lost/Sent = Pct  Address
  0                                             server1.example.microsoft.co
m [fec0::f282:204:5aff:fe56:1006%1]
                              0/ 100 =  0%   |
  1    0ms    0/ 100 =  0%    0/ 100 =  0%  fec0::f282:2b0:d0ff:fee9:4143%1

Trace complete.
```

The following Pathping command line options support IPv6:

- **-4**

  Forces Pathping to use an IPv4 address when the DNS name query for a host name returns both IPv4 and IPv6 addresses.

- **-6**

  Forces Pathping to use an IPv6 address when the DNS name query for a host name returns both IPv4 and IPv6 addresses.

NOTE:

The Pathping **-g** *host-list* command line option is not supported for IPv6.

For more information about Pathping command line options, search for "pathping" in the Windows .NET Server Help and Support Center.

Netstat

The Netstat utility is used to display active TCP connections, ports on which the computer is listening, Ethernet statistics, the IPv4 routing table, IPv4 statistics (for the IP, ICMP, TCP, and UDP protocols), the IPv6 routing table, and IPv6 statistics (for the IPv6, ICMPv6, TCP over IPv6, and UDP over IPv6 protocols).

The following is an example display of the Netstat utility on a computer running a member of the Windows .NET Server 2003 family with the IPv6 protocol installed:

```
F:\>netstat -s

IPv4 Statistics

  Packets Received                    = 187107
  Received Header Errors              = 0
  Received Address Errors             = 84248
  Datagrams Forwarded                 = 0
  Unknown Protocols Received          = 0
  Received Packets Discarded          = 0
  Received Packets Delivered          = 186194
  Output Requests                     = 27767
  Routing Discards                    = 0
  Discarded Output Packets            = 0
  Output Packet No Route              = 0
  Reassembly Required                 = 0
  Reassembly Successful               = 0
  Reassembly Failures                 = 0
  Datagrams Successfully Fragmented   = 0
  Datagrams Failing Fragmentation     = 0
  Fragments Created                   = 0


IPv6 Statistics

  Packets Received                    = 53118
  Received Header Errors              = 0
  Received Address Errors             = 0
  Datagrams Forwarded                 = 0
  Unknown Protocols Received          = 0
  Received Packets Discarded          = 0
  Received Packets Delivered          = 0
  Output Requests                     = 60695
  Routing Discards                    = 0
  Discarded Output Packets            = 0
  Output Packet No Route              = 0
  Reassembly Required                 = 0
  Reassembly Successful               = 0
  Reassembly Failures                 = 0
```

```
Datagrams Successfully Fragmented   = 0
Datagrams Failing Fragmentation     = 0
Fragments Created                   = 0
```

ICMPv4 Statistics

	Received	Sent
Messages	682	881
Errors	0	0
Destination Unreachable	2	201
Time Exceeded	0	0
Parameter Problems	0	0
Source Quenches	0	0
Redirects	0	0
Echos	340	340
Echo Replies	340	340
Timestamps	0	0
Timestamp Replies	0	0
Address Masks	0	0
Address Mask Replies	0	0

ICMPv6 Statistics

	Received	Sent
Messages	309	80
Errors	0	0
Destination Unreachable	193	0
Echos	4	0
Echo Replies	0	4
MLD Reports	0	6
Router Solicitations	0	7
Router Advertisements	54	0
Neighbor Solicitations	31	32
Neighbor Advertisements	27	31

TCP Statistics for IPv4

```
Active Opens                    = 128
Passive Opens                   = 106
Failed Connection Attempts      = 0
Reset Connections               = 3
Current Connections             = 16
```

```
      Segments Received                    = 22708
      Segments Sent                        = 26255
      Segments Retransmitted               = 37

   TCP Statistics for IPv6

      Active Opens                         = 74
      Passive Opens                        = 72
      Failed Connection Attempts           = 1
      Reset Connections                    = 0
      Current Connections                  = 14
      Segments Received                    = 52809
      Segments Sent                        = 59813
      Segments Retransmitted               = 3

   UDP Statistics for IPv4

      Datagrams Received     = 160982
      No Ports               = 2158
      Receive Errors         = 2
      Datagrams Sent         = 591

   UDP Statistics for IPv6

      Datagrams Received     = 0
      No Ports               = 0
      Receive Errors         = 0
      Datagrams Sent         = 744
```

For more information about Netstat command line options, search for "netstat" in the Windows .NET Server Help and Support Center.

IPV6 COMMAND LINE UTILITIES

The Windows .NET Server 2003 family includes the following IPv6 command line utilities:

- Netsh.exe (with the **interface ipv6, interface ipv6 6to4, interface ipv6 isatap,** and **interface portproxy** contexts)
- Ipsec6.exe

Netsh.exe

You can use the Netsh.exe command-line and scripting utility to configure networking components on the local computer or remote computers. You can run Netsh commands from the command prompt, interactively from a Netsh command prompt, or by creating a script file to run a batch of Netsh commands. You can also use the Netsh utility to save a computer's current network configuration in a script file for either archival and restoration purposes or to configure other servers.

Netsh supports multiple components through the addition of Netsh helper dynamic link libraries (DLLs). A Netsh helper DLL extends Netsh functionality by providing additional commands to monitor or configure a specific networking component. For example, Ipv6mon.dll provides commands to configure IPv6 and subcomponents of the IPv6 protocol. Each Netsh helper DLL provides a context—a group of commands for a specific networking component. Within each context, subcontexts might exist. For example, within the **interface ipv6** context, the **6to4** and **isatap** subcontexts group 6to4 and ISATAP configuration commands.

For more information about the Netsh utility, search for "netsh overview" in the Windows .NET Server Help and Support Center.

Netsh interface ipv6

Although IPv6 was designed to be self-configuring for most IPv6 hosts, there is still a need to configure specific configuration parameters based on the role of the computer running a member of the Windows .NET Server 2003 family on the network. For example, a simple host computer with a single LAN interface should not require any additional configuration. All configuration for addresses and routes for basic connectivity is provided through router discovery. However, a computer acting as a router or PortProxy server must be manually configured.

If additional configuration is needed, using the commands in the **netsh interface ipv6** context is the only way to configure the IPv6 protocol provided with the Windows .NET Server 2003 family. There are no dialog boxes for configuring the **Microsoft TCP/IP version 6** protocol in the Network Connections folder.

For more information about the syntax for a specific **netsh interface ipv6** command, either type the command without the parameters to obtain command-line help, or search for "netsh interface ipv6" in the Windows .NET Server Help and Support Center.

Useful commands to gather information about the IPv6 configuration of a computer running the IPv6 protocol for the Windows .NET Server 2003 family are the following:

- Netsh interface ipv6 show interface
- Netsh interface ipv6 show address
- Netsh interface ipv6 show routes
- Netsh interface ipv6 show neighbors
- Netsh interface ipv6 show destinationcache

Netsh interface ipv6 show interface

This command displays the list of IPv6 interfaces. Here is an example:

```
Idx  Met   MTU   State        Name
---  ----  ----  ----------   -----
  3    0   1500  Connected    Local Area Connection
  2    1   1280  Connected    Automatic Tunneling Pseudo-Interface
  1    0   1500  Connected    Loopback Pseudo-Interface
```

Netsh interface ipv6 show address

This command displays the list of IPv6 addresses for each interface. Here is an example:

```
Interface 3: Local Area Connection

Addr Type  DAD State  Valid Life   Pref. Life  Address
---------  ---------  ----------   ----------  -----------------------------------
Public     Preferred  29d23h58m51s 6d23h58m51s
fec0::f282:204:5aff:fe56:1006
Anonymous  Preferred  6d56m49s          54m2s
3ffe:2900:d005:f282:b8df:3ec8:8a61:a06b
Public     Preferred  29d23h58m51s 6d23h58m51s
3ffe:2900:d005:f282:204:5aff:fe56:1006
Link       Preferred  infinite     infinite fe80::204:5aff:fe56:1006


Interface 2: Automatic Tunneling Pseudo-Interface

Addr Type  DAD State  Valid Life   Pref. Life   Address
---------  ---------  ----------   ----------   -----------------------------------
Link       Preferred  infinite     infinite    fe80::5efe:157.60.137.151
```

```
Interface 1: Loopback Pseudo-Interface

Addr Type  DAD State  Valid Life   Pref. Life   Address
---------  ---------  ----------   ----------   -----------------------------------
Loopback   Preferred  infinite     infinite     ::1
Link       Preferred  infinite     infinite     fe80::1
```

Netsh interface ipv6 show routes

This command displays the list of IPv6 routes in the IPv6 routing table. Here is an example:

```
Publish  Type      Met  Prefix                    Idx  Gateway/Interface Name
-------  --------  ---  ----------------------    ---  -----------------------
no       Autoconf    8  fec0:0:0:f282::/64          3  Local Area Connection
no       Autoconf    8  3ffe:2900:d005:f282::/64    3  Local Area Connection
no       Autoconf  256  ::/0                        3  fe80::210:ffff:fed6:58c0
```

By default, host and multicast routes are not displayed. To see all the IPv6 routes, use the **netsh interface ipv6 show routes level=verbose** command.

Netsh interface ipv6 show neighbors

This command displays the contents of the neighbor cache, sorted by interface. Here is an example:

```
Interface 3: Local Area Connection

Internet Address                            Physical Address   Type
----------------------------------------    ----------------   -------------
fe80::210:ffff:fed6:58c0                    00-10-ff-d6-58-c0  Stale (router)
fe80::204:5aff:fe56:1006                    00-04-5a-56-10-06  Permanent
3ffe:2900:d005:f282:204:5aff:fe56:1006      00-04-5a-56-10-06  Permanent
3ffe:2900:d005:f282:b8df:3ec8:8a61:a06b     00-04-5a-56-10-06  Permanent
fec0::f282:204:5aff:fe56:1006               00-04-5a-56-10-06  Permanent


Interface 2: Automatic Tunneling Pseudo-Interface

Internet Address                            Physical Address   Type
----------------------------------------    ----------------   -------------
fe80::5efe:157.60.137.151                   127.0.0.1          Permanent
```

```
Interface 1: Loopback Pseudo-Interface

Internet Address                         Physical Address   Type
---------------------------------------- ----------------   -------------
fe80::1                                                     Permanent
::1                                                         Permanent
```

Netsh interface ipv6 show destinationcache

This command displays the contents of the destination cache, sorted by interface. Here is an example:

```
Interface 3: Local Area Connection

PMTU Destination Address                        Next Hop Address
---- -------------------------------------      ------------------------
1500 fec0:0:0:ffff::3                           fe80::210:ffff:fed6:58c0
1500 fec0:0:0:ffff::2                           fe80::210:ffff:fed6:58c0
1500 fec0:0:0:ffff::1                           fe80::210:ffff:fed6:58c0
```

Netsh interface ipv6 6to4

The commands in the **Netsh interface ipv6 6to4** context are used to configure the behavior or to display the configuration of the 6to4 component on either a 6to4 host or a 6to4 router.

For more information about the syntax for a specific **netsh interface ipv6 6to4** command, either type the command without the parameters to obtain command-line help or search for "netsh interface ipv6" in the Windows .NET Server Help and Support Center. The syntax for the commands in the **netsh interface ipv6 6to4** context is included in the topic titled "Netsh commands for Interface IPv6: Command-line reference."

Netsh interface ipv6 isatap

The commands in the **netsh interface ipv6 isatap** context are used to configure the behavior or display the configuration of the ISATAP component on an ISATAP router. For more information about the syntax for a specific **netsh interface ipv6 isatap** command, either type the command without the parameters to obtain command-line help or search for "netsh interface ipv6" in the Windows .NET Server Help and Support Center. The syntax for the commands in the **netsh interface ipv6 isatap** context is included in the topic titled "Netsh commands for Interface IPv6: Command-line reference."

Netsh interface portproxy

The commands in the **netsh interface portproxy** context are used to configure PortProxy behavior or to display its configuration. For more information about the syntax for a specific **netsh interface portproxy** command, either type the command without the parameters to obtain command-line help or search for "netsh interface portproxy" in the Windows .NET Server Help and Support Center.

Ipsec6.exe

You can use Ipsec6.exe to configure IPSec policies and security associations for IPSec-protected IPv6 traffic. For more information about Ipsec6.exe, search for "ipsec6" in the Windows .NET Server Help and Support Center. The syntax for the Ipsec6.exe commands is included in the topic titled "IPv6 utilities."

For an example of using Ipsec6.exe to configure IPSec security policies and associations for two link-local hosts, see Appendix E, "Setting up an IPv6 Test Lab."

NOTE:
The IPSec support for the IPv6 protocol for the Windows .NET Server 2003 family is not designed for production use. The Ipsec6.exe utility is provided for experimentation purposes and will be removed in a future version of the Windows operating system.

TESTING FOR UNDERSTANDING

To test your understanding of the IPv6 protocol for the Windows .NET Server 2003 family, answer the following questions. See Appendix D to check your answers.

1. List and describe the features of the IPv6 protocol that allow for IPv4 and IPv6 coexistence.

2. How do you configure the IPv6 protocol for the Windows .NET Server 2003 family after it has been installed?

3. Under what circumstances will a Windows .NET Server IPv6 router advertise itself as a default router?

4. List and describe the types of network communication in which both the client and server components are IPv6-enabled in the Windows .NET Server 2003 family.

5. List the two ways to install the IPv6 protocol for the Windows .NET Server 2003 family.

6. List how the common TCP/IP utilities have been enhanced to support IPv6 in the Windows .NET Server 2003 family.

Chapter 3

IPv6 Addressing

At the end of this chapter, you should be able to:

- Describe the IPv6 address space and state why the address length of 128 bits was chosen.

- Describe IPv6 address syntax, including zero suppression and compression and prefixes.

- Enumerate and describe the function of the different types of unicast IPv6 addresses.

- Describe the format of multicast IPv6 addresses.

- Describe the function of anycast IPv6 addresses.

- Describe how IPv6 interface identifiers are derived.

- List and compare the different addressing concepts between IPv4 addresses and IPv6 addresses.

THE IPV6 ADDRESS SPACE

The most obvious distinguishing feature of IPv6 is its use of much larger addresses. The size of an address in IPv6 is 128 bits, a bit-string that is four times longer than the 32-bit IPv4 address. A 32-bit address space allows for 2^{32}, or 4,294,967,296, possible addresses. A 128-bit address space allows for 2^{128}, or 340,282,366,920,938,463,463,374,607,431,768,211,456 (or 3.4×10^{38}), possible addresses.

In the late 1970s, when the IPv4 address space was designed, it was unimaginable that it could ever be exhausted. However, due to changes in technology and an allocation practice that did not anticipate the recent explosion of hosts on the Internet, the IPv4 address space was consumed to the point that by 1992, it was clear a replacement would be necessary.

With IPv6, it is even harder to conceive that the IPv6 address space will ever be consumed. To help put this number in perspective, a 128-bit address space provides 665,570,793,348,866,943,898,599 (6.65×10^{23}) addresses for every square meter of the Earth's surface.

It is important to remember that the decision to make the IPv6 address 128 bits in length was not so that every square meter of the Earth could have 6.65×10^{23} addresses. Rather, the relatively large size of the IPv6 address is designed to be divided into hierarchical routing domains that reflect the topology of the modern-day Internet. The use of 128 bits allows for multiple levels of hierarchy and flexibility in designing hierarchical addressing and routing that is currently lacking on the IPv4-based Internet.

ADDRESSES PER SQUARE METER OF THE EARTH

The number of 6.65×10^{23} addresses for every square meter of the Earth's surface is derived from the fact that the surface of the Earth is approximately 197,399,019 square miles and there are 2.59×10^{6} square meters per square mile. So, the Earth's surface is $197,399,019 \times 2.59 \times 10^{6}$, or 511,263,971,197,990 square meters.

Therefore, there are 340,282,366,920,938,463,463,374,607,431,768, 211,456 / 511,263,971,197,990, or 665,570,793,348,866,943,898,599 (or 6.65×10^{23}) addresses for each square meter of the Earth's surface.

It is easy to get lost in the vastness of the IPv6 address space. As we will discover, the unthinkably large 128-bit IPv6 address that is assigned to an interface on a typical IPv6 host is composed of a 64-bit subnet identifier and a 64-bit interface identifier (a 50-50 split between subnet space and interface space). The 64 bits of subnet identifier leave enough addressing room to satisfy the addressing requirements of three levels of Internet service providers (ISPs) between your organization and the backbone of the Internet and the addressing needs of your organization. The 64 bits of interface identifier accommodate the mapping of current and future link-layer media access control (MAC) addresses.

Current Allocation

Similar to the way in which the IPv4 address space was divided into unicast addresses (using Internet address classes) and multicast addresses, the IPv6 address space is divided on the basis of the value of high-order bits. The high-order bits and their fixed values are known as a Format Prefix (FP).

Table 3-1 lists the allocation of the IPv6 address space by FPs as defined in RFC 2373.

Table 3-1. CURRENT ALLOCATION OF THE IPv6 ADDRESS SPACE

Allocation	Format Prefix (FP)	Fraction of the Address Space
Reserved	0000 0000	1/256
Unassigned	0000 0001	1/256
Reserved for Network Service Access Point (NSAP) allocation	0000 001	1/128
Unassigned	0000 010	1/128
Unassigned	0000 011	1/128
Unassigned	0000 1	1/32
Unassigned	0001	1/16
Aggregatable global unicast addresses	001	1/8
Unassigned	010	1/8
Unassigned	011	1/8
Unassigned	100	1/8
Unassigned	101	1/8
Unassigned	110	1/8
Unassigned	1110	1/16
Unassigned	1111 0	1/32
Unassigned	1111 10	1/64
Unassigned	1111 110	1/128
Unassigned	1111 1110 0	1/512
Link-local unicast addresses	1111 1110 10	1/1024
Site-local unicast addresses	1111 1110 11	1/1024
Multicast addresses	1111 1111	1/256

The current set of unicast addresses that can be used with IPv6 nodes consists of aggregatable global unicast addresses, link-local unicast addresses, and site-local unicast addresses. These addresses represent only 12.7 percent of the entire IPv6 address space.

IPv6 ADDRESS SYNTAX

IPv4 addresses are represented in dotted-decimal format. The 32-bit IPv4 address is divided along 8-bit boundaries. Each set of 8 bits is converted to its decimal equivalent and separated by periods. For IPv6, the 128-bit address is divided along 16-bit boundaries, and each 16-bit block is converted to a 4-digit hexadecimal number and separated by colons. The resulting representation is called *colon hexadecimal.*

The following is an IPv6 address in binary form:

00100001110110100000000001101001100000000000000000000010111100111011
00000010101010100000000001111111111111110001010001001110001011010

The 128-bit address is divided along 16-bit boundaries:

0010000111011010   0000000011010011   0000000000000000   0010111100111011

0000001010101010   0000000011111111   1111111000101000   1001110001011010

Each 16-bit block is converted to hexadecimal and delimited with colons. The result is:

21DA:00D3:0000:2F3B:02AA:00FF:FE28:9C5A

IPv6 address representation is further simplified by suppressing the leading zeros within each 16-bit block. However, each block must have at least a single digit. With leading zero suppression, the result is:

21DA:D3:0:2F3B:2AA:FF:FE28:9C5A

NUMBER SYSTEM CHOICE FOR IPV6

Hexadecimal (the $Base_{16}$ numbering system), rather than decimal (the $Base_{10}$ numbering system), is used for IPv6 because it is easier to convert between hexadecimal and binary than it is to convert between decimal and binary. Each hexadecimal digit represents four binary digits.

With IPv4, decimal is used to make the IPv4 addresses more palatable for humans and a 32-bit address becomes 4 decimal numbers separated by the period (.) character. With IPv6, dotted decimal representation would result in 16 decimal numbers separated by the period (.) character. IPv6 addresses are so large that there is no attempt to make them palatable to most humans, with the exception of some types of IPv6 addresses that contain embedded IPv4 addresses. Configuration of typical

continued

Number System Choice for IPv6 *continued*

end systems is automated and end users will almost always use names rather than IPv6 addresses. Therefore, the addresses are expressed in a way to make them more palatable to computers and IPv6 network administrators who understand the semantics and relationship of hexadecimal and binary numbers.

Table 3-2 lists the conversion between binary, hexadecimal, and decimal numbers.

Table 3-2. **CONVERTING BETWEEN BINARY, HEXADECIMAL, AND DECIMAL NUMBERS**

Binary	*Hexadecimal*	*Decimal*
0000	0	0
0001	1	1
0010	2	2
0011	3	3
0100	4	4
0101	5	5
0110	6	6
0111	7	7
1000	8	8
1001	9	9
1010	A	10
1011	B	11
1100	C	12
1101	D	13
1110	E	14
1111	F	15

Compressing Zeros

Some types of IPv6 addresses contain long sequences of zeros. To further simplify the representation of IPv6 addresses, a single contiguous sequence of 16-bit blocks set to 0 in the colon hexadecimal format can be compressed to ::, known as a *double colon*.

For example, the link-local address of FE80:0:0:0:2AA:FF:FE9A:4CA2 can be compressed to FE80::2AA:FF:FE9A:4CA2. The multicast address FF02:0:0:0:0:0:0:2 can be compressed to FF02::2.

NOTE:

You cannot use zero compression to include part of a 16-bit block. For example, you cannot express FF02:30:0:0:0:0:0:5 as FF02:3::5, but FF02:30::5 is correct.

HOW MANY BITS IN ::?

To determine how many 0 bits are represented by the ::, you can count the number of blocks in the compressed address, subtract this number from 8, and then multiply the result by 16. For example, in the address FF02::2, there are two blocks (the "FF02" block and the "2" block.) The number of bits expressed by the :: is 96 (96 = (8 − 2) × 16). Zero compression can be used only once in a given address. Otherwise, you could not determine the number of 0 bits represented by each instance of ::.

IPv6 Prefixes

The prefix is the part of the address where the bits have fixed values or are the bits of a route or subnet identifier. Prefixes for IPv6 subnet identifiers and routes are expressed in the same way as Classless Inter-Domain Routing (CIDR) notation for IPv4. An IPv6 prefix is written in *address/prefix-length* notation.

For example, 21DA:D3::/48 is a route prefix and 21DA:D3:0:2F3B::/64 is a subnet prefix. As described earlier in this chapter, the 64-bit prefix is used for individual subnets to which nodes are attached. All subnets have a 64-bit prefix. Any prefix that is less than 64 bits is a route or address range that is summarizing a portion of the IPv6 address space.

NOTE:

IPv4 implementations commonly use a dotted decimal representation of the network prefix known as the subnet mask. A subnet mask is not used for IPv6. Only the prefix length notation is supported.

An IPv6 prefix is relevant only for routes or address ranges, not for individual unicast addresses. In IPv4, it is common to express an IPv4 address with its prefix length. For example, 192.168.29.7/24 (equivalent to 192.168.29.7 with the subnet mask 255.255.255.0) denotes the IPv4 address 192.168.29.7 with a 24-bit subnet mask. Because IPv4 addresses are no longer class-based, you cannot assume the class-based subnet mask based on the value of the leading octet. The prefix length is included so that you can determine which bits identify the subnet and which bits identify the host on the subnet. Because the number of bits used to identify the subnet in IPv4 is variable, the prefix length is needed to separate the subnet ID from the host ID.

In IPv6, however, there is no notion of a variable length subnet identifier. At the individual IPv6 subnet level for currently defined unicast IPv6 addresses, the number of bits used to identify the subnet is always 64 and the number of bits used to identify the host on the subnet is always 64. Therefore, while unicast IPv6 addresses written with their prefix lengths are permitted in RFC 2373, in practice their prefix lengths are always 64 and therefore do not need to be expressed. For example, there is no need to express the IPv6 unicast address FEC0::2AC4:2AA:FF:FE9A:82D4 as FEC0::2AC4:2AA:FF:FE9A:82D4/64. Due to the 50-50 split of subnet and interface identifiers, the unicast IPv6 address FEC0::2AC4:2AA:FF:FE9A:82D4 implies that the subnet identifier is FEC0:0:0:2AC4::/64.

TYPES OF IPV6 ADDRESSES

There are three types of IPv6 addresses:

1. Unicast

   A unicast address identifies a single interface within the scope of the type of address. The scope of an address is the region of the IPv6 network over which the address is unique. With the appropriate unicast routing topology, packets addressed to a unicast address are delivered to a single interface. To accommodate load-balancing systems, RFC 2373 allows for multiple interfaces to use the same address as long as they appear as a single interface to the IPv6 implementation on the host.

2. Multicast

   A multicast address identifies zero or more interfaces. With the appropriate multicast routing topology, packets addressed to a multicast address are delivered to all interfaces identified by the address.

3. Anycast

   An anycast address identifies multiple interfaces. With the appropriate unicast routing topology, packets addressed to an anycast address are delivered to a single interface—the nearest interface that is identified by the address. The nearest interface is defined as being the closest in terms of routing distance. A multicast address is used for one-to-many communication, with delivery to multiple interfaces. An anycast address is used for one-to-one-of-many communication, with delivery to a single interface.

In all cases, IPv6 addresses identify interfaces, not nodes. A node is identified by any unicast address assigned to any one of its interfaces.

NOTE:

RFC 2373 does not define a broadcast address. All types of IPv4 broadcast addressing are performed in IPv6 using multicast addresses. For example, the subnet and limited broadcast addresses from IPv4 are replaced with the link-local scope all-nodes multicast address of FF02::1.

UNICAST IPV6 ADDRESSES

The following types of addresses are unicast IPv6 addresses:

- Aggregatable global unicast addresses
- Link-local addresses
- Site-local addresses
- Special addresses
- Compatibility addresses
- NSAP addresses

Aggregatable Global Unicast Addresses

Aggregatable global unicast addresses, also known as global addresses, are identified by the FP of 001. IPv6 global addresses are equivalent to public IPv4 addresses. They are globally routable and reachable on the IPv6 portion of the Internet.

As the name implies, aggregatable global unicast addresses are designed to be aggregated or summarized to produce an efficient routing infrastructure. Unlike the current IPv4-based Internet, which is a mixture of both flat and hierarchical routing, the IPv6-based Internet has been designed from its foundation to support efficient, hierarchical addressing and routing. The scope of a global address is the entire IPv6 Internet.

Figure 3-1 shows the structure of an aggregatable global unicast address.

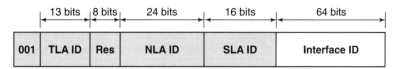

Figure 3-1. *The structure of an aggregatable global unicast address*

The fields in the aggregatable global unicast address are:

TLA ID — Top-Level Aggregation Identifier. The size of this field is 13 bits. The TLA ID identifies the highest level in the routing hierarchy. TLA IDs are administered by the Internet Assigned Numbers Authority (IANA) and allocated to local Internet registries that, in turn, allocate individual TLA IDs to large, long-haul ISPs. A 13-bit field allows up to 8,192 different TLA IDs. Routers in the highest level of the IPv6 Internet routing hierarchy (called default-free routers) do not have a default route—only routes with 16-bit prefixes corresponding to the allocated TLA IDs and additional entries for routes based on the TLA ID assigned to the routing region where the router is located.

Res — Bits that are reserved for future use in expanding the size of either the TLA ID or the NLA ID (defined next). The size of this field is 8 bits.

NLA ID — Next-Level Aggregation Identifier. The size of this field is 24 bits. The NLA ID allows an ISP to create multiple levels of addressing hierarchy within its network to both organize addressing and routing for downstream ISPs and identify organization sites. The structure of the ISP's network is not visible to the default-free routers. The combination of the 001 FP, the TLA ID, the Res field, and the NLA ID form a 48-bit prefix that is assigned to an organization's site that is connecting to the IPv6 portion of the Internet. A site is an organization network or portion of an organization's network that has a defined geographical location (such as an office, an office complex, or a campus).

SLA ID — Site-Level Aggregation Identifier. The SLA ID is used by an individual organization to identify subnets within its site. The size of this field is 16 bits. The organization can use these 16 bits within its site to create 65,536 subnets or create multiple levels of addressing hierarchy and an efficient routing infrastructure. With 16 bits of subnetting flexibility, an aggregatable global unicast prefix assigned to an organization is equivalent to that organization being allocated an IPv4 Class A network ID (assuming that the last octet is used for identifying nodes on subnets). The structure of the organization's network is not visible to the ISP.

Interface ID — Indicates the interface on a specific subnet. The size of this field is 64 bits. The interface ID in IPv6 is equivalent to the node ID or host ID in IPv4.

BILLIONS OF SITES

Another way to gauge the practical size of the IPv6 address space is to examine the number of sites that can connect to the IPv6 Internet. With the current FP of 001 and the current definition of the TLA ID (13 bits long) and NLA ID (24 bits long), it is possible to define 2^{37} or 137,438,953,472 possible 48-bit prefixes to assign to sites connected to the Internet. This large number of sites is possible even when we are using only 1/8th of the entire IPv6 address space.

By comparison, using the Internet address classes originally defined for IPv4, it was possible to assign 2,113,389 network IDs to organizations connected to the Internet. The number 2,113,389 is derived from adding up all the possible Class A, Class B, and Class C network IDs and then subtracting the network IDs used for the private address space. Even with the adoption of CIDR to make more efficient use of unassigned Class A and Class B network IDs, the number of possible sites connected to the Internet is not substantially increased nor does it approach the number of possible sites that can be connected to the IPv6 Internet.

Topologies Within Global Addresses

The fields within the global address create a three-level topological structure, as shown in Figure 3-2.

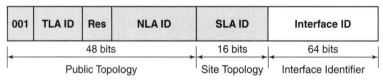

Figure 3-2. *The topological structure of the global address*

The public topology is the collection of larger and smaller ISPs that provide access to the IPv6 Internet. The site topology is the collection of subnets within an organization's site. The interface identifier specifies a unique interface on a subnet within an organization's site.

Local-Use Unicast Addresses

There are two types of local-use unicast addresses:

1. Link-local addresses are used between on-link neighbors and for Neighbor Discovery processes.

2. Site-local addresses are used between nodes communicating with other nodes in the same organization.

Link-Local Addresses

Link-local addresses, identified by the FP of 1111 1110 10, are used by nodes when communicating with neighboring nodes on the same link. For example, on a single link IPv6 network with no router, link-local addresses are used to communicate between hosts on the link. Link-local addresses are equivalent to Automatic Private IP Addressing (APIPA) IPv4 addresses autoconfigured on Microsoft Windows .NET Server 2003 family, Windows XP, Windows 2000, Windows Millennium Edition, and Windows 98 computers using the 169.254.0.0/16 prefix. The scope of a link-local address is the local link.

Figure 3-3 shows the structure of the link-local address.

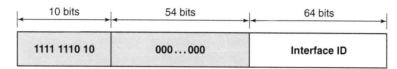

Figure 3-3. *The structure of the link-local address*

A link-local address is required for Neighbor Discovery processes and is always automatically configured, even in the absence of all other unicast addresses. For more information about the address autoconfiguration process for link-local addresses, see Chapter 8, "Address Autoconfiguration."

Link-local addresses always begin with FE80. With the 64-bit interface identifier, the prefix for link-local addresses is always FE80::/64. An IPv6 router never forwards link-local traffic beyond the link.

Site-Local Addresses

Site-local addresses, identified by the FP of 1111 1110 11, are equivalent to the IPv4 private address space (10.0.0.0/8, 172.16.0.0/12, and 192.168.0.0/16). For example, private intranets that do not have a direct, routed connection to the IPv6 Internet can use site-local addresses without conflicting with global addresses. Site-local addresses are not reachable from other sites, and routers must not forward site-local traffic outside the site. Site-local addresses can be used in addition to global addresses. The scope of a site-local address is the site.

Figure 3-4 shows the structure of the site-local address.

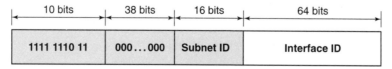

Figure 3-4. *The structure of the site-local address*

Unlike link-local addresses, site-local addresses are not automatically configured and must be assigned either through stateless or stateful address autoconfiguration. For more information, see Chapter 8, "Address Autoconfiguration."

The first 48 bits are always fixed for site-local addresses, beginning with FEC0::/48. After the 48 fixed bits is a 16-bit subnet identifier (Subnet ID field) that provides 16 bits with which you can create subnets within your organization. With 16 bits, you can have up to 65,536 subnets in a flat subnet structure, or you can divide the high-order bits of the Subnet ID field to create a hierarchical and aggregatable routing infrastructure. After the Subnet ID field is a 64-bit Interface ID field that identifies a specific interface on a subnet.

The global address and site-local address share the same structure beyond the first 48 bits of the address. In global addresses, the SLA ID field identifies the subnet within an organization. For site-local addresses, the Subnet ID field performs the same function. Because of this, you can create a subnetted routing infrastructure that is used for both site-local and global addresses.

For example, a specific subnet of your organization can be assigned the global prefix 3FFE:FFFF:4D1C:221A::/64 and the site-local prefix FEC0:0:0:221A::/64 where the subnet is effectively identified by the SLA ID/Subnet ID value of 221A. While the subnet identifier is the same for both prefixes, routes for both prefixes must still be propagated throughout the routing infrastructure so that addresses based on both prefixes are reachable.

Special IPv6 Addresses

The following are special IPv6 addresses:

- Unspecified address
  The unspecified address (0:0:0:0:0:0:0:0 or ::) is used only to indicate the absence of an address. It is equivalent to the IPv4 unspecified address of 0.0.0.0. The unspecified address is typically used as a source address when a unique address has not yet been determined. The unspecified address is never assigned to an interface or used as a destination address.

- Loopback address
  The loopback address (0:0:0:0:0:0:0:1 or ::1) is used to identify a loopback interface, enabling a node to send packets to itself. It is equivalent to the IPv4 loopback address of 127.0.0.1. Packets addressed to the loopback address must never be sent on a link or forwarded by an IPv6 router.

Compatibility Addresses

To aid in the migration from IPv4 to IPv6 and the coexistence of both types of hosts, the following addresses are defined:

- IPv4-compatible address
  The IPv4-compatible address, 0:0:0:0:0:0:*w.x.y.z* or ::*w.x.y.z* (where *w.x.y.z* is the dotted decimal representation of a public IPv4 address), is used by IPv6/IPv4 nodes that are communicating with IPv6 over an IPv4 infrastructure that uses public IPv4 addresses, such as the Internet.

- IPv4-mapped address
  The IPv4-mapped address, 0:0:0:0:0:FFFF:*w.x.y.z* or ::FFFF: *w.x.y.z*, is used to represent an IPv4-only node to an IPv6 node. Windows .NET Server 2003 family and Windows XP IPv6 do not support the use of IPv4-mapped addresses.

- 6over4 address
  An address of the type [*64-bit prefix*]:0:0:WWXX:YYZZ, where WWXX: YYZZ is the colon hexadecimal representation of *w.x.y.z* (a public or private IPv4 address), is used to represent a host for the tunneling mechanism known as 6over4.

- 6to4 address
  An address of the type 2002:WWXX:YYZZ:[*SLA ID*]:[*Interface ID*], where WWXX:YYZZ is the colon hexadecimal representation of *w.x.y.z* (a public IPv4 address), is used to represent a node for the tunneling mechanism known as 6to4.

- ISATAP address
  An address of the type [*64-bit prefix*]:0:5EFE:*w.x.y.z*, where *w.x.y.z* is a public or private IPv4 address, is used to represent a node for the address assignment mechanism known as Intra-Site Automatic Tunnel Addressing Protocol (ISATAP).

For more information about IPv6 compatibility addresses, see Chapter 11, "Coexistence and Migration."

NSAP Addresses

To provide a way of mapping Open Systems Interconnect (OSI) NSAP addresses to IPv6 addresses, NSAP addresses use the FP of 0000001 and map the last 121 bits of the NSAP address to an IPv6 address. For more information about the four types of NSAP address mappings, see RFC 1888. Figure 3-5 shows the structure of NSAP addresses for IPv6.

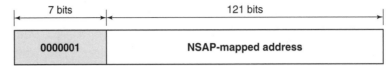

Figure 3-5. *The structure of NSAP addresses for IPv6*

MULTICAST IPV6 ADDRESSES

In IPv6, multicast traffic operates in the same way that it does in IPv4. Arbitrarily located IPv6 nodes can listen for multicast traffic on an arbitrary IPv6 multicast address. IPv6 nodes can listen to multiple multicast addresses at the same time. Nodes can join or leave a multicast group at any time.

IPv6 multicast addresses have the FP of 1111 1111. Therefore, an IPv6 multicast address always begins with FF. Multicast addresses cannot be used as source addresses or as intermediate destinations in a Routing header. Beyond the FP, multicast addresses include additional structure to identify flags, their scope, and the multicast group. Figure 3-6 shows the structure of the IPv6 multicast address.

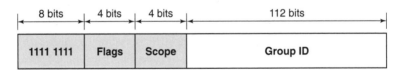

Figure 3-6. *The structure of the IPv6 multicast address*

The fields in the multicast address are:

Flags — Indicates flags set on the multicast address. The size of this field is 4 bits. As of RFC 2373, the only flag defined is the Transient (T) flag, which uses the low-order bit of the Flags field. When set to 0, the T flag indicates that the multicast address is a permanently assigned (well-known) multicast address allocated by IANA. When set to 1, the T flag indicates that the multicast address is a transient (non-permanently-assigned) multicast address.

Scope — Indicates the scope of the IPv6 network for which the multicast traffic is intended to be delivered. The size of this field is 4 bits. In addition to information provided by multicast routing protocols, routers use the multicast scope to determine whether multicast traffic can be forwarded.

Table 3-3 lists the values for the Scope field assigned in RFC 2373.

Table 3-3. DEFINED VALUES FOR THE SCOPE FIELD

Scope Field Value	Scope
0	Reserved
1	Node-local scope
2	Link-local scope
5	Site-local scope
8	Organization-local scope
E	Global scope
F	Reserved

For example, traffic with the multicast address of FF02::2 has a link-local scope. An IPv6 router never forwards this traffic beyond the local link.

Group ID – Identifies the multicast group and is unique within the scope. The size of this field is 112 bits. Permanently assigned group IDs are independent of the scope. Transient group IDs are relevant only to a specific scope. Multicast addresses from FF01:: through FF0F:: are reserved, well-known addresses.

To identify all nodes for the node-local and link-local scopes, the following addresses are defined:

■   FF01::1 (node-local scope all-nodes multicast address)

■   FF02::1 (link-local scope all-nodes multicast address)

To identify all routers for the node-local, link-local, and site-local scopes, the following addresses are defined:

■   FF01::2 (node-local scope all-routers multicast address)

■   FF02::2 (link-local scope all-routers multicast address)

■   FF05::2 (site-local scope all-routers multicast address)

For the current list of permanently assigned IPv6 multicast addresses, see *http://www.iana.org/assignments/ipv6-multicast-addresses*.

IPv6 multicast addresses replace all forms of IPv4 broadcast addresses. The IPv4 network broadcast (in which all host bits are set to 1 in a classful environment), subnet broadcast (in which all host bits are set to 1 in a non-classful environment), and limited broadcast (255.255.255.255) addresses are replaced by the link-local scope all-nodes multicast address (FF02:01) in IPv6.

Recommended Multicast IPv6 Addresses

With 112 bits in the Group ID field, it is possible to have 2^{112} group IDs. Because of the way in which IPv6 multicast addresses are mapped to Ethernet multicast MAC addresses, RFC 2373 recommends assigning the group ID from the low-order 32 bits of the IPv6 multicast address and setting the remaining original Group ID field bits to 0. By using only the low-order 32 bits, each group ID maps to a unique Ethernet multicast MAC address. Figure 3-7 shows the structure of the recommended IPv6 multicast address.

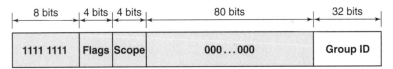

Figure 3-7. *The structure of the recommended IPv6 multicast address*

Solicited-Node Address

The solicited-node address facilitates the efficient querying of network nodes during link-layer address resolution—the resolving of a link-layer address of a known IPv6 address. In IPv4, the ARP Request frame is sent to the MAC-level broadcast, disturbing all nodes on the network segment, including those that are not running IPv4. IPv6 uses the Neighbor Solicitation message to perform link-layer address resolution. However, instead of using the local-link scope all-nodes multicast address as the Neighbor Solicitation message destination, which would disturb all IPv6 nodes on the local link, the solicited-node multicast address is used. The solicited-node multicast address is constructed from the prefix FF02::1:FF00:0/104 and the last 24 bits of a unicast IPv6 address.

For example, Node A is assigned the link-local address of FE80::2AA:FF:FE28:9C5A and is also listening on the corresponding solicited-node multicast address of FF02::1:FF28:9C5A. (An underline is used to highlight the correspondence of the last six hexadecimal digits.) Node B on the local link must resolve Node A's link-local address FE80::2AA:FF:FE28:9C5A to its corresponding link-layer address. Node B sends a Neighbor Solicitation message to the solicited-node multicast address of FF02::1:FF28:9C5A. Because Node A is listening on this multicast address, it processes the Neighbor Solicitation message and sends a unicast Neighbor Advertisement message in reply.

The result of using the solicited-node multicast address is that link-layer address resolutions, a common occurrence on a link, are not using a mechanism that disturbs all network nodes. By using the solicited-node address, very few nodes are disturbed during address resolution. In practice, due to the relationship between the link-layer MAC address, the IPv6 interface ID, and the solicited-node address, the solicited-node address acts as a pseudo-unicast address for very efficient address resolution. For more information, see "IPv6 Interface Identifiers" in this chapter.

ANYCAST IPV6 ADDRESSES

An anycast address is assigned to multiple interfaces. Packets addressed to an anycast address are forwarded by the routing infrastructure to the nearest interface to which the anycast address is assigned. In order to facilitate delivery, the routing infrastructure must be aware of the interfaces that have anycast addresses assigned to them and their distance in terms of routing metrics. This awareness is accomplished by the propagation of host routes throughout the routing infrastructure of the portion of the network that cannot summarize the anycast address using a route prefix.

For example, for the anycast address 3FFE:2900:D005:6187:2AA:FF:FE89:6B9A, host routes for this address are propagated within the routing infrastructure of the organization assigned the 48-bit prefix 3FFE:2900:D005::/48. Because a node assigned this anycast address can be placed anywhere on the organization's intranet, source routes for all nodes assigned this anycast address are needed in the routing tables of all routers within the organization. Outside the organization, this anycast address is summarized by the 3FFE:2900:D005::/48 prefix that is assigned to the organization. Therefore, the host routes needed to deliver IPv6 packets to the nearest anycast group member within an organization's intranet are not needed in the routing infrastructure of the IPv6 Internet.

As of RFC 2373, anycast addresses are used only as destination addresses and are assigned only to routers. Anycast addresses are assigned out of the unicast address space and the scope of an anycast address is the scope of the type of unicast address from which the anycast address is assigned. It is not possible to determine if a given destination unicast address is also an anycast address. The only nodes that have this awareness are the routers that use host routes to forward the anycast traffic to the nearest anycast group member and the anycast group members themselves.

Subnet-Router Anycast Address

The Subnet-Router anycast address is defined in RFC 2373 and is required. It is created from the subnet prefix for a given interface. When the Subnet-Router anycast address is constructed, the bits in the subnet prefix are fixed at their appropriate values and the remaining bits are set to 0. Figure 3-8 shows the structure of the Subnet-Router anycast address.

Figure 3-8. *The structure of the Subnet-Router anycast address*

All router interfaces attached to a subnet are assigned the Subnet-Router anycast address for that subnet. The Subnet-Router anycast address is used to communicate with the nearest router connected to a specified subnet.

IPV6 ADDRESSES FOR A HOST

An IPv4 host with a single network adapter typically has a single IPv4 address assigned to that adapter. An IPv6 host, however, usually has multiple IPv6 addresses assigned to each adapter. The interfaces on a typical IPv6 host are assigned the following unicast addresses:

- A link-local address for each interface
- Additional unicast addresses for each interface (which could be a site-local address and one or multiple global addresses)
- The loopback address (::1) for the loopback interface

Typical IPv6 hosts are always logically multihomed because they always have at least two addresses with which they can receive packets—a link-local address for local link traffic and a routable site-local or global address.

Additionally, each interface on an IPv6 host is listening for traffic on the following multicast addresses:

- The node-local scope all-nodes multicast address (FF01::1)
- The link-local scope all-nodes multicast address (FF02::1)
- The solicited-node address for each unicast address
- The multicast addresses of joined groups

IPv6 ADDRESSES FOR A ROUTER

The interfaces on an IPv6 router are assigned the following unicast addresses:

- A link-local address for each interface

- Additional unicast addresses for each interface (which could be a site-local address and one or multiple global addresses)

- The loopback address (::1) for the loopback interface

Additionally, the interfaces of an IPv6 router are assigned the following anycast addresses:

- A Subnet-Router anycast address for each subnet

- Additional anycast addresses (optional)

Additionally, the interfaces of an IPv6 router are listening for traffic on the following multicast addresses:

- The node-local scope all-nodes multicast address (FF01::1)

- The node-local scope all-routers multicast address (FF01::2)

- The link-local scope all-nodes multicast address (FF02::1)

- The link-local scope all-routers multicast address (FF02::2)

- The site-local scope all-routers multicast address (FF05::2)

- The solicited-node address for each unicast address

- The multicast addresses of joined groups

SUBNETTING THE IPv6 ADDRESS SPACE

Just as in IPv4, the IPv6 address space can be divided by using high-order bits that do not already have fixed values to create subnetted network prefixes. These are used either to summarize a level in the routing or addressing hierarchy (with a prefix length less than 64), or to define a specific subnet or network segment (with a prefix length of 64). IPv4 subnetting differs from IPv6 subnetting in the definition of the host ID portion of the address. In IPv4, the host ID can be of varying length, depending on the subnetting scheme. For currently defined unicast IPv6 addresses, the host ID is the interface ID portion of the IPv6 unicast address and is always a fixed size of 64 bits.

Subnetting for NLA IDs

If you are an ISP, subnetting the IPv6 address space consists of using subnetting techniques to divide the NLA ID portion of a global address in a manner that allows for route summarization and delegation of the remaining address space for different portions of your network, for downstream providers, or for individual customers. The global address has a 24-bit NLA ID field to be used by the various layers of ISPs between a top-level aggregator (a global ISP identified by the TLA ID) and a customer site.

For a global address allocated to a top-level aggregator, the first 16 bits of the address are fixed and correspond to the FP (set to 001) and the TLA ID (13 bits in length). The TLA ID is followed by the Res portion, which consists of 8 reserved bits set to 0. Therefore, for subnetting of the NLA ID portion of a global address, the first 24 bits are fixed. In a global address, the Res bits are never shown due to the suppression of leading zeros in IPv6 colon hexadecimal notation.

Subnetting the NLA ID portion of a global address requires a two-step procedure:

1. Determine the number of bits to be used for the subnetting.

2. Enumerate the new subnetted network prefixes.

The subnetting technique described here assumes that subnetting is done by dividing the 24-bit address space of the NLA ID using the high-order bits in the NLA ID that do not already have fixed values. While this method promotes hierarchical addressing and routing, it is not required. For example, you can also create a flat addressing space for the NLA ID by numbering the subnets from 0 to 16,777,215.

Step 1: Determining the Number of Subnetting Bits

The number of bits being used for subnetting determines the possible number of new subnetted network prefixes that can be allocated to portions of your network based on geographical, customer segment, or other divisions. In a hierarchical routing infrastructure, you need to determine how many network prefixes, and therefore how many bits, you need at each level in the hierarchy. The more bits you choose for the various levels of the hierarchy, the fewer bits you will have available to enumerate individual subnets in the last level of the hierarchy. The last level in the hierarchy is used to assign 48-bit prefixes to customer sites.

For example, a network designer at a large ISP decides to implement a two-level hierarchy reflecting a geographical/customer segment structure and uses 8 bits for the geographical level and 8 bits for the customer segment level.

This means that each customer segment in each geographical location has only 8 bits of subnetting space left $(24 - 8 - 8)$, or only $256 (= 2^8)$ 48-bit prefixes per customer segment.

On any given level in the hierarchy, you will have a number of bits that are already fixed by the next level up in the hierarchy (f), a number of bits used for subnetting at the current level in the hierarchy (s), and a number of bits remaining for the next level down in the hierarchy (r). At all times, $f + s + r = 24$. This relationship is shown in Figure 3-9.

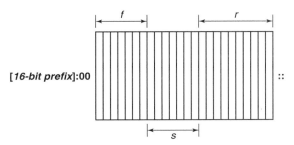

Figure 3-9. *The subnetting of an NLA ID*

Step 2: Enumerating Subnetted Network Prefixes

Based on the number of bits used for subnetting, you must list the new subnetted network prefixes. There are two main approaches:

■ Hexadecimal — Enumerate new subnetted network prefixes by using hexadecimal representations of the NLA ID and increment.

■ Decimal — Enumerate new subnetted network prefixes by using decimal representations of the NLA ID and increment. The decimal subnetting technique is included here for those who are more comfortable dealing with decimal numbers (Base_{10}).

Either method produces the same result: an enumerated list of subnetted network prefixes.

Creating the enumerated list of subnetted network prefixes by using the hexadecimal method

1. Based on s (the number of bits chosen for subnetting), and m (the prefix length of the network prefix being subnetted), calculate the following:

$$f = m - 24$$

f is the number of bits within the NLA ID that are already fixed.

$$n = 2^s$$

n is the number of network prefixes that are obtained.

$$i = 2^{24-(f+s)}$$

i is the incremental value between each successive NLA ID expressed in hexadecimal form.

$$l = 24 + f + s$$

l is the prefix length of the new subnetted network prefixes.

2. Create a three-column table with n entries. The first column is the network prefix number (starting with 1), the second column is the value of F (the hexadecimal representation of the NLA ID), and the third column is the new subnetted network prefix.

3. In the first table entry, the entry for the NLA ID column is F and the subnetted network prefix is the original network prefix with the new prefix length. To obtain F, combine the last two hexadecimal digits of the second hexadecimal block with the four hexadecimal digits of the third hexadecimal block of the NLA ID being subnetted to form a 6-digit hexadecimal number. Remember to include zeros that may not be present due to leading zero suppression. For example, for the global address prefix 3000:4D:C00::/38, F is 0x4D0C00.

4. In the next table entry, for the NLA ID column, increase the value of F by i. For example, in the second table entry, the NLA ID is $F + i$.

5. For the subnetted network prefix column, convert the NLA ID into two separate 16-bit blocks in colon hexadecimal notation and place them after the 16-bit prefix to express the new subnetted network prefix. For example, for the second table entry, the subnetted network prefix is [*16-bit prefix*]:[$F + i$ (expressed in colon hexadecimal notation)]::/l.

6. Repeat steps 4 and 5 until the table is complete.

For example, to perform a 3-bit subnetting of the global network prefix 3000:4D:C00::/38, we first calculate the values of the number of prefixes, the increment, and the new prefix length. Our starting values are F = 0x4D0C00, s = 3, and f = 38 − 24 = 14. The number of prefixes is 8 ($n = 2^3$). The increment is 0x80 ($i = 2^{24-(14+3)}$ = 128 = 0x80). The new prefix length is 41 (l = 38 + 3).

Next, we construct a table with 8 entries. The subnetted network prefix for network prefix 1 is 3000:4D:C00::/41. Additional entries in the table are successive increments of i in the NLA ID portion of the network prefix, as shown in Table 3-4.

Table 3-4. THE HEXADECIMAL SUBNETTING TECHNIQUE FOR NETWORK PREFIX 3000:4D:C00::/38

Network Prefix Number	NLA ID (hexadecimal)	Subnetted Network Prefix
1	4D0C00	3000:4D:C00::/41
2	4D0C80	3000:4D:C80::/41
3	4D0D00	3000:4D:D00::/41
4	4D0D80	3000:4D:D80::/41
5	4D0E00	3000:4D:E00::/41
6	4D0E80	3000:4D:E80::/41
7	4D0F00	3000:4D:F00::/41
8	4D0F80	3000:4D:F80::/41

NOTE:
RFC 2373 allows the use of subnetted network prefixes where the bits being used for subnetting are set to all zeros (the all-zeros subnetted network prefix) and all ones (the all-ones subnetted network prefix) for any portion of the IPv6 network prefix being subnetted.

Creating the enumerated list of subnetted network prefixes using the decimal method

1. Based on s (the number of bits chosen for subnetting), and m (the prefix length of the network prefix being subnetted), and F (the hexadecimal value of the NLA ID being subnetted), calculate the following:

   $$f = m - 24$$

   f is the number of bits within the NLA ID that are already fixed.

   $$n = 2^s$$

   n is the number of network prefixes that are obtained.

   $$i = 2^{24-(f+s)}$$

   i is the incremental value between each successive NLA ID expressed in decimal form.

$$l = 24 + f + s$$

l is the prefix length of the new subnetted network prefixes.

D = decimal representation of *F*

2. Create a four-column table with *n* entries. The first column is the network prefix number (starting with 1), the second column is the decimal representation of the NLA ID portion of the new subnetted network prefix, the third column is the hexadecimal representation of the NLA ID portion of the new subnetted network prefix, and the fourth column is the new subnetted network prefix.

3. In the first table entry, the decimal representation of the NLA ID is *D*, the hexadecimal representation of the NLA ID is *F*, and the subnetted network prefix is the original network prefix with the new prefix length.

4. In the next table entry, for the second column, increase the value of the decimal representation of the NLA ID by *i*. For example, in the second table entry, the decimal representation of the subnet ID is *D* + *i*.

5. For the third column, convert the decimal representation of the NLA ID to hexadecimal.

6. For the fourth column, convert the NLA ID into two separate 16-bit blocks in colon hexadecimal notation and place them after the 16-bit prefix to express the new subnetted network prefix. For example, for the second table entry, the subnetted network prefix is [*16-bit prefix*]:[*F* + *i* (expressed in colon hexadecimal notation)]::/*l*.

7. Repeat steps 4 through 6 until the table is complete.

For example, to perform a 3-bit subnetting of the global network prefix 3000:4D:C00::/38, we first calculate the values of the number of prefixes, the increment, and the new prefix length. Our starting values are *F* = 0x4D0C00, *s* = 3, and *f* = 38 − 24 = 14. The number of prefixes is 8 (*n* = 2^3). The increment is 128 (*i* = $2^{24-(14+3)}$ = 128). The new prefix length is 41 (*l* = 38 + 3). The decimal representation of the starting NLA ID is 5049344 (*D* = 0x4D0C00 = 5049344).

Next, we construct a table with 8 entries. The subnetted network prefix for network prefix 1 is 3000:4D:C00::/41. Additional entries in the table are successive increments of *i* in the NLA ID portion of the network prefix, as shown in Table 3-5.

Table 3-5. THE DECIMAL SUBNETTING TECHNIQUE FOR NETWORK PREFIX 3000:4D:C00::/38

Network Prefix Number	Decimal Representation of NLA ID	Hexadecimal Representation of NLA ID	Subnetted Network Prefix
1	5049344	4D0C00	3000:4D:C00::/41
2	5049472	4D0C80	3000:4D:C80::/41
3	5049600	4D0D00	3000:4D:D00::/41
4	5049728	4D0D80	3000:4D:D80::/41
5	5049856	4D0E00	3000:4D:E00::/41
6	5049984	4D0E80	3000:4D:E80::/41
7	5050112	4D0F00	3000:4D:F00::/41
8	5050240	4D0F80	3000:4D:F80::/41

Subnetting for SLA IDs/Subnet IDs

For most network administrators within an organization, subnetting the IPv6 address space consists of using subnetting techniques to divide the SLA ID portion of the global address or the Subnet ID portion of the site-local address in a manner that allows for route summarization and delegation of the remaining address space to different portions of an IPv6 intranet. The global address has a 16-bit SLA ID field to be used by organizations within their sites. The site-local address has a 16-bit Subnet ID field to be used by organizations within a site.

In both cases, the first 48 bits of the address are fixed. For the global address, the first 48 bits are fixed and allocated by an ISP and correspond to the TLA and NLA ID portions of the global address. For the site-local address, the first 48 bits are fixed at FEC0::/48. In the discussion that follows, the term subnet ID refers to either the SLA ID portion of the global address or the Subnet ID portion of a site-local address.

Subnetting the subnet ID portion of a global or site-local address space requires a two-step procedure:

1. Determine the number of bits to be used for the subnetting.

2. Enumerate the new subnetted network prefixes.

The subnetting technique described here assumes that subnetting is done by dividing the 16-bit address space of the subnet ID using the high-order bits in the subnet ID. While this method promotes hierarchical addressing and routing, it is not required. For example, in a small organization with a small number of subnets, you can also create a flat addressing space for the subnet ID by numbering the subnets starting at 0.

As described in the "Local-Use Unicast Addresses" section of this chapter, you can use the same subnetting scheme and use the same subnet ID for both site-local and global address network prefixes.

Step 1: Determining the Number of Subnetting Bits

The number of bits being used for subnetting determines the possible number of new subnetted network prefixes that can be allocated to portions of your network based on geographical or departmental divisions. In a hierarchical routing infrastructure, you need to determine how many network prefixes, and therefore how many bits, you need at each level in the hierarchy. The more bits you choose for the various levels of the hierarchy, the fewer bits you will have available to enumerate individual subnets in the last level of the hierarchy.

For example, a network administrator decides to implement a two-level hierarchy reflecting a geographical/departmental structure and uses 4 bits for the geographical level and 6 bits for the departmental level. This means that each department in each geographical location has only 6 bits of subnetting space left $(16 - 6 - 4)$, or only $64 (= 2^6)$ subnets per department.

On any given level in the hierarchy, you will have a number of bits that are already fixed by the next level up in the hierarchy (f), a number of bits used for subnetting at the current level in the hierarchy (s), and a number of bits remaining for the next level down in the hierarchy (r). At all times, $f + s + r = 16$. This relationship is shown in Figure 3-10.

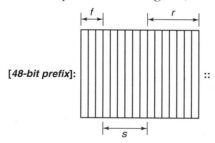

Figure 3-10. *The subnetting of a Subnet ID*

Step 2: Enumerating Subnetted Network Prefixes

Based on the number of bits used for subnetting, you must list the new subnetted network prefixes. There are two main approaches:

- Hexadecimal — Enumerate new subnetted network prefixes by using hexadecimal representations of the subnet ID and increment.

- Decimal — Enumerate new subnetted network prefixes by using decimal representations of the subnet ID and increment.

Either method produces the same result: an enumerated list of subnetted network prefixes.

Creating the enumerated list of subnetted network prefixes using the hexadecimal method

1. Based on s (the number of bits chosen for subnetting), m (the prefix length of the network prefix being subnetted), and F (the hexadecimal value of the subnet being subnetted), calculate the following:

   $$f = m - 48$$

   f is the number of bits within the subnet ID that are already fixed.

   $$n = 2^s$$

   n is the number of network prefixes that are obtained.

   $$i = 2^{16-(f+s)}$$

   i is the incremental value between each successive subnet ID expressed in hexadecimal form.

   $$l = 48 + f + s$$

   l is the prefix length of the new subnetted network prefixes.

2. Create a two-column table with n entries. The first column is the network prefix number (starting with 1) and the second column is the new subnetted network prefix.

3. In the first table entry, based on F, the hexadecimal value of the subnet ID being subnetted, the subnetted network prefix is [*48-bit prefix*]:*F*::/*l*.

4. In the next table entry, increase the value within the subnet ID portion of the site-local or global address by i. For example, in the second table entry, the subnetted prefix is [*48-bit prefix*]:*F* + *i*::/*l*.

5. Repeat step 4 until the table is complete.

For example, to perform a 3-bit subnetting of the site-local network prefix FEC0:0:0:C000::/51, we first calculate the values of the number of prefixes, the increment, and the new prefix length. Our starting values are $F = 0xC000$, $s = 3$, and $f = 51 - 48 = 3$. The number of prefixes is 8 ($n = 2^3$). The increment is 0x400 ($i = 2^{16-(3+3)} = 1024 = 0x400$). The new prefix length is 54 ($l = 48 + 3 + 3$).

Next, we construct a table with 8 entries. The entry for the network prefix 1 is FEC0:0:0:C000::/54. Additional entries in the table are successive increments of i in the subnet ID portion of the network prefix, as shown in Table 3-6.

Table 3-6. The Hexadecimal Subnetting Technique for Network Prefix FEC0:0:0:C000::/51

Network Prefix Number	Subnetted Network Prefix
1	FEC0:0:0:C000::/54
2	FEC0:0:0:C400::/54
3	FEC0:0:0:C800::/54
4	FEC0:0:0:CC00::/54
5	FEC0:0:0:D000::/54
6	FEC0:0:0:D400::/54
7	FEC0:0:0:D800::/54
8	FEC0:0:0:DC00::/54

Creating the enumerated list of subnetted network prefixes using the decimal method

1. Based on s (the number of bits chosen for subnetting), and m (the prefix length of the network prefix being subnetted), and F (the hexadecimal value of the subnet ID being subnetted), calculate the following:

   $$f = m - 48$$

   f is the number of bits within the subnet ID that are already fixed.

   $$n = 2^s$$

   n is the number of network prefixes that are obtained.

   $$i = 2^{16-(f+s)}$$

   i is the incremental value between each successive subnet ID.

   $$l = 48 + f + s$$

   l is the prefix length of the new subnetted network prefixes.

   D = decimal representation of F

2. Create a three-column table with n entries. The first column is the network prefix number (starting with 1), the second column is the decimal representation of the subnet ID portion of the new network prefix, and the third column is the new subnetted network prefix.

3. In the first table entry, the decimal representation of the subnet ID is D and the subnetted network prefix is [*48-bit prefix*]:*F*::/*l*.

4. In the next table entry, for the second column, increase the value of the decimal representation of the subnet ID by i. For example, in the second table entry, the decimal representation of the subnet ID is $D + i$.

5. For the third column, convert the decimal representation of the subnet ID to hexadecimal and construct the prefix from [*48-bit prefix*]:[*subnet ID*]::/*l*. For example, in the second table entry, the subnetted network prefix is [*48-bit prefix*]:[*D + i* (converted to hexadecimal)]::/*l*.

6. Repeat steps 4 and 5 until the table is complete.

For example, to perform a 3-bit subnetting of the site-local network prefix FEC0:0:0:C000::/51, we first calculate the values of the number of prefixes, the increment, the new prefix length, and the decimal representation of the starting subnet ID. Our starting values are $F = 0xC000$, $s = 3$, and $f = 51 - 48 = 3$. The number of prefixes is 8 ($n = 2^3$). The increment is 1024 ($i = 2^{16-(3+3)}$). The new prefix length is 54 ($l = 48 + 3 + 3$). The decimal representation of the starting subnet ID is 49152 ($D = 0xC000 = 49152$).

Next, we construct a table with 8 entries. The entry for the network prefix 1 is 49152 and FEC0:0:0:C000::/54. Additional entries in the table are successive increments of *i* in the subnet ID portion of the network prefix, as shown in Table 3-7.

Table 3-7. THE DECIMAL SUBNETTING TECHNIQUE FOR NETWORK PREFIX FEC0:0:0:C000::/51

Network Prefix Number	Decimal Representation of Subnet ID	Subnetted Network Prefix
1	49152	FEC0:0:0:C000::/54
2	50176	FEC0:0:0:C400::/54
3	51200	FEC0:0:0:C800::/54
4	52224	FEC0:0:0:CC00::/54
5	53248	FEC0:0:0:D000::/54
6	54272	FEC0:0:0:D400::/54
7	55296	FEC0:0:0:D800::/54
8	56320	FEC0:0:0:DC00::/54

IPv6 INTERFACE IDENTIFIERS

The last 64 bits of a currently defined IPv6 unicast address are the interface identifier that is unique to the 64-bit prefix of the IPv6 address. In IPv4, the host or node ID portion of an IPv4 address is a logical identifier of an interface on an IPv4 subnet. IPv4 host IDs are of variable length depending on the subnetting scheme and how many interfaces you want to allow on a given subnet. For example, with an 8-bit host ID, there were $2^8 - 2$ or 254 possible host IDs (the all-zeros and all-ones combinations are reserved).

In IPv6, the interface ID is of fixed length. This length was not fixed at 64 bits to allow up to 2^{64} possible hosts on the same subnet. Rather, the IPv6 interface ID is 64 bits long to accommodate the mapping of current 48-bit MAC addresses used by most LAN technologies such as Ethernet and the mapping of 64-bit MAC addresses of IEEE 1394 (also known as FireWire) and future LAN technologies.

The ways in which an interface identifier is determined are the following:

■ As defined in RFC 2373, all unicast addresses that use the prefixes 001 through 111 must also use a 64-bit interface identifier that is derived from the Extended Unique Identifier (EUI)-64 address. The 64-bit EUI-64 address is defined by the Institute of Electrical and Electronic Engineers (IEEE). EUI-64 addresses are either assigned to a network adapter or derived from IEEE 802 addresses.

■ As defined in RFC 3041, it might have a temporarily assigned, randomly generated interface identifier to provide a level of anonymity.

■ It is assigned during stateful address autoconfiguration (for example, via Dynamic Host Configuration Protocol version 6 (DHCPv6)). Stateful address autoconfiguration standards and protocols are in progress.

■ As defined in RFC 2472, an interface identifier can be based on link-layer addresses or serial numbers, or randomly generated when configuring a Point-to-Point Protocol (PPP) interface and an EUI-64 address is not available.

■ It is assigned during manual address configuration.

EUI-64 Address-based Interface Identifiers

The most common way to derive an IPv6 interface identifier is through the EUI-64 address, a new type of MAC address for network adapters. To gain an understanding of EUI-64 addresses, it is useful to review the current MAC address format known as IEEE 802 addresses.

IEEE 802 Addresses

Network adapters for common LAN technologies such as Ethernet, Token Ring, and Fiber Data Distributed Interface (FDDI) use a 48-bit address called an IEEE 802 address. It consists of a 24-bit company ID (also called the manufacturer ID) and a 24-bit extension ID (also called the board ID). The combination of the company ID, which is uniquely assigned to each manufacturer of network adapters, and the extension ID, which is uniquely assigned to each network adapter at the time of manufacture, produces a globally unique 48-bit address. This 48-bit address is also called the physical, hardware, or media access control (MAC) address.

Figure 3-11 shows the structure of the 48-bit IEEE 802 address for Ethernet.

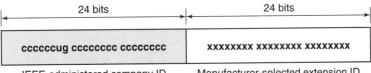

Figure 3-11. *The structure of the 48-bit IEEE 802 address for Ethernet*

Defined bits within the IEEE 802 address for Ethernet are:

Universal/Local (U/L) — The next-to-the low-order bit in the first byte is usedto indicate whether the address is universally or locally administered. If the U/L bit is set to 0, the IEEE (through the designation of a unique company ID) has administered the address. If the U/L bit is set to 1, the address is locally administered. In this case, the network administrator has overridden the manu-factured address and specified a different address. The U/L bit is designated by the **u** in Figure 3-11.

Individual/Group (I/G) — The low-order bit of the first byte is used to indicate whether the address is an individual address (unicast) or a group address (multicast). When set to 0, the address is a unicast address. When set to 1, the address is a multicast address. The I/G bit is designated by the **g** in Figure 3-11.

For a typical 802.x network adapter address, both the U/L and I/G bits are set to 0, corresponding to a universally administered, unicast MAC address.

IEEE EUI-64 Addresses

The IEEE EUI-64 address represents a new standard for network interface ad-dressing. The company ID is still 24-bits long, but the extension ID is 40 bits, creating a much larger address space for a network adapter manufacturer. The EUI-64 address uses the U/L and I/G bits in the same way as the IEEE 802 address.

Figure 3-12 shows the structure of the EUI-64 address.

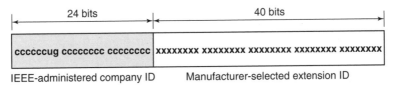

Figure 3-12. *The structure of the EUI-64 address*

Mapping IEEE 802 Addresses to EUI-64 Addresses

To create an EUI-64 address from an IEEE 802 address, the 16 bits of 11111111 11111110 (0xFFFE) are inserted into the IEEE 802 address between the com-pany ID and the extension ID, as shown in Figure 3-13.

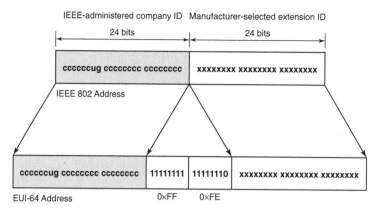

Figure 3-13. *The mapping of IEEE 802 addresses to EUI-64 addresses*

Obtaining Interface Identifiers for IPv6 Addresses

To obtain the 64-bit interface identifier for IPv6 unicast addresses, the U/L bit in the EUI-64 address is complemented (if it is a 1 in the EUI-64 address, it is set to 0; and if it is a 0 in the EUI-64 address, it is set to 1).

The main reason for complementing the U/L bit is to provide greater compressibility of locally administered EUI-64 addresses. It is common practice when assigning locally administered addresses to number them in a simple way. For example, on a point-to-point link, you may assign one interface on the link the locally administered EUI-64 address of 02-00-00-00-00-00-00-01 and the other interface the locally administered EUI-64 address of 02-00-00-00-00-00-00-02. If the U/L bit is not complemented, the corresponding link-local addresses for these two interfaces become FE80::200:0:0:1 and FE80::200:0:0:2. By complementing the U/L bit, the corresponding link-local addresses for these two interfaces become FE80::1 and FE80::2.

Figure 3-14 shows the conversion of an EUI-64 address to an IPv6 interface identifier.

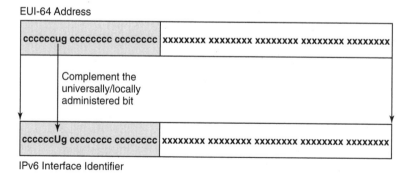

Figure 3-14. *The conversion of an EUI-64 address to an IPv6 interface identifier*

> **NOTE:**
> Because the U/L bit is complemented when converting an EUI-64 address to an IPv6 interface identifier, the resulting bit in the IPv6 interface identifier has the opposite interpretation of the IEEE-defined U/L bit. If the seventh bit of the IPv6 interface identifier is set to 0, it is locally administered. If the seventh bit of the IPv6 interface identifier is set to 1, it is universally administered.

Converting IEEE 802 Addresses to IPv6 Interface Identifiers

To obtain an IPv6 interface identifier from an IEEE 802 address, you must first map the IEEE 802 address to an EUI-64 address, and then complement the U/L bit. Figure 3-15 shows this conversion process for a universally administered, unicast IEEE 802 address.

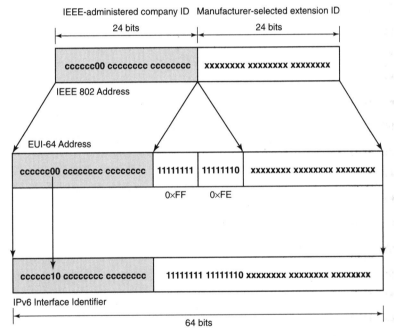

Figure 3-15. *The conversion of an IEEE 802 address to an IPv6 interface identifier*

IEEE 802 Address Conversion Example

Host A has the Ethernet MAC address of 00-AA-00-3F-2A-1C. First, it is converted to EUI-64 format by inserting FF-FE between the third and fourth bytes, yielding 00-AA-00-FF-FE-3F-2A-1C. Then, the U/L bit, which is the seventh bit in the first byte, is complemented. The first byte in binary form is 00000000. When the seventh bit is complemented, it becomes 00000010 (0x02). The final result is

02-AA-00-FF-FE-3F-2A-1C which, when converted to colon hexadecimal notation, becomes the interface identifier 2AA:FF:FE3F: 2A1C. As a result, the link-local address that corresponds to the network adapter with the MAC address of 00-AA-00-3F-2A-1C is FE80::2AA:FF:FE3F:2A1C.

NOTE:

When complementing the U/L bit, add 0x2 to the first byte if the EUI-64 address is universally administered, and subtract 0x2 from the first byte if the EUI-64 address is locally administered.

Temporary Address Interface Identifiers

In today's IPv4-based Internet, a typical Internet user dials an ISP and obtains an IPv4 address using PPP and the Internet Protocol Control Protocol (IPCP). Each time the user dials, a different IPv4 address might be obtained. Therefore, it is not easy to track a dial-up user's traffic on the Internet based on the user's IP address.

For IPv6-based dial-up connections, the user is assigned a 64-bit prefix, at the time of connection, by using router discovery, an exchange of Router Solicitation and Router Advertisement messages. If the interface identifier is always based on the EUI-64 address (as derived from the static IEEE 802 address), it is possible to identify the traffic of a specific node regardless of the prefix assigned at the time of connection. The use of the same 64-bit interface identifier allows identification of a user's traffic whether they are accessing the Internet from home or from work. This makes it easy for Internet merchants and malicious users to track a specific user and their use of the Internet.

To address this concern to provide the same level of anonymity as that provided with IPv4, an alternative derivation of the IPv6 interface identifier that is randomly generated and changes over time is discussed in RFC 3041.

The initial interface identifier is generated using random number techniques. For IPv6 systems that do not have the ability to store any history information for generating future values of the interface identifier, a new random interface identifier is generated each time the IPv6 protocol is initialized. For IPv6 systems that do have storage capabilities, a history value is stored and when the IPv6 protocol is initialized, a new interface identifier is created through the following process:

1. Retrieve the history value from storage and append the interface identifier based on the EUI-64 address of the adapter.

2. Compute the Message Digest-5 (MD5) hash over the quantity in step 1. The MD5 hash computation will produce a 128-bit value.

3. Store the low-order 64 bits of the MD5 hash computed in step 2 as the history value for the next computation of the interface identifier.

4. Take the high-order 64 bits of the MD5 hash computed in step 2 and set the seventh bit to zero. The seventh bit corresponds to the U/L bit, which, when set to 0, indicates a locally administered interface identifier. The result is the interface identifier.

The resulting IPv6 address, based on this random interface identifier, is known as a *temporary address*. Temporary addresses are generated for public address prefixes that use stateless address autoconfiguration. Temporary addresses are used for the lower of the following values of the valid and preferred lifetimes:

■ The lifetimes included in the Prefix Information option in the received Router Advertisement message.

■ Local default values of 1 week for valid lifetime and 1 day for preferred lifetime.

After the temporary address valid lifetime expires, a new interface identifier and temporary address is generated. For more information about router discovery, see Chapter 6, "Neighbor Discovery." For more information about stateless address autoconfiguration and valid and preferred lifetimes, see Chapter 8, "Address Autoconfiguration."

MAPPING IPv6 MULTICAST ADDRESSES TO ETHERNET ADDRESSES

When sending IPv6 multicast packets on an Ethernet link, the corresponding destination MAC address is 0x33-33-mm-mm-mm-mm, where mm-mm-mm-mm is a direct mapping of the last 32 bits of the IPv6 multicast address. Figure 3-16 shows the mapping of an IPv6 multicast address to an Ethernet multicast address.

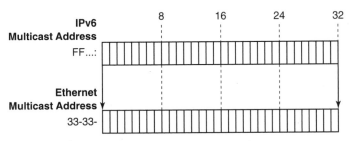

Figure 3-16. *The mapping of IPv6 multicast addresses to Ethernet multicast addresses*

Ethernet network adapters maintain a table of interesting destination MAC addresses. If an Ethernet frame with an interesting destination MAC address is received, it is passed to upper layers for additional processing. By default, this table contains the MAC-level broadcast address (0xFF-FF-FF-FF-FF-FF) and the unicast MAC address assigned to the adapter. To facilitate efficient delivery of multicast traffic, additional multicast destination addresses can be added or removed from the table. For every multicast address being listened to by the host, there is a corresponding entry in the table of interesting MAC addresses.

For example, an IPv6 host with the Ethernet MAC address of 00-AA-00-3F-2A-1C (link-local address of FE80::2AA:FF:FE3F:2A1C) adds the following multicast MAC addresses to the table of interesting destination MAC addresses on the Ethernet adapter:

- The address of 33-33-00-00-00-01, which corresponds to the link-local scope all-nodes multicast address of FF02::1.

- The address of 33-33-FF-3F-2A-1C, which corresponds to the solicited-node address of FF02::1:FF3F:2A1C. Remember that the solicited-node address is the prefix FF02::1:FF00:0/104 and the last 24 bits of the unicast IPv6 address.

Additional multicast addresses on which the host is listening are added and removed from the table as needed.

IPV4 ADDRESSES AND IPV6 EQUIVALENTS

To summarize the relationships between IPv4 addressing and IPv6 addressing, Table 3-8 lists both IPv4 addresses and addressing concepts and their IPv6 equivalents.

Table 3-8. IPV4 ADDRESSING CONCEPTS AND THEIR IPV6 EQUIVALENTS

IPv4 Address	*IPv6 Address*
Internet address classes	Not applicable in IPv6
Multicast addresses (224.0.0.0/4)	IPv6 multicast addresses (FF00::/8)
Broadcast addresses	Not applicable in IPv6
Unspecified address is 0.0.0.0	Unspecified address is ::
Loopback address is 127.0.0.1	Loopback address is ::1

continued

Table 3-8 *continued*

IPv4 Address	IPv6 Address
Public IP addresses	Aggregatable global unicast addresses
Private IP addresses (10.0.0.0/8, 172.16.0.0/12, and 192.168.0.0/16)	Site-local addresses (FEC0::/48)
APIPA addresses (169.254.0.0/16)	Link-local addresses (FE80::/64)
Text representation: Dotted decimal notation	Text representation: Colon hexadecimal format with suppression of leading zeros and zero compression. IPv4-compatible addresses are expressed in dotted decimal notation.
Network bits representation: Subnet mask in dotted decimal notation or prefix length	Network bits representation: Prefix length notation only

REFERENCES

RFC 1888 — "OSI NSAPs and IPv6"

RFC 2373 — "IP Version 6 Addressing Architecture"

RFC 2472 — "IP Version 6 over PPP"

RFC 3041 — "Privacy Extensions for Stateless Address Autoconfiguration in IPv6"

TESTING FOR UNDERSTANDING

To test your understanding of IPv6 addressing, answer the following questions. See Appendix D, "Testing for Understanding Answers" to check your answers.

1. Why is the IPv6 address length 128 bits?

2. Define the Format Prefixes (FPs) for commonly used unicast addresses.

3. Express FEC0:0000:0000:0001:02AA:0000:0000:0007A more efficiently.

4. How many bits are expressed by "::" in the addresses 3341::1:2AA: 9FF:FE56:24DC and FF02::2?

5. Describe the difference between unicast, multicast, and anycast addresses in terms of a host sending packets to zero or more interfaces.

6. Why are no broadcast addresses defined for IPv6?

7. Define the structure, including field sizes, of the aggregatable global unicast address.

8. Define the scope for each of the different types of typically used unicast addresses.

9. Explain how global and site-local addressing can share the same subnetting infrastructure within an organization.

10. Define the structure, including field sizes, of the multicast address.

11. Why does RFC 2373 recommend using only the last 32 bits of the IPv6 multicast address for the multicast group ID?

12. Explain how the solicited-node multicast address acts as a pseudo-unicast address.

13. How do routers know the nearest location of an anycast group member?

14. Perform a 4-bit subnetting on the site-local prefix FEC0:0:0:3D80::/57.

15. What is the IPv6 interface identifier for the universally administered, unicast IEEE 802 address of 0C-1C-09-A8-F9-CE? What is the corresponding link-local address? What is the corresponding solicited-node multicast address?

16. What is the IPv6 interface identifier for the locally administered, unicast EUI-64 address of 02-00-00-00-00-00-00-09? What is the corresponding link-local address?

17. What is the site-local scope multicast address corresponding to the Ethernet multicast MAC address of 33-33-00-0A-4F-11?

18. For each type of address, identify how the address begins in colon hexadecimal notation.

Type of Address	Begins with...
Link-local unicast address	FE80
Site-local unicast address	
Global address	
Multicast address	
Link-local scope multicast address	
Site-local scope multicast address	
Solicited-node multicast address	
IPv4-compatible address	
IPv4-mapped address	
6to4 address	

Chapter 4

The IPv6 Header

At the end of this chapter, you should be able to:

■ Describe the structure of an IPv6 packet.

■ List and describe the fields in the IPv4 header.

■ List and describe the fields in the IPv6 header.

■ Compare and contrast the fields in the IPv4 header with the fields in the IPv6 header.

■ List and describe each IPv6 extension header.

■ Describe the IPv6 maximum transmission unit (MTU).

■ Describe the new pseudo-header used for upper-layer checksums.

STRUCTURE OF AN IPV6 PACKET

An IPv6 packet consists of an IPv6 header, extension headers, and an upper-layer protocol data unit. Figure 4-1 shows the structure of an IPv6 packet.

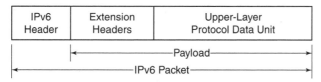

Figure 4-1. *The structure of an IPv6 packet*

The components of an IPv6 packet are the following:

■ **IPv6 Header**
The IPv6 header is always present and is a fixed size of 40 bytes. The fields in the IPv6 header are described in "IPv6 Header" in this chapter.

■ **Extension Headers**

Zero or more extension headers can be present and are of varying lengths. A Next Header field in the IPv6 header indicates the first extension header. Within each extension header is another Next Header field, indicating the next extension header. The last extension header indicates the header for the upper-layer protocol—such as Transmission Control Protocol (TCP), User Datagram Protocol (UDP), or Internet Control Message Protocol version 6 (ICMPv6)—contained within the upper-layer protocol data unit.

The IPv6 header and extension headers replace the existing IPv4 header and its options. The new extension header format allows IPv6 to be enhanced to support future needs and capabilities. Unlike options in the IPv4 header, IPv6 extension headers have no maximum size and can expand to accommodate all of the extension data needed for IPv6 communication. IPv6 extension headers are described in "IPv6 Extension Headers" in this chapter.

■ **Upper-Layer Protocol Data Unit**

The upper-layer protocol data unit (PDU) typically consists of an upper-layer protocol header and its payload (for example, an ICMPv6 message, a TCP segment, or a UDP message).

The IPv6 packet payload is the combination of the IPv6 extension headers and the upper-layer PDU. Normally, it can be up to 65,535 bytes long. IPv6 packets with payloads larger than 65,535 bytes in length, known as *jumbograms,* can also be sent.

IPV4 HEADER

Before examining the IPv6 header, you might find it helpful, for contrasting purposes, to review the IPv4 header shown in Figure 4-2.

The fields in the IPv4 header are:

■ **Version**

The Version field indicates the version of IP and is set to 4. The size of this field is 4 bits.

■ **Internet Header Length**

The Internet Header Length (IHL) field indicates the number of 4-byte blocks in the IPv4 header. The size of this field is 4 bits. Because an IPv4 header is a minimum of 20 bytes in size, the smallest value of the IHL field is 5. IPv4 options can extend the minimum IPv4 header size in increments of 4 bytes. If an IPv4 option is not an integral

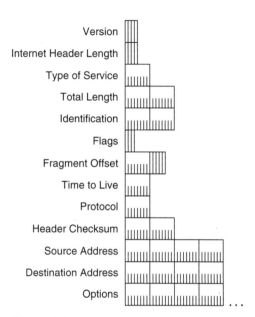

Figure 4-2. *The structure of the IPv4 header*

multiple of 4 bytes in length, the remaining bytes are padded with padding options, making the entire IPv4 header an integral multiple of 4 bytes. With a maximum IHL value of 0xF, the maximum size of the IPv4 header including options is 60 bytes (15 × 4).

- **Type of Service**

  The Type of Service field indicates the desired service expected by this packet for delivery through routers across the IPv4 inter-network. The size of this field is 8 bits, including bits for precedence, delay, throughput, reliability, and cost characteristics. RFC 2474 provides an alternate definition of the 8 bits of the Type of Service field in terms of a Differentiated Services (DS) field that provides information on non-default router handling without the need for a signaling protocol or the maintenance of state at each router.

- **Total Length**

  The Total Length field indicates the total length of the IPv4 packet (IPv4 header + IPv4 payload) and does not include link-layer framing. The size of this field is 16 bits, which can indicate an IPv4 packet that is up to 65,535 bytes long.

- **Identification**

  The Identification field identifies this specific IPv4 packet. The size of this field is 16 bits. The Identification field is selected by the source node of the IPv4 packet. If the IPv4 packet is fragmented, all of the fragments retain the Identification field value so that the destination node can group the fragments for reassembly.

- **Flags**

  The Flags field identifies flags for the fragmentation process. The size of this field is 3 bits; however, only 2 bits are defined for current use. There are two flags—one to indicate whether the IPv4 packet can be fragmented and another to indicate whether more fragments follow the current fragment.

- **Fragment Offset**

  The Fragment Offset field indicates the position of the fragment relative to the beginning of the original IPv4 payload. The size of this field is 13 bits.

- **Time-to-Live**

  The Time-to-Live (TTL) field indicates the maximum number of links on which an IPv4 packet can travel before being discarded. The size of this field is 8 bits. The TTL field was originally defined as a time count for the number of seconds the packet could exist on the network. An IPv4 router determined the length of time required (in seconds) to forward the IPv4 packet and decremented the TTL accordingly. Modern routers almost always forward an IPv4 packet in less than a second, and are required by RFC 791 to decrement the TTL by at least one. Therefore, the TTL becomes a maximum link count with the value set by the sending node. When the TTL equals 0, an ICMPv4 Time Exceeded-Time to Live Exceeded in Transit message is sent to the source of the packet and the packet is discarded.

- **Protocol**

  The Protocol field identifies the upper-layer protocol. The size of this field is 8 bits. For example, a value of 6 in this field identifies TCP as the upper-layer protocol, a decimal value of 17 identifies UDP, and a value of 1 identifies ICMPv4. The Protocol field is used to identify the upper-layer protocol that is to receive the IPv4 packet payload.

- **Header Checksum**

  The Header Checksum field provides a checksum on the IPv4 header only. The size of this field is 16 bits. The IPv4 payload is not included in the checksum calculation as the IPv4 payload usually contains its own checksum. Each IPv4 node that receives IPv4 packets verifies the IPv4 header checksum, and silently discards the IPv4 packet if checksum verification fails. When a router forwards an IPv4 packet, it must decrement the TTL. Therefore, the Header Checksum value is recomputed at each hop between source and destination.

■ **Source Address**
The Source Address field stores the IPv4 address of the originating host. The size of this field is 32 bits.

■ **Destination Address**
The Destination Address field stores the IPv4 address of the destination host. The size of this field is 32 bits.

■ **Options**
The Options field stores one or more IPv4 options. The size of this field is a multiple of 32 bits (4 bytes). If an IPv4 option does not use all 32 bits, padding options must be added so that the IPv4 header is an integral number of 4-byte blocks that can be indicated by the IHL field.

IPV6 HEADER

The IPv6 header is a streamlined version of the IPv4 header. It eliminates fields that are either unneeded or rarely used, and adds a field that provides better support for real-time traffic. Figure 4-3 shows the structure of the IPv6 header as described in RFC 2460.

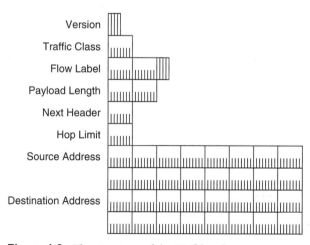

Figure 4-3. *The structure of the IPv6 header*

The fields in the IPv6 header are:

■ **Version**

The Version field indicates the version of IP and is set to 6. The size of this field is 4 bits. While the purpose of the Version field is defined in the same way for both IPv4 and IPv6, its value is not used to pass the packet to an IPv4 or IPv6 protocol layer. This identification is done through a protocol identification field in the link-layer header. For example, a common link-layer encapsulation for Ethernet called Ethernet II uses a 16-bit EtherType field to identify the Ethernet frame payload. For IPv4 packets, the EtherType field is set to 0x800. For IPv6 packets, the EtherType field is set to 0x86DD. Thus, the determination of the protocol of the Ethernet payload occurs before the packet is passed to the appropriate protocol layer.

■ **Traffic Class**

The Traffic Class field indicates the IPv6 packet's class or priority. The size of this field is 8 bits. This field provides functionality similar to the IPv4 Type of Service field. In RFC 2460, the values of the Traffic Class field are not defined. However, an IPv6 implementation is required to provide a means for an application layer protocol to specify the value of the Traffic Class field for experimentation. Like the Type of Service field in the IPv4 header, RFC 2474 provides an alternate definition of the Traffic Class field in the form of the Differentiated Services (DS) field.

■ **Flow Label**

The Flow Label field indicates that this packet belongs to a specific sequence of packets between a source and destination, requiring special handling by intermediate IPv6 routers. The size of this field is 20 bits. The flow label is used for non-default quality-of-service (QoS) connections, such as those needed by real-time data (voice and video). For default router handling, the Flow Label field is set to 0. There can be multiple flows between a source and destination, as distinguished by separate non-zero flow labels. Like the Traffic Class field, exact details of the Flow Label field's use are not yet defined.

■ **Payload Length**

The Payload Length field indicates the length of the IPv6 payload. The size of this field is 16 bits. The Payload Length field includes the extension headers and the upper-layer PDU. With 16 bits, an IPv6 payload of up to 65,535 bytes can be indicated. For payload lengths greater than 65,535 bytes, the Payload Length field is set to 0 and the Jumbo Payload option is used in the Hop-by-Hop Options extension header, which is covered later in this chapter.

■ **Next Header**

The Next Header field indicates either the type of the first extension header (if present) or the protocol in the upper-layer PDU (such as TCP, UDP, or ICMPv6). The size of this field is 8 bits. When indicating an upper-layer protocol, the Next Header field uses the same values that are used in the IPv4 Protocol field.

■ **Hop Limit**

The Hop Limit field indicates the maximum number of links over which the IPv6 packet can travel before being discarded. The size of this field is 8 bits. The Hop Limit field is similar to the IPv4 TTL field, except that there is no historical relation to the amount of time (in seconds) that the packet is queued at the router. When Hop Limit equals 0 at a router, the router sends an ICMPv6 Time Exceeded-Hop Limit Exceeded in Transit message to the source and discards the packet.

■ **Source Address**

The Source Address field indicates the IPv6 address of the originating host. The size of this field is 128 bits.

■ **Destination Address**

The Destination Address field indicates the IPv6 address of the current destination node. The size of this field is 128 bits. In most cases the Destination Address field is set to the final destination address. However, if a Routing extension header is present, the Destination Address field might be set to the address of the next intermediate destination.

Network Monitor Capture

Here is an example of an IPv6 header, as displayed by Network Monitor (capture 04_01 in the \NetworkMonitorCaptures folder on the companion CD-ROM):

```
+ Frame: Base frame properties
+ ETHERNET:  EType = IPv6
  IP6:  Proto = ICMP6; Len = 40
      IP6: Version = 6 (0x6)
      IP6: Traffic Class = 0 (0x0)
      IP6: Flow Label = 0 (0x0)
      IP6: Payload Length = 40 (0x28)
      IP6: Next Header = 58 (ICMP6)
```

```
    IP6: Hop Limit = 128 (0x80)
    IP6: Source Address = fe80::260:97ff:fe02:6e8f
    IP6: Destination Address = fe80::260:97ff:fe02:6d3d
    IP6: Payload: Number of data bytes remaining = 40 (0x0028)
+ ICMP6: Echo Request; ID = 0, Seq = 24
```

This ICMPv6 Echo Request packet uses the default Traffic Class and Flow Label, a Hop Limit of 128, and is sent between two hosts using link-local addresses.

Values of the Next Header Field

Table 4-1 lists typical values of the Next Header field for an IPv6 header or an IPv6 extension header. Each of the IPv6 extension headers is covered later in the chapter.

Table 4-1. **TYPICAL VALUES OF THE NEXT HEADER FIELD**

Value (Decimal)	Header
0	Hop-by-Hop Options header
6	TCP
17	UDP
41	Encapsulated IPv6 header
43	Routing header
44	Fragment header
50	Encapsulating Security Payload header
51	Authentication header
58	ICMPv6
59	No next header
60	Destination Options header

For the most current list of the reserved values for the IPv4 Protocol and IPv6 Next Header fields, see *http://www.iana.org/assignments/protocol-numbers*.

In looking at the value of the Next Header field to indicate no next header, it would seem to make more sense to set its value to 0, rather than 59. However, the designers of IPv6 wanted to optimize the processing of IPv6 packets at intermediate routers. The only extension header that must be processed at every intermediate router is the Hop-by-Hop Options header. To optimize the test of whether the Hop-by-Hop Options header is present, its Next Header value is set to 0. In router hardware, it is easier to test for a value of 0 than to test for a value of 59.

Comparing the IPv4 and IPv6 Headers

In comparing the IPv4 and IPv6 headers, you can see the following:

■ The number of fields has dropped from 12 (including options) in the IPv4 header to 8 in the IPv6 header.

■ The number of fields that must be processed by an intermediate router has dropped from 6 to 4, making the forwarding of normal IPv6 packets more efficient.

■ Seldom-used fields such as fields supporting fragmentation and options in the IPv4 header have been moved to extension headers in the IPv6 header.

■ The size of the IPv6 header has doubled from 20 bytes for a minimum-sized IPv4 header to 40 bytes. However, the new IPv6 header contains source and destination addresses that are four times longer than IPv4 source and destination addresses.

Table 4-2 lists the individual differences between the IPv4 and IPv6 header fields.

Table 4-2. IPv4 Header Fields and Corresponding IPv6 Equivalents

IPv4 Header Field	*IPv6 Header Field*
Version	Same field but with a different version number.
Internet Header Length	Removed in IPv6. IPv6 does not include a Header Length field because the IPv6 header is always a fixed length of 40 bytes. Each extension header is either a fixed length or indicates its own length.
Type of Service	Replaced by the IPv6 Traffic Class field.
Total Length	Replaced by the IPv6 Payload Length field, which indicates only the size of the payload.
Identification Flags Fragment Offset	Removed in IPv6. Fragmentation information is not included in the IPv6 header. It is contained in a Fragment extension header.
Time-to-Live	Replaced by the IPv6 Hop Limit field.
Protocol	Replaced by the IPv6 Next Header field.
Header Checksum	Removed in IPv6. In IPv6, the link layer performs bit-level error detection for the entire IPv6 packet.

continued

Table 4-2 *continued*

IPv4 Header Field	IPv6 Header Field
Source Address	The field is the same except that IPv6 addresses are 128 bits in length.
Destination Address	The field is the same except that IPv6 addresses are 128 bits in length.
Options	Removed in IPv6. IPv6 extension headers replace IPv4 options.

The one new field in the IPv6 header that is not included in the IPv4 header is the Flow Label field.

The result of the new IPv6 header is a reduction in the critical router loop, the set of instructions that must be executed to determine how to forward a packet. To forward a normal IPv4 packet, a router typically performs the following in its critical router loop:

1. Verify the Header Checksum field by performing its own checksum calculation and comparing its result with the result stored in the IPv4 header. While this step is required by RFC 1812, modern high-speed routers commonly skip it.

2. Verify the value of the Version field. While this step is not required by RFC 791 or 1812, doing so saves network bandwidth, as a packet containing an invalid version number is not propagated across the IPv4 internetwork only to be discarded by the destination node.

3. Decrement the value of the TTL field. If its new value is less than 1, send an ICMPv4 Time Exceeded-Time to Live Exceeded in Transit message to the source of the packet and then discard the packet. If not, place the new value in the TTL field.

4. Check for the presence of IPv4 header options. If present, process them.

5. Use the value of the Destination Address field and the contents of the local routing table to determine a forwarding interface and a next-hop IPv4 address. If a route is not found, send an ICMPv4 Destination Unreachable-Host Unreachable message to the source of the packet and discard the packet.

6. If the IPv4 maximum transmission unit (MTU) of the forwarding interface is less than the value of the Total Length field and the

Don't Fragment (DF) flag is set to 0, perform IPv4 fragmentation. If the MTU of the forwarding interface is less than the value of the Total Length field and the DF flag is set to 1, send an ICMPv4 Destination Unreachable-Fragmentation Needed And DF Set message to the source of the packet and discard the packet.

7. Recalculate the new header checksum and place its new value in the Header Checksum field.

8. Forward the packet by using the appropriate forwarding interface.

NOTE:
This critical router loop for IPv4 routers is a simplified list of items that an IPv4 router typically performs when forwarding. This list is not meant to imply any specific implementation nor an optimized order in which to process IPv4 packets for forwarding.

To forward a normal IPv6 packet, a router typically performs the following in its critical router loop:

1. Verify the value of the Version field. Although this step is not required by RFC 2460, doing so saves network bandwidth, because a packet containing an invalid version number is not propagated across the IPv6 internetwork only to be discarded by the destination node.

2. Decrement the value of the Hop Limit field. If its new value is less than 1, send an ICMPv6 Time Exceeded-Hop Limit Exceeded in Transit message to the source of the packet and discard the packet. If not, place the new value in the Hop Limit field.

3. Check the Next Header field for a value of 0. If 0, process the Hop-by-Hop Options header.

4. Use the value of the Destination Address field and the contents of the local routing table to determine a forwarding interface and a next-hop IPv6 address. If a route is not found, send an ICMPv6 Destination Unreachable-No Route To Destination message to the source of the packet and then discard the packet.

5. If the link MTU of the forwarding interface is less than (40 + the value of the Payload Length field), send an ICMPv6 Packet Too Big message to the source of the packet and discard the packet.

6. Forward the packet by using the appropriate forwarding interface.

NOTE:

This critical router loop for IPv6 routers is a simplified list of items that an IPv6 router typically performs when forwarding. This list is not meant to imply any specific implementation nor an optimized order in which to process packets for forwarding.

As you can see, the process to forward an IPv6 packet is much simpler than for an IPv4 packet, as it does not have to verify and recalculate a header checksum, perform fragmentation, or process options not intended for the router.

IPV6 EXTENSION HEADERS

The IPv4 header includes all options. Therefore, each intermediate router must check for their existence and process them when present. This can cause performance degradation in the forwarding of IPv4 packets. With IPv6, delivery and forwarding options are moved to extension headers. The only extension header that must be processed at each intermediate router is the Hop-by-Hop Options extension header. This increases IPv6 header processing speed and improves the performance of forwarding IPv6 packets.

RFC 2460 specifies that the following IPv6 extension headers must be supported by all IPv6 nodes:

- Hop-by-Hop Options header

- Destination Options header

- Routing header

- Fragment header

- Authentication header

- Encapsulating Security Payload header

With the exception of the Authentication header and Encapsulating Security Payload header, all the above IPv6 extension headers are defined in RFC 2460.

In a typical IPv6 packet, no extension headers are present. If special handling is required by either intermediate routers or the destination, the sending host adds one or more extension headers.

Each extension header must fall on a 64-bit (8-byte) boundary. Extension headers of a fixed size must be an integral multiple of 8 bytes. Extension headers of variable size contain a Header Extension Length field and must use padding as needed to ensure that their size is an integral multiple of 8 bytes.

The Next Header field in the IPv6 header and zero or more extension headers form a chain of pointers. Each pointer indicates the type of header that comes after the immediate header until the upper-layer protocol is ultimately identified. Figure 4-4 shows the chain of pointers formed by the Next Header field for various IPv6 packets.

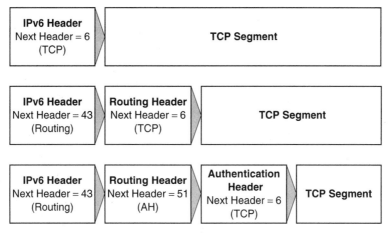

Figure 4-4. *The chain of pointers formed by the Next Header field*

Extension Headers Order

Extension headers are processed in the order in which they are present. Because the only extension header that is processed by every node on the path is the Hop-by-Hop Options header, it must be first. There are similar rules for other extension headers. In RFC 2460, it is recommended that extension headers be placed after the IPv6 header in the following order:

1. Hop-by-Hop Options header
2. Destination Options header (for intermediate destinations when the Routing header is present)
3. Routing header
4. Fragment header
5. Authentication header
6. Encapsulating Security Payload header
7. Destination Options header (for the final destination)

Hop-by-Hop Options Header

The Hop-by-Hop Options header is used to specify delivery parameters at each hop on the path to the destination. It is identified by the value of 0 in the IPv6 header's Next Header field. Figure 4-5 shows the structure of the Hop-by-Hop Options header.

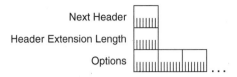

Figure 4-5. *The structure of the Hop-by-Hop Options header*

The Hop-by-Hop Options header consists of a Next Header field, a Header Extension Length field, and an Options field that contains one or more options. The value of the Header Extension Length field is the number of 8-byte blocks in the Hop-by-Hop Options extension header, not including the first 8 bytes. Therefore, for an 8-byte Hop-by-Hop Options header, the value of the Header Extension Length field is 0. Padding options are used to ensure 8-byte boundaries.

AN IPV6 ROUTER OPTIMIZATION

The interpretation of the Header Extension Length field in the Hop-by-Hop Options header is another example of how the designers of IPv6 wanted to optimize processing of IPv6 packets at intermediate routers. For those packets with a Hop-by-Hop Options header, one of the first operations is to determine the size of the header. If the Header Extension Length field were defined to be the number of 8-byte blocks in the header, its minimum value would be 1 (the minimum-sized Hop-by-Hop Options header is 8 bytes long). To ensure robustness in an IPv6 forwarding implementation, a field whose valid values begin at 1 would have to be checked for the invalid value of 0 before additional processing could be done.

With the current definition of the Header Extension Length field, 0 is a valid value and no testing of invalid values needs to be done. The number of bytes in the Hop-by-Hop Options header is calculated from the following formula: (header extension length + 1) × 8.

An option is a set of fields that either describes a specific characteristic of the packet delivery or provides padding. Options are sent in the Hop-by-Hop Options header and Destination Options header (described later in this chapter). Each option is encoded in the type-length-value (TLV) format that is commonly used in TCP/IP protocols. Figure 4-6 shows the structure of an option.

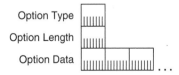

Figure 4-6. *The structure of an option*

The Option Type field both identifies the option and determines the way it is handled by the processing node. The Option Length field indicates the number of bytes in the option, not including the Option Type and Option Length fields. The option data is the specific data associated with the option.

An option might have an alignment requirement to ensure that specific fields within the option fall on desired boundaries. For example, it is easier to process an IPv6 address if it falls on an 8-byte boundary. Alignment requirements are expressed by using the notation $xn + y$, indicating that the option must begin at a byte boundary equal to an integral multiple of x bytes plus y bytes from the start of the header. For example, the alignment requirement $4n + 2$ indicates that the option must begin at a byte boundary of (an integral multiple of 4 bytes) + 2 bytes. In other words, the option must begin at the byte boundary of 6, 10, 14, and so on, relative to the start of the Hop-by-Hop Options or Destination Options headers. To accommodate alignment requirements, padding typically appears before an option and appears between each option when multiple options are present.

Option Type Field

Within the Option Type field, the two high-order bits indicate how the option is handled when the node processing the option does not recognize the option type. Table 4-3 lists the defined values of these two bits and their purpose.

Table 4-3. VALUES OF THE TWO HIGH-ORDER BITS IN THE OPTION TYPE FIELD

Value (Binary)	Action Taken
00	Skip the option
01	Silently discard the packet
10	Discard the packet and send an ICMPv6 Parameter Problem message to the sender if the Destination Address field in the IPv6 header is a unicast or multicast address
11	Discard the packet and send an ICMPv6 Parameter Problem message to the sender if the Destination Address field in the IPv6 header is not a multicast address

The third-highest-order bit of the Option Type indicates whether the option data can change (= 1) or not change (= 0) in the path to the destination.

Pad1 Option

The Pad1 option is defined in RFC 2460 and is used to insert a single byte of padding so that the Hop-by-Hop Options or Destination Options headers fall on 8-byte boundaries and to accommodate the alignment requirements of options. The Pad1 option has no alignment requirements. Figure 4-7 shows the Pad1 option.

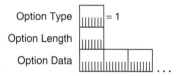

Figure 4-7. *The structure of the Pad1 option*

The Pad1 option consists of a single byte; Option Type is set to 0, and it has no length or value fields. With Option Type set to 0, the option is skipped if not recognized and it is not allowed to change in transit.

PadN Option

The PadN option is defined in RFC 2460 and is used to insert two or more bytes of padding so that the Hop-by-Hop Options or Destination Options headers fall on 8-byte boundaries and to accommodate the alignment requirements of options. The PadN option has no alignment requirements. Figure 4-8 shows the PadN option.

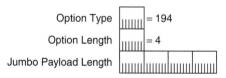

Figure 4-8. *The structure of the PadN option*

The PadN option consists of the Option Type field (set to 1), the Length field (set to the number of padding bytes present), and 0 or more bytes of padding. With the Option Type field set to 1, the option is skipped if not recognized and it is not allowed to change in transit.

Jumbo Payload Option

The Jumbo Payload option is defined in RFC 2675 and is used to indicate a payload size that is greater than 65,535 bytes. The Jumbo Payload option has the alignment requirement of 4n + 2. Figure 4-9 shows the Jumbo Payload option.

```
   Option Type  |||||| = 194
 Option Length  |||||| = 4
Jumbo Payload Length  ||||||||||||||||||||||||||
```

Figure 4-9. *The structure of the Jumbo Payload option*

With the Jumbo Payload option, the Payload Length field in the IPv6 header no longer indicates the size of the IPv6 packet payload. Instead, the Jumbo Payload Length field in the Jumbo Payload option indicates the size, in bytes, of the IPv6 packet payload. With a 32-bit Jumbo Payload Length field, payload sizes of up to 4,294,967,295 bytes can be indicated. An IPv6 packet with a payload size greater than 65,535 bytes is known as a *jumbogram*. With the Option Type field set to 194 (0xC2 hexadecimal, binary 11000010), the packet is discarded and an ICMPv6 Parameter Problem message is sent if the option is not recognized and the destination address is not a multicast address, and the option is not allowed to change in transit. Microsoft implementations of IPv6 do not support the use of jumbograms.

Router Alert Option

The Router Alert option (Option Type 5) is defined in RFC 2711 and is used to indicate to a router that the contents of the packet require additional processing. The Router Alert option has the alignment requirement of 2n + 0. Figure 4-10 shows the structure of the Router Alert option.

Figure 4-10. *The structure of the Router Alert option*

The Router Alert option is used for Multicast Listener Discovery (MLD) and the Resource ReSerVation Protocol (RSVP). With the Option Type field set to 5, the option is skipped if not recognized and it is not allowed to change in transit.

Network Monitor Capture

Here is an example of a Hop-by-Hop Options header as displayed by Network Monitor (capture 04_02 in the \NetworkMonitorCaptures folder on the companion CD-ROM):

```
+ Frame: Base frame properties
+ ETHERNET:  EType = IPv6
  IP6: Hop Opts; Proto = ICMP6; Len = 24
      IP6: Version = 6 (0x6)
      IP6: Traffic Class = 0 (0x0)
      IP6: Flow Label = 0 (0x0)
      IP6: Payload Length = 32 (0x20)
      IP6: Next Header = 0 (Hop-by-Hop Options Header)
      IP6: Hop Limit = 1 (0x1)
      IP6: Source Address = fe80::2b0:d0ff:fee9:4143
      IP6: Destination Address = ff02::1:ffe9:4143
      IP6: Hop-by-Hop Options Header
```

```
IP6: Next Header = 58 (ICMP6)
IP6: Length = 0 (0x0)
IP6: Router Alert Option
    IP6: Type = 5
        IP6: 00...... = Skip option if not recognized
        IP6: ..0..... = Option data does not change enroute
    IP6: Length = 2 (0x2)
    IP6: Router Alert Value = 0 (0x0)
IP6: Padding (2 bytes)
    IP6: Type = 1 (PadN)
        IP6: 00...... = Skip option if not recognized
        IP6: ..0..... = Option data does not change enroute
    IP6: Length = 0 (0x0)
IP6: Payload: Number of data bytes remaining = 24 (0x0018)
+ ICMP6: Multicast Listener Report
```

Notice the use of the Router Alert option (option type 5) and the PadN option (option type 1) to pad the entire Hop-by-Hop Options header to 8 bytes (1-byte Next Header field + 1-byte Option Length field + 4-byte Router Alert option + 2-byte PadN option).

Destination Options Header

The Destination Options header is used to specify packet delivery parameters for either intermediate destinations or the final destination. This header is identified by the value of 60 in the previous header's Next Header field. The Destination Options header has the same structure as the Hop-by-Hop Options header, as shown in Figure 4-11.

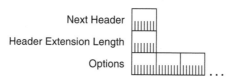

Figure 4-11. *The structure of the Destination Options header*

The Destination Options header is used in two ways:

1. If a Routing header is present, it specifies delivery or processing options at each intermediate destination. In this case, the Destination Options header occurs before the Routing header.

2. If no Routing header is present, or if this header occurs after the Routing header, this header specifies delivery or processing options at the final destination.

Binding Update Option

The Binding Update destination option (Option Type 198) is defined in the Internet draft titled "Mobility Support in IPv6" and is used by a mobile IPv6 node to update another node with its new care-of address. The Binding Update option in the Destination Options header (for the final destination) can be included in an existing packet sent to the destination or in a packet that contains just the Destination Options header. In the latter case, the Next Header field in the Destination Options header is set to 59, indicating no next header. The Binding Update option has the alignment requirement of 4n + 2. Figure 4-12 shows the structure of the Binding Update option.

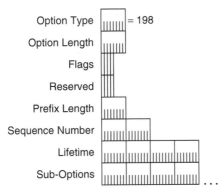

Figure 4-12. *The structure of the Binding Update option*

The fields in the Binding Update option are:

■ **Option Type**
   With the Option Type field set to 198 (0xC6 hexadecimal, 11000110 binary), the packet is discarded and an ICMPv6 Parameter Problem message is sent if the option is not recognized and the destination address is not a multicast address, and the option is not allowed to change in transit.

■ **Option Length**
   The Option Length field indicates the length of the option in bytes, not including the Option Type and Option Length fields. The Option Length field includes the sub-options, if present.

■ **Flags**
   As defined in version 13 of the Internet draft "Mobility Support in IPv6," there are four 1-bit flags as follows (starting from the high-order bit):

   ❑   Acknowledge (A): Set to indicate that the sender is requesting a binding acknowledgement.

❑   Home Registration (H): Set to indicate that the sender is requesting the receiver to be the mobile node's home agent.

❑   Router (R): Set to indicate that the mobile node is a router. This flag can be set only if the Home Registration (H) flag is also set.

❑   Duplicate Address Detection (D): Set to indicate that the sender is requesting the receiver to perform duplicate address detection for the mobile node's home address. This flag can be set only if the Acknowledge (A) and Home Registration (H) flags are also set.

■   **Reserved**
The Reserved field contains reserved bits that are set to 0. The size of this field is 4 bits.

■   **Prefix Length**
The Prefix Length field indicates the length of the subnet prefix in the Home Address field in the Home Address destination option (described later in this chapter). A binding update includes both the Binding Update and Home Address options. The remaining low-order bits in the Home Address option's Home Address field are the interface identifier of the mobile node's home address. The home agent uses this interface identifier to determine all the types of addresses used on the home link (such as link-local, site-local, and global), and performs duplicate address detection if indicated. The Prefix Length field is set only when the Home Registration (H) flag is also set. The size of this field is 8 bits.

■   **Sequence Number**
The Sequence Number field indicates the sequence of the binding update and is used by the mobile node to match a binding update with a corresponding binding acknowledgement. The size of this field is 16 bits.

■   **Lifetime**
The Lifetime field indicates the number of seconds that the binding is valid. A value of 0xFFFFFFFF indicates infinity. A value of 0 indicates that the binding is invalid and must be deleted. The size of this field is 32 bits.

■   **Sub-Options**
Sub-options can include additional optional information and allow the binding update to be extended in the future. Sub-options use

the TLV format, in the same way that options do. The current sub-options defined for the Binding Update option are:

❑   The Unique Identifier sub-option consists of an 8-bit Type field (set to 2), an 8-bit Length field (set to 2), and a 16-bit Unique Identifier field. The Unique Identifier sub-option is used to match a binding update with a binding request.

❑   The Alternate Care-of Address sub-option consists of an 8-bit Type field (set to 4), an 8-bit Length field (set to 16), and a 128-bit Alternate Care-of Address field. The Alternate Care-of Address sub-option is included when the mobile node wants to indicate a care-of address that is different from the source address of the packet containing the binding update.

Binding Acknowledgement Option

The Binding Acknowledgement destination option (Option Type 7) is defined in the Internet draft titled "Mobility Support in IPv6" and is used to acknowl-edge the receipt of a binding update (a packet that contains the Binding Up-date option) when the Acknowledge (A) flag is set. Like the Binding Update option, the Binding Acknowledgement option can be included in an existing packet being sent to the mobile node or in a packet that contains just the Destination Options header. The Binding Acknowledgement option has the alignment requirement of 4n + 3. Figure 4-13 shows the structure of the Bind-ing Acknowledgement option.

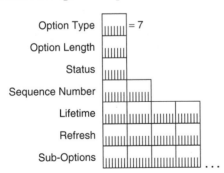

Figure 4-13. *The structure of the Binding Acknowledgement option*

The fields in the Binding Acknowledgement option are:

■   **Option Type**
With the Option Type field set to 7 (binary 00000111), the option is skipped if not recognized and is not allowed to change in transit.

■ **Option Length**

The Option Length field indicates the length of the option in bytes, not including the Option Type and Option Length fields. The Option Length field includes the sub-options, if present.

■ **Status**

The Status field indicates the status of the binding update. Status field values less than 128 indicate successful acceptance of the binding update by the receiving node. Status field values greater than 127 indicate failure of the binding update. The size of this field is 8 bits. Table 4-4 lists the values of the Status field defined in version 13 of the Internet draft titled "Mobility Support in IPv6."

Table 4-4. **VALUES OF THE STATUS FIELD**

Status Field Value (Decimal)	Description
0	Binding update accepted
128	Reason unspecified
130	Administratively prohibited
131	Insufficient resources
132	Home registration not supported
133	Not home subnet
136	Incorrect interface identifier length
137	Not home agent for this mobile node
138	Duplicate address detection failed

■ **Sequence Number**

The Sequence Number field indicates the binding update for this binding acknowledgement and is set to the Sequence Number field in the received Binding Update option. The size of this field is 16 bits.

■ **Lifetime**

The Lifetime field indicates the number of seconds that the sending node will maintain the binding for the mobile node. If the sending node is the mobile node's home agent, the Lifetime field also indicates the number of seconds the sending node is the home agent. This field is relevant only if the binding update was received successfully. The size of this field is 32 bits.

- **Refresh**

  The Refresh field indicates an interval, in seconds, at which the mobile node should update its binding with the sending node. This field is relevant only if the binding update was successfully received. The size of this field is 32 bits.

- **Sub-Options**

  Sub-options can include additional optional information and allow the binding acknowledgement to be extended in the future. There are currently no sub-options defined for the Binding Acknowledgement option.

Binding Request Option

The Binding Request destination option (Option Type 8) is defined in the Internet draft titled "Mobility Support in IPv6" and is used to request the binding from a mobile node. Like the Binding Update option, the Binding Request option can be included in an existing packet being sent to the mobile node or in a packet that contains just the Destination Options header. The Binding Request option has no alignment requirements. Figure 4-14 shows the structure of the Binding Request option.

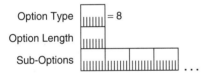

Figure 4-14. *The structure of the Binding Request option*

The fields in the Binding Request option are:

- **Option Type**

  With the Option Type field set to 8 (binary 00001000), the option is skipped if not recognized and is not allowed to change in transit.

- **Option Length**

  Indicates the length of the option in bytes, not including the Option Type and Option Length fields. The Option Length field includes the sub-options, if present. The presence of sub-options is detected through the value of the Option Length field. If the Option Length field is greater than 0, sub-options are present.

- **Sub-Options**

  Sub-options can include additional optional information and allow the binding request to be extended in the future. The only sub-option defined for the binding request is the Unique Identifier sub-option, which is used to match a binding request to a binding update.

Home Address Option

The Home Address destination option (Option Type 201) is defined in the Internet draft titled "Mobility Support in IPv6" and is used to indicate the home address of the mobile node. The Home Address option is included in the binding update. The Home Address option has the alignment requirement of 8n + 6. Figure 4-15 shows the structure of the Home Address option.

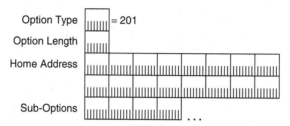

Figure 4-15. *The structure of the Home Address option*

The fields in the Home Address option are:

- **Option Type**
  With the Option Type field set to 201 (0xC9 hexadecimal, 11001001 binary), the packet is discarded and an ICMPv6 Parameter Problem message is sent if the option is not recognized and the destination address is not a multicast address, and the option is not allowed to change in transit.

- **Option Length**
  The Option Length field indicates the length of the option in bytes, not including the Option Type and Option Length fields. The Option Length field includes the sub-options, if present. The presence of sub-options is detected through the value of the Option Length field. If the Option Length field is greater than 16, sub-options are present.

- **Home Address**
  The Home Address field indicates the home address of the mobile node. The size of this field is 128 bits.

- **Sub-Options**
  Sub-options can include additional optional information and allow the Home Address option to be extended in the future. There are currently no sub-options defined for the Home Address option.

Network Monitor Capture

Here is an example of the Home Address option in the Destination Options header as displayed by Network Monitor (capture 04_03 in the

\NetworkMonitorCaptures folder on the companion CD-ROM):

```
+ Frame: Base frame properties
+ ETHERNET:  EType = IPv6
  IP6: Dest Opts; Len = 0
      IP6: Version = 6 (0x6)
      IP6: Traffic Class = 0 (0x0)
      IP6: Flow Label = 0 (0x0)
      IP6: Payload Length = 40 (0x28)
      IP6: Next Header = 60 (Destination Options Header)
      IP6: Hop Limit = 255 (0xFF)
      IP6: Source Address = 3ffe:2900:d005:4f:2c0:4fff:fe68:38c5
      IP6: Destination Address = 3ffe:2900:d005:1d4a:2c0:4fff:fe09:2f31
      IP6: Destination Options Header
         IP6: Next Header = 59 (None)
         IP6: Length = 4 (0x4)
       + IP6: Padding (4 bytes)
       + IP6: Binding Update Option
       + IP6: Padding (6 bytes)
         IP6: Home Address Option
             IP6: Type = 201
                 IP6: 11...... = Discard packet if not recognized, and
                                 send ICMP if not multicast
                 IP6: ..0..... = Option data does not change enroute
             IP6: Length = 16 (0x10)
             IP6: Home Address = 3ffe:2900:d005:6:2c0:4fff:fe68:38c5
```

Notice how the value of the Next Header field in the Destination Options header is set to 59, indicating no next header. Also notice the use of two PadN options to pad the entire Destination Options header to a multiple of 8 bytes (1-byte Next Header field + 1-byte Length field + 4-byte PadN option + 10-byte Binding Update option + 6-byte PadN option + 18-byte Home Address option = 40 bytes). Also notice how the PadN options are used to enforce the Binding Update option's alignment requirement of 4n + 2 (the Binding Update option begins at the byte offset of 6 [= (4 × 1) + 2]) and the Home Address option alignment requirement of 8n + 6 (the Home Address option begins at the byte offset of 22 [= (8 × 2) + 6]).

Summary of Option Types

Table 4-5 lists the different option types for options in Hop-by-Hop Options and Destination Options headers.

Table 4-5. OPTION TYPES

Option Type	Option and Where It Is Used	Alignment Requirement
0	Pad1 option: Hop-by-Hop and Destination Options headers	None
1	PadN option: Hop-by-Hop and Destination Options headers	None
194 (0xC2)	Jumbo Payload option: Hop-by-Hop Options header	$4n + 2$
5	Router Alert option: Hop-by-Hop Options header	$2n + 0$
198 (0xC6)	Binding Update option: Destination Options header	$4n + 2$
7	Binding Acknowledgement option: Destination Options header	$4n + 3$
8	Binding Request option: Destination Options header	None
201 (0xC9)	Home Address option: Destination Options header	$8n + 6$

Routing Header

IPv4 defines strict source routing, in which each intermediate destination must be only one hop away, and loose source routing, in which each intermediate destination can be one or more hops away. IPv6 source nodes can use the Routing header to specify a source route, which is a list of intermediate destinations for the packet to travel to on its path to the final destination. The Routing header is identified by the value of 43 in the previous header's Next Header field. Figure 4-16 shows the structure of the Routing header.

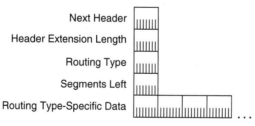

Figure 4-16. *The structure of the Routing header*

The Routing header consists of a Next Header field, a Header Extension Length field (defined in the same way as the Hop-by-Hop Options extension header), a Routing Type field, a Segments Left field that indicates the number of intermediate destinations that are still to be visited, and routing type-specific data.

RFC 2460 also defines Routing Type 0, used for loose source routing. Figure 4-17 shows the structure of the Routing Type 0 header.

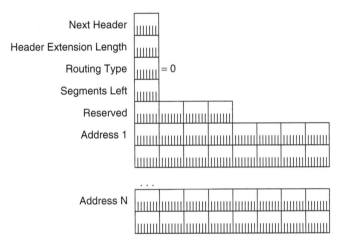

Figure 4-17. *The structure of the Routing Type 0 header*

For Routing Type 0, the routing type-specific data consists of a 32-bit Reserved field and a list of intermediate destination addresses, including the final destination address. When the packet is initially sent, the destination address is set to the first intermediate destination, and the routing type-specific data is the list of additional intermediate destinations and the final destination. The Segments Left field is set to the total number of addresses included in the routing type-specific data.

When the IPv6 packet reaches an intermediate destination, the Routing header is processed and:

1. The current destination address and the address in the (N − Segments Left + 1) position in the list of addresses are swapped, where N is the total number of addresses in the Routing header.

2. The Segments Left field is decremented.

3. The packet is forwarded.

By the time the packet arrives at the final destination, the Segments Left field has been set to 0 and the list of intermediate addresses visited in the path to the destination is recorded in the Routing header.

Network Monitor Capture

Here is an example of the Routing header as displayed by Network Monitor (capture 04_04 in the \NetworkMonitorCaptures folder on the companion CD-ROM):

```
+ Frame: Base frame properties
+ ETHERNET:  EType = IPv6
  IP6: Routing (1 left of 1); Proto = ICMP6; Len = 40
      IP6: Version = 6 (0x6)
      IP6: Traffic Class = 0 (0x0)
      IP6: Flow Label = 0 (0x0)
      IP6: Payload Length = 64 (0x40)
      IP6: Next Header = 43 (Routing Header)
      IP6: Hop Limit = 127 (0x7F)
      IP6: Source Address = fec0::2:2b0:d0ff:fee9:4143
      IP6: Destination Address = fec0::2:260:97ff:fe02:6e8f
      IP6: Routing Header
          IP6: Next Header = 58 (ICMP6)
          IP6: Length = 2 (0x2)
          IP6: Type = 0 (0x0)
          IP6: Segments Left = 1 (0x1)
          IP6: Reserved
          IP6: Route
              IP6: Address = fec0::1:260:8ff:fe52:f9d8
      IP6: Payload: Number of data bytes remaining = 40 (0x0028)
+ ICMP6: Echo Request; ID = 0, Seq = 15642
```

In this simple example of the Routing header, an ICMPv6 Echo Request message is sent from the source FEC0::2:2B0:D0FF:FEE9:4143 to the destination FEC0::1:260:8FF:FE52:F9D8 using the intermediate destination of FEC0::2: 260:97FF:FE02:6E8F.

Fragment Header

The Fragment header is used for IPv6 fragmentation and reassembly services. This header is identified by the value of 44 in the previous header's Next Header field. Figure 4-18 shows the structure of the Fragment header.

The Fragment header includes a Next Header field, a 13-bit Fragment Offset field, a More Fragments flag, and a 32-bit Identification field. The Fragment Offset, More Fragments flag, and Identification fields are used in the same way as the corresponding fields in the IPv4 header. Because the use of the

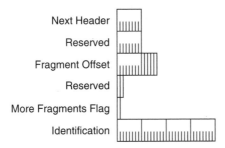

Figure 4-18. *The structure of the Fragment header*

Fragment Offset field is defined for 8-byte fragment blocks, the Fragment header cannot be used for jumbograms. The maximum number that can be expressed with the 13-bit Fragment Offset field is 8,191. Therefore, Fragment Offset can be used to indicate only a fragment data starting position of up to 8,191 × 8, or 65,528.

In IPv6, only source nodes can fragment payloads. If the payload submitted by the upper-layer protocol is larger than the link or path MTU, then IPv6 fragments the payload at the source and uses the Fragment header to provide re-assembly information. An IPv6 router will never fragment an IPv6 packet being forwarded.

Because the IPv6 internetwork will not transparently fragment payloads, data sent from applications that do not have an awareness of the destination path MTU will not be able to sense when data needing fragmentation by the source is discarded by IPv6 routers. This can be a problem for unicast or multicast traffic sent as a UDP message or other types of message streams that do not use TCP.

DIFFERENCES IN FRAGMENTATION FIELDS

There are some subtle differences between the fragmentation fields in IPv4 and IPv6. In IPv4, the fragmentation flags are the three high-order bits of the 16-bit quantity composed of the combination of the fragmentation flags and the Fragment Offset field. In IPv6, the bits used for fragmentation flags are the three low-order bits of the 16-bit quantity composed of the combination of the fragmentation flags and the Fragment Offset field. In IPv4, the Identification field is 16 bits rather than 32 bits in IPv6, and in IPv6 there is no Don't Fragment flag. Because IPv6 routers never perform fragmentation, the Don't Fragment flag would always be set to 1 for all IPv6 packets, and therefore does not need to be included.

IPv6 Fragmentation Process

When an IPv6 packet is fragmented, it is initially divided into unfragmentable and fragmentable parts:

■ The unfragmentable part of the original IPv6 packet must be processed by intermediate nodes between the fragmenting node and the destination. This part consists of the IPv6 header, the Hop-by-Hop Options header, the Destination Options header for intermediate destinations, and the Routing header.

■ The fragmentable part of the original IPv6 packet must be processed only at the final destination node. This part consists of the Authentication header, the Encapsulating Security Payload header, the Destination Options header for the final destination, and the upper-layer PDU.

Next, the IPv6 fragment packets are formed. Each fragment packet consists of the unfragmentable part, a fragment header, and a portion of the fragmentable part. Figure 4-19 shows the IPv6 fragmentation process for a packet fragmented into three fragments.

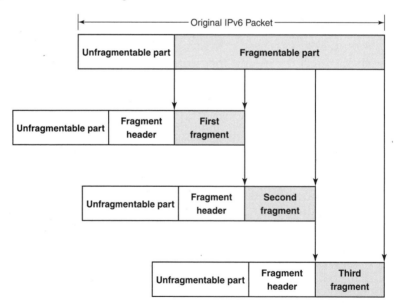

Figure 4-19. *The IPv6 fragmentation process*

In each fragment, the Next Header field in the Fragment header indicates the first header or the upper-layer protocol in the original fragmentable part. The Fragment Offset field in the Fragment header indicates the offset, in 8-byte units known as fragment blocks, of this fragment relative to the original pay-load. The More Fragments flag is set on all fragment packets except the last fragment packet. All fragment packets created from the same IPv6 packet must contain the same Identification field value.

Fragmentation of IPv6 packets can occur when the upper-layer protocol of the sending host submits a packet to IPv6 that is larger than the path MTU to the destination. Examples of IPv6 fragmentation are when a UDP application that is not aware of a path MTU sends large packets to a destination, or when a TCP application sends a packet before it is made aware of a path MTU update that lowers the path MTU. In this latter case, IPv6 is aware of the new path MTU, but TCP is not. TCP submits the TCP segment by using the old, larger value of the path MTU and IPv6 fragments the TCP segment to fit the new, lower path MTU value. Once TCP is made aware of the new path MTU, subsequent TCP segments are not fragmented.

IPv6 packets sent to IPv4 destinations that undergo IPv6-to-IPv4 header translation may receive a path MTU update of less than 1,280. In this case, the sending host sends IPv6 packets with a Fragment header in which the Fragment Offset field is set to 0 and the More Fragments flag is not set, and a smaller pay-load size of 1,272 bytes. The Fragment header is included so that the IPv6-to-IPv4 translator can use the Identification field in the Fragment header to perform IPv4 fragmentation to reach the IPv4 destination.

Network Monitor Capture

Here is an example of a Fragment header as displayed by Network Monitor (frame 3 of capture 04_05 in the \NetworkMonitorCaptures folder on the companion CD-ROM):

```
+ Frame: Base frame properties
+ ETHERNET:  EType = IPv6
  IP6: Fragment (id 5 at 0xb50+); Proto = ICMP6; Len = 1448
      IP6: Version = 6 (0x6)
      IP6: Traffic Class = 0 (0x0)
      IP6: Flow Label = 0 (0x0)
      IP6: Payload Length = 1456 (0x5B0)
      IP6: Next Header = 44 (Fragment Header)
      IP6: Hop Limit = 128 (0x80)
      IP6: Source Address = fe80::210:5aff:feaa:20a2
      IP6: Destination Address = fe80::250:daff:fed8:c153
      IP6: Fragment Header
          IP6: Next Header = 58 (ICMP6)
          IP6: Reserved
          IP6: Offset = 2896 (0xB50)
```

```
      IP6: ..............1 = More fragments
      IP6: Identifier = 5 (0x5)
  IP6: Payload: Number of data bytes remaining = 1448 (0x05A8)
```

This is a fragment of a payload using the identification number of 5 and starts in byte position 2,896 relative to the fragmentable portion of the original IPv6 payload.

IPv6 Reassembly Process

The fragment packets are forwarded by the intermediate IPv6 router(s) to the destination IPv6 address. The fragment packets can take different paths to the destination and arrive in a different order in which they are sent. To reassemble the fragment packets into the original payload, IPv6 uses the Source Address and Destination Address fields in the IPv6 header and the Identification field in the Fragment header to group the fragments. Figure 4-20 shows the IPv6 reassembly process.

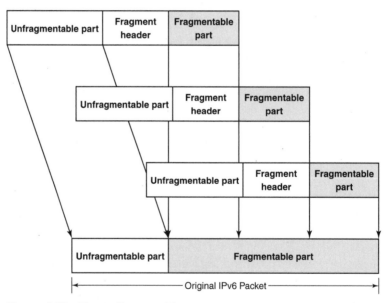

Figure 4-20. *The IPv6 reassembly process*

After all the fragments arrive, the original payload length is calculated and the Payload Length field in the IPv6 header for the reassembled packet is updated. Additionally, the Next Header field of the last header of the unfragmentable part is set to the Next Header field of the Fragment header of the first fragment.

RFC 2460 recommends a reassembly time of 60 seconds before abandoning reassembly and discarding the partially reassembled packet. If the first fragment has arrived and reassembly has not completed, the reassembling host sends an ICMPv6 Time Exceeded-Fragment Reassembly Time Exceeded message to the source of the fragment.

Authentication Header

The Authentication header provides data authentication (verification of the node that sent the packet), data integrity (verification that the data was not modified in transit), and anti-replay protection (assurance that captured packets cannot be retransmitted and accepted as valid data) for the IPv6 packet including the fields in the IPv6 header that do not change in transit across an IPv6 internetwork. The Authentication header, described in RFC 2402, is part of the security architecture for IP, as defined in RFC 2401. The Authentication header is identified by the value of 51 in the previous header's Next Header field. Figure 4-21 shows the structure of the Authentication header.

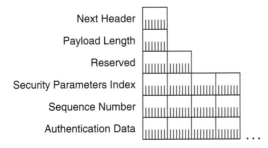

Figure 4-21. *The structure of the Authentication header*

The Authentication header contains a Next Header field, a Payload Length field (the number of 4-byte blocks in the Authentication header, not counting the first two), a Reserved field, a Security Parameters Index (SPI) field that helps identify a specific IP Security (IPSec) security association (SA), a Sequence Number field that provides anti-replay protection, and an Authentication Data field that contains an integrity value check (ICV). The ICV provides data authentication and data integrity.

The Authentication header does not provide data confidentiality services for the upper-layer PDU by encrypting the data so that it cannot be viewed without the encryption key. To obtain data authentication and data integrity for the entire IPv6 packet and data confidentiality for the upper-layer PDU, you can use both the Authentication header and the Encapsulating Security Payload header and trailer.

Details about how the Authentication header provides data authentication and integrity through cryptographic techniques are beyond the scope of this book.

Encapsulating Security Payload Header and Trailer

The Encapsulating Security Payload (ESP) header and trailer, described in RFC 2406, provide data confidentiality, data authentication, data integrity, and replay protection services to the encapsulated payload. The ESP header provides no security services for the IPv6 header or extension headers that occur before the ESP header. The ESP header and trailer are identified by the value of 50 in the previous header's Next Header field. Figure 4-22 shows the structure of the ESP header and trailer.

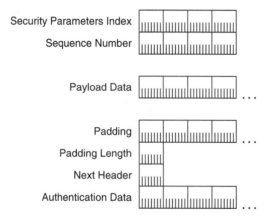

Figure 4-22. *The structure of the Encapsulating Security Payload header and trailer*

The ESP header contains an SPI field that helps identify the IPSec SA, and a Sequence Number field that provides anti-replay protection. The ESP trailer contains the Padding, Padding Length, Next Header, and Authentication Data fields. The Padding field is used to ensure 4-byte boundaries for the ESP payload and appropriate data block boundaries for encryption algorithms. The Padding Length field indicates the size of the Padding field in bytes. The Authentication Data field contains the ICV.

Details about how the ESP header and trailer provide data confidentiality, authentication, and integrity through cryptographic techniques are beyond the scope of this book.

IPv6 MTU

IPv6 requires that the link layer support a minimum MTU size of 1,280 bytes. Link layers that do not support this MTU size must provide a link-layer fragmentation and reassembly scheme that is transparent to IPv6. For link layers that can support a configurable MTU size, RFC 2460 recommends that they be configured with an MTU size of at least 1,500 bytes (the IPv6 MTU for Ethernet II encapsulation). An example of a configurable MTU is the Maximum Receive Unit (MRU) of a PPP link.

Like IPv4, IPv6 provides a Path MTU Discovery process that uses the ICMPv6 Packet Too Big message described in the "Path MTU Discovery" section of Chapter 5, "ICMPv6." Path MTU Discovery allows the transmission of IPv6 packets that are larger than 1,280 bytes.

IPv6 source hosts can fragment payloads of upper-layer protocols that are larger than the path MTU by using the process and Fragment header previously described. However, the use of IPv6 fragmentation is highly discouraged. An IPv6 node must be able to reassemble a fragmented packet that is at least 1,500 bytes in size.

Table 4-6 lists commonly used LAN and WAN technologies and their defined IPv6 MTUs.

Table 4-6. **IPv6 MTUs FOR COMMON LAN AND WAN TECHNOLOGIES**

LAN or WAN Technology	*IPv6 MTU*
Ethernet (Ethernet II encapsulation)	1,500
Ethernet (IEEE 802.3 SubNetwork Access Protocol [SNAP] encapsulation)	1,492
Token Ring	Varies
FDDI	4,352
Attached Resource Computer Network (ARCNet)	9,072
PPP	1,500
X.25	1,280
Frame Relay	1,592
Asynchronous Transfer Mode (ATM) (Null or SNAP encapsulation)	9,180

For more information about LAN and WAN encapsulations for IPv6 packets, see Appendix A, "Link-Layer Support for IPv6."

UPPER-LAYER CHECKSUMS

The current implementation of TCP, UDP, and ICMP for IPv4 incorporates into their checksum calculation a pseudo-header that includes both the IPv4 Source Address and Destination Address fields. This checksum calculation must be modified for TCP, UDP, and ICMPv6 traffic sent over IPv6 to include IPv6 addresses. Figure 4-23 shows the structure of the new IPv6 pseudo-header that must be used by TCP, UDP, and ICMPv6 checksum calculations. IPv6 uses the same algorithm as IPv4 for computing the checksum value.

The IPv6 pseudo-header includes the Source Address, the Destination Address, an Upper Layer Packet Length field that indicates the length of the upper-layer PDU, and a Next Header field that indicates the upper-layer protocol for which the checksum is being calculated.

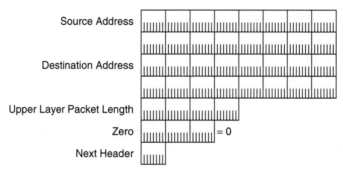

Figure 4-23. *The structure of the new IPv6 pseudo-header*

REFERENCES

RFC 791 – "Internet Protocol"

RFC 1812 – "Requirements for IP Version 4 Routers"

RFC 2401 – "Security Architecture for the Internet Protocol"

RFC 2402 – "IP Authentication Header"

RFC 2406 – "IP Encapsulating Security Payload (ESP)"

RFC 2460 – "Internet Protocol, Version 6 (IPv6)"

RFC 2474 – "Definition of the Differentiated Services Field (DS Field)"

RFC 2675 – "IPv6 Jumbograms"

RFC 2711 – "IPv6 Router Alert Option"

Internet draft – "Mobility Support in IPv6"

TESTING FOR UNDERSTANDING

To test your understanding of the IPv6 header, answer the following questions. See Appendix D, "Testing for Understanding Answers" to check your answers.

1. Why does the IPv6 header not include a checksum?

2. What is the IPv6 equivalent to the IHL field in the IPv4 header?

3. How does the combination of the Traffic Class and Flow Label fields provide better support for QoS traffic?

4. Which extension headers are fragmentable and why? Which extension headers are not fragmentable and why?

5. Describe a situation that results in an IPv6 packet that contains a Fragment Header in which the Fragment Offset field is set to 0 and the More Fragments flag is not set.

6. Describe how the new upper-layer checksum calculation affects transport layer protocols such as TCP and UDP.

7. If the minimum MTU for IPv6 packets is 1,280 bytes, then how are 1,280-byte packets sent on a link that supports only 512-byte frames?

Chapter 5

ICMPv6

At the end of this chapter, you should be able to:

■ Explain the purpose of ICMPv6 and the structure of all ICMPv6 messages.

■ Describe the two types of ICMPv6 messages and how to distinguish them.

■ Define the four types of ICMPv6 error messages.

■ Explain the two types of ICMPv6 informational messages used for diagnostics.

■ Enumerate the common ICMPv4 messages and give their ICMPv6 equivalents.

■ Describe the path MTU discovery process for IPv6.

OVERVIEW OF ICMPv6

Like IPv4, the specification for the IPv6 header and extension headers does not provide facilities for reporting errors. Instead, IPv6 uses an updated version of the Internet Control Message Protocol (ICMP) named ICMP version 6 (ICMPv6). ICMPv6 has the common IPv4 ICMP functions of reporting delivery and forwarding errors, and providing a simple echo service for troubleshooting. ICMPv6 is defined in RFC 2463 and is required for an IPv6 implementation.

The ICMPv6 protocol also provides a packet structure framework for the following:

■ **Neighbor Discovery**
Neighbor Discovery (ND) is a series of five ICMPv6 messages that manage node-to-node communication on a link. ND replaces Address Resolution Protocol (ARP), ICMPv4 Router Discovery, and the ICMPv4 Redirect message. ND is described in more detail in Chapter 6, "Neighbor Discovery."

■ **Multicast Listener Discovery**
Multicast Listener Discovery (MLD) is a series of three ICMPv6 messages that are equivalent to version 2 of the Internet Group Management Protocol (IGMP) for IPv4 to manage subnet multicast membership. MLD is described in more detail in Chapter 7, "Multicast Listener Discovery."

Types of ICMPv6 Messages

There are two types of ICMPv6 messages:

■ **Error messages**
Error messages report errors in the forwarding or delivery of IPv6 packets by either the destination node or an intermediate router. The high-order bit of the 8-bit Type field for all ICMPv6 error messages is set to 0. Therefore, valid values for the Type field for ICMPv6 error messages are in the range of 0 through 127. ICMPv6 error messages include Destination Unreachable, Packet Too Big, Time Exceeded, and Parameter Problem.

■ **Informational messages**
Informational messages provide diagnostic functions and additional host functionality such as MLD and ND. The high-order bit of the 8-bit Type field for all ICMPv6 informational messages is set to 1. Therefore, valid values for the Type field for ICMPv6 information messages are in the range of 128 through 255. ICMPv6 informational messages described in RFC 2463 include Echo Request and Echo Reply.

ICMPv6 Header

An ICMPv6 header is identified by a Next Header value of 58 in the immediately preceding header. Figure 5-1 shows the structure of ICMPv6 messages.

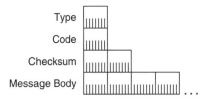

Figure 5-1. *The structure of ICMPv6 messages*

The fields in the ICMPv6 header are:

- **Type**
  Indicates the type of ICMPv6 message. The size of this field is 8 bits. In ICMPv6 error messages, the high-order bit is set to 0. In ICMPv6 informational messages, the high-order bit is set to 1.

- **Code**
  Differentiates among multiple messages within a given message type. The size of this field is 8 bits. For the first, or only, message for a given type, the value of the Code field is 0.

- **Checksum**
  Stores a checksum of the ICMPv6 message. The size of this field is 16 bits. The IPv6 pseudo-header is added to the front of the ICMPv6 message when calculating the checksum. For more information about the IPv6 pseudo-header, see "Upper Layer Checksums" in Chapter 4, "The IPv6 Header."

- **Message body**
  Contains ICMPv6 message-specific data.

ICMPv6 Error Messages

ICMPv6 error messages report forwarding or delivery errors by either a router or the destination host, and consist of the following messages:

- Destination Unreachable (ICMPv6 Type 1)

- Packet Too Big (ICMPv6 Type 2)

- Time Exceeded (ICMPv6 Type 3)

- Parameter Problem (ICMPv6 Type 4)

To conserve network bandwidth, ICMPv6 error messages are not sent for every error encountered. Instead, ICMPv6 error messages are rate limited. Rate limiting can be based on either of the following:

- **A timer**
  The rate is one error message per source or any source for every T milliseconds (ms). RFC 2463 suggests a value of 1000 ms.

- **A percentage of bandwidth**
  The rate of error messages sent per interface is some percentage P of the link's bandwidth. RFC 2463 suggests a value of 2%.

In Windows XP and the Windows .NET Server 2003 family, IPv6 sends up to two ICMPv6 error messages per second per source.

Destination Unreachable

A router or a destination host sends an ICMPv6 Destination Unreachable message when the packet cannot be forwarded to the destination node or upper-layer protocol. Figure 5-2 shows the structure of the Destination Unreachable message.

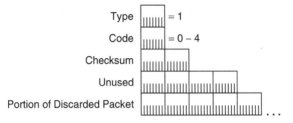

Figure 5-2. *The structure of the Destination Unreachable message*

In the Destination Unreachable message, the Type field is set to 1 and the Code field is set to a value in the range of 0 through 4. Following the Checksum field is a 32-bit Unused field and the leading portion of the discarded packet, sized so that the entire IPv6 packet containing the ICMPv6 message is no larger than 1,280 bytes (the minimum IPv6 MTU). The number of bytes of the discarded packet included in the message varies if there are IPv6 extension headers present. For an ICMPv6 message without extension headers, up to 1,232 bytes of the discarded packet are included (1,280 less a 40-byte IPv6 header and an 8-byte ICMPv6 Destination Unreachable header).

Table 5-1 lists the value of the Code field for the various Destination Unreachable messages as defined in RFC 2463 and the Internet draft titled "IPv6 Scoped Address Architecture."

Table 5-1. ICMPv6 DESTINATION UNREACHABLE MESSAGES

Code Field Value	Description
0 - No Route to Destination	No route matching the destination was found in the routing table.
1 - Communication with Destination Administratively Prohibited	The communication with the destination is prohibited by administrative policy. This is typically sent when the packet is discarded by a firewall.

continued

Table 5-1 *continued*

Code Field Value	Description
2 - Beyond Scope of Source Address	The destination is beyond the scope of the source address. A router sends this when the packet is forwarded using an interface that is not within the scoped zone of the source address. This message is defined in the Internet draft titled "IPv6 Scoped Address Architecture."
3 - Address Unreachable	The destination address is unreachable. This is typically sent because of an inability to resolve the destination's link-layer address.
4 - Port Unreachable	The destination port was unreachable. This is typically sent when an IPv6 packet containing a UDP message arrived at the destination but there were no applications listening on the destination UDP port.

Network Monitor Capture

Here is an example of a Destination Unreachable-No Route to Destination message as displayed by Network Monitor (capture 05_01 in the \NetworkMonitorCaptures folder on the companion CD-ROM):

```
+ Frame: Base frame properties
+ ETHERNET: EType = IPv6
     IP6: Version = 6 (0x6)
     IP6: Traffic Class = 0 (0x0)
     IP6: Flow Label = 0 (0x0)
     IP6: Payload Length = 88 (0x58)
     IP6: Next Header = 58 (ICMP6)
     IP6: Hop Limit = 128 (0x80)
     IP6: Source Address = fec0::2:201:2ff:fe44:87d1
     IP6: Destination Address = fec0::2:260:97ff:fe02:6e8f
     IP6: Payload: Number of data bytes remaining = 88 (0x0058)
   ICMP6: Destination Unreachable (No route)
     ICMP6: Type = 1 (Destination Unreachable)
     ICMP6: Code = 0 (No route)
     ICMP6: Checksum = 0xD498
     ICMP6: Unused
     ICMP6: Data: Number of data bytes remaining = 80 (0x0050)
```

Packet Too Big

An ICMPv6 Packet Too Big message is sent when the packet cannot be forwarded because the link MTU on the forwarding interface of a router is smaller than the size of the IPv6 packet. Figure 5-3 shows the structure of the Packet Too Big message.

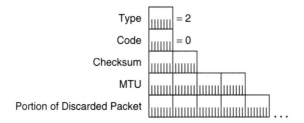

Type   = 2
Code   = 0
Checksum
MTU
Portion of Discarded Packet

Figure 5-3. *The structure of the Packet Too Big message*

In the Packet Too Big message, the Type field is set to 2 and the Code field is set to 0. Following the Checksum field is a 32-bit MTU field that stores the link MTU of the interface over which the packet was being forwarded. Next is the leading portion of the discarded packet, sized so that the entire IPv6 packet containing the ICMPv6 message is no larger than 1,280 bytes. The Packet Too Big message is used for the IPv6 Path MTU Discovery process described in the "Path MTU Discovery" section of this chapter.

Network Monitor Capture

Here is an example of a Packet Too Big message as displayed by Network Monitor (frame 2 of capture 05_02 in the \NetworkMonitorCaptures folder on the companion CD-ROM):

```
+ Frame: Base frame properties
+ ETHERNET:  EType = IPv6
+ IP6: Proto = ICMP6; Len = 1240
  ICMP6: Packet Too Big (MTU = 1280)
      ICMP6: Type = 2 (Packet Too Big)
      ICMP6: Code = 0 (0x0)
      ICMP6: Checksum = 0xAD3D
      ICMP6: MTU = 1280 (0x500)
      ICMP6: Data: Number of data bytes remaining = 1232 (0x04D0)
```

This message was sent by a router attempting to forward a 1,500-byte Echo Request message over an interface that supported only a 1,280-byte IPv6 MTU.

Time Exceeded

A router typically sends an ICMPv6 Time Exceeded message when the Hop Limit field in the IPv6 header becomes zero after decrementing its value during the forwarding process. Figure 5-4 shows the structure of the Time Exceeded message.

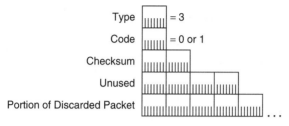

Figure 5-4. *The structure of the Time Exceeded message*

In the Time Exceeded message, the Type field is set to 3 and the Code field is set to:

- 0 (Hop Limit Exceeded in Transit) by a router when the Hop Limit field in the IPv6 header is decremented to 0, or in the rare instance when the value of the Hop Limit field in the IPv6 header of an arriving packet is 0.

- 1 (Fragment Reassembly Time Exceeded) by a host when the fragmentation reassembly time of the destination host expires. RFC 2460 specifies a reassembly time of 60 seconds.

Following the Checksum field is a 32-bit Unused field and the leading portion of the discarded packet, sized so that the entire IPv6 packet containing the ICMPv6 message is no larger than 1,280 bytes.

The receipt of a Time Exceeded-Hop Limit Exceeded in Transit message indicates that either the value of the Hop Limit field of outgoing packets is not large enough to reach the destination, or that a routing loop exists. A recommended value for the Hop Limit field set by the sending node is twice the diameter of the network, where the diameter is the maximum number of links between the farthest ends of the network. A routing loop is a condition on a network in which packets are forwarded in a loop between two or more routers.

Parameter Problem

An ICMPv6 Parameter Problem message is sent either by a router or by the destination. This occurs when there is an error in the IPv6 header or an extension header that prevents IPv6 from performing additional processing. Figure 5-5 shows the structure of the Parameter Problem message.

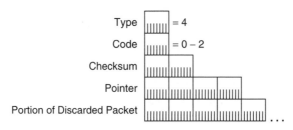

Figure 5-5. *The structure of the Parameter Problem message*

In the Parameter Problem message, the Type field is set to 4 and the Code field has a value in the range of 0 through 2. Following the Checksum field is the 32-bit Pointer field that indicates the byte offset (starting at 0) in the IPv6 packet at which the error was encountered. Following the Pointer field is the leading portion of the discarded packet, sized so that the entire ICMPv6 message is no larger than 1,280 bytes. The Pointer field value is set to the correct offset even when the location of the error is not within the portion of the discarded packet. When the receiving host recognizes an error in the portion of the packet beyond an Encapsulating Security Payload (ESP) extension header, the offset indicates the byte position in the decrypted packet, not the encrypted packet as sent on the network.

Table 5-2 shows the Code field values for Parameter Problem messages.

Table 5-2. ICMPv6 PARAMETER PROBLEM MESSAGES

Code Field Value	Description
0 - Erroneous Header Field Encountered	An error in a field within the IPv6 header or an extension header was encountered.
1 - Unrecognized Next Header Type Encountered	An unrecognized Next Header field value was encountered. This is equivalent to the ICMPv4 Destination Unreachable-Protocol Unreachable message.
2 - Unrecognized IPv6 Option Encountered	An unrecognized IPv6 option was encountered.

The Parameter Problem-Unrecognized IPv6 Option Encountered message is used when both of the following are true:

■   An option in a Hop-by-Hop Options header or a Destination Options header is not recognized.

■   Within the option's Option Type field, the 2 high-order bits are set to either 10 (binary) or 11 (binary).

For more information about the Option Type field, see "Hop-by-Hop Options Header" in Chapter 4, "The IPv6 Header."

ICMPV6 INFORMATIONAL MESSAGES

The ICMPv6 informational messages defined in RFC 2463 provide a simple diagnostic capability to aid in troubleshooting and consist of the following messages:

- Echo Request (ICMPv6 Type 128)
- Echo Reply (ICMPv6 Type 129)

Additional ICMPv6 informational messages are used for ND and MLD. For more information, see Chapter 6, "Neighbor Discovery" and Chapter 7, "Multicast Listener Discovery."

Echo Request

An ICMPv6 Echo Request message is sent to a destination to solicit an immediate Echo Reply message. The Echo Request/Echo Reply message facility provides a simple diagnostic function to aid in the troubleshooting of a variety of reachability and routing problems. Figure 5-6 shows the structure of the Echo Request message.

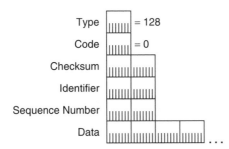

Figure 5-6. *The structure of the Echo Request message*

In the Echo Request message, the Type field is set to 128 and the Code field is set to 0. Following the Checksum field are the 16-bit Identifier and the 16-bit Sequence Number fields. The Identifier and Sequence Number fields are set by the sending host so that they can be used to match an incoming Echo Reply message with a sent Echo Request message. The Data field is zero or more bytes of optional data that is also set by the sending host.

Network Monitor Capture

Here is an example of an Echo Request message as displayed by Network Monitor (frame 1 of capture 05_03 in the \NetworkMonitorCaptures folder on the companion CD-ROM):

```
+ Frame: Base frame properties
+ ETHERNET:  EType = IPv6
+ IP6: Proto = ICMP6; Len = 40
  ICMP6: Echo Request; ID = 0, Seq = 24
      ICMP6: Type = 128 (Echo Request)
      ICMP6: Code = 0 (0x0)
      ICMP6: Checksum = 0xCB4D
      ICMP6: Identifier = 0 (0x0)
      ICMP6: Sequence Number = 24 (0x18)
      ICMP6: Data: Number of data bytes remaining = 32 (0x0020)
```

Echo Reply

An ICMPv6 Echo Reply message is sent in response to the receipt of an ICMPv6 Echo Request message. Figure 5-7 shows the structure of the Echo Reply message.

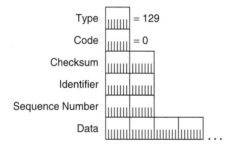

Figure 5-7. *The structure of the Echo Reply message*

In the Echo Reply message, the Type field is set to 129 and the Code field is set to 0. Following the Checksum field are the 16-bit Identifier and the 16-bit Sequence Number fields. The Identifier, Sequence Number, and Data fields are set with the same values as those in the Echo Request message that prompted the Echo Reply.

Echo Request messages can be sent to a multicast address. As specified in RFC 2463, an Echo Request message sent to a multicast address should be answered with an Echo Reply message, sent from a unicast address assigned to the interface on which the Echo Request was received.

Network Monitor Capture

Here is an example of an Echo Reply message as displayed by Network Monitor (frame 2 of capture 05_03 in the \NetworkMonitorCaptures folder on the companion CD-ROM):

```
+ Frame: Base frame properties
+ ETHERNET:  EType = IPv6
+ IP6: Proto = ICMP6; Len = 40
  ICMP6: Echo Reply; ID = 0, Seq = 24
      ICMP6: Type = 129 (Echo Reply)
      ICMP6: Code = 0 (0x0)
      ICMP6: Checksum = 0xCA4D
      ICMP6: Identifier = 0 (0x0)
      ICMP6: Sequence Number = 24 (0x18)
      ICMP6: Data: Number of data bytes remaining = 32 (0x0020)
```

This Echo Reply message was sent in response to the previously displayed Echo Request message. Notice how the Identifier, Sequence Number, and Data fields (actual contents of the Data field are not shown) match the original Echo Request message.

COMPARING ICMPv4 AND ICMPv6 MESSAGES

Table 5-3 lists commonly used ICMPv4 messages and their ICMPv6 equivalents listed in order of the ICMPv4 Type and Code fields.

Table 5-3. ICMPv4 MESSAGES AND THEIR ICMPv6 EQUIVALENTS

ICMPv4 Message	*ICMPv6 Equivalent*
Destination Unreachable-Network Unreachable (Type 3, Code 0)	Destination Unreachable-No Route to Destination (Type 1, Code 0)
Destination Unreachable-Host Unreachable (Type 3, Code 1)	Destination Unreachable-Address Unreachable (Type 1, Code 3)
Destination Unreachable-Protocol Unreachable (Type 3, Code 2)	Parameter Problem-Unrecognized Next Header Type Encountered (Type 4, Code 1)

continued

Table 5-1 *continued*

ICMPv4 Message	ICMPv6 Equivalent
Destination Unreachable-Port Unreachable (Type 3, Code 3)	Destination Unreachable-Port Unreachable (Type 1, Code 4)
Destination Unreachable-Fragmentation Needed and DF Set (Type 3, Code 4) (as specified in RFC 1191)	Packet Too Big (Type 2, Code 0)
Destination Unreachable-Communication with Destination Host Administratively Prohibited (Type 3, Code 10)	Destination Unreachable-Communication with Destination Administratively Prohibited (Type 1, Code 1)
Source Quench (Type 4, Code 0)	This message is not present in IPv6.
Redirect (Type 5, Code 0)	Neighbor Discovery Redirect message (Type 137, Code 0). For more information, see Chapter 6, "Neighbor Discovery."
Time Exceeded-TTL Exceeded in Transit (Type 11, Code 0)	Time Exceeded-Hop Limit Exceeded in Transit (Type 3, Code 0)
Time Exceeded-Fragment Reassembly Time Exceeded (Type 11, Code 1)	Time Exceeded-Fragment Reassembly Time Exceeded (Type 3, Code 1)
Parameter Problem (Type 12, Code 0)	Parameter Problem (Type 4, Code 0 or Code 2)

NOTE:

The comparisons between the ICMPv4 Destination Unreachable-Network Unreachable and Destination Unreachable-Host Unreachable messages and their IPv6 equivalents are based on the historical definitions of these messages. In common practice, the ICMPv4 Destination Unreachable-Network Unreachable message is not used because in a classless addressing environment, the network of the destination cannot be determined from the destination address. Instead, the ICMPv4 Destination Unreachable-Host Unreachable message is sent when a route is not found for the destination.

PATH MTU DISCOVERY

Sending the largest possible packets maximizes efficient use of network capacity when bulk data transfers are performed. Because IPv6 routers no longer support fragmentation, the sending host must either fragment its payload (not recommended) or discover the maximum-sized packet that can be sent to the destination and send unfragmented packets at that size.

The path maximum transmission unit (PMTU) is the smallest link MTU supported by any link in the path between a source and a destination. The link MTU is the maximum-sized link-layer payload that can be sent on the link. This corresponds to the maximum-sized packet that can be sent on the link, but differs from the maximum-sized frame that can be sent on the link. The maximum-sized frame includes the link-layer header and trailer. For example, for Ethernet links using Ethernet II encapsulation, the link MTU is 1,500 bytes and the maximum-sized frame is 1,526 bytes (which includes the Ethernet preamble, source and destination addresses, the EtherType field, and the Frame Check Sequence field). For more information about the Ethernet II header and trailer, see Appendix A.

IPv6 packets with a maximum size of the PMTU of the current path do not require fragmentation by the sending host and are successfully forwarded by all routers on the path. To discover the PMTU of the current path, the sending node relies on the receipt of ICMPv6 Packet Too Big messages. The PMTU is discovered through the following process:

1. The sending node assumes that the destination PMTU is the link MTU of the interface on which the traffic is being forwarded.

2. The sending node sends IPv6 packets at the assumed PMTU size.

3. If a router on the path is unable to forward the packet because it is using an interface with a link MTU that is smaller than the size of the packet, it sends an ICMPv6 Packet Too Big message back to the sending node and discards the IPv6 packet. The ICMPv6 Packet Too Big message contains the link MTU of the interface on which forwarding failed.

4. The sending node sets the new assumed PMTU for packets being sent to the destination to the value of the MTU field in the ICMPv6 Packet Too Big message.

The sending node starts again at step 2 and repeats steps 2 through 4 for as many times as are necessary to discover the PMTU. The PMTU is determined when either no additional ICMPv6 Packet Too Big messages are received or an acknowledgment or response packet is received from the destination.

In RFC 1981, it is recommended that IPv6 nodes support PMTU discovery. Those that do not must use the minimum link MTU of 1,280 bytes as the PMTU for all destinations.

Changes in PMTU

Due to changes in routing topology, the path between source and destination might change over time. When a new path requires a lower PMTU, the PMTU process described in the "Path MTU Discovery" section begins at step 3 and repeats steps 2 through 4 until the new PMTU is discovered.

Decreases in path MTU are immediately discovered through the receipt of ICMPv6 Packet Too Big messages. Increases in path MTU must be detected by the sending node. As described in RFC 1981, the sending node can attempt to send a larger IPv6 packet after a minimum of 5 minutes (10 minutes are recommended) upon receiving an ICMPv6 Packet Too Big message.

Figure 5-8 summarizes the PMTU discovery process of a node using the IPv6 protocol for the Windows .NET Server 2003 family.

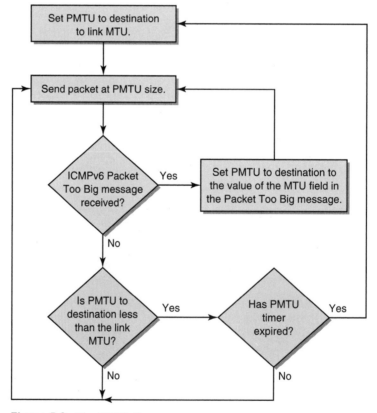

Figure 5-8. *The PMTU discovery process*

REFERENCES

RFC 1191 — "Path MTU Discovery"

RFC 1981 — "Path MTU Discovery for IP version 6"

RFC 2460 — "Internet Protocol, Version 6 (IPv6)"

RFC 2463 — "Internet Control Message Protocol (ICMPv6) for the Internet Protocol Version 6 (IPv6)"

Internet draft — "IPv6 Scoped Address Architecture"

TESTING FOR UNDERSTANDING

To test your understanding of ICMPv6, answer the following questions. See Appendix D to check your answers.

1. How do you distinguish ICMPv6 error messages from ICMPv6 informational messages?

2. Which fields of the Echo Request message are echoed in the Echo Reply message?

3. For a maximum-sized IPv6 packet with a Fragment extension header sent on an Ethernet link, how many bytes of the original payload are returned in an ICMPv6 Destination Unreachable message?

4. How can you tell whether a returned packet was discarded by a firewall that is enforcing network policy or a router that could not resolve the link-layer address of the destination?

5. Why is the MTU field in the ICMPv6 Packet Too Big message 4 bytes long when the Next Hop MTU field in the ICMPv4 Destination Unreachable-Fragmentation Needed and DF Set message is only 2 bytes long?

6. Why isn't the ICMPv6 Parameter Problem-Unrecognized Option message sent when the 2 high-order bits of an option's Option Type field are set to either 00 (binary) or 01 (binary)?

7. Based on the IPv6 design requirement to minimize processing at IPv6 routers, why is there no equivalent to the ICMPv4 Source Quench message in IPv6?

Chapter 6

Neighbor Discovery

At the end of this chapter, you should be able to:

- Describe the functions of the IPv6 Neighbor Discovery (ND) protocol.

- List and describe the function and format of ND options.

- List and describe the function and format of ND messages.

- Describe which ND messages use which ND options.

- Describe the details of the address resolution, neighbor unreachability detection, duplicate address detection, router discovery, and redirect processes.

- Describe the host sending algorithm in terms of host data structures and ND messages.

NEIGHBOR DISCOVERY OVERVIEW

IPv6 Neighbor Discovery (ND) is a set of messages and processes that determine relationships between neighboring nodes. ND replaces ARP, ICMP router discovery, and the ICMP Redirect message used in IPv4. ND also provides additional functionality.

ND is used by nodes to:

- Resolve the link-layer address of a neighboring node to which an IPv6 packet is being forwarded.

- Determine when the link-layer address of a neighboring node has changed.

- Determine whether a neighbor is still reachable.

ND is used by hosts to:

- Discover neighboring routers.

■   Autoconfigure addresses, address prefixes, routes, and other configuration parameters.

ND is used by routers to:

■   Advertise their presence, host configuration parameters, routes, and on-link prefixes.

■   Inform hosts of a better next-hop address to forward packets for a specific destination.

IPv6 ND processes include the following:

■   **Router discovery**
During router discovery, a host discovers the local routers on an attached link. This process is equivalent to ICMPv4 router discovery. For more information, see the "Router Discovery" section in this chapter.

■   **Prefix discovery**
Prefix discovery is the process by which hosts discover the network prefixes for local link destinations. This is similar to the exchange of the ICMPv4 Address Mask Request and Address Mask Reply messages. For more information, see the "Router Discovery" section in this chapter.

■   **Parameter discovery**
The parameter discovery process enables hosts to discover additional operating parameters, including the link MTU and the default hop limit for outgoing packets. For more information, see the "Router Discovery" section in this chapter.

■   **Address autoconfiguration**
During address autoconfiguration, IP addresses are configured for interfaces in either the presence or absence of a stateful address configuration server, such as a Dynamic Host Configuration Protocol version 6 (DHCPv6) server. For more information, see Chapter 8, "Address Autoconfiguration."

■   **Address resolution**
Address resolution is the process by which nodes resolve a neighbor's IPv6 address to its link-layer address. It is equivalent to ARP in IPv4. For more information, see the "Address Resolution" section in this chapter.

- **Next-hop determination**

  During next-hop determination, a node determines the IPv6 address of the neighbor to which a packet is being forwarded, based on the destination address. The next-hop address is either the destination address or the address of an on-link default router. For more information, see "Host Sending Algorithm" in this chapter.

- **Neighbor unreachability detection**

  The neighbor unreachability detection process is the means by which a node determines that the IPv6 layer of a neighbor is no longer receiving packets. For more information, see the "Neighbor Unreachability Detection" section in this chapter.

- **Duplicate address detection**

  During duplicate address detection, a node determines that an address considered for use is not already in use by a neighboring node. This process is equivalent to using gratuitous ARP frames in IPv4. For more information, see the "Duplicate Address Detection" section in this chapter.

- **Redirect function**

  The redirect function is the process of informing a host of a better first-hop IPv6 address to reach a destination. It is equivalent to the use of the ICMPv4 Redirect message. For more information, see the "Redirect Function" section in this chapter.

  ND is described in RFC 2461.

Neighbor Discovery Message Format

ND messages use the ICMPv6 message structure and ICMPv6 types 133 through 137. ND messages consist of an ND message header, composed of an ICMPv6 header and ND message-specific data, and zero or more ND options. Figure 6-1 shows the format of an ND message.

Figure 6-1. *The format of an ND message*

There are five different ND messages:

1. Router Solicitation (ICMPv6 type 133)

2. Router Advertisement (ICMPv6 type 134)

3. Neighbor Solicitation (ICMPv6 type 135)

4. Neighbor Advertisement (ICMPv6 type 136)

5. Redirect (ICMPv6 type 137)

ND message options provide additional information, indicating MAC addresses, on-link network prefixes, on-link MTU information, redirection data, mobility information, and specific routes.

To ensure that ND messages that are received have originated from a node on the local link, all ND messages are sent with a hop limit of 255. When an ND message is received, the Hop Limit field in the IPv6 header is checked. If it is not set to 255, the message is silently discarded. Verifying that the ND message has a hop limit of 255 provides protection from ND-based network attacks that are launched from off-link nodes. With a hop limit of 255, a router could not have forwarded the ND message from an off-link node.

NEIGHBOR DISCOVERY OPTIONS

ND options are formatted in type-length-value (TLV) format. Figure 6-2 shows the TLV format.

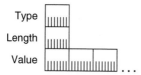

Figure 6-2. *The TLV format for ND options*

The 8-bit Type field indicates the type of ND option. Table 6-1 lists the ND option types defined in RFC 2461, the Internet draft titled "Mobility Support in IPv6," and the Internet draft titled "Default Router Preferences and More-Specific Routes."

Table 6-1. **IPV6 ND OPTION TYPES**

Type	*Option Name*	*Source Document*
1	Source Link-Layer Address	RFC 2461
2	Target Link-Layer Address	RFC 2461
3	Prefix Information	RFC 2461

continued

Table 6-1 *continued*

Type	Option Name	Source Document
4	Redirected Header	RFC 2461
5	MTU	RFC 2461
7	Advertisement Interval	"Mobility Support in IPv6" draft
8	Home Agent Information	"Mobility Support in IPv6" draft
9	Route Information	"Default Router Preferences and More-Specific Routes" draft

The 8-bit Length field indicates the length of the entire option in 8-byte blocks. All ND options must fall on 8-byte boundaries. The variable length Value field contains the data for the option.

Source and Target Link-Layer Address Options

The Source Link-Layer Address option indicates the link-layer address of the ND message sender. The Source Link-Layer Address option is included in the Neighbor Solicitation, Router Solicitation, and Router Advertisement messages. The Source Link-Layer Address option is not included when the source address of the ND message is the unspecified address (::).

Figure 6-3 shows the structure of the Source Link-Layer Address option.

Figure 6-3. *The structure of the Source Link-Layer Address option*

The Target Link-Layer Address option indicates the link-layer address of the neighboring node to which IPv6 packets should be directed. The Target Link-Layer Address option is included in the Neighbor Advertisement and Redirect messages.

Figure 6-4 shows the structure of the Target Link-Layer Address option.

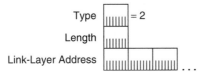

Figure 6-4. *The structure of the Target Link-Layer Address option*

The Source Link-Layer Address option and the Target Link-Layer Address option have the same format.

The Type field is set to 1 for a Source Link-Layer Address option and 2 for a Target Link-Layer Address option. The Length field is set to the number of 8-byte blocks in the entire option. The Link-Layer Address field is a variable-length field that contains the link-layer address of the source or target. Each link layer defined for IPv6 must specify the way in which the link-layer address is formatted in the Source and Target Link-Layer Address options.

For example, RFC 2464 defines how IPv6 packets are sent over Ethernet networks. It also includes the format of the Source and Target Link-Layer Address ND options. For Ethernet, the link-layer address is 48-bits (6-bytes) in length. Figure 6-5 shows the Target Link-Layer Address option for Ethernet.

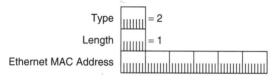

Figure 6-5. *The Target Link-Layer Address option for Ethernet*

Network Monitor Capture

Here is an example of a Source Link-Layer Address option used in a Neighbor Solicitation message as displayed by Network Monitor (frame 1 of capture 06_01 in the \NetworkMonitorCaptures folder on the companion CD-ROM):

```
+ Frame: Base frame properties
+ ETHERNET:  EType = IPv6
+ IP6: Proto = ICMP6; Len = 32
  ICMP6: Neighbor Solicitation; Target = fe80::260:97ff:fe02:6ea5
      ICMP6: Type = 135 (Neighbor Solicitation)
      ICMP6: Code = 0 (0x0)
      ICMP6: Checksum = 0x0F35
      ICMP6: Reserved
      ICMP6: Target Address = fe80::260:97ff:fe02:6ea5
      ICMP6: Source Link-Layer Address = 00 10 5A AA 20 A2
          ICMP6: Type = 1 (0x1)
          ICMP6: Length = 1 (0x1)
          ICMP6: Source Link-Layer Address = 00 10 5A AA 20 A2
```

Prefix Information Option

The Prefix Information option is sent in Router Advertisement messages to indicate both address prefixes and information about address autoconfiguration. There can be multiple Prefix Information options included in a Router Advertisement message, indicating multiple address prefixes.

Figure 6-6 shows the structure of the Prefix Information option.

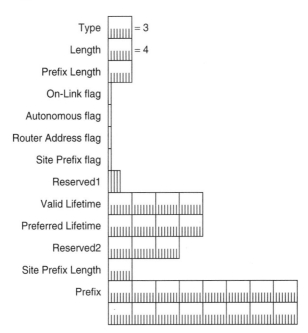

Figure 6-6. *The structure of the Prefix Information option*

The fields in the Prefix Information option are:

■ **Type**
The value of this field is 3.

■ **Length**
The value of this field is 4. (The entire option is 32 bytes in length.)

■ **Prefix Length**
The Prefix Length field indicates the number of leading bits in the Prefix field that comprise the address prefix. The size of this field is 8 bits. The Prefix Length field has a value from 0 through 128. Because typical prefixes advertised are for subnet identifiers, the Prefix Length field is usually set to 64.

■ **On-link flag**
The On-link flag indicates, when set to 1, that the addresses implied by the included prefix are available on the link on which this Router Advertisement message was received. When set to 0, it is not assumed that the addresses that match the prefix are available on-link. The size of this field is 1 bit.

■ **Autonomous flag**

The Autonomous flag indicates, when set to 1, that the included prefix is used to create an autonomous (or stateless) address configuration. When set to 0, the included prefix is not used to create a stateless address configuration. The size of this field is 1 bit.

■ **Router Address flag**

The Router Address flag indicates, when set to 1, that the Prefix field also contains an IPv6 address assigned to the sending router. The Router Address flag and the included prefix allow a receiving mobile node to discover the global address(es) of its home agent (the sending router). The size of this field is 1 bit. This flag is described in the Internet draft titled "Mobility Support in IPv6."

■ **Site Prefix flag**

The Site Prefix flag indicates, when set to 1, that the site prefix defined by the Prefix field and the Site Prefix Length field be used to update the site prefix table. The site prefix table is maintained by the host and is utilized to prefer the use of site-local addresses when a global address matches a site prefix. This flag is described in the Internet draft titled "Site Prefixes in Neighbor Discovery."

■ **Reserved1**

The Reserved1 field is a 4-bit field reserved for future use and set to 0.

■ **Valid Lifetime**

The Valid Lifetime field indicates the number of seconds that an address, based on the included prefix and using stateless address configuration, remains valid. The size of this field is 32 bits. The Valid Lifetime field also indicates the number of seconds that the included prefix is valid for on-link determination. For an infinite valid lifetime, the Valid Lifetime field is set to 0xFFFFFFFF.

■ **Preferred Lifetime**

The Preferred Lifetime field indicates the number of seconds that an address, based on the included prefix and using stateless address autoconfiguration, remains in a preferred state. The size of this field is 32 bits. Stateless autoconfiguration addresses that are still valid are either in a preferred or deprecated state. In the preferred state, the address can be used for unrestricted communication. In the deprecated state, the use of the address is not recommended for new communications. However, existing communications using a deprecated address can continue. An address goes from the preferred state to the deprecated state when its preferred lifetime expires. For an infinite preferred lifetime, the Preferred Lifetime field is set to 0xFFFFFFFF.

■ **Reserved2**
The Reserved2 field is a 24-bit field reserved for future use and set to 0.

■ **Site Prefix Length**
The Site Prefix Length field indicates the number of leading bits in the Prefix field that define a site prefix. The length of this field is 8 bits. This field is significant only if the Site Prefix flag is set to 1. This field is described in the Internet draft titled "Site Prefixes in Neighbor Discovery."

■ **Prefix**
The Prefix field indicates the prefix for the IPv6 address derived through stateless autoconfiguration. The size of this field is 128 bits. Bits in the Prefix field—up to a count equaling the value of the Prefix Length field—are significant for creating the prefix. The combination of the Prefix Length field and the Prefix field unambiguously defines the prefix which, when combined with the interface identifier for the node, creates an IPv6 address. The link-local prefix should not be sent and is ignored by the receiving host.

Network Monitor Capture
Here is an example of a Prefix Information option used in a Router Advertisement message as displayed by Network Monitor (capture 06_02 in the \NetworkMonitorCaptures folder on the companion CD-ROM):

```
+ Frame: Base frame properties
+ ETHERNET:  EType = IPv6
+ IP6: Proto = ICMP6; Len = 96
  ICMP6: Router Advertisement
        ICMP6: Type = 134 (Router Advertisement)
        ICMP6: Code = 0 (0x0)
        ICMP6: Checksum = 0xBAA5
        ICMP6: Current Hop Limit = 0 (0x0)
        ICMP6: 0....... = Not managed address config
        ICMP6: .0...... = Not other stateful config
        ICMP6: ..0..... = Not a Mobile IP Home Agent
        ICMP6: Route Preference = Medium (0)
        ICMP6: Router Lifetime = 0 (0x0)
        ICMP6: Reachable Time = 0 (0x0)
```

```
          ICMP6: Retransmission Timer = 0 (0x0)
      + ICMP6: Source Link-Layer Address = 00 B0 D0 23 47 33
      + ICMP6: MTU = 1500 (0x5DC)
        ICMP6: Prefix = fec0:0:0:2::
          ICMP6: Type = 3 (0x3)
          ICMP6: Length = 4 (0x4)
          ICMP6: Prefix Length = 64 (0x40)
          ICMP6: 0....... = No on-link specification
          ICMP6: .0...... = Not autonomous address config
          ICMP6: ..0..... = No router address
          ICMP6: ...0.... = Not a site prefix
          ICMP6: .......1 = Route prefix provided
          ICMP6: Valid Lifetime = 4294967295 (0xFFFFFFFF)
          ICMP6: Preferred Lifetime = 4294967295 (0xFFFFFFFF)
          ICMP6: Reserved
          ICMP6: Site Prefix Length = 0 (0x0)
          ICMP6: Prefix = fec0:0:0:2::
      + ICMP6: Prefix = fec0:0:0:1::
```

Redirected Header Option

The Redirected Header option is sent in Redirect messages to specify the IPv6 packet that caused the router to send a Redirect message. It can contain all or part of the redirected IPv6 packet, depending on the size of the IPv6 packet that was initially sent.

Figure 6-7 shows the structure of the Redirected Header option.

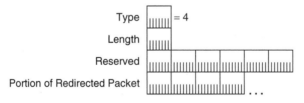

Figure 6-7. *The structure of the Redirected Header option*

The fields in the Redirected Header option are:

■ **Type**
The value of this field is 4.

■ **Length**
The value of this field is the number of 8-byte blocks in the entire option.

- **Reserved**

  The Reserved field is a 48-bit field reserved for future use and set to 0.

- **Portion of redirected packet**

  This field contains either the IPv6 packet or a portion of the IPv6 packet that caused the Redirect message to be sent. The amount of the original packet that is included is the leading portion of the packet so that the entire Redirect message is no more than 1,280 bytes in length.

Network Monitor Capture

Here is an example of a Redirected Header option used in a Redirect message as displayed by Network Monitor (capture 06_03 in the \NetworkMonitorCaptures folder on the companion CD-ROM):

```
+ Frame: Base frame properties
+ ETHERNET: EType = IPv6
+ IP6: Proto = ICMP6; Len = 128
  ICMP6: Redirect
      ICMP6: Type = 137 (Redirect)
      ICMP6: Code = 0 (0x0)
      ICMP6: Checksum = 0x76D4
      ICMP6: Reserved
      ICMP6: Target Address = fe80::2b0:d0ff:fe23:4735
      ICMP6: Destination Address = 3000::1
      ICMP6: Redirected Packet: Number of data bytes remaining = 80 (0x50)
          ICMP6: Type = 4 (0x4)
          ICMP6: Length = 11 (0xB)
          ICMP6: Reserved
          ICMP6: Redirected Packet: Number of data bytes remaining =
                 80 (0x0050)
```

MTU Option

The MTU option is sent in Router Advertisement messages to indicate the IPv6 MTU of the link. This option is typically used when the IPv6 MTU for a link is not well known or needs to be set due to a translational or mixed-media bridging configuration. The MTU option overrides the IPv6 MTU reported by the interface hardware.

In bridged or Layer-2 switched environments, it is possible to have different link-layer technologies with different link-layer MTUs on the same link.

In this case, differences in IPv6 MTUs between nodes on the same link are not detected through Path MTU Discovery. The MTU option is used to indicate the highest IPv6 MTU supported by all link-layer technologies on the link.

Figure 6-8 shows a switched configuration where the MTU option is used to solve a mixed media problem.

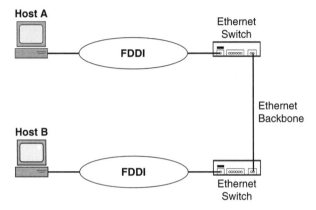

Figure 6-8. *A mixed media configuration*

Two IPv6 hosts, Host A and Host B, are connected to two different Ethernet (Layer 2) switches using FDDI ports. The two switches are connected by an Ethernet backbone. When Host A and Host B negotiate a TCP connection, each reports a TCP maximum segment size of 4,312 (the FDDI IPv6 MTU of 4,352, minus 40 bytes of IPv6 header). However, when TCP data on the connection begins to flow, the switches silently discard IPv6 packets larger than 1,500 bytes that are sent between Host A and Host B.

With the MTU option, the router for the network segment (not shown) reports an IPv6 MTU of 1,500 in the Router Advertisement message for all hosts on the link. When both Host A and Host B adjust their IPv6 MTU from 4,352 to 1,500, maximum-sized TCP segments sent between them are not discarded by the intermediate switches.

Figure 6-9 shows the structure of the MTU option.

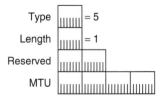

Figure 6-9. *The structure of the MTU option*

The fields in the MTU option are:

- **Type**

  The value of this field is 5.

- **Length**

  The value of this field is 1. (There are 8 bytes in the entire option.)

- **Reserved**

  The Reserved field is a 16-bit field reserved for future use and set to 0.

- **MTU**

  The MTU field indicates the IPv6 MTU that should be used by the host for the link on which the Router Advertisement was received. The size of this field is 32 bits. The value in the MTU field is ignored if it is larger than the link MTU.

Network Monitor Capture

Here is an example of an MTU option used in a Router Advertisement message as displayed by Network Monitor (capture 06_02 in the \NetworkMonitorCaptures folder on the companion CD-ROM):

```
+ Frame: Base frame properties
+ ETHERNET:  EType = IPv6
+ IP6: Proto = ICMP6; Len = 96
  ICMP6: Router Advertisement
      ICMP6: Type = 134 (Router Advertisement)
      ICMP6: Code = 0 (0x0)
      ICMP6: Checksum = 0xBAA5
      ICMP6: Current Hop Limit = 0 (0x0)
      ICMP6: 0....... = Not managed address config
      ICMP6: .0...... = Not other stateful config
      ICMP6: ..0..... = Not a Mobile IP Home Agent
      ICMP6: Route Preference = Medium (0)
      ICMP6: Router Lifetime = 0 (0x0)
      ICMP6: Reachable Time = 0 (0x0)
      ICMP6: Retransmission Timer = 0 (0x0)
    + ICMP6: Source Link-Layer Address = 00 B0 D0 23 47 33
      ICMP6: MTU = 1500 (0x5DC)
          ICMP6: Type = 5 (0x5)
          ICMP6: Length = 1 (0x1)
          ICMP6: Reserved
```

```
            ICMP6: MTU = 1500 (0x5DC)
   +  ICMP6: Prefix = fec0:0:0:2::
   +  ICMP6: Prefix = fec0:0:0:1::
```

Advertisement Interval Option

The Advertisement Interval option is sent in Router Advertisement messages to specify the interval at which the router (acting as a home agent) sends unsolicited multicast router advertisements. The Advertisement Interval option is described in the Internet draft titled "Mobility Support in IPv6."

Figure 6-10 shows the structure of the Advertisement Interval option.

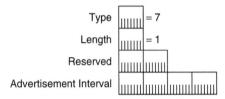

Figure 6-10. *The structure of the Advertisement Interval option*

The fields in the Advertisement Interval option are:

- **Type**
  The value of this field is 7.

- **Length**
  Because the size of the entire option is fixed at 8 bytes, the value in the Length field is always set to 1.

- **Reserved**
  This is a 16-bit field reserved for future use and set to 0.

- **Advertisement Interval**
  The Advertisement Interval field specifies the maximum time in milliseconds between consecutive unsolicited multicast Router Advertisement messages to be sent by the home agent. The size of this field is 32 bits.

Home Agent Information Option

The Home Agent Information option is sent in Router Advertisement messages sent by a home agent to specify the home agent's configuration. The Home Agent Information option is described in the Internet draft titled "Mobility Support in IPv6."

Figure 6-11 shows the structure of the Home Agent Information option.

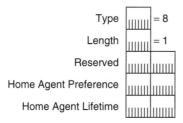

Figure 6-11. *The structure of the Home Agent Information option*

The fields in the Home Agent Information option are:

- **Type**
  The value of this field is 8.

- **Length**
  Because the size of the entire option is fixed at 8 bytes, the value of this field is always set to 1.

- **Reserved**
  The Reserved field is a 16-bit field reserved for future use and set to 0.

- **Home Agent Preference**
  The Home Agent Preference field indicates the preference for the sending home agent. The preference is used in ordering addresses returned to a mobile node by the home agent. The size of this field is 16 bits.

- **Home Agent Lifetime**
  The Home Agent Lifetime field indicates the lifetime of the home agent in seconds. The size of this field is 16 bits.

Route Information Option

The Route Information option is sent in Router Advertisement messages to specify individual routes for receiving hosts to add to their local routing table. The Route Information option is described in the Internet draft titled "Default Route Preferences and More-Specific Routes."

Figure 6-12 shows the structure of the Route Information option.

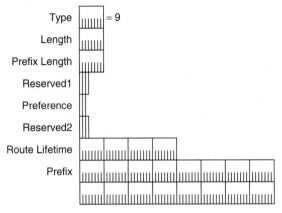

Figure 6-12. *The structure of the Route Information option*

The fields in the Route Information option are:

- **Type**
  The value of this field is 9.

- **Length**
  The value of the Length field depends on the prefix length of the route and the corresponding size of the Prefix field. If the prefix length is 0 (and there is no Prefix field), the value of the Length field is 1. If the prefix length is greater than 0 and less than 65, the length of the Prefix field is 64 bits and the value of the Length field is 2. If the prefix length is greater than 64, the length of the Prefix field is 128 bits and the value of the Length field is 3.

- **Prefix Length**
  The Prefix Length field indicates the number of leading bits in the Prefix field that are significant for the route. Valid values range from 0 to 128. The size of this field is 8 bits.

- **Reserved1**
  The Reserved1 field is a 3-bit field reserved for future use and set to 0.

- **Preference**
  The Preference field indicates the level of preference for this route as sent from the advertising router. If multiple routers advertise the same prefix using a Route Information option, you can configure the routers so that they advertise the route with different preference levels. Valid values in binary are 01 (High), 00 (Medium), and 11 (Low). The size of this field is 2 bits.

■ **Reserved2**

The Reserved2 field is a 3-bit field reserved for future use and set to 0.

■ **Route Lifetime**

The Route Lifetime field indicates the amount of time in seconds that the prefix is valid for route determination. The size of this field is 32 bits. For an infinite route lifetime, the Route Lifetime field is set to 0xFFFFFFFF.

■ **Prefix**

The Prefix field indicates the route prefix. The size of the Prefix field can be 0, 64, or 128 bits depending on the value of the Prefix Length field. If the prefix length is 0, the size of the Prefix field is 0. If the prefix length is greater than 0 and less than 65, the size of the Prefix field is 64 bits. If the prefix length is greater than 64, the size of the Prefix field is 128 bits. The prefix length indicates the number of high-order bits in the prefix that are relevant for route determination. All bits in the Prefix field past the prefix length must be set to 0.

A typical use of the Route Information option is to enable hosts to make better forwarding decisions when sending data. Figure 6-13 shows a simple network configuration where the Route Information option can be useful.

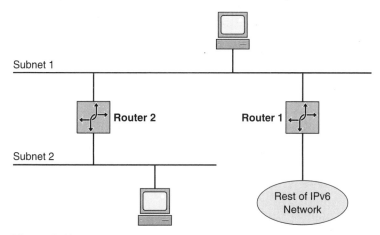

Figure 6-13. *An example configuration in which the Route Information option is used*

Without the Route Information option, you would typically configure the routers so that only Router 1 advertises itself as a default router on Subnet 1. Hosts on Subnet 1 sending traffic to hosts on Subnet 2 would have to rely on Redirect messages from Router 1 to inform them that the best next-hop address to reach hosts on Subnet 2 is actually Router 2. For more information, see "Redirect Function" in this chapter.

Using the Route Information option, Router 2 is configured to advertise the prefix of Subnet 2. Upon receipt of router advertisements from both routers, hosts on Subnet 1 automatically add a default route with Router 1 as its next-hop address and a specific route for the Subnet 2 prefix with Router 2 as its next-hop address. Now, all the hosts on Subnet 2 are reachable by hosts on Subnet 1 without having to rely on redirects from Router 1.

NEIGHBOR DISCOVERY MESSAGES

All of the functions of IPv6 ND are performed with the following messages:

- Router Solicitation
- Router Advertisement
- Neighbor Solicitation
- Neighbor Advertisement
- Redirect

Router Solicitation

The Router Solicitation message is sent by IPv6 hosts to discover the presence of IPv6 routers on the link. A host sends a multicast Router Solicitation message to prompt IPv6 routers to respond immediately, rather than waiting for a pseudo-periodic Router Advertisement message.

For example, assuming that the local link is Ethernet, in the Ethernet header of the Router Solicitation message:

- The Source Address field is set to the MAC address of the sending network adapter.
- The Destination Address field is set to 33-33-00-00-00-02.

In the IPv6 header of the Router Solicitation message:

- The Source Address field is set to either a link-local IPv6 address assigned to the sending interface or the IPv6 unspecified address (::).
- The Destination Address field is set to the link-local scope all-routers multicast address (FF02::2).
- The Hop Limit field is set to 255.

Figure 6-14 shows the structure of the Router Solicitation message.

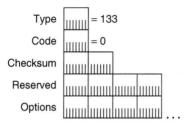

Figure 6-14. *The structure of the Router Solicitation message*

The fields in the Router Solicitation message are:

■ **Type**
The value of this field is 133.

■ **Code**
The value of this field is 0.

■ **Checksum**
The value of this field is the ICMPv6 checksum.

■ **Reserved**
This is a 32-bit field reserved for future use and set to 0.

■ **Source Link-Layer Address option**
When present, the Source Link-Layer Address option contains the link-layer address of the sender. For an Ethernet node, the Source Link-Layer Address option contains the Ethernet MAC address of the sending host. The address in the Source Link-Layer Address option is used by the receiving router to determine the unicast MAC address of the host to which the corresponding unicast Router Advertisement is sent.

Network Monitor Capture

Here is an example of a Router Solicitation message as displayed by Network Monitor (capture 06_04 in the \NetworkMonitorCaptures folder on the companion CD-ROM):

```
+ Frame: Base frame properties
+ ETHERNET: ETYPE = IPv6
  IP6: Proto = ICMP6; Len = 16
      IP6: Version = 6 (0x6)
      IP6: Traffic Class = 0 (0x0)
      IP6: Flow Label = 0 (0x0)
```

```
                       IP6: Payload Length = 16 (0x10)
                       IP6: Next Header = 58 (ICMP6)
                       IP6: Hop Limit = 255 (0xFF)
                       IP6: Source Address = fe80::2b0:d0ff:fe23:4733
                       IP6: Destination Address = ff02::2
                       IP6: Payload: Number of data bytes remaining = 16 (0x0010)
                 ICMP6: Router Solicitation
                       ICMP6: Type = 133 (Router Solicitation)
                       ICMP6: Code = 0 (0x0)
                       ICMP6: Checksum = 0x4B20
                       ICMP6: Reserved
                       ICMP6: Source Link-level Address = 00 B0 D0 23 47 33
                           ICMP6: Type = 1 (0x1)
                           ICMP6: Length = 1 (0x1)
                           ICMP6: Source Link-level Address = 00 B0 D0 23 47 33
```

Router Advertisement

IPv6 routers send the Router Advertisement message pseudo-periodically and in response to the receipt of a Router Solicitation message. It contains the information required by hosts to determine the link prefixes, the link MTU, specific routes, whether or not to use address autoconfiguration, and the duration for which addresses created through address autoconfiguration are valid and preferred.

For example, assuming that the local link is Ethernet, in the Ethernet header of the Router Advertisement message:

■ The Source Address field is set to the MAC address of the sending network adapter.

■ The Destination Address field is set to either 33-33-00-00-00-01 or the unicast MAC address of the host that sent a Router Solicitation from a unicast address.

In the IPv6 header of the Router Advertisement message:

■ The Source Address field is set to the link-local address assigned to the sending interface.

■ The Destination Address field is set to either the link-local scope all-nodes multicast address (FF02::1) or the unicast IPv6 address of the host that sent the Router Solicitation message from a unicast address.

■ The Hop Limit field is set to 255.

Figure 6-15 shows the structure of the Router Advertisement message.

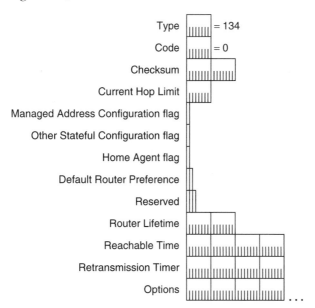

Figure 6-15. *The structure of the Router Advertisement message*

The fields in the Router Advertisement message are:

- **Type**
  The value of this field is 134.

- **Code**
  The value of this field is 0.

- **Checksum**
  The value of this field is the ICMPv6 checksum.

- **Current Hop Limit**
  The Current Hop Limit field indicates the default value of the Hop Limit field in the IPv6 header for packets sent by hosts that receive this Router Advertisement message. The size of this field is 8 bits. A current hop limit of 0 indicates that the default value of the Hop Limit field is not specified by the router.

- **Managed Address Configuration flag**
  The Managed Address Configuration flag indicates, when set to 1, that hosts receiving this Router Advertisement message must use a stateful address configuration protocol (for example, DHCPv6) to obtain addresses in addition to the addresses that might be derived from stateless address autoconfiguration. The size of this field is 1 bit.

- **Other Stateful Configuration flag**

  The Other Stateful Configuration flag indicates, when set to 1, that hosts receiving this Router Advertisement message must use a stateful address configuration protocol (for example, DHCPv6) to obtain non-address configuration information. The size of this field is 1 bit.

- **Home Agent flag**

  The Home Agent flag indicates, when set to 1, that the advertising router is also functioning as a home agent for IPv6 mobility. The size of this field is 1 bit. This flag is described in the Internet draft titled "Mobility Support in IPv6."

- **Default Router Preference**

  The Default Router Preference field indicates the level of preference for this router as the default router. If multiple routers advertise themselves as default routers, you can configure the routers so that they advertise with different preference levels. Valid values in binary are 01 (High), 00 (Medium), and 11 (Low). If the preference is set to 10, the receiving host should assume a value of 0 for the Router Lifetime field, effectively disabling the advertising router as a default router. The size of this field is 2 bits. This field is described in the Internet draft "Default Router Preferences and More-Specific Routes."

  A typical configuration that can use the default router preference is a subnet that has two routers connected to the Internet or an organization intranet—one router is the primary router and another router is a slower, secondary router intended to provide fault tolerance for the primary router. Both routers advertise themselves as default routers; however, the primary router advertises a default router preference of 01 (High) and the secondary router advertises a default router preference of 00 (Medium). If the primary router becomes unavailable, the hosts on the subnet will use the secondary router until the primary router becomes available.

- **Reserved**

  This is a 3-bit field reserved for future use and set to 0.

- **Router Lifetime**

  The Router Lifetime field indicates the lifetime (in seconds) of the router as the default router. The size of this field is 16 bits. The maximum Router Lifetime value is 65,535 seconds (about 18.2 hours). A value of 0 indicates that the router cannot be considered a default router; however, all other information contained in the Router Advertisement is still valid.

- **Reachable Time**

  The Reachable Time field indicates the amount of time (in milliseconds) that a node can consider a neighboring node reachable after receiving a reachability confirmation. The size of this field is 32 bits. A value of 0 indicates that the router does not specify the reachable time. For more information, see "Neighbor Unreachability Detection" in this chapter.

- **Retransmission Timer**

  The Retransmission Timer field indicates the amount of time (in milliseconds) between retransmissions of Neighbor Solicitation messages. The size of this field is 32 bits. The retransmission timer is used during neighbor unreachability detection. A value of 0 indicates that the router does not specify the retransmission timer value.

- **Source Link-Layer Address option**

  When present, the Source Link-Layer Address option contains the link-layer address of the interface on which the Router Advertisement message was sent. This option can be omitted when the router is load-balancing across multiple link-layer addresses.

- **MTU option**

  When present, the MTU option contains the MTU of the link. It is typically sent on links that have a variable MTU or in switched environments that have multiple link-layer technologies on the same link.

- **Prefix Information options**

  When present, Prefix Information options contain the on-link prefixes that are used for address autoconfiguration. The link-local prefix is never sent as a Prefix Information option.

- **Advertisement Interval option**

  When present, the Advertisement Interval option contains the interval for subsequent unsolicited multicast Router Advertisement messages sent from the router acting as the home agent.

- **Home Agent Information option**

  When present, the Home Agent Information option contains the preference and lifetime of the home agent.

- **Route Information options**

  When present, Route Information options contain routes to add to the local routing table for more efficient host forwarding decisions.

Network Monitor Capture

Here is an example of a Router Advertisement message as displayed by Network Monitor (capture 06_02 in the \NetworkMonitorCaptures folder on the companion CD-ROM):

```
+ Frame: Base frame properties
+ ETHERNET:  EType = IPv6
  IP6: Proto = ICMP6; Len = 96
     IP6: Version = 6 (0x6)
     IP6: Traffic Class = 0 (0x0)
     IP6: Flow Label = 0 (0x0)
     IP6: Payload Length = 96 (0x0060)
     IP6: Next Header = 58 (ICMP6)
     IP6: Hop Limit = 255 (0xFF)
     IP6: Source Address = fe80::2b0:d0ff:fe23:4733
     IP6: Destination Address = ff02::1
     IP6: Payload: Number of data bytes remaining = 96 (0x0060)
  ICMP6: Router Advertisement
     ICMP6: Type = 134 (Router Advertisement)
     ICMP6: Code = 0 (0x0)
     ICMP6: Checksum = 0xBAA5
     ICMP6: Current Hop Limit = 0 (0x0)
     ICMP6: 0....... = Not managed address config
     ICMP6: .0...... = Not other stateful config
     ICMP6: ..0..... = Not a Mobile IP Home Agent
     ICMP6: Route Preference = Medium (0)
     ICMP6: Router Lifetime = 0 (0x0)
     ICMP6: Reachable Time = 0 (0x0)
     ICMP6: Retransmission Timer = 0 (0x0)
   + ICMP6: Source Link-Layer Address = 00 B0 D0 23 47 33
   + ICMP6: MTU = 1500 (0x5DC)
   + ICMP6: Prefix = fec0:0:0:2::
   + ICMP6: Prefix = fec0:0:0:1::
```

Neighbor Solicitation

The Neighbor Solicitation message is sent by IPv6 hosts to discover the link-layer address of an on-link IPv6 node. It typically includes the link-layer address of the sender. Typical Neighbor Solicitation messages are multicast for address resolution and unicast when the reachability of a neighboring node is being verified.

For example, assuming that the local link is Ethernet, in the Ethernet header of the Neighbor Solicitation message:

■ The Source Address field is set to the MAC address of the sending network adapter.

■ For a multicast Neighbor Solicitation message, the Destination Address field is set to the Ethernet MAC address that corresponds to the solicited-node address of the target. For a unicast Neighbor Solicitation message, the Destination Address field is set to the unicast MAC address of the neighbor.

In the IPv6 header of the Neighbor Solicitation message:

■ The Source Address field is set to either a unicast IPv6 address assigned to the sending interface or, during duplicate address detection, the unspecified address (::).

■ For a multicast Neighbor Solicitation, the Destination Address field is set to the solicited-node address of the target. For a unicast Neighbor Solicitation, the Destination Address field is set to the unicast address of the target.

■ The Hop Limit field is set to 255.

Figure 6-16 shows the structure of the Neighbor Solicitation message.

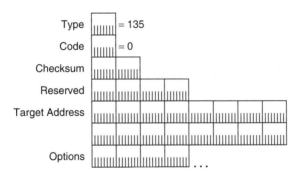

Figure 6-16. *The structure of the Neighbor Solicitation message*

The fields in the Neighbor Solicitation message are:

■ **Type**
The value of this field is 135.

- **Code**

  The value of this field is 0.

- **Checksum**

  The value of this field is the ICMPv6 checksum.

- **Reserved**

  This is a 32-bit field reserved for future use and set to 0.

- **Target Address**

  The Target Address field indicates the IP address of the target. The size of this field is 128 bits.

- **Source Link-Layer Address option**

  When present, the Source Link-Layer Address option contains the link-layer address of the sender. For an Ethernet node, the Source Link-Layer Address option contains the Ethernet MAC address of the sending node. The receiving node uses the address in the Source Link-Layer Address option to determine the unicast MAC address of the node to which the corresponding Neighbor Advertisement is sent. During duplicate address detection, when the source IPv6 address is the unspecified address (::), the Source Link-Layer Address option is not included.

Network Monitor Capture

Here is an example of a Neighbor Solicitation message as displayed by Network Monitor (frame 1 of capture 06_01 in the \NetworkMonitorCaptures folder on the companion CD-ROM):

```
+ Frame: Base frame properties
  ETHERNET:  EType = IPv6
    + ETHERNET: Destination address : 3333FF026EA5
    + ETHERNET: Source address : 00105AAA20A2
      ETHERNET: Ethernet Type : 0x86DD
  IP6: Proto = ICMP6; Len = 32
      IP6: Version = 6 (0x6)
      IP6: Traffic Class = 0 (0x0)
      IP6: Flow Label = 0 (0x0)
      IP6: Payload Length = 32 (0x20)
      IP6: Next Header = 58 (ICMP6)
      IP6: Hop Limit = 255 (0xFF)
```

```
IP6: Source Address = fe80::210:5aff:feaa:20a2
IP6: Destination Address = ff02::1:ff02:6ea5
IP6: Payload: Number of data bytes remaining = 32 (0x0020)
ICMP6: Neighbor Solicitation; Target = fe80::260:97ff:fe02:6ea5
    ICMP6: Type = 135 (Neighbor Solicitation)
    ICMP6: Code = 0 (0x0)
    ICMP6: Checksum = 0x0F35
    ICMP6: Reserved
    ICMP6: Target Address = fe80::260:97ff:fe02:6ea5
    ICMP6: Source Link-Layer Address = 00 10 5A AA 20 A2
        ICMP6: Type = 1 (0x1)
        ICMP6: Length = 1 (0x1)
        ICMP6: Source Link-Layer Address = 00 10 5A AA 20 A2
```

Notice how the last 24 bits of the target address (FE80::260:97FF:FE02:
6EA5) correspond to the last 24 bits of the solicited-node destination address
(FF02::1:FF02:6EA5) (corresponding bits underlined). Also notice how the last
32 bits of the solicited-node destination address (FF02::1:FF02:6EA5) correspond
to the last 32 bits of the Ethernet destination address (3333FF026EA5) (corresponding bits underlined).

Neighbor Advertisement

An IPv6 node sends the Neighbor Advertisement message in response to a
Neighbor Solicitation message. An IPv6 node also sends unsolicited Neighbor
Advertisements to inform neighboring nodes of changes in link-layer addresses
or the node's role. The Neighbor Advertisement contains information required
by nodes to determine the type of Neighbor Advertisement message, the sender's
role on the network, and typically the link-layer address of the sender.

For example, assuming that the local link is Ethernet, in the Ethernet
header of the Neighbor Advertisement message:

- The Source Address field is set to the MAC address of the sending
  network adapter.

- The Destination Address field is set, for a solicited Neighbor Advertisement, to the unicast MAC address of the initial Neighbor Solicitation sender. For an unsolicited Neighbor Advertisement, the
  Destination Address field is set to 33-33-00-00-00-01, the Ethernet
  MAC address corresponding to the link-local scope all-nodes
  multicast address.

In the IPv6 header of the Neighbor Advertisement message:

■ The Source Address field is set to a unicast address assigned to the sending interface.

■ The Destination Address field is set, for a solicited Neighbor Advertisement, to the unicast IP address of the sender of the initial Neighbor Solicitation. For an unsolicited Neighbor Advertisement, the Destination Address field is set to the link-local scope all-nodes multicast address (FF02::1).

■ The Hop Limit field is set to 255.

Figure 6-17 shows the structure of the Neighbor Advertisement message.

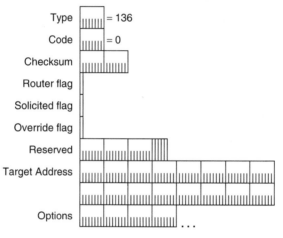

Figure 6-17. *The structure of the Neighbor Advertisement message*

The fields in the Neighbor Advertisement message are:

■ **Type**
The value of this field is 136.

■ **Code**
The value of this field is 0.

■ **Checksum**
The value of this field is the ICMPv6 checksum.

■ **Router flag**
The Router flag indicates the role of the sender of the Neighbor Advertisement message. The size of this field is 1 bit. The Router flag

is set to 1 when the sender is a router and 0 when the sender is not. The Router flag is used by the neighbor unreachability detection process to determine when a router changes to a host.

- **Solicited flag**

  The Solicited flag indicates, when set to 1, that the Neighbor Advertisement message was sent in response to a Neighbor Solicitation message. The size of this field is 1 bit. The Solicited flag is used as a reachability confirmation during neighbor unreachability detection. The Solicited flag is set to 0 for both multicast Neighbor Advertisements and unsolicited unicast Neighbor Advertisements.

- **Override flag**

  The Override flag indicates, when set to 1, that the link-layer address in the included Target Link-Layer Address option should override the link-layer address in the existing neighbor cache entry. The size of this field is 1 bit. If the Override flag is set to 0, the enclosed link-layer address updates a neighbor cache entry only if the link-layer address is not known. The Override flag is set to 0 for a solicited anycast address or a proxied advertisement. The Override flag is set to 1 in other solicited and unsolicited advertisements. For more information about the neighbor cache, see the "Neighbor Discovery Processes" section in this chapter.

- **Reserved**

  This is a 29-bit field reserved for future use and set to 0.

- **Target Address**

  The Target Address field indicates the address being advertised. The size of this field is 128 bits. For solicited Neighbor Advertisement messages, the target address is set to the value of the Target Address field in the corresponding Neighbor Solicitation. For unsolicited Neighbor Advertisement messages, the target address is the address whose link-layer address or role has changed.

- **Target Link-Layer Address option**

  When present, the Target Link-Layer Address option contains the link-layer address of the target, which is the sender of the Neighbor Advertisement. For an Ethernet node, the Target Link-Layer Address option contains the Ethernet MAC address of the sending node. The address in the Target Link-Layer Address option is used by receiving nodes to determine the unicast MAC address of the advertising node.

Network Monitor Capture

Here is an example of a solicited Neighbor Advertisement message as displayed by Network Monitor (frame 2 of capture 06_01 in the \NetworkMonitorCaptures folder on the companion CD-ROM):

```
+ Frame: Base frame properties
+ ETHERNET:  EType = IPv6
  IP6: Proto = ICMP6; Len = 32
      IP6: Version = 6 (0x6)
      IP6: Traffic Class = 0 (0x0)
      IP6: Flow Label = 0 (0x0)
      IP6: Payload Length = 32 (0x20)
      IP6: Next Header = 58 (ICMP6)
      IP6: Hop Limit = 255 (0xFF)
      IP6: Source Address = fe80::260:97ff:fe02:6ea5
      IP6: Destination Address = fe80::210:5aff:feaa:20a2
      IP6: Payload: Number of data bytes remaining = 32 (0x0020)
  ICMP6: Neighbor Advertisement; Target = fe80::260:97ff:fe02:6ea5
      ICMP6: Type = 136 (Neighbor Advertisement)
      ICMP6: Code = 0 (0x0)
      ICMP6: Checksum = 0x89AC
      ICMP6: 0............................ = Not router
      ICMP6: .1........................... = Solicited
      ICMP6: ..1.......................... = Override
      ICMP6: Target Address = fe80::260:97ff:fe02:6ea5
      ICMP6: Target Link-Layer Address = 00 60 97 02 6E A5
          ICMP6: Type = 2 (0x2)
          ICMP6: Length = 1 (0x1)
          ICMP6: Target Link-Layer Address = 00 60 97 02 6E A5
```

Redirect

The Redirect message is sent by an IPv6 router to inform an originating host of a better first-hop address for a specific destination. Redirect messages are sent only by routers for unicast traffic, are unicast only to originating hosts, and are processed only by hosts.

For example, assuming that the local link is Ethernet, in the Ethernet header of the Redirect message:

- The Source Address field is set to the MAC address of the sending network adapter.

■ The Destination Address field is set to the unicast MAC address of the originating sender.

In the IPv6 header of the Redirect message:

■ The Source Address field is set to a unicast address that is assigned to the sending interface.

■ The Destination Address field is set to the unicast IP address of the originating host.

■ The Hop Limit field is set to 255.

Figure 6-18 shows the structure of the Redirect message.

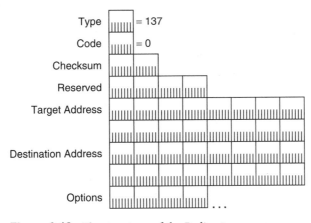

Figure 6-18. *The structure of the Redirect message*

The fields in the Redirect message are:

■ **Type**
The value of this field is 137.

■ **Code**
The value of this field is 0.

■ **Checksum**
The value of this field is the ICMPv6 checksum.

■ **Reserved**
This is a 32-bit field reserved for the future and set to 0.

■ **Target Address**
The Target Address field indicates the better next-hop address for packets addressed to the node in the Destination Address field. The

size of this field is 128 bits. For off-link traffic, the Target Address field is set to the link-local address of a local router. For on-link traffic, the Target Address field is set to the Destination Address field in the Redirect message.

■ **Destination Address**

The Destination Address field contains the destination address of the packet that caused the router to send the Redirect message. The size of this field is 128 bits. Upon receipt at the originating host, the Target Address and Destination Address fields are used to update forwarding information for the destination. Subsequent packets sent to the destination by the host are forwarded to the address in the Target Address field.

■ **Target Link-Layer Address option**

The Target Link-Layer Address option contains the link-layer address of the target (the node to which subsequent packets should be sent). The Target Link-Layer Address option can be included when known by the router, although it is not typically sent.

■ **Redirected Header option**

The Redirected Header option includes the leading portion of the original packet that caused the Redirect message to be sent, sized so that the entire IPv6 packet containing the Redirect message is no larger than 1,280 bytes.

Network Monitor Capture

Here is an example of a Redirect message as displayed by Network Monitor (capture 06_03 in the \NetworkMonitorCaptures folder on the companion CD-ROM):

```
+ Frame: Base frame properties
  ETHERNET:  EType = IPv6
    + ETHERNET: Destination address : 00600852F9D8
    + ETHERNET: Source address : 00B0D0234733
      ETHERNET: Frame Length : 182 (0x00B6)
      ETHERNET: Ethernet Type : 0x86DD
      ETHERNET: Ethernet Data: Number of data bytes remaining
                            = 168 (0x00A8)
  IP6: Proto = ICMP6; Len = 128
    IP6: Version = 6 (0x6)
    IP6: Traffic Class = 0 (0x0)
    IP6: Flow Label = 0 (0x0)
    IP6: Payload Length = 128 (0x80)
    IP6: Next Header = 58 (ICMP6)
```

```
    IP6: Hop Limit = 255 (0xFF)
    IP6: Source Address = fe80::2b0:d0ff:fe23:4733
    IP6: Destination Address = fe80::260:8ff:fe52:f9d8
    IP6: Payload: Number of data bytes remaining = 128 (0x0080)
ICMP6: Redirect
    ICMP6: Type = 137 (Redirect)
    ICMP6: Code = 0 (0x0)
    ICMP6: Checksum = 0x76D4
    ICMP6: Reserved
    ICMP6: Target Address = fe80::2b0:d0ff:fe23:4735
    ICMP6: Destination Address = 3000::1
    ICMP6: Redirected Packet: Number of data bytes remaining
                            = 88 (0x0058)
        ICMP6: Type = 4 (0x4)
        ICMP6: Length = 11 (0xB)
        ICMP6: Reserved
        ICMP6: Redirected Packet: Number of data bytes remaining
                                = 80 (0x0050)
```

Summary of Neighbor Discovery Messages and Options

Table 6-2 lists each ND message and the options that might be included with the message.

Table 6-2. ND MESSAGES AND THE OPTIONS THAT MIGHT BE INCLUDED

ND Message	ND Options that Might be Included
Router Solicitation	Source Link-Layer Address option: Used to inform the router of the link-layer address of the host for the unicast Router Advertisement response.
Router Advertisement	Source Link-Layer Address option: Used to inform the receiving host(s) of the link-layer address of the router.
	Prefix Information option(s): Used to inform the receiving host(s) of on-link prefixes and whether to autoconfigure stateless addresses.
	MTU option: Used to inform the receiving host(s) of the IPv6 MTU of the link.

continued

Table 6-2 *continued*

ND Message	ND Options that Might be Included
	Advertisement Interval option: Used to inform the receiving host how often the router (the home agent) is sending unsolicited multicast router advertisements.
	Home Agent Information option: Used to advertise the home agent's preference and lifetime.
	Route Information option(s): Used to inform the receiving host(s) of specific routes to add to a local routing table.
Neighbor Solicitation	Source Link-Layer Address option: Used to inform the receiving node of the link-layer address of the sender.
Neighbor Advertisement	Target Link-Layer Address option: Used to inform the receiving node(s) of the link-layer address corresponding to the Target Address field.
Redirect	Redirected Header option: Used to include all or a portion of the packet that was redirected.
	Target Link-Layer Address option: Used to inform the receiving node(s) of the link-layer address corresponding to the Target Address field.

NEIGHBOR DISCOVERY PROCESSES

The ND protocol provides message exchanges for the following processes:

- Address resolution (including duplicate address detection)
- Router discovery (includes prefix and parameter discovery)
- Neighbor unreachability detection
- Redirect function

For information about address autoconfiguration, see Chapter 8, "Address Autoconfiguration." For information about next-hop determination, see the "Host Sending Algorithm" section in this chapter.

Conceptual Host Data Structures

To facilitate interactions between neighboring nodes, RFC 2461 defines the following conceptual host data structures as an example of how to store information for ND processes:

■ **Neighbor cache**

The neighbor cache stores the on-link IP address of each neighbor, its corresponding link-layer address, and an indication of the neighbor's reachability state. The neighbor cache is equivalent to the ARP cache in IPv4.

■ **Destination cache**

The destination cache stores information on next-hop IP addresses for destinations to which traffic has recently been sent. Each entry in the destination cache contains the destination IP address (either local or remote), the previously resolved next-hop IP address, and the path MTU for the destination.

■ **Prefix list**

The prefix list contains on-link prefixes. Each entry in the prefix list defines a range of IP addresses for destinations that are directly reachable (neighbors). This list is populated from prefixes advertised by routers using the Router Advertisement message.

■ **Default router list**

IP addresses corresponding to on-link routers that have sent Router Advertisement messages and are eligible to be default routers are included in the default router list.

Figure 6-19 shows the conceptual host data structures defined in RFC 2461. RFC 2461 defines these data structures as an example of an IPv6 host conceptual model. An IPv6 implementation is not required to create these exact data structures as long as the external behavior of the host is consistent with RFC 2461. For example, the IPv6 protocol for the Windows .NET Server 2003 family and Windows XP uses a destination cache and neighbor cache. A routing table is used, rather than a prefix list and default router list, to determine the next-hop address for a given destination. For more information about how IPv6 determines the next-hop address using the conceptual RFC 2461 data structures, see the "Host Sending Algorithm" section in this chapter.

To view the destination cache on a computer running a member of the Windows .NET Server 2003 family or Windows XP, type **netsh interface ipv6 show destinationcache** at a command prompt. To view the neighbor cache, type

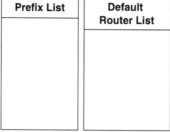

Destination Cache			Neighbor Cache		
Destination	Next-Hop Address	PMTU	IP Address	Link-Layer Address	Reachability

Prefix List	Default Router List

Figure 6-19. *The conceptual host data structures defined in RFC 2461*

netsh interface ipv6 show neighbors at a command prompt. To view the routing table, type **netsh interface ipv6 show routes** at a command prompt.

Address Resolution

The address resolution process for IPv6 nodes consists of an exchange of Neighbor Solicitation and Neighbor Advertisement messages to resolve the link-layer address of the on-link next-hop address for a given destination. The sending host sends a multicast Neighbor Solicitation message on the appropriate interface. The multicast address of the Neighbor Solicitation message is the solicited-node multicast address derived from the target IP address. The Neighbor Solicitation message includes the link-layer address of the sending host in the Source Link-Layer Address option. For information about how a host determines the next-hop address for a destination, see "Host Sending Algorithm" in this chapter.

When the target host receives the Neighbor Solicitation message, it updates its own neighbor cache based on the source address of the Neighbor Solicitation message and the link-layer address in the Source Link-Layer Address option. Next, the target node sends a unicast Neighbor Advertisement to the Neighbor Solicitation sender. The Neighbor Advertisement includes the Target Link-Layer Address option.

After receiving the Neighbor Advertisement from the target, the sending host updates its neighbor cache with an entry for the target based on the information in the Target Link-Layer Address option. At this point, unicast IPv6 traffic between the sending host and the target of the Neighbor Solicitation can be sent.

Address Resolution Example-Part 1

Host A has an Ethernet MAC address of 00-10-5A-AA-20-A2 and a corresponding link-local address of FE80::210:5AFF:FEAA:20A2. Host B has an Ethernet MAC address of 00-60-97-02-6E-A5 and a corresponding link-local address of FE80::260:97FF:FE02:6EA5. To send a packet to Host B, Host A must first use address resolution to resolve Host B's link-layer address.

Based on Host B's IP address, Host A sends a multicast Neighbor Solicitation message to the solicited-node address of FF02::1:FF02:6EA5, as shown in Figure 6-20.

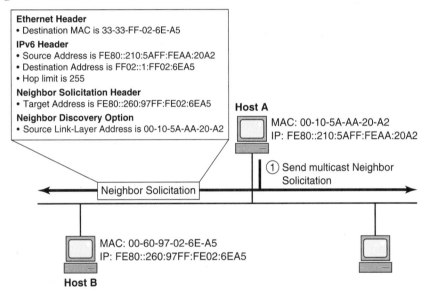

Figure 6-20. *The multicast Neighbor Solicitation message*

Network Monitor Capture

Here is the Neighbor Solicitation message for this example as displayed by Network Monitor (frame 1 of capture 06_01 in the \NetworkMonitorCaptures folder on the companion CD-ROM):

```
+ Frame: Base frame properties
+ ETHERNET:  EType = IPv6
     ETHERNET: Destination address : 3333FF026EA5
     ETHERNET: Source address : 00105AAA20A2
     ETHERNET: Frame Length : 86 (0x0056)
     ETHERNET: Ethernet Type : 0x86DD
     ETHERNET: Ethernet Data: Number of data bytes remaining = 72 (0x0048)
```

```
IP6: Proto = ICMP6; Len = 32
    IP6: Version = 6 (0x6)
    IP6: Traffic Class = 0 (0x0)
    IP6: Flow Label = 0 (0x0)
    IP6: Payload Length = 32 (0x20)
    IP6: Next Header = 58 (ICMP6)
    IP6: Hop Limit = 255 (0xFF)
    IP6: Source Address = fe80::210:5aff:feaa:20a2
    IP6: Destination Address = ff02::1:ff02:6ea5
    IP6: Payload: Number of data bytes remaining = 31 (0x001F)
ICMP6: Neighbor Solicitation; Target = fe80::260:97ff:fe02:6ea5
    ICMP6: Type = 135 (Neighbor Solicitation)
    ICMP6: Code = 0 (0x0)
    ICMP6: Checksum = 0x0F35
    ICMP6: Reserved
    ICMP6: Target Address = fe80::260:97ff:fe02:6ea5
    ICMP6: Source Link-Layer Address = 00 10 5A AA 20 A2
        ICMP6: Type = 1 (0x1)
        ICMP6: Length = 1 (0x1)
        ICMP6: Source Link-Layer Address = 00 10 5A AA 20 A2
```

Address Resolution Example-Part 2

Host B, having registered the multicast MAC address of 33-33-FF-02-6E-A5 with its Ethernet adapter, receives and processes the Neighbor Solicitation message. Host B responds with a unicast Neighbor Advertisement message, as shown in Figure 6-21.

Network Monitor Capture

Here is the Neighbor Advertisement message for this example as displayed by Network Monitor (frame 2 of capture 06_01 in the \NetworkMonitorCaptures folder on the companion CD-ROM):

```
+ Frame: Base frame properties
+ ETHERNET:  EType = IPv6
   + ETHERNET: Destination address : 00105AAA20A2
   + ETHERNET: Source address : 006097026EA5
     ETHERNET: Frame Length : 86 (0x0056)
     ETHERNET: Ethernet Type : 0x86DD
     ETHERNET: Ethernet Data: Number of data bytes remaining = 72 (0x0048)
  IP6: Proto = ICMP6; Len = 32
    IP6: Version = 6 (0x6)
    IP6: Traffic Class = 0 (0x0)
```

```
      IP6: Flow Label = 0 (0x0)

      IP6: Payload Length = 32 (0x20)

      IP6: Next Header = 58 (ICMP6)

      IP6: Hop Limit = 255 (0xFF)

      IP6: Source Address = fe80::260:97ff:fe02:6ea5

      IP6: Destination Address = fe80::210:5aff:feaa:20a2

      IP6: Payload: Number of data bytes remaining = 32 (0x0020)
ICMP6: Neighbor Advertisement; Target = fe80::260:97ff:fe02:6ea5

      ICMP6: Type = 136 (Neighbor Advertisement)

      ICMP6: Code = 0 (0x0)

      ICMP6: Checksum = 0x89AC

      ICMP6: 0............................. = Not router

      ICMP6: .1............................ = Solicited

      ICMP6: ..1........................... = Override

      ICMP6: Target Address = fe80::260:97ff:fe02:6ea5

      ICMP6: Target Link-Layer Address = 00 60 97 02 6E A5

          ICMP6: Type = 2 (0x2)

          ICMP6: Length = 1 (0x1)

          ICMP6: Target Link-Layer Address = 00 60 97 02 6E A5
```

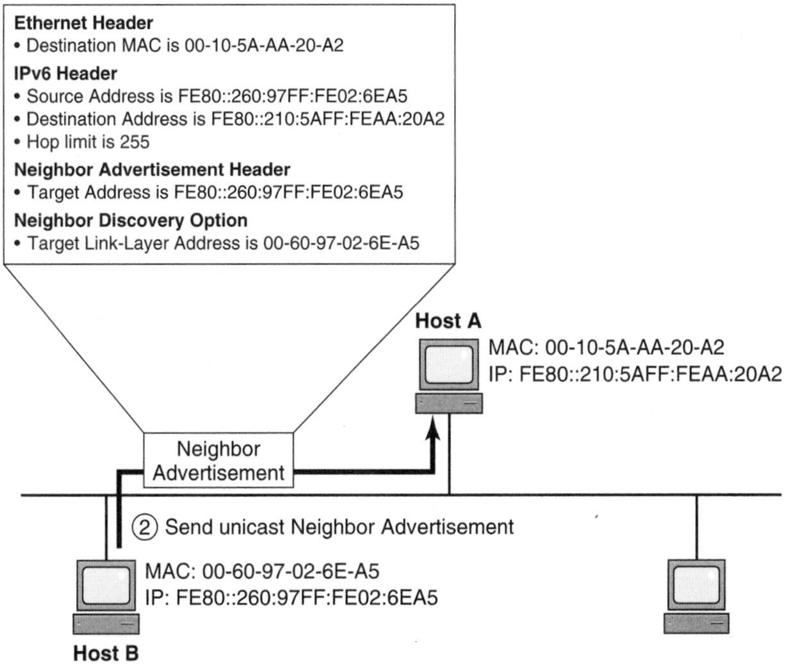

Figure 6-21. *The unicast Neighbor Advertisement message*

Neighbor Unreachability Detection

A neighboring node is reachable if there has been a recent confirmation that IPv6 packets sent to the neighboring node were received and processed by the neighboring node. Neighbor unreachability does not necessarily verify the end-to-end reachability of the destination. Because a neighboring node can be a host or router, the neighboring node might not be the final destination of the packet. Neighbor unreachability verifies only the reachability of the first hop to the destination.

One of the ways that reachability is confirmed is through the sending of a unicast Neighbor Solicitation message and the receipt of a solicited Neighbor Advertisement message. A solicited Neighbor Advertisement message, which has its Solicited flag set to 1, is sent only in response to a Neighbor Solicitation message. Unsolicited Neighbor Advertisement or Router Advertisement messages are not considered proof of reachability. The exchange of Neighbor Solicitation and Neighbor Advertisement messages confirms only the reachability of the node that sent the Neighbor Advertisement from the node that sent the Neighbor Solicitation. It does not confirm the reachability of the node that sent the Neighbor Solicitation from the node that sent the Neighbor Advertisement.

For example, if Host A sends a unicast Neighbor Solicitation to Host B and Host B sends a solicited unicast Neighbor Advertisement to Host A, Host A considers Host B reachable. Because there is no confirmation in this exchange that Host A actually received the Neighbor Advertisement, Host B does not consider Host A reachable. To confirm reachability of Host A from Host B, Host B must send its own unicast Neighbor Solicitation to Host A and receive a solicited unicast Neighbor Advertisement from Host A.

Here is an example of an exchange of ND messages to establish neighbor reachability by two nodes (HOST_A and HOST_B) for each other as displayed by Network Monitor (capture 06_05 in the \NetworkMonitorCaptures folder on the companion CD-ROM):

```
1      8.356000      HOST_A      HOST_B          ICMP6
       Neighbor Solicitation; Target = fe80::210:5aff:feaa:20a2
2      8.357000      HOST_B      HOST_A          ICMP6
       Neighbor Advertisement; Target = fe80::210:5aff:feaa:20a2
3      8.527000      HOST_B      HOST_A          ICMP6
       Neighbor Solicitation; Target = fe80::250:daff:fed8:c153
4      8.527000      HOST_A      HOST_B          ICMP6
       Neighbor Advertisement; Target = fe80::250:daff:fed8:c153
```

In frames 1 and 2, HOST_A establishes the reachability of HOST_B. In frames 3 and 4, HOST_B establishes the reachability of HOST_A.

> **NOTE:**
> The Network Monitor frame summary lines have been wrapped for
> improved readability.

Another method of determining reachability is when upper-layer protocols indicate that the communication using the next-hop address is making
forward progress. For TCP traffic, forward progress is determined when
acknowledgement segments for sent data are received. The end-to-end reachability confirmed by the receipt of TCP acknowledgments implies the reachability of the first hop to the destination. The TCP module provides these indications
to the IPv6 protocol module on an ongoing basis.

Other protocols, such as UDP, might not have a method of determining
or indicating the forward progress of communication. In this case, the exchange
of Neighbor Solicitation and Neighbor Advertisement messages is used to confirm reachability.

Neighbor Cache Entry States

The reachability of a neighboring node is determined by monitoring the state
of the neighboring node's entry in the neighbor cache.

Figure 6-22 shows the states of a neighbor cache entry.

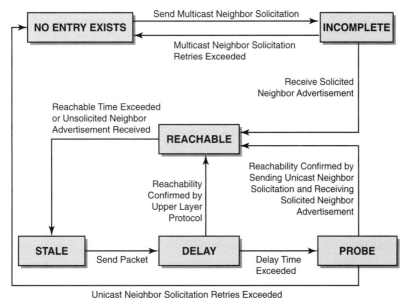

Figure 6-22. *The states of a neighbor cache entry*

RFC 2461 defines the following states for a neighbor cache entry:

■ **INCOMPLETE**

IPv6 address resolution, which uses a solicited-node multicast Neighbor Solicitation message, is in progress. The INCOMPLETE state is entered when a new neighbor cache entry is created but does not yet have the node's corresponding link-layer address. The number of multicast neighbor solicitations sent before abandoning the address resolution process and removing the neighbor cache entry is set by a configurable variable. RFC 2461 uses the variable name of MAX_MULTICAST_SOLICIT and recommends a value of 3.

■ **REACHABLE**

Reachability has been confirmed by receipt of a solicited unicast Neighbor Advertisement message. The neighbor cache entry stays in the REACHABLE state until the number of milliseconds indicated in the Reachable Time field in the Router Advertisement message (or a host default value) elapses. As long as upper layer protocols such as TCP indicate that communication is making forward progress, the entry stays in the REACHABLE state. Each time an indication of forward progress is made, the reachable time for the entry is refreshed.

■ **STALE**

Reachable time (the duration since the last reachability confirmation was received) has elapsed. The neighbor cache entry goes into the STALE state after the value (milliseconds) in the Reachable Time field in the Router Advertisement message (or a host default value) elapses and remains in this state until a packet is sent to the neighbor. The STALE state is also entered when an unsolicited neighbor advertisement that advertises the link-layer address is received.

■ **DELAY**

To allow time for upper layer protocols to provide reachability confirmation before sending Neighbor Solicitation messages, the state of the neighbor cache entry enters the DELAY state and waits a configurable period of time. RFC 2461 uses the variable name of DELAY_FIRST_PROBE_TIME and recommends a value of 5 seconds. If no reachability confirmation is received by the delay time, then the entry enters the PROBE state and a unicast Neighbor Solicitation message is sent.

■   **PROBE**

Reachability confirmation is in progress for a neighbor cache entry that was in either the STALE state or the DELAY state. Unicast Neighbor Solicitation messages are sent at intervals corresponding to the Retransmission Timer field in the Router Advertisement message received by this host (or a default host value). The number of Neighbor Solicitations sent before abandoning the reachability detection process and removing the neighbor cache entry is set by a configurable variable. RFC 2461 uses the variable name of MAX_UNICAST_SOLICITS and recommends a value of 3.

Depending on the IPv6 implementation, any entry can go from any state to the NO ENTRY EXISTS state at any time (not shown in Figure 6-21).

If the unreachable neighbor is a router, the host chooses another router from the default router list and performs both address resolution and neighbor unreachability detection on it.

If a router becomes a host, it should send a multicast Neighbor Advertisement message with the Router flag set to 0. If a host receives a Neighbor Advertisement message from a router where the Router flag is set to 0, the host removes that router from the default router list and, if necessary, chooses another router.

Neighbor Unreachability Detection and Dead Gateway Detection

The TCP/IP (IPv4) protocol for the Windows .NET Server 2003 family and Windows XP supports an algorithm known as dead gateway detection. Dead gateway detection detects the failure of the current default gateway by monitoring the number of failing TCP connections. When 25% of the active TCP connections have failed and been switched to another default gateway, the default gateway of the host is switched to another default gateway.

Dead gateway detection provides some default gateway fault tolerance for hosts on subnets containing multiple default routers. However, dead gateway detection:

■   Monitors only TCP traffic. If connectivity fails for other types of traffic, the default gateway is not switched.

■   Can cause the default gateway configuration to change when a remote router fails. Remote routers in the path between the host and the destination that fail might also cause TCP connections forwarded along that path to fail and for the host to switch its default gateway. Because dead gateway detection relies on an end-to-end protocol (such as TCP), a host can switch its default gateway even when the current default gateway is fully operational.

Neighbor unreachability detection is an improvement over dead gateway detection because it:

■ Provides for host-based default router fault tolerance for all types of traffic, not just TCP. Although forward progress indicators are used for TCP traffic, other protocols can rely on an exchange of Neighbor Solicitation and Neighbor Advertisement messages to determine reachability.

■ Detects whether the neighboring default router is operational. Neighbor unreachability detection will not cause the default router configuration to change because of a failing remote router.

Duplicate Address Detection

IPv4 nodes use ARP Request messages and a method called gratuitous ARP to detect a duplicate unicast IPv4 address on the local link. Similarly, IPv6 nodes use the Neighbor Solicitation message to detect duplicate address use on the local link.

With IPv4 gratuitous ARP, the Source Protocol Address and Target Protocol Address fields in the ARP Request message header are set to the IPv4 address for which duplication is being detected. In IPv6 duplicate address detection, the Target Address field in the Neighbor Solicitation message is set to the IPv6 address for which duplication is being detected.

Duplicate address detection differs from address resolution in the following ways:

■ In the duplicate address detection Neighbor Solicitation message, the Source Address field in the IPv6 header is set to the unspecified address (::). The address being queried for duplication cannot be used until it is determined that there are no duplicates.

■ In the Neighbor Advertisement reply to a duplicate address detection Neighbor Solicitation message, the Destination Address in the IPv6 header is set to the link-local scope all-nodes multicast address (FF02::1). The Solicited flag in the Neighbor Advertisement message is set to 0. Because the sender of the duplicate address detection Neighbor Solicitation message is not using the desired IP address, it cannot receive unicast Neighbor Advertisements. Therefore, the Neighbor Advertisement is multicast.

Upon receipt of the multicast Neighbor Advertisement with the Target Address field set to the IP address for which duplication is being detected, the node disables the use of the duplicate IP address on the interface. If the node does not receive a Neighbor Advertisement that defends the use of the address, it initializes the address on the interface.

An IPv6 node does not perform duplicate address detection for anycast addresses. Anycast addresses are not unique to a node.

Duplicate Address Detection Example-Part 1

Host B has a site-local address of FEC0::2:260:8FF:FE52:F9D8. Host A is attempting to use the site-local address of FEC0::2:260:8FF:FE52:F9D8. However, before Host A can use this address, it must verify its uniqueness through duplicate address detection.

Host A sends a solicited-node multicast Neighbor Solicitation message to the address FF02::1:FF52:F9D8, as shown in Figure 6-23.

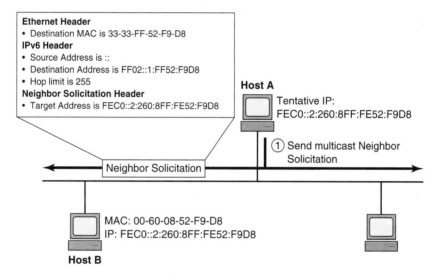

Figure 6-23. *A multicast Neighbor Solicitation message for duplicate address detection*

Network Monitor Capture

Here is the Neighbor Solicitation message for this example as displayed by Network Monitor (frame 1 of capture 06_06 in the \NetworkMonitorCaptures folder on the companion CD-ROM):

```
+ Frame: Base frame properties
  ETHERNET: ETYPE = IPv6
    + ETHERNET: Destination address : 3333FF52F9D8
    + ETHERNET: Source address : 00B0D0234733
      ETHERNET: Frame Length : 78 (0x004E)
      ETHERNET: Ethernet Type : 0x86DD
      ETHERNET: Ethernet Data: Number of data bytes remaining = 64 (0x0040)
```

```
IP6: Proto = ICMP6; Len = 24
    IP6: Version = 6 (0x6)
    IP6: Traffic Class = 0 (0x0)
    IP6: Flow Label = 0 (0x0)
    IP6: Payload Length = 24 (0x18)
    IP6: Next Header = 58 (ICMP6)
    IP6: Hop Limit = 255 (0xFF)
    IP6: Source Address = ::
    IP6: Destination Address = ff02::1:ff52:f9d8
    IP6: Payload: Number of data bytes remaining = 24 (0x0018)
ICMP6: Neighbor Solicitation; Target = fec0::2:260:8ff:fe52:f9d8
    ICMP6: Type = 135 (Neighbor Solicitation)
    ICMP6: Code = 0 (0x0)
    ICMP6: Checksum = 0x7E2F
    ICMP6: Reserved
    ICMP6: Target Address = fec0::2:260:8ff:fe52:f9d8
```

Notice the use of the unspecified address (::) in the Source Address field in the IPv6 header and the lack of the Source Link-Layer Address option.

Duplicate Address Detection Example-Part 2

Host B, having registered the multicast MAC address of 33-33-FF-52-F9-D8 with its Ethernet adapter, receives and processes the Neighbor Solicitation message. Host B notes that the source address is the unspecified address. Host B then responds with a multicast Neighbor Advertisement message, as shown in Figure 6-24.

Network Monitor Capture

Here is the Neighbor Advertisement message for this example as displayed by Network Monitor (frame 2 of capture 06_06 in the \NetworkMonitorCaptures folder on the companion CD-ROM):

```
+ Frame: Base frame properties
  ETHERNET: ETYPE = IPv6
    + ETHERNET: Destination address : 333300000001
    + ETHERNET: Source address : 00600852F9D8
      ETHERNET: Frame Length : 86 (0x0056)
      ETHERNET: Ethernet Type : 0x86DD
      ETHERNET: Ethernet Data: Number of data bytes remaining =
                               72 (0x0048)
  IP6: Proto = ICMP6; Len = 32
    IP6: Version = 6 (0x6)
```

```
    IP6: Traffic Class = 0 (0x0)
    IP6: Flow Label = 0 (0x0)
    IP6: Payload Length = 32 (0x20)
    IP6: Next Header = 58 (ICMP6)
    IP6: Hop Limit = 255 (0xFF)
    IP6: Source Address = fec0::2:260:8ff:fe52:f9d8
    IP6: Destination Address = ff02::1
    IP6: Payload: Number of data bytes remaining = 32 (0x0020)
ICMP6: Neighbor Advertisement; Target = fec0::2:260:8ff:fe52:f9d8
    ICMP6: Type = 136 (Neighbor Advertisement)
    ICMP6: Code = 0 (0x0)
    ICMP6: Checksum = 0x4F79
    ICMP6: 0............................. = Not router
    ICMP6: .0............................ = Not solicited
    ICMP6: ..1........................... = Override
    ICMP6: Target Address = fec0::2:260:8ff:fe52:f9d8
    ICMP6: Target Link-Layer Address = 00 60 08 52 F9 D8
        ICMP6: Type = 2 (0x2)
        ICMP6: Length = 1 (0x1)
        ICMP6: Target Link-Layer Address = 00 60 08 52 F9 D8
```

Notice the use of the link-local scope all-nodes multicast address as the destination address and the values of the Solicited and Override flags.

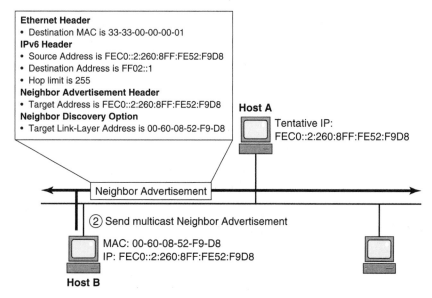

Figure 6-24. *The multicast Neighbor Advertisement message*

Router Discovery

Router discovery is the process through which nodes attempt to discover the set of routers on the local link. Router discovery in IPv6 is similar to ICMP router discovery for IPv4 described in RFC 1256. ICMP router discovery is a set of ICMP messages that allow IPv4 hosts to determine the presence of local routers, determine which local router is automatically configured as a default gateway, and to automatically switch to a different router as their default gateway when the current default gateway becomes unavailable.

An important difference between ICMPv4 router discovery and IPv6 router discovery is the mechanism through which a new default router is selected when the current one becomes unavailable. In ICMPv4 router discovery, the Router Advertisement message includes an Advertisement Lifetime field. Advertisement Lifetime is the time after which the router can be considered unavailable. In the worst case, a router can become unavailable and hosts will not attempt to discover a new default router until the Router Advertisement time has elapsed.

IPv6 has a Router Lifetime field in the Router Advertisement message. This field indicates the length of time that the router can be considered a default router. However, if the current default router becomes unavailable, the condition is detected through neighbor unreachability detection instead of the Router Lifetime field in the Router Advertisement message. Because neighbor unreachability detection determines that the router is no longer reachable, a new router is chosen immediately from the default router list or the host sends a Router Solicitation message to determine if additional default routers are present on the link. For more information, see the "Neighbor Unreachability Detection" section in this chapter.

In addition to configuring a default router, IPv6 router discovery also configures the following:

- The default setting for the Hop Limit field in the IPv6 header.

- A determination of whether the node should use a stateful address protocol, such as Dynamic Host Configuration Protocol for IPv6 (DHCPv6), for addresses and other configuration parameters.

- The timers used in neighbor unreachability detection and the retransmission of Neighbor Solicitations.

- The list of network prefixes defined for the link. Each network prefix contains both the IPv6 network prefix and its valid and preferred lifetimes. If indicated, a network prefix combined with the interface identifier creates a stateless IP address configuration for the receiving interface. A network prefix also defines the range of addresses for nodes on the local link.

- The MTU of the local link.

- Specific routes to add to the routing table.

The IPv6 router discovery processes are the following:

- IPv6 routers pseudo-periodically send a Router Advertisement message on the local link advertising their existence as routers. They also provide configuration parameters such as default hop limit, MTU, prefixes, and routes. For more information about how often routers send pseudo-periodic router advertisements, see section 6.2.4 of RFC 2461.

- Active IPv6 hosts on the local link receive the Router Advertisement m essages and use the contents to maintain the default router and prefix lists, autoconfigure addresses, add routes, and configure other parameters.

- A host that is starting sends a Router Solicitation message to the link-local scope all-routers multicast address (FF02::2). If the starting host is already configured with a unicast address, the Router Solicitation is sent with a unicast source address. Otherwise, the Router Solicitation is sent with an unspecified source address (::). Upon receipt of a Router Solicitation message, all routers on the local link send a Router Advertisement message to either the unicast address of the host that sent the Router Solicitation (if the source address of the Router Solicitation is a unicast address), or to the link-local scope all-nodes multicast address (FF02::1) (if the source address of the Router Solicitation message is unspecified). The host receives the Router Advertisement messages and uses their contents to build the default router and prefix lists and set other configuration parameters. The number of Router Solicitations sent before abandoning the router discovery process is set by a configurable variable. RFC 2461 uses the variable name of MAX_RTR_SOLICITATIONS and recommends a value of 3.

Router Discovery Example-Part 1

Host A has the Ethernet MAC address of 00-B0-D0-E9-41-43. The router has an Ethernet MAC address of 00-10-FF-D6-58-C0 and a corresponding link-local address of FE80::210:FFFF:FED6:58C0. To forward packets to off-link destinations, Host A must discover the presence of the router.

As part of the startup process, Host A sends a multicast Router Solicitation message to the address FF02::2 before it has confirmed the use of its corresponding link-local address, as shown in Figure 6-25.

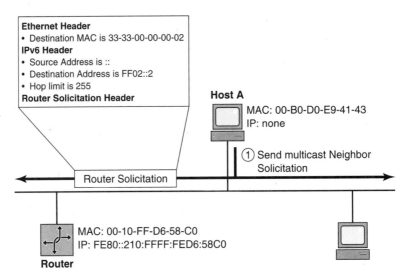

Figure 6-25. *The multicast Router Solicitation message*

Network Monitor Capture

Here is the Router Solicitation message for this example as displayed by Network Monitor (frame 1 of capture 06_07 in the \NetworkMonitorCaptures folder on the companion CD-ROM):

```
+ Frame: Base frame properties
+ ETHERNET:  EType = IPv6
    + ETHERNET: Destination address : 333300000002
    + ETHERNET: Source address : 00B0D0E94143
      ETHERNET: Frame Length : 62 (0x003E)
      ETHERNET: Ethernet Type : 0x86DD
      ETHERNET: Ethernet Data: Number of data bytes remaining = 48 (0x0030)
 IP6: Proto = ICMP6; Len = 8
      IP6: Version = 6 (0x6)
      IP6: Traffic Class = 0 (0x0)
      IP6: Flow Label = 0 (0x0)
      IP6: Payload Length = 8 (0x8)
      IP6: Next Header = 58 (ICMP6)
      IP6: Hop Limit = 255 (0xFF)
```

```
    IP6: Source Address = ::
    IP6: Destination Address = ff02::2
    IP6: Payload: Number of data bytes remaining = 8 (0x0008)
ICMP6: Router Solicitation
    ICMP6: Type = 133 (Router Solicitation)
    ICMP6: Code = 0 (0x0)
    ICMP6: Checksum = 0x7BB8
    ICMP6: Reserved
```

Notice the use of the unspecified address (::) as the source and that the Source Link-Layer Address option is not included.

Router Discovery Example-Part 2

The router, having registered the multicast MAC address of 33-33-00-00-00-02 with its Ethernet adapter, receives and processes the Router Solicitation. The router responds with a multicast Router Advertisement message containing configuration parameters and local link prefixes, as shown in Figure 6-26.

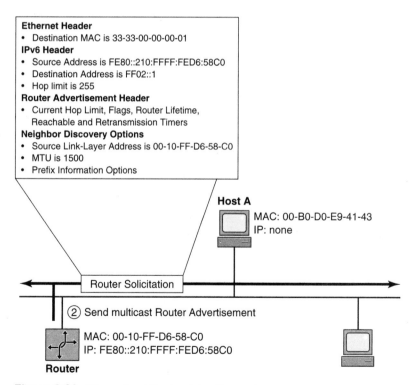

Figure 6-26. *The unicast Router Advertisement message*

Network Monitor Capture

Here is the Router Advertisement message for this example as displayed by
Network Monitor (frame 4 of capture 06_07 in the \NetworkMonitorCaptures
folder on the companion CD-ROM):

```
+ Frame: Base frame properties
+ ETHERNET:  EType = IPv6
    + ETHERNET: Destination address : 333300000001
    + ETHERNET: Source address : 0010FFD658C0
      ETHERNET: Frame Length : 142 (0x008E)
      ETHERNET: Ethernet Type : 0x86DD
      ETHERNET: Ethernet Data: Number of data bytes remaining =
                                128 (0x0080)
  IP6: Proto = ICMP6; Len = 88
      IP6: Version = 6 (0x6)
      IP6: Traffic Class = 7 (0x7)
      IP6: Flow Label = 0 (0x0)
      IP6: Payload Length = 88 (0x58)
      IP6: Next Header = 58 (ICMP6)
      IP6: Hop Limit = 255 (0xFF)
      IP6: Source Address = fe80::210:ffff:fed6:58c0
      IP6: Destination Address = ff02::1
      IP6: Payload: Number of data bytes remaining = 88 (0x0058)
  ICMP6: Router Advertisement
      ICMP6: Type = 134 (Router Advertisement)
      ICMP6: Code = 0 (0x0)
      ICMP6: Checksum = 0x4DDB
      ICMP6: Current Hop Limit = 64 (0x40)
      ICMP6: 0....... = Not managed address config
      ICMP6: .0...... = Not other stateful config
      ICMP6: ..0..... = Not a Mobile IP Home Agent
      ICMP6: Default Router Preference = Medium (0)
      ICMP6: Router Lifetime = 1800 (0x708)
      ICMP6: Reachable Time = 0 (0x0)
      ICMP6: Retransmission Timer = 0 (0x0)
      ICMP6: Source Link-Layer Address = 00 10 FF D6 58 C0
          ICMP6: Type = 1 (0x1)
          ICMP6: Length = 1 (0x1)
          ICMP6: Source Link-Layer Address = 00 10 FF D6 58 C0
      ICMP6: Prefix = 3ffe:2900:d005:f282::
          ICMP6: Type = 3 (0x3)
```

```
                ICMP6: Length = 4 (0x4)
                ICMP6: Prefix Length = 64 (0x40)
                ICMP6: 1....... = On-link determination allowed
                ICMP6: .1...... = Autonomous address configuration
                ICMP6: ..0..... = No router address
                ICMP6: ...0.... = Not a site prefix
                ICMP6: Valid Lifetime = 2592000 (0x278D00)
                ICMP6: Preferred Lifetime = 604800 (0x93A80)
                ICMP6: Reserved
                ICMP6: Site Prefix Length = 0 (0x0)
                ICMP6: Prefix = 3ffe:2900:d005:f282::
          ICMP6: Prefix = fec0:0:0:f282::
                ICMP6: Type = 3 (0x3)
                ICMP6: Length = 4 (0x4)
                ICMP6: Prefix Length = 64 (0x40)
                ICMP6: 1....... = On-link determination allowed
                ICMP6: .1...... = Autonomous address configuration
                ICMP6: ..0..... = No router address
                ICMP6: ...0.... = Not a site prefix
                ICMP6: Valid Lifetime = 2592000 (0x278D00)
                ICMP6: Preferred Lifetime = 604800 (0x93A80)
                ICMP6: Reserved
                ICMP6: Site Prefix Length = 0 (0x0)
                ICMP6: Prefix = fec0:0:0:f282::
```

This Router Advertisement contains two prefixes—one for 3FFE:2900:
D005:F282::/64 and one for FEC0:0:0:F282::/64. Notice how both the global
prefix and the site-local prefix use the same subnet identifier (F282).

Redirect Function

Routers use the redirect function to inform originating hosts of a better first-hop
neighbor to which traffic should be forwarded for a specific destination. There
are two instances where redirect is used:

1. A router informs an originating host of the IP address of a router
   available on the local link that is "closer" to the destination. "Closer"
   is a routing metric function used to reach the destination network
   segment. This condition can occur when there are multiple routers on a network segment, and the originating host chooses a
   default router and it is not the better ("closer") one to use to reach
   the destination.

   2. A router informs an originating host that the destination is a neighbor (it is on the same link as the originating host). This condition can occur when the prefix list of a host does not include the prefix of the destination. Because the destination does not match a prefix in the list, the originating host forwards the packet to its default router.

The following steps occur in the IPv6 redirect process:

   1. The originating host forwards a unicast packet to its default router.

   2. The router processes the packet and notes that the address of the originating host is a neighbor. Additionally, it notes that both the originating host's address and the next-hop address are on the same link.

   3. The router sends the originating host a Redirect message. In the Target Address field of the Redirect message is the next-hop address of the node to which the originating host should send subsequent packets addressed to the destination.

   4. The router forwards the packet to the appropriate next-hop address, using address resolution if needed to obtain the link-layer address of the next hop.

   For packets redirected to a router, the Target Address field is set to the link-local address of the router. For packets redirected to a host, the Target Address field is set to the destination address of the packet originally sent.

   The Redirect message includes the Redirected Header option. It might also include the Target Link-Layer Address option.

   5. Upon receipt of the Redirect message, the originating host updates the destination address entry in the destination cache with the address in the Target Address field. If the Target Link-Layer Address option is included in the Redirect message, its contents are used to create or update the corresponding neighbor cache entry.

Redirect messages are sent only by the first router in the path between the originating host and the destination. Hosts never send Redirect messages and routers never update routing tables based on the receipt of a Redirect message. Like ICMPv6 error messages, Redirect messages are rate limited.

Redirect Example-Part 1

Host A has the Ethernet MAC address of 00-AA-00-11-11-11 and a corresponding link-local address of FE80::2AA:FF:FE11:1111. Host A also has the site-local address of FEC0::1:2AA:FF:FE11:1111. Router 2 has the Ethernet MAC address of 00-AA-00-22-22-22 and a corresponding link-local address of FE80::2AA:FF:FE22:2222. Router 2 also has the site-local address of FEC0::1:2AA:FF:FE22:2222. Router 3 has the Ethernet MAC address of 00-AA-00-33-33-33 and a corresponding link-local address of FE80::2AA:FF:FE33:3333. Router 3 also has the site-local address of FEC0::1:2AA:FF:FE33:3333. Host A sends a packet to an off-link host at FEC0::2:2AA:FF:FE99:9999 (not shown) and uses Router 2 as its current default router. However, Router 3 is the better router to use to reach this destination.

Host A performs address resolution if needed and sends the packet destined to FEC0::2:2AA:FF:FE99:9999 to Router 2, as shown in Figure 6-27.

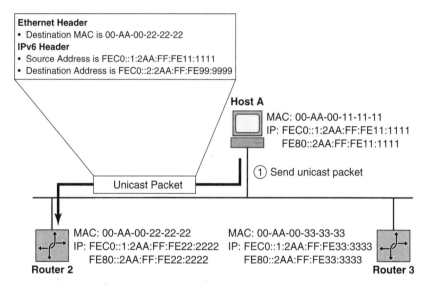

Figure 6-27. *The unicast packet sent to the router*

Redirect Example-Part 2

Router 2 receives the packet from Host A and notes that Host A is a neighbor. It also notes that Host A and the next-hop address for the destination are on the same link. To inform Host A that subsequent packets to the destination of FEC0::2:2AA:EE:FE99:9999 should be sent to Router 3, Router 2 performs address resolution if needed and sends a Redirect message to Host A, as shown in Figure 6-28.

Redirect Example-Part 3

Based on the contents of its local routing table, Router 2 performs address resolution if needed and forwards the unicast packet received from Host A to Router 3, as shown in Figure 6-29.

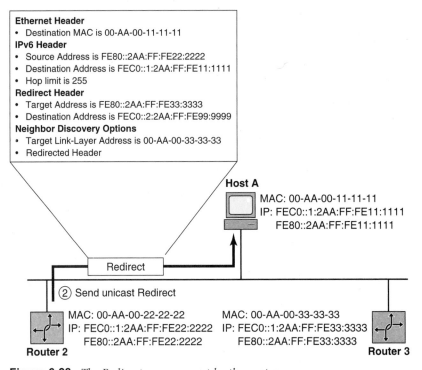

Figure 6-28. *The Redirect message sent by the router*

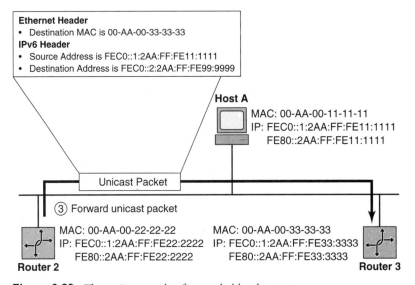

Figure 6-29. *The unicast packet forwarded by the router*

HOST SENDING ALGORITHM

The process by which an IPv6 host sends a unicast IPv6 packet uses a combination of the local host's conceptual data structures and the ND protocol. An IPv6 host uses the following algorithm when sending a unicast packet to an arbitrary destination:

1. Check the destination cache for an entry matching the destination address.

2. If an entry matching the destination address is found in the destination cache, obtain the next-hop address from the destination cache entry. If the destination is a mobile IPv6 node, the destination cache entry might contain a pointer to a care-of destination cache entry. If so, the next-hop address is obtained from the care-of destination cache entry. For more information about IPv6 mobility support, see Chapter 12, "IPv6 Mobility." Go to step 4.

   If an entry matching the destination address is not found in the destination cache, determine if the destination address matches a prefix in the prefix list.

   > If the destination address matches a prefix in the prefix list, the next-hop address is set to the destination address. Go to step 3.

   > If the destination address does not match a prefix in the prefix list, check to see if there is a default router.

   > > If there is no default router (and there are no routers in the default router list), the next-hop address is set to the destination address.

3. Update the destination cache.

4. Check the neighbor cache for an entry matching the next-hop address.

5. If an entry matching the next-hop address is found in the neighbor cache, use the link-layer address of the matching entry.

   If an entry matching the next-hop address is not found in the neighbor cache, use address resolution to obtain the link-layer address for the next-hop address.

   > If address resolution fails, indicate an error.

6. Send the packet by using the link-layer address of the neighbor cache entry.

   Figure 6-30 shows the host sending algorithm in flowchart form.

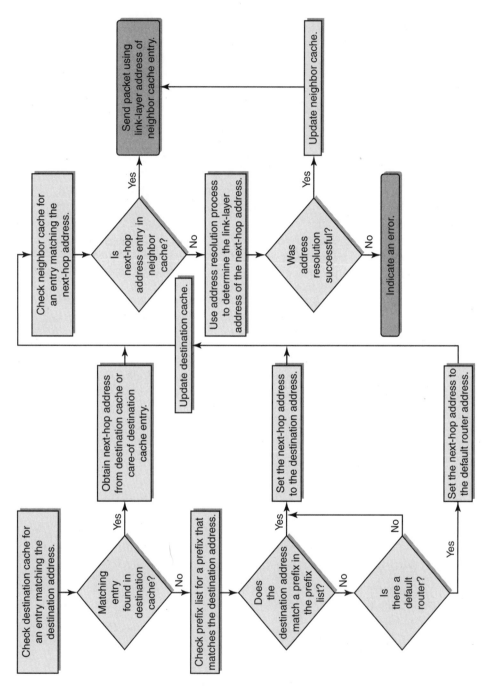

Figure 6-30. *The host sending algorithm*

Because the IPv6 protocol for the Windows .NET Server 2003 family and Windows XP uses a routing table in place of a prefix list and default router list, the host-sending algorithm uses a different method to determine the next-hop address for the destination. For more information, see "End-to-End IPv6 Delivery Process" in Chapter 10, "IPv6 Routing."

IPv4 NEIGHBOR MESSAGES AND FUNCTIONS AND IPV6 EQUIVALENTS

Table 6-3 lists IPv4 neighbor messages, components, and functions and their IPv6 equivalents.

Table 6-3. IPv4 NEIGHBOR MESSAGES, COMPONENTS, AND FUNCTIONS AND THEIR IPV6 EQUIVALENTS

IPv4	*IPv6*
ARP Request message	Neighbor Solicitation message
ARP Reply message	Neighbor Advertisement message
ARP cache	Neighbor cache
Gratuitous ARP	Duplicate address detection
Router Solicitation message (optional)	Router Solicitation message (required)
Router Advertisement message (optional)	Router Advertisement message (required)
Redirect message	Redirect message

REFERENCES

RFC 1256 – "ICMP Router Discovery Messages"

RFC 2461 – "Neighbor Discovery for IP Version 6 (IPv6)"

RFC 2464 – "Transmission of IPv6 Packets over Ethernet Networks"

Internet draft – "Mobility Support in IPv6"

Internet draft – "Site Prefixes in Neighbor Discovery"

Internet draft – "Default Router Preferences and More-Specific Routes"

TESTING FOR UNDERSTANDING

To test your understanding of IPv6 ND, answer the following questions. See Appendix D to check your answers.

1. List the IPv4 facilities that are replaced by the IPv6 ND protocol.

2. List the capabilities of the IPv6 ND protocol that are not present in IPv4.

3. List the five different ND messages and the options that can be included with them.

4. Describe the interpretation of the Length field in ND options.

5. What is the value of the Length field for a maximum-sized Redirected Header option (assuming no IPv6 extension headers are present)?

6. Describe how you would use the MTU option to provide seamless connectivity between Ethernet nodes and ATM nodes on a transparently bridged link.

7. Why is the Source Link-Layer Address option not included in the Neighbor Solicitation message sent during duplicate address detection?

8. Describe the configuration parameters and their corresponding fields sent in the Router Advertisement message (not including options). Describe the configuration parameters and their corresponding fields sent in the Prefix Information option.

9. Under what circumstances is an unsolicited Neighbor Advertisement message sent?

10. What are the differences in address resolution and duplicate address detection node behavior for anycast addresses?

11. Why is the response to a duplicate address detection sent as multicast? Who sends the response, the offending or defending node?

12. Why is the value of the Hop Limit field set to 255 for all ND messages?

13. Describe the purpose of each of the host data structures described in RFC 2461.

14. What field in the Redirect message contains the next-hop address of the better router to use for packets addressed to a specific destination? Describe how the contents of that field are used to update the conceptual host data structures for subsequent data sent to the destination.

15. Under what circumstances does a router send a Router Advertisement?

16. For Host A and Host B on the same link, why is the exchange of a Neighbor Solicitation message (sent by Host A to Host B) and a Neighbor Advertisement message (sent by Host B to Host A) not considered by Host B as proof that Host A is reachable?

17. What is the next-hop address of a destination set to for a host that does not have a prefix matching the destination address or a default router?

Chapter 7

Multicast Listener Discovery

At the end of this chapter, you should be able to:

- Describe the purpose of the IPv6 Multicast Listener Discovery (MLD) protocol.
- Describe how IPv6 hosts and routers support multicast communication.
- Describe the structure of an MLD message packet.
- Describe the structure and purpose of each type of MLD message.

OVERVIEW OF MULTICAST LISTENER DISCOVERY

Multicast Listener Discovery (MLD) is the IPv6 equivalent of Internet Group Management Protocol version 2 (IGMPv2) defined in RFC 2236 for IPv4. MLD is a set of messages exchanged by routers and hosts, enabling routers to discover the set of multicast addresses for which there are listening hosts for each attached subnet. Like IGMPv2, MLD allows routers to discover the list of multicast addresses for which there is at least one listener on each subnet, and not the list of individual multicast listeners for each multicast address. MLD is described in RFC 2710.

> **NOTE:**
> A specification for IGMPv3 exists as an Internet draft ("Internet Group Management Protocol, Version 3") and is close to becoming an Internet standards track RFC, replacing IGMPv2. When this occurs, MLD for IPv6 will also be updated to include the features of IGMPv3 for IPv6 multicast hosts and routers.

IPv6 Multicast Overview

In IPv4, multicast support is optional. In IPv6, multicast support is required. This section provides an overview of IPv6 multicast concepts.

In addition to unicast and anycast support, IPv6 also provides a mechanism to send and receive IPv6 multicast traffic. IPv6 multicast traffic is sent to a single destination address but is received and processed by multiple IPv6 hosts, regardless of their location on the network. Hosts listen to a specific IPv6 multicast address and receive all packets to that address. Multicast is more efficient than IPv6 unicast for one-to-many delivery of data. Instead of having multiple unicast packets sent, only one packet is sent.

The additional elements of IPv6 multicast include the following:

- The set of hosts listening on a specific IPv6 multicast address is called a multicast group.

- Multicast group membership is dynamic, and hosts can join and leave the group at any time.

- There are no limitations to the size of a multicast group.

- A multicast group can span IPv6 routers across multiple subnets. This configuration requires IPv6 multicast support on IPv6 routers and the ability for hosts to register themselves with the router. Host registration is accomplished by using MLD.

- A host can send traffic to a multicast address without being a member of the group.

IPv6 multicast addresses are defined by the FP 1111 1111 (0xFF) and can have different scopes. For more information about IPv6 multicast addresses, see Chapter 3, "IPv6 Addressing."

In an IPv6 multicast-enabled network, any host can send multicast traffic to any multicast address, and any host can receive multicast traffic from any multicast address regardless of their location. To facilitate this capability, the hosts and routers of the network must support multicast traffic.

Host Support for Multicast

For a host to send IPv6 multicast packets, it must:

- **Determine the IPv6 multicast address to use.**
  The IPv6 multicast address can be hard-coded by the application or obtained through a mechanism that allocates a unique multicast address.

■ **Place the IPv6 multicast packet on the medium.**

The sending host must construct an IPv6 packet containing the destination IPv6 multicast address and place it on the medium. In the case of Ethernet and FDDI, the destination MAC address is created from the IPv6 multicast address as described in Chapter 3, "IPv6 Addressing."

For a host to receive IPv6 multicast packets, it must:

■ **Inform IPv6 to receive multicast traffic.**

To determine the IPv6 multicast address to use, the application must first determine whether to create a multicast group or use an existing multicast group. To join an existing group, the application can use a hard-coded multicast address or an address derived from a universal resource locator (URL) string.

After the multicast address is determined, an application must inform IPv6 to receive multicast packets for a specified multicast address. For example, the application can use Windows Sockets functions to notify IPv6 of the multicast groups joined. If multiple applications use the same IPv6 multicast address, then IPv6 must pass a copy of the multicast packet to each application. IPv6 must track which applications use which multicast addresses, as applications join or leave multicast groups. Additionally, for a multihomed host, IPv6 must track the application membership of multicast groups for each interface.

■ **Register the multicast MAC address with the network adapter.**

If the network technology supports hardware-based multicasting, then the network adapter is instructed to pass up packets for a specific multicast address. In the case of shared access technologies such as Ethernet and FDDI, IPv6 instructs the network adapter to listen for and pass to higher protocol layers all frames with a multicast MAC address corresponding to the IPv6 multicast address. The IPv6 protocol included in Windows XP and the Windows .NET Server 2003 family uses an **NdisRequest( )** function to instruct the network adapter to listen for and pass to higher protocol layers all frames with a specific multicast destination MAC address.

■ **Inform local routers.**

The host must inform local subnet routers that it is listening for multicast traffic at a specific multicast address. The protocol that registers multicast group information for IPv6 is MLD. The host sends an MLD Multicast Listener Report message to register membership in a specific multicast group. All multicast group membership is reported, except for the multicast group for the link-local scope all-nodes multicast address (FF02::1).

Even though an IPv6 multicast router would never forward traffic destined to a link-local scope multicast address beyond the local link, multicast group membership for link-local scope multicast addresses is still reported. This is done so that multicast-aware Layer 2 switches and bridges can properly forward IPv6 link-local multicast traffic to nodes on different LAN segments of a link.

Router Support for Multicast

To forward IPv6 multicast packets to only those subnets for which there are group members, an IPv6 multicast router must be able to:

- Receive all IPv6 multicast traffic.

- Forward IPv6 multicast traffic.

- Receive and process MLD Multicast Listener Report and Multicast Listener Done messages.

- Query attached subnets for host membership status.

- Communicate group membership to other IPv6 multicast routers.

Receive All IPv6 Multicast Traffic

For shared access technologies, such as Ethernet and FDDI, the normal listening mode for network adapters is unicast listening mode. The listening mode is the way that the network adapter analyzes the destination MAC address of incoming frames to decide to process them further. In unicast listening mode, the only frames that are considered for further processing are in a table of interesting destination MAC addresses on the network adapter. Typically, the only interesting addresses are the MAC-level broadcast address (0xFF-FF-FF-FF-FF-FF) and the unicast address of the adapter. The unicast address is also known as the MAC, physical, or hardware address.

However, for an IPv6 multicast router to receive all multicast traffic on a subnet, it must place the network adapter connected to the subnet in a special listening mode called multicast promiscuous mode. When an adapter is placed in multicast promiscuous mode, it analyzes the IEEE-defined I/G bit to determine whether the frame requires further processing. For more information on the I/G bit in IEEE 802 addresses, see Chapter 3, "IPv6 Addressing."

The values of the I/G bit are the following:

- If the I/G bit is set to 0, the address is a unicast (or individual) address.

- If the I/G bit is set to 1, the address is a multicast (or group) address. The multicast bit is also set to 1 for the MAC-level broadcast address.

When the network adapter is placed in multicast promiscuous listening mode, any frames with the I/G bit set to 1 are passed to higher protocol layers for further processing.

Multicast promiscuous mode is different than promiscuous mode. In promiscuous mode, all frames—regardless of the destination MAC address—are passed to higher protocol layers for processing. Promiscuous mode is used by protocol analyzers, also known as network sniffers, such as the full version of Microsoft Network Monitor that is part of the Microsoft Systems Management Server.

Most network adapters support multicast promiscuous mode. A network adapter that supports promiscuous mode might not support multicast promiscuous mode. Consult your network adapter documentation or manufacturer for information about whether your network adapter supports multicast promiscuous mode. Network adapters of hosts are typically not placed in multicast promiscuous mode.

Forward IPv6 Multicast Traffic

The ability to forward IPv6 multicast packets is a router capability. When multicast forwarding is enabled, IPv6 multicast packets that have a scope larger than link-local are analyzed to determine over which interfaces the packet is to be forwarded. The analysis is done by comparing the source address and destination multicast address to entries in an IPv6 multicast forwarding table. Upon receipt of an IPv6 multicast packet that has a scope larger than link-local, the Hop Limit field in the IPv6 header is decremented by 1. If the hop limit is less than 1 after decrementing, the multicast packet is silently discarded. If the hop limit is greater than 0 after decrementing, the multicast forwarding table is checked. If an entry in the multicast forwarding table is found that matches the destination IPv6 multicast address, the IPv6 multicast packet is forwarded with its new hop limit over the appropriate interfaces.

The multicast forwarding process does not distinguish between hosts on locally attached subnets who are receiving multicast traffic or hosts on a subnet that is downstream from the locally attached subnet across another router. In other words, a multicast router might forward a multicast packet on a subnet for which there are no hosts listening. The multicast packet is forwarded because another router on that subnet indicated that a host in its direction is receiving the multicast traffic.

The multicast forwarding table does not record each multicast group member or the number of multicast group members. It records only that there is at least one multicast group member for a specific multicast address.

The IPv6 protocol included in Windows XP and the Windows .NET Server 2003 family does not support IPv6 multicast forwarding.

Receive and Process MLD Multicast Listener Report and Multicast Listener Done Messages

Multicast routers receive MLD Multicast Listener Report messages from all hosts on all locally attached subnets. This information is used to track multicast group membership by placing entries in the multicast forwarding table. Because multicast routers have placed their network adapters in multicast promiscuous mode, they receive all MLD Multicast Listener Report messages sent to any multicast address.

To improve the *leave latency,* which is the time between when the last host on a subnet has left the group and when no more multicast traffic for that group is forwarded to that subnet, an IPv6 host that might be the last member of a group on a subnet sends an MLD Multicast Listener Done message. After sending multicast-address-specific queries to the group reported in the MLD Multicast Listener Done message and receiving no response, the IPv6 router can determine that there are no more group members on that subnet.

Query Attached Subnets for Host Membership Status

To compensate for the loss of MLD Multicast Listener Report and Multicast Listener Done messages, IPv6 multicast routers periodically send MLD Multicast Listener Query messages on the local subnet. A host that is still a member of a multicast group might respond to the query with an MLD Multicast Listener Report message. To keep multiple hosts on a particular subnet from sending MLD Multicast Listener Report messages for the same group, a random response timer is used on the hosts to delay the transmission of the MLD Multicast Listener Report message. If another host sends the message on that subnet before the response timer expires, a message is not sent by the other hosts on that subnet.

Communicate Group Membership to Other IPv6 Multicast Routers

To create multicast-enabled IPv6 networks containing more than one router, multicast routers must communicate group membership information to each other so group members can receive IPv6 multicast traffic regardless of their location on the IPv6 network.

Multicast routers exchange host membership information by using a multicast routing protocol such as the Protocol Independent Multicast (PIM) protocol. Group membership is communicated either explicitly, by exchanging multicast address and subnet information, or implicitly, by informing upstream routers that no group members exist downstream from the source of the multicast traffic.

The goals of a multicast routing protocol include the following:

■ Forward traffic away from the source to prevent loops.

■ Minimize or eliminate multicast traffic to subnets that do not need the traffic.

■ Minimize CPU and memory load on the router for scalability.

■ Minimize the overhead of the routing protocol.

■ Minimize the *join latency,* which is the time it takes for the first group member on a subnet to begin receiving traffic sent to the group.

Multicast routing is more complex than unicast routing. With unicast routing, unicast traffic is forwarded to a unique destination. Unicast routes can summarize ranges of unique destinations. Unicast routes in the network are comparatively consistent and need to be updated only when the topology of the IPv6 network changes.

With multicast routing, multicast traffic is forwarded to an ambiguous group destination. Multicast addresses represent individual multicast groups, and in general, cannot be summarized in the multicast forwarding table. The location of group members is not consistent, and the multicast forwarding tables of multicast routers might need to be updated whenever a multicast group member joins or leaves a multicast group.

Just as unicast routing protocols update the unicast IPv6 routing table, multicast routing protocols update the IPv6 multicast forwarding table of a router.

MLD PACKET STRUCTURE

Unlike IGMPv2, MLD uses ICMPv6 messages instead of defining a separate message structure. Figure 7-1 shows the structure of an MLD message packet.

IPv6 Header Next Header = 0 (Hop-by-Hop Options)	**Hop-by-Hop Options Header** IPv6 Router Alert Option Next Header = 58 (ICMPv6)	**MLD Message**

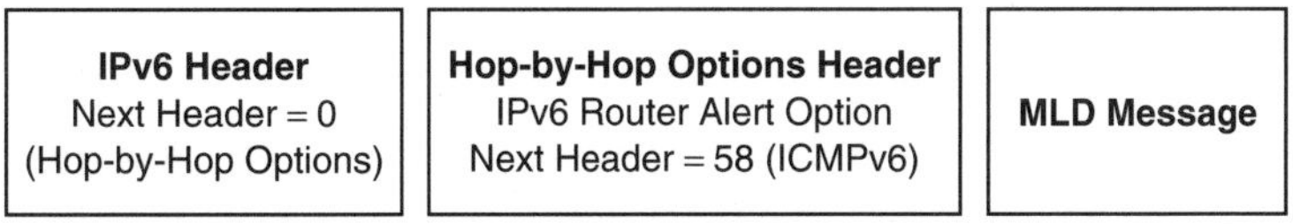

Figure 7-1. *The structure of an MLD message packet*

An MLD message packet consists of an IPv6 header, a Hop-by-Hop Options extension header, and the MLD message. The Hop-by-Hop Options extension header contains the IPv6 Router Alert Option described in RFC 2711. It is used to ensure that routers process MLD messages that are sent to multicast addresses for which the router is not a group member.

MLD MESSAGES

There are three types of MLD messages:

1. Multicast Listener Query (ICMPv6 Type 130)

2. Multicast Listener Report (ICMPv6 Type 131)

3. Multicast Listener Done (ICMPv6 Type 132)

All three MLD messages share the same message structure.

Multicast Listener Query

An IPv6 multicast-capable router uses the Multicast Listener Query message to query a link for multicast group membership. It is equivalent to the IGMPv2 Host Membership Query message. There are two types of Multicast Listener Query messages:

1. General query

   The general query is used to periodically query all hosts on a subnet for the presence of multicast group members of any multicast address. The only multicast address that is not reported is the link-local scope all-nodes multicast address (FF02::1).

2. Multicast-address-specific query

   The multicast-address-specific query is used to query all hosts on a subnet that are members of a specific multicast group.

The two message types are distinguished by the Destination Address field in the IPv6 header and the Multicast Address field within the Multicast Listener Query message.

In the IPv6 header of a Multicast Listener Query message:

■ The Hop Limit field is set to 1.

■ The Source Address field is set to the link-local address of the interface on which the query is being sent.

■ The Destination Address field is the specific multicast address being queried. For the general query, the Destination Address field is set to the link-local scope all-nodes multicast address (FF02::1). For the multicast-address-specific query, the Destination Address field is set to the specific multicast address being queried.

Figure 7-2 shows the structure of the Multicast Listener Query message.

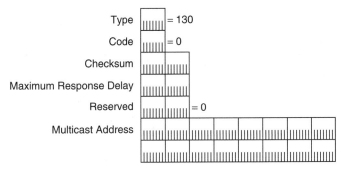

Type = 130
Code = 0
Checksum
Maximum Response Delay
Reserved = 0
Multicast Address

Figure 7-2. *The structure of the Multicast Listener Query message*

The fields in the Multicast Listener Query message are:

■ **Type**
The value of this field is 130.

■ **Code**
The value of this field is 0.

■ **Checksum**
The value of this field is the ICMPv6 checksum.

■ **Maximum Response Delay**
The Maximum Response Delay field indicates the maximum amount of time in milliseconds within which a multicast group member must report its membership by using an MLD Multicast Listener Report message. The size of this field is 16 bits.

When a host that is a group member of a given multicast address receives a Multicast Listener Query, the host uses the value of the Maximum Response Delay field to calculate a random response time less than or equal to the current value of the field. Each host on the subnet that could report its membership sets a different random response time. The host on the subnet whose random response time expires first sends the Multicast Listener Report message. When the other hosts that could report group membership for the multicast address receive the Multicast Listener Report message, they abandon the attempt to send their own Multicast Listener Report message. This process results typically in only one host member reporting group membership for a given multicast address on each subnet.

- **Reserved**
  This is a 16-bit field reserved for future use and set to 0.

- **Multicast Address**
  For the general query, the Multicast Address field is set to the unspecified address (::). For the multicast-address-specific query, the Multicast Address field is set to the specific multicast address that is being queried. The size of this field is 128 bits.

Multicast Listener Report

The Multicast Listener Report message is used by a listening node to either immediately report its interest in receiving multicast traffic at a specific multicast address or respond to a Multicast Listener Query message (either a general or multicast-address-specific query). It is equivalent to the IGMPv2 Host Membership Report message.

In the IPv6 header of a Multicast Listener Report message:

- The Hop Limit field is set to 1.

- The Source Address field is set to the link-local address of the interface on which the report is being sent. If the Multicast Listener Report message is for a solicited-node multicast address corresponding to a unicast address for which duplicate address detection is not yet complete, the source address is set to the unspecified address (::).

- The Destination Address field is the specific multicast address being reported.

Figure 7-3 shows the structure of the Multicast Listener Report message.

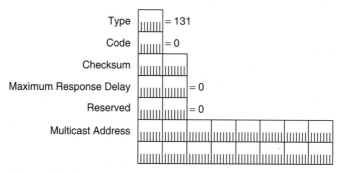

Figure 7-3. *The structure of the Multicast Listener Report message*

The fields in the Multicast Listener Report message are:

- **Type**
  The value of this field is 131.

- **Code**
  The value of this field is 0.

- **Checksum**
  The value of this field is the ICMPv6 checksum.

- **Maximum Response Delay**
  This field is not used in the Multicast Listener Report message and is set to 0.

- **Reserved**
  This is a 16-bit field reserved for future use and set to 0.

- **Multicast Address**
  The Multicast Address field is set to the specific multicast address that is being reported.

Network Monitor Capture

Here is an example of a Multicast Listener Report message as displayed by Network Monitor (capture 07_01 in the \NetworkMonitorCaptures folder on the companion CD-ROM):

```
+ Frame: Base frame properties
+ ETHERNET:  EType = IPv6
   + ETHERNET: Destination address : 3333FFB17480
   + ETHERNET: Source address : 00902766C140
     ETHERNET: Frame Length : 86 (0x0056)
     ETHERNET: Ethernet Type : 0x86DD
     ETHERNET: Ethernet Data: Number of data bytes remaining = 72 (0x0048)
  IP6: Hop Opts; Proto = ICMP6; Len = 24
     IP6: Version = 6 (0x6)
     IP6: Traffic Class = 0 (0x0)
     IP6: Flow Label = 0 (0x0)
     IP6: Payload Length = 32 (0x20)
     IP6: Next Header = 0 (Hop-by-Hop Options Header)
     IP6: Hop Limit = 1 (0x1)
     IP6: Source Address = fe80::290:27ff:fe66:c140
     IP6: Destination Address = ff02::1:ffb1:7480
     IP6: Hop-by-Hop Options Header
```

```
         IP6: Next Header = 58 (ICMP6)
         IP6: Length = 0 (0x0)
         IP6: Router Alert Option
             IP6: Type = 5
                 IP6: 00...... = Skip option if not recognized
                 IP6: ..0..... = Option data does not change enroute
             IP6: Length = 2 (0x2)
             IP6: Router Alert Value = 0 (0x0)
         IP6: Padding (2 bytes)
             IP6: Type = 1 (PadN)
                 IP6: 00...... = Skip option if not recognized
                 IP6: ..0..... = Option data does not change enroute
             IP6: Length = 0 (0x0)
     IP6: Payload: Number of data bytes remaining = 24 (0x0018)
ICMP6: Multicast Listener Report
     ICMP6: Type = 131 (Multicast Listener Report)
     ICMP6: Code = 0 (0x0)
     ICMP6: Checksum = 0xAD88
     ICMP6: Maximum Response Delay = 0 (0x0)
     ICMP6: Unused
     ICMP6: Multicast Address = ff02::1:ffb1:7480
```

Notice the mapping of the destination IPv6 multicast address (FF02::1:<u>FFB1:7480</u>) and the destination MAC multicast address (3333<u>FFB17480</u>) (corresponding bits underlined), and the use of the Hop-by-Hop Options header and the IPv6 Router Alert option (Option Type 5).

Multicast Listener Done

The Multicast Listener Done message is equivalent to the IGMPv2 Leave Group message and is used to inform the local routers that there might not be any more group members of a specific multicast address on the subnet. A local router verifies that there are no more group members on the subnet.

The Multicast Listener Done message is sent when the group member that responded to the last Multicast Listener Query message for the multicast address on the subnet leaves the multicast group. Notice that the group member sending the Multicast Listener Done message might not truly be the last group member on the subnet. This is why membership for the group is verified by a local router. This simple method of reporting what might be the last group member prevents a host from having to track the presence of other multicast group members on their subnet for each multicast group for which the host is a member.

Because IPv6 multicast routers do not track how many group members are on a subnet for a given multicast group, every subnet must be treated as if there were multiple group members present. The host that sends the Multicast Listener Done message might not be the last group member. Therefore, upon receiving a Multicast Listener Done message, the multicast querying router on the subnet immediately sends multicast-address-specific queries for the multicast address being reported in the Multicast Listener Done message. If there are additional group members, one of them will send a Multicast Listener Report message.

In the IPv6 header of a Multicast Listener Done message:

■ The Hop Limit field is set to 1.

■ The Source Address field is set to the link-local address of the interface on which the report is being sent.

■ The Destination Address field is set to the link-local scope all-routers multicast address (FF02::2).

Figure 7-4 shows the structure of the Multicast Listener Done message.

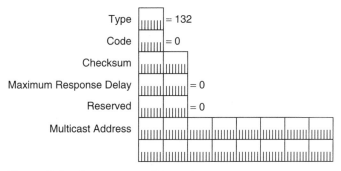

Figure 7-4. *The structure of the Multicast Listener Done message*

The fields in the Multicast Listener Done message are:

■ **Type**
The value of this field is 132.

■ **Code**
The value of this field is 0.

■ **Checksum**
The value of this field is the ICMPv6 checksum.

- **Maximum Response Delay**
  This field is not used in the Multicast Listener Done message and is set to 0.

- **Reserved**
  This is a 16-bit field reserved for future use and set to 0.

- **Multicast Address**
  The Multicast Address field is set to the specific multicast address for which there may be no more listeners on the subnet.

SUMMARY OF MLD

Table 7-1 lists IGMPv2 messages and their corresponding MLD equivalents.

Table 7-1. IGMPv2 MESSAGES AND THEIR MLD EQUIVALENTS

IGMPv2 Message	MLD Equivalent
Host Membership Query (Type 17)	Multicast Listener Query
Host Membership Report (Type 22)	Multicast Listener Report
Leave Group (Type 23)	Multicast Listener Done

REFERENCES

RFC 2236 – "Internet Group Management Protocol, Version 2"

RFC 2710 – "Multicast Listener Discovery (MLD) for IPv6"

RFC 2711 – "IPv6 Router Alert Option"

TESTING FOR UNDERSTANDING

To test your understanding of MLD, answer the following questions. See Appendix D to check your answers.

1. Why is the IPv6 Router Alert option used in the Hop-by-Hop Options header for MLD messages?

2. Which addresses are used as the source address in MLD messages?

3. How do you distinguish a general query from a multicast-address-specific query in the Multicast Listener Query message?

4. For which multicast addresses are Multicast Listener Report messages never sent?

5. In which MLD message is the value of the Maximum Response Delay field significant?

6. Describe the use of the Multicast Address field for each MLD message.

Chapter 8

Address Autoconfiguration

At the end of this chapter, you should be able to:

- Describe the use of address autoconfiguration in IPv6.

- Describe the states of an autoconfigured address and their relation to preferred and valid lifetimes.

- Describe the types of autoconfiguration.

- Explain the details of the stateless address autoconfiguration process.

- Describe the automatically configured addresses for a host running the IPv6 protocol for the Windows .NET Server 2003 family and Windows XP.

ADDRESS AUTOCONFIGURATION OVERVIEW

One of the most useful aspects of IPv6 is its ability to automatically configure itself, even without the use of a stateful address autoconfiguration protocol such as DHCPv6. By default, an IPv6 host can configure a link-local address for each interface. By using router discovery, a host can also determine the addresses of routers, other configuration parameters, additional addresses, and on-link prefixes. Included in the Router Advertisement message is an indication of whether a stateful address autoconfiguration protocol should be used.

NOTE:
DHCPv6 standards are in progress and are not discussed in this chapter.

Autoconfigured Address States

Autoconfigured addresses are in one or more of the following states:

■ **Tentative**

The address is in the process of being verified as unique. Verification occurs through duplicate address detection. A node cannot receive unicast traffic to a tentative address. It can, however, receive and process multicast Neighbor Advertisement messages sent in response to the Neighbor Solicitation message that has been sent during duplicate address detection.

■ **Valid**

The address can be used for sending and receiving unicast traffic. The valid state includes both the preferred and deprecated states. The sum of the times that an address remains in the tentative, preferred, and deprecated states is determined by the Valid Lifetime field in the Prefix Information option of a Router Advertisement message.

❑ **Preferred**

The address is valid, its uniqueness has been verified, and it can be used for unlimited communications. A node can send and receive unicast traffic to and from a preferred address. The period of time that an address can remain in the tentative and preferred states is determined by the Preferred Lifetime field in the Prefix Information option of a Router Advertisement message.

❑ **Deprecated**

The address is valid, its uniqueness has been verified, but its use is discouraged for new communication. Existing communication sessions can still use a deprecated address. A node can send and receive unicast traffic to and from a deprecated address.

■ **Invalid**

The address can no longer be used to send or receive unicast traffic. An address enters the invalid state after the valid lifetime expires.

Figure 8-1 shows the states of an autoconfigured address and their relationship to the preferred and valid lifetimes.

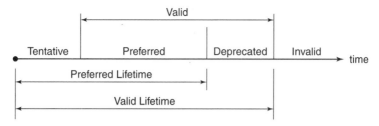

Figure 8-1. *The states of an autoconfigured address*

NOTE:

With the exception of autoconfiguration for link-local addresses, address autoconfiguration is specified only for hosts. Routers must obtain address and configuration parameters through another means, such as manual configuration.

Types of Autoconfiguration

There are three types of autoconfiguration:

- **Stateless**
  Configuration of addresses is based on the receipt of Router Advertisement messages. These messages have the Managed Address Configuration and Other Stateful Configuration flags set to 0 and include one or more Prefix Information options, each with its Autonomous flag set to 1.

- **Stateful**
  Configuration is based on the use of a stateful address autoconfiguration protocol, such as DHCPv6, to obtain addresses and other configuration options. A host uses stateful address autoconfiguration when it receives a Router Advertisement message with no Prefix Information options and either the Managed Address Configuration flag or the Other Stateful Configuration flag is set to 1. A host will also use stateful address autoconfiguration when there are no routers present on the local link.

- **Both**
  Configuration is based on the receipt of Router Advertisement messages that include Prefix Information options, each with its Autonomous flag set to 1, and have the Managed Address Configuration or Other Stateful Configuration flags set to 1.

219

For all types of autoconfiguration, a link-local address is always configured automatically.

AUTOCONFIGURATION PROCESS

The address autoconfiguration process defined in RFC 2462 for the physical interface of an IPv6 node is the following:

1. A tentative link-local address is derived based on the link-local prefix of FE80::/64 and a EUI-64-derived interface identifier.

2. Using duplicate address detection to verify the uniqueness of the tentative link-local address, a Neighbor Solicitation message is sent with the Target Address field that is set to the tentative link-local address.

3. If a Neighbor Advertisement message (sent in response to the Neighbor Solicitation message) is received, this indicates that another node on the local link is using the tentative link-local address and address autoconfiguration stops. At this point, manual configuration must be performed on the node.

4. If no Neighbor Advertisement message (sent in response to the Neighbor Solicitation message) is received, the tentative link-local address is assumed to be unique and valid. The link-local address is initialized for the interface. The link-layer multicast address of the solicited-node address corresponding to the link-local address is registered with the network adapter.

For an IPv6 host, the address autoconfiguration continues as follows:

1. The host sends a Router Solicitation message. While routers pseudo-periodically send router advertisements, the host sends a Router Solicitation message to request an immediate router advertisement, rather than waiting until the next router advertisement. By default, up to three Router Solicitation messages are sent.

2. If no Router Advertisement messages are received, the host uses a stateful address autoconfiguration protocol to obtain addresses and other configuration parameters.

3. If a Router Advertisement message is received, the hop limit, reachable time, retransmission timer, and the MTU (if the MTU option is present) are set.

4. For each Prefix Information option present:

   If the On-Link flag is set to 1, the prefix is added to the prefix list.

> If the Autonomous flag is set to 1, the prefix and an appropriate interface identifier are used to derive a tentative address.

> Duplicate address detection is used to verify the uniqueness of the tentative address.

>> If the tentative address is in use, the use of the address is not initialized for the interface.

>> If the tentative address is not in use, the address is initialized. This includes setting the valid and preferred lifetimes based on the Valid Lifetime and Preferred Lifetime fields in the Prefix Information option. If needed, it also includes registering the link-layer multicast address of the solicited-node address corresponding to the new address with the network adapter.

5. If the Managed Address Configuration flag in the Router Advertisement message is set to 1, a stateful address autoconfiguration protocol is used to obtain additional addresses.

6. If the Other Stateful Configuration flag in the Router Advertisement message is set to 1, a stateful address autoconfiguration protocol is used to obtain additional configuration parameters.

> Figures 8-2 and 8-3 show the address autoconfiguration process for a host.

IPv6 Protocol for the Windows .NET Server 2003 Family and Windows XP Autoconfiguration Specifics

RFC 2462 does not require a specific order for sending the initial router solicitation and performing duplicate address detection for the derived link-local address. The IPv6 protocol for the Windows .NET Server 2003 family and Windows XP sends the Router Solicitation message before performing duplicate address detection on the EUI-64-derived link-local address. In this way, duplicate address detection and router discovery are done in parallel to save time during the physical interface initialization process.

If the EUI-64-derived link-local address is a duplicate, stateless address autoconfiguration for the IPv6 protocol for the Windows .NET Server 2003 family and Windows XP can continue with the receipt of a multicast Router Advertisement message containing site-local or global prefixes. The attempted link-local address is shown with a "Duplicate" state in the display of the **netsh interface ipv6 show address** command and a site-local or global address—rather than the duplicate link-local address—is used for neighbor discovery processes.

The IPv6 protocol for the Windows .NET Server 2003 family and Windows XP does not support stateful address autoconfiguration or DHCPv6.

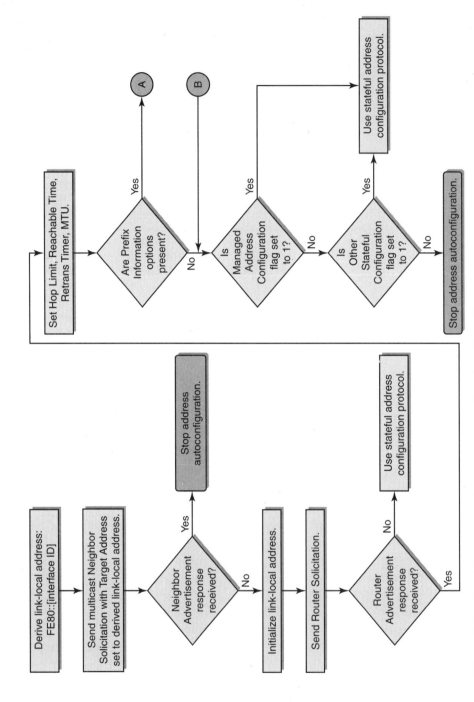

Figure 8-2. *The address autoconfiguration process for a host (Part 1)*

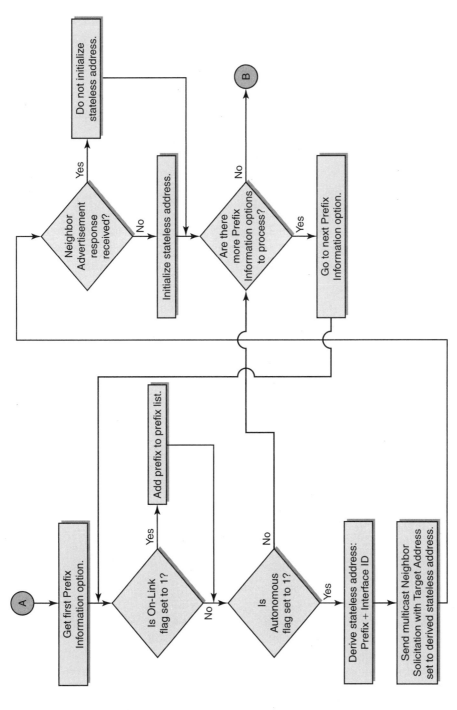

Figure 8-3. *The address autoconfiguration process for a host (Part 2)*

Autoconfigured Addresses for the IPv6 Protocol for the Windows .NET Server 2003 Family and Windows XP

By default, the following IPv6 addresses are automatically configured for the IPv6 protocol for the Windows .NET Server 2003 family and Windows XP:

■ Link-local addresses using EUI-64-derived interface identifiers are assigned to all LAN interfaces.

■ If included as a site-local prefix in a Prefix Information option of a router advertisement, a site-local address using an EUI-64-derived interface identifier is assigned to the LAN interface that received the router advertisement.

■ If included as a global prefix in a Prefix Information option of a router advertisement, a global address using an EUI-64-derived interface identifier is assigned to the LAN interface that received the router advertisement.

■ If included as a global prefix in a Prefix Information option of a router advertisement, a global address using a randomly derived temporary interface identifier is assigned to the LAN interface that received the router advertisement.

■ If public IPv4 addresses are assigned to interfaces of the computer and there are no global autoconfiguration prefixes received in Router Advertisement messages, corresponding 6to4 addresses using 6to4-derived interface identifiers are assigned to the 6to4 Tunneling Pseudo Interface. 6to4 is described in RFC 3056.

■ For all IPv4 addresses that are assigned to interfaces of the computer, corresponding link-local addresses using Intra-site Automatic Tunnel Addressing Protocol (ISATAP)-derived interface identifiers are assigned to the Automatic Tunneling Pseudo-Interface. ISATAP is described in the Internet draft "Intra-Site Automatic Tunnel Addressing Protocol (ISATAP)".

■ If included as a site-local prefix in a Prefix Information option of a router advertisement received on the Automatic Tunneling Pseudo-Interface, a site local address using the ISATAP-derived interface identifier corresponding to the IPv4 address that is the best source to use to reach the ISATAP router is assigned to the Automatic Tunneling Pseudo-Interface.

■ If included as a global prefix in a Prefix Information option of a router advertisement received on the Automatic Tunneling Pseudo-Interface, a global address using the ISATAP-derived interface identifier corresponding to the IPv4 address that is the best source to use to reach the ISATAP router is assigned to the Automatic Tunneling Pseudo-Interface.

■ The loopback address (::1) and the link-local address FE80::1 are assigned to the Loopback Pseudo-Interface.

NOTE:

In order to receive a Router Advertisement message on the Automatic Tunneling Pseudo-Interface, the host must be able to resolve the name "isatap" to an IPv4 address. This is done through normal name resolution mechanisms including DNS and NetBIOS name queries. Once resolved, the host sends a Router Solicitation message encapsulated in an IPv4 header to the ISATAP router. The ISATAP router then sends a Router Advertisement message encapsulated in an IPv4 header to the host.

For more information about ISATAP and 6to4, see Chapter 11, "Coexistence and Migration."

The following is an example of the display of the **netsh interface ipv6 show address** command for a host running Windows .NET Standard Server that received a Router Advertisement message containing the prefixes FEC0:0:0: F282::/64 and 3FFE:2900:D005:F282::/64 on its LAN interface (interface index 3):

```
Interface 3: Local Area Connection


Addr Type  DAD State  Valid Life Pref. Life Address
---------  ---------  ---------- ---------- ---------------------------------------
Public     Preferred     2591813     604613 fec0::f282:201:2ff:fe44:87d1
Anonymous  Preferred      604613      86046 3ffe:2900:d005:f282:ed46:5dd4:5439:2e1c
Public     Preferred     2591813     604613 3ffe:2900:d005:f282:201:2ff:fe44:87d1
Link       Preferred  4294967295 4294967295 fe80::201:2ff:fe44:87d1


Interface 2: Automatic Tunneling Pseudo-Interface


Addr Type  DAD State  Valid Life Pref. Life Address
---------  ---------  ---------- ---------- ---------------------------------------
Link       Preferred  4294967295 4294967295 fe80::5efe:157.54.138.19
```

```
Interface 1: Loopback Pseudo-Interface


Addr Type  DAD State  Valid Life Pref. Life Address
---------  ---------  ---------- ---------- ----------------------------------------
Loopback   Preferred  4294967295 4294967295 ::1
Link       Preferred  4294967295 4294967295 fe80::1
```

Network Monitor Capture

The following Network Monitor capture summary (capture 08_01 in the \NetworkMonitorCaptures folder on the companion CD-ROM) shows the IPv6 traffic for an example interface startup process for a computer running Windows XP.

```
Frame  Time        Source          Destination      Protocol/Desc
1      15.671975   HOST            3333FF234733     ICMP6
       Multicast Listener Report
2      15.671975   HOST            333300000002     ICMP6
       Router Solicitation
3      15.671975   HOST            3333FF234733     ICMP6
       Neighbor Solicitation; Target = fe80::2b0:d0ff:fe23:4733
4      15.671975   ROUTER          333300000001     ICMP6
       Router Advertisement
5      16.171979   HOST            3333FF972C32     ICMP6
       Multicast Listener Report
6      16.171979   HOST            3333FF234733     ICMP6
       Neighbor Solicitation; Target = fec0::f282:2b0:d0ff:fe23:4733
7      16.171979   HOST            3333FF972C32     ICMP6
       Neighbor Solicitation;
       Target = 3ffe:2900:d005:f282:1cfc:d6c6:8897:2c32
8      16.171979   HOST            3333FF234733     ICMP6
       Neighbor Solicitation;
       Target = 3ffe:2900:d005:f282:2b0:d0ff:fe23:4733
9      17.187610   HOST            3333FF234733     ICMP6
       Multicast Listener Report
10     21.672014   HOST            3333FF972C32     ICMP6
       Multicast Listener Report
```

The interface startup process is the following:

■ Frame 1 is an MLD Multicast Listener Report message for the solicited-node multicast address FF02::1:FF23:4733. This solicited-node multicast address is used for all IPv6 addresses that are derived from the EUI-64 address of the network adapter.

- Frame 2 is the initial router solicitation.

- Frame 3 is duplicate address detection on the EUI-64-derived link-local address FE80::2B0:D0FF:FE23:4733.

- Frame 4 is the router advertisement sent in response to the router solicitation (Frame 2). The router advertisement is sent to the link-local scope all-nodes multicast address because the router solicitation (Frame 2) was sent from the unspecified address (::). This router advertisement contains two Prefix Information options—one for the global prefix 3FFE:2900:D005:F282::/64 and one for the site-local prefix FEC0:0:0:F282::/64.

- Frame 5 is an MLD Multicast Listener Report message for the solicited-node multicast address FF02::1:FF97:2C32. This solicited-node multicast address is used for all temporary IPv6 addresses that are randomly derived.

- Frame 6 is duplicate address detection on the EUI-64-derived site-local address FEC0::F282:2B0:D0FF:FE23:4733.

- Frame 7 is duplicate address detection on the randomly derived temporary global address 3FFE:2900:D005:F282:1CFC:D6C6:8897:2C32.

- Frame 8 is duplicate address detection on the EUI-64-derived global address 3FFE:2900:D005:F282:2B0:D0FF:FE23:4733.

- Frame 9 is an additional MLD Multicast Listener Report message for the solicited-node multicast address FF02::1:FF23:4733.

- Frame 10 is an additional MLD Multicast Listener Report message for the solicited-node multicast address FF02::1:FF97:2C32.

In addition to autoconfigured addresses, the IPv6 protocol for the Windows .NET Server 2003 family and Windows XP also supports the manual configuration of IPv6 addresses using the **netsh interface ipv6 set address** command.

REFERENCES

RFC 2462 – "IPv6 Stateless Address Autoconfiguration"

RFC 3056 – "Connection of IPv6 Domains via IPv4 Clouds"

Internet draft – "Intra-Site Automatic Tunnel Addressing Protocol (ISATAP)"

TESTING FOR UNDERSTANDING

To test your understanding of IPv6 address autoconfiguration, answer the following questions. See Appendix D to check your answers.

1. List and describe the states of an IPv6 autoconfigured address.

2. What is the formula for calculating the amount of time an autoconfigured address remains in the deprecated state?

3. How does a router obtain addresses other than link-local addresses?

4. According to RFC 2462, what addresses are autoconfigured for LAN interfaces on hosts when duplicate address detection for the EUI-64-derived link-local address fails? What is the behavior for the IPv6 protocol for the Windows .NET Server 2003 family and Windows XP?

5. A host computer is running Windows .NET Standard Server and is assigned the IPv4 address 172.30.90.65 on its single LAN interface. IPv6 on this computer starts up and receives a Router Advertisement message on its LAN interface that contains both a site-local prefix (FEC0:0:0:29D8::/64) and a global prefix (3FFE:FFFF:A3:29D8::/64). List and describe the autoconfigured addresses for all interfaces on this host.

Chapter 9

IPv6 and Name Resolution

At the end of this chapter, you should be able to:

- Describe the DNS support for IPv6 name-to-address and address-to-name resolution defined in RFC 1886.

- Describe the IPv6 name resolution support provided by the Windows .NET Server 2003 family.

NAME RESOLUTION FOR IPv6

For IPv6, it is more important than ever that names be used to reference network resources rather than addresses. With IPv4, it is hard enough to remember an IPv4 address as a series of four decimal numbers. An IPv6 address can have up to 32 hexadecimal digits. It is unreasonable to expect end users to remember or reliably type an IPv6 address when attempting to access a resource. Therefore, name resolution support for IPv6 addresses is a critically important part of an IPv6 deployment.

DNS ENHANCEMENTS FOR IPv6

In RFC 1886, a new DNS resource record type, AAAA (also known as "quad A"), is used for resolving a fully qualified domain name to an IPv6 address. AAAA records use the DNS record type of 28. AAAA records are comparable to the host address (A) resource records used for IPv4 name resolution. The resource record type is named AAAA because 128-bit IPv6 addresses are four times longer than 32-bit IPv4 addresses.

The AAAA resource record in a typical DNS database file has the following structure:

```
Name    IN    AAAA    Address
```

Where *Name* is the fully qualified domain name and *Address* is the IPv6 address associated with the name. The following is an example of an AAAA resource record:

```
host1.microsoft.com    IN    AAAA    FEC0::1:2AA:FF:FE3F:2A1C
```

To receive IPv6 address resolution data in the DNS query answer sections of the DNS query response, a host must specify either an AAAA query (by setting the Question Type field in a DNS query question entry to 0x1C [28 in decimal]) or a general query (by setting the Question Type field in a DNS query question entry to 0xFF [255 in decimal]).

RFC 1886 also describes the IP6.INT domain created for IPv6 reverse queries. Also called pointer queries, reverse queries determine a host name based on the address. To create the namespace for reverse queries, each hexadecimal digit in the fully expressed 32-digit IPv6 address becomes a separate level in the reverse domain hierarchy in inverse order.

For example, the reverse lookup domain name for the address FEC0:: 1:2AA:FF:FE3F:2A1C (fully expressed as FEC0:0000:0000:0001:02AA:00FF:FE3F: 2A1C) is C.1.A.2.F.3.E.F.F.F.0.0.A.A.2.0.1.0.0.0.0.0.0.0.0.0.0.0.0.0.C.E.F.IP6.INT.

An example pointer (PTR) record is the following (folded for readability):

```
C.1.A.2.F.3.E.F.F.F.0.0.A.A.2.0.1.0.0.0.0.0.0.0.0.0.0.0.0.0.C.E.F.IP6.INT.
    IN    PTR    host1.microsoft.com
```

The DNS support defined in RFC 1886 is a simple way to both map host names to IPv6 addresses and provide reverse name resolution. It is a direct translation of IPv4 name and reverse name resolution techniques to IPv6.

NOTE:

DNS support for IPv6 is also described in RFC 2874, "DNS Extensions to Support IPv6 Address Aggregation and Renumbering." However, elements of this RFC are being designated by the IETF as experimental and are not described in this book.

NAME RESOLUTION SUPPORT IN THE WINDOWS .NET SERVER 2003 FAMILY

Name resolution support for the IPv6 protocol for the Windows .NET Server 2003 family consists of the following:

■ Static entries in the Hosts file

■ DNS Server service support for AAAA records and PTR records in the IP6.INT domain

■ DNS resolver support for AAAA records

■ DNS dynamic update for AAAA records

■ Address selection rules that determine which set of addresses to use for communication

Although DNS queries may result in records for both IPv4 and IPv6 addresses, all DNS traffic is sent as IPv4 packets.

Unlike the IPv4 protocol for the Windows .NET Server 2003 family, IPv6 does not support the Network Basic Input Output System (NetBIOS). Therefore, all of the methods associated with NetBIOS name resolution (the NetBIOS name cache, Windows Internet Name Service [WINS], NetBIOS name broadcasts, and entries in the Lmhosts file) result only in IPv4 addresses.

For more information on the IPv6 protocol for the Windows .NET Server 2003 family and Windows XP support for DNS, see Chapter 2, "IPv6 Protocol for the Windows .NET Server 2003 family and Windows XP."

Hosts File

The Hosts file stored in the *SystemRoot*\System32\Drivers\Etc folder now supports static entries for IPv6 addresses. Each entry must be of the form

```
address      name
```

where *address* is an IPv6 address and *name* is a name associated with the address. The address and name are not case sensitive and must be separated by at least one space or tab character.

The following is an example entry:

```
3ffe:ffff:6c2b:f282:204:5aff:fe56:f62      ipv6test
```

By default, the Hosts file is checked before name resolution using DNS is attempted.

DNS Server Service

The DNS Server service in the Windows .NET Server 2003 family and in Windows 2000 Server supports the manual creation of AAAA static records and DNS dynamic update of AAAA records. For DNS dynamic update, the zones in which records are dynamically updated by DNS clients must be configured to allow dynamic updates. For the Windows 2000 DNS Server service, you must manually configure the zone to allow DNS updates from the **General** tab from the properties of the zone in the DNS snap-in. For the Windows .NET Server 2003 family DNS Server service, you can enable dynamic updates when the zone file is created with the New Zone Wizard.

To manually create an AAAA record for the Windows 2000 Server DNS Server service, you must select **Other New Records** when creating a new DNS record in the DNS snap-in. In the **Resource Record Type** dialog box, click **IPv6 Host** as the resource record type, and then click **Create Record**. You must type the IPv6 address as eight separate text blocks corresponding to the eight hexadecimal blocks of an uncompressed IPv6 address. You cannot use double-colon (::) to compress a block of zeros.

To manually create an AAAA record for the Windows .NET Server 2003 family DNS Server service, you must select **Other New Records** when creating a new DNS record in the DNS snap-in. In the **Resource Record Type** dialog box, click **IPv6 Host (AAAA)** as the resource record type, and then click **Create Record**. You can type the IPv6 address as a single string and use double-colon to compress a block of zeros.

The Windows .NET Server DNS Server service supports DNS traffic over IPv6, including name queries and dynamic updates.

DNS Resolver

The DNS resolver, the DNS client on each host that queries for DNS names and processes the result of DNS queries, now supports the parsing of both A and AAAA records in DNS query responses. The DNS resolver supports queries and responses over IPv6. DNS queries by default are sent using the well-known site-local IPv6 addresses of FEC0:0:0:FFFF::1, FEC0:0:0:FFFF::2, and FEC0:0:0:FFFF::3. You can also manually configure the addresses of your IPv6-enabled DNS servers by using the **netsh interface ipv6 add dns** command.

DNS Dynamic Update

The IPv6 protocol for the Windows .NET Server 2003 family supports DNS dynamic update to automatically register AAAA records over either IPv4 or IPv6 for the following addresses:

- Site-local addresses with EUI-64 and ISATAP-derived interface identifiers.
- Global addresses with EUI-64 and ISATAP-derived interface identifiers.

Global addresses with randomly derived interface identifiers (temporary addresses), 6to4 addresses assigned to the 6to4 Tunneling Pseudo-Interface, the loopback address, and link-local addresses are not registered with DNS.

DNS dynamic update for LAN connections for IPv4 and IPv6 is controlled by the **Register This Connection's Address In DNS** check box on the **DNS** tab from the advanced settings of the **Internet Protocol (TCP/IP)** protocol in the Network Connections folder. This check box is enabled by default.

PTR records for host names in the IP6.INT reverse domain are not registered automatically. You can configure them manually for the Windows .NET Server 2003 family or Windows 2000 DNS Server service by adding PTR records to the appropriate zone file(s) using the DNS snap-in.

Address Selection Rules

After the querying node obtains the set of addresses corresponding to the name by using DNS, the node must determine the set of addresses to choose as the source and destination for subsequent communication. This is typically not an issue in today's prevalent IPv4-only environment. However, in an environment in which IPv4 and IPv6 coexist, the set of addresses returned in a DNS query might contain multiple IPv4 and IPv6 addresses. The querying host is configured with at least one IPv4 address and (typically) multiple IPv6 addresses. Deciding which type of address (IPv4 vs. IPv6), and then the scope of the address (public vs. private for IPv4 and link-local vs. site-local vs. global vs. coexistence for IPv6), for both the source and the destination addresses is not an easy task. Default address selection rules are being investigated and are described in the Internet draft titled "Default Address Selection for IPv6."

By default, the address selection rules for the IPv6 protocol for the Windows .NET Server 2003 family favor the use of IPv6 addresses over IPv4 addresses. You can view the default address selection rules for the IPv6 protocol for the Windows .NET Server 2003 family by using the **netsh interface ipv6 show prefixpolicy** command to display the prefix policy table. You can modify the entries in the prefix policy table by using the **netsh interface ipv6 add/set/delete prefixpolicy** commands. For information on how to set the precedence, the source address label, and the destination address label, see the Internet draft titled "Default Address Selection for IPv6."

REFERENCES

RFC 1886 – "DNS Extensions to support IP version 6"

RFC 2874 – "DNS Extensions to Support IPv6 Address Aggregation and Renumbering"

Internet draft – "Default Address Selection for IPv6"

TESTING FOR UNDERSTANDING

To test your understanding of IPv6 name resolution, answer the following questions. See Appendix D to check your answers.

1. Why is the RFC 1886-defined DNS record for IPv6 name resolution named the "AAAA" record?

2. What is the benefit to using the Windows .NET Server 2003 family DNS Server service over the Windows 2000 DNS Server service when manually configuring AAAA records?

3. A host computer is running Windows .NET Standard Server and is assigned the IPv4 address 172.30.90.65 on its single LAN interface. IPv6 on this computer starts up and receives a Router Advertisement message on its Automatic Tunneling Pseudo-Interface that contains both a site-local prefix (FEC0:0:0:C140::/64) and a global prefix (3FFE:FFFF:A3:C140::/64). List the IPv6 addresses for the AAAA records registered with DNS by this host.

4. Describe the importance of address selection rules for a node running both IPv4 and IPv6 that is using a DNS infrastructure containing both A and AAAA records.

Chapter 10

IPv6 Routing

At the end of this chapter, you should be able to:

- Describe the contents of the IPv6 routing table.

- Explain the end-to-end IPv6 packet delivery process.

- Understand dynamic routing and the routing protocols developed for use with IPv6.

- Describe static routing support in the IPv6 protocol for the Windows .NET Server 2003 family and Windows XP.

ROUTING IN IPv6

Similar to IPv4 nodes, typical IPv6 nodes use a local IPv6 routing table to determine how to forward packets. IPv6 routing table entries are created by default when IPv6 initializes and additional entries are added either by the receipt of Router Advertisement messages containing on-link prefixes and routes, or through manual configuration.

IPv6 Routing Table

A routing table is present on all nodes running the IPv6 protocol for the Windows .NET Server 2003 family and Windows XP. The routing table stores information about IPv6 network prefixes and how they can be reached (either directly or indirectly). Before the IPv6 routing table is checked, the destination cache is checked for an entry matching the destination address in the IPv6 packet being forwarded. If an entry for the destination address is not in the destination cache, the routing table is used to determine:

1. **The interface to be used for the forwarding (the next-hop interface)**
   The interface identifies the physical or logical interface that is used to forward the packet to either its destination or the next router.

2. **The next-hop address**

   For a direct delivery (in which the destination is on a local link), the next-hop address is the destination address in the packet. For an indirect delivery (in which the destination is not on a local link), the next-hop address is the address of a router.

   After the next-hop interface and address are determined, the destination cache is updated. Subsequent packets forwarded to the destination use the destination cache entry, rather than having to check the routing table.

IPv6 Routing Table Entry Types

IPv6 routing table entries can be used to store the following types of routes:

■ **Directly attached network routes**

   These routes are network prefixes for subnets that are directly attached and typically have a 64-bit prefix length.

■ **Remote network routes**

   These routes are network prefixes for subnets that are not directly attached but are available across other routers. Remote network routes can be subnet network prefixes (typically with a 64-bit prefix length) or a prefix for an address space (typically with a prefix length less than 64).

■ **Host routes**

   A host route is a route to a specific IPv6 address. Host routes allow routing to occur on a per-IPv6 address basis. For host routes, the route prefix is a specific IPv6 address with a 128-bit prefix length. In contrast, both types of network routes have prefixes that have a prefix length less than 128 bits.

■ **Default route**

   The default route is used when a more specific network or host route is not found. The default route prefix is ::/0.

Route Determination Process

To determine which routing table entry is used for the forwarding decision, IPv6 uses the following process:

1. For each entry in a routing table, compare the bits in the network prefix to the same bits in the destination address for the number of bits indicated in the prefix length of the route. For the number of bits in the prefix length for the route, if all the bits in the network prefix match all the bits in the destination IPv6 address the route is a match for the destination.

2. The list of matching routes is compiled. The route that has the largest prefix length (the route that matched the most high-order bits with the destination address) is chosen. The longest matching route is the most specific route to the destination. If multiple entries with the longest match are found (multiple routes to the same network prefix, for example), the router uses the lowest metric to select the best route. If multiple entries exist that are the longest match and the lowest metric, IPv6 can choose which routing table entry to use.

For any given destination, the above procedure results in finding matching routes in the following order:

1. A host route that matches the entire destination address

2. A network route with the longest prefix length that matches the destination

3. The default route (the network prefix ::/0)

The result of the route determination process is the selection of a single route in the routing table. The selected route yields a next-hop interface and address. If the route determination process on the sending host fails to find a route, IPv6 assumes that the destination is locally reachable. If the route determination process on a router fails to find a route, IPv6 sends an ICMPv6 Destination Unreachable-No Route to Destination message to the sending host and discards the packet.

Example IPv6 Routing Table for Windows XP and the Windows .NET Server 2003 family

To view the IPv6 routing table on a computer running a member of the Windows .NET Server 2003 family or Windows XP, type **netsh interface ipv6 show routes** at a command prompt. Here is the display of the **netsh interface ipv6 show routes** command for a computer with three network adapters that is acting as a default router for two subnets configured with site-local address prefixes and that has a default route pointing to a default router on a third subnet:

```
Publish  Type       Met   Prefix           Idx  Gateway/Interface Name
-------  -------    ----   --------------   ---  ------------------------
yes      Autoconf     8    fec0:0:0:1::/64    3  Local Area Connection
yes      Autoconf     8    fec0:0:0:2::/64    4  Local Area Connection 2
yes      Autoconf     8    fec0:0:0:3::/64    5  Local Area Connection 3
yes      Manual     256    ::/0               5  fe80::210:ffff:fed6:58c0
```

Each entry in the IPv6 routing table for Windows XP and the Windows .NET Server 2003 family has the following fields:

■ Whether the route is published (advertised in a Routing Advertisement message).

■ The route type.

■ A metric used to select between multiple routes with the same prefix. The lowest metric is the most desirable matching route.

■ The prefix.

■ The interface index indicating the interface over which packets matching the address prefix are reachable.

   The interface indexes can be viewed from the display of the **netsh interface ipv6 show interface** command.

■ A next-hop IPv6 address or an interface name.

   For remote network routes, a next-hop IPv6 address is listed. For directly attached network routes, the name of the interface from which the address prefix is directly reachable is listed.

Routes configured by user applications have the route type of Manual. Routes configured by the IPv6 protocol have the route type of Autoconf. The IPv6 routing table is built automatically, based on the current IPv6 configuration of your computer. A route for the link-local prefix (FE80::/64) is never present in the IPv6 routing table.

The first, second, and third routes are for the 64-bit site-local address prefixes of locally attached subnets. An Ethernet network adapter named Local Area Connection (interface index 3) is connected to the subnet FEC0:0:0:1::/64, a second Ethernet network adapter named Local Area Connection 2 (interface index 4) is connected to the subnet FEC0:0:0:2::/64, and a third Ethernet network adapter named Local Area Connection 3 (interface index 5) is connected to the subnet FEC0:0:0:3::/64.

The fourth route is the default route (prefix of ::/0). The default route matches all destinations. If the default route is the longest matching route for the destination, the packet is forwarded to the IPv6 address FE80::210:FFFF:FED6:58C0 by using the Ethernet network adapter named Local Area Connection 3 (interface index 5).

When determining the forwarding or next-hop IPv6 address from a route in the routing table:

■ If the Gateway/Interface Name column of the route table entry indicates an interface name, then the destination is a neighbor and the next-hop address is set to the destination address of the IPv6 packet.

■   If the Gateway/Interface Name column of the route table entry indicates an address (the address of a neighboring router), then the destination is remote and the next-hop address is set to the address in the Gateway/Interface Name column.

For example, when traffic is sent to FEC0:0:0:2:2AA:FF:FE90:4D3C, the longest matching route is the route for the directly attached network FEC0:0:0:2::/64. The forwarding IP address is set to the destination address of FEC0:0:0:2:2AA:FF: FE90:4D3C and the interface is the interface that corresponds to interface index 4 (the Ethernet network adapter named Local Area Connection 2). When traffic is sent to FEC0:0:0:9:2AA:FF:FE03:21A6, the longest matching route is the default route (::/0). The forwarding IP address is set to the router address of FE80::210: FFFF:FED6:58C0 and the interface is the interface that corresponds to interface index 5 (the Ethernet network adapter named Local Area Connection 3).

END-TO-END IPV6 DELIVERY PROCESS

The following sections describe the process of forwarding an IPv6 packet from the sending host, across one or more IPv6 routers, and to the final destination. This example assumes that the Hop-by-Hop Options, Destination Options, and Routing extension headers are not present.

IPv6 on the Sending Host

The process by which an IPv6 host sends an IPv6 packet uses a combination of the local host's data structures and the Neighbor Discovery protocol. An IPv6 host uses the following algorithm when sending a packet to an arbitrary destination:

1.   Set the Hop Limit field value to either a default or application-specified value.

2.   Check the destination cache for an entry matching the destination address. You can view the destination cache with the **netsh interface ipv6 show destinationcache** command.

3.   If an entry matching the destination address is found in the destination cache, obtain the next-hop address and interface from the destination cache entry. If the destination is a mobile IPv6 node, the destination cache entry may contain a pointer to a care-of destination cache entry. If so, the next-hop address is obtained from the care-of destination cache entry. For more information about IPv6 mobility support, see Chapter 12, "IPv6 Mobility." Go to step 7.

4. Check the local IPv6 routing table for the longest matching route with the lowest metric to the destination address. If there are multiple longest matching routes with the lowest metric, IPv6 chooses a route to use.

5. Based on the longest matching route with the lowest metric, determine the next-hop interface and address used for forwarding the packet.

    If no route is found, IPv6 assumes that the destination is directly reachable. The next-hop address is set to the destination address and an interface is chosen.

6. Update the destination cache.

7. Check the neighbor cache for an entry matching the next-hop address. You can view the neighbor cache by using the **netsh interface ipv6 show neighbors** command.

8. If an entry matching the next-hop address is found in the neighbor cache, obtain the link-layer address.

9. If an entry matching the next-hop address is not found in the neighbor cache, use address resolution to obtain the link-layer address for the next-hop address.

    If address resolution is not successful, indicate an error.

10. Send the packet by using the link-layer address of the neighbor cache entry.

    Figure 10-1 shows the sending host process.

IPv6 on the Router

An IPv6 router uses the following algorithm when receiving and forwarding a packet to an arbitrary unicast or anycast destination:

1. Perform optional header error checks such as ensuring that the Version field is set to 6 and that the source address is not the loopback address (::1) or a multicast address.

2. Verify whether the destination address in the IPv6 packet corresponds to an address assigned to a router interface.

    If so, the router processes the IPv6 packet as the destination host (see step 3 in "IPv6 on the Destination Host" in this chapter).

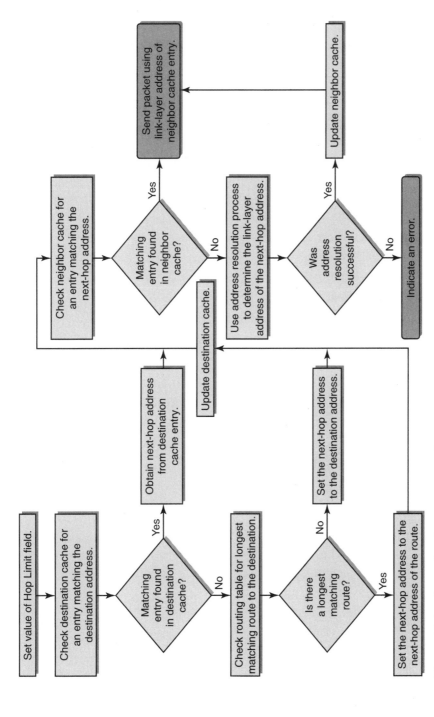

Figure 10-1. *The sending host process*

3. Decrement the value of the Hop Limit field by 1.

If the value of the Hop Limit field is less than 1, the router sends an ICMPv6 Time Exceeded-Hop Limit Exceeded in Transit message to the sender and discards the packet.

4. If the value of the Hop Limit field is greater than 0, update the Hop Limit field in the IPv6 header of the packet.

5. Check the destination cache for an entry matching the destination address.

6. If an entry matching the destination address is found in the destination cache, obtain the next-hop interface and address from the destination cache entry. Go to step 9.

7. Check the local IPv6 routing table for the longest matching route to the destination IPv6 address.

8. Based on the longest matching route, determine the next hop interface and address used for forwarding the packet.

If no route is found, send an ICMPv6 Destination Unreachable-No Route to Destination message to the sending host and discard the packet.

9. Update the destination cache.

10. If the interface on which the packet was received is the same as the interface on which the packet is being forwarded, the interface is a point-to-point link, and the Destination Address field matches a prefix assigned to the interface, send an ICMPv6 Destination Unreachable-Address Unreachable message to the sending host and discard the packet. This prevents the needless "ping-pong" forwarding of IPv6 packets between the two interfaces on a point-to-point link for a packet whose destination matches the prefix of the point-to-point link but does not match the address of either interface. This condition and its solution are described in the Internet draft titled "Avoiding ping-pong packets on point-to-point links."

11. If the interface on which the packet was received is the same as the interface on which the packet is being forwarded, and the Source Address field matches a prefix assigned to the interface, send a Redirect message to the sending host (subject to rate limiting).

12. Compare the link MTU of the next-hop interface to the size of the IPv6 packet being forwarded.

If the link MTU is smaller than the packet size, send an ICMPv6 Packet Too Big message to the sending host and discard the packet.

13. Check the neighbor cache for an entry matching the next-hop address.

14. If an entry matching the next-hop address is found in the neighbor cache, obtain the link-layer address.

15. If an entry matching the next-hop address is not found in the neighbor cache, use address resolution to obtain the link-layer address for the next-hop address.

    If address resolution is not successful, send an ICMPv6 Destination Unreachable-Address Unreachable message to the sending host and discard the packet.

16. Send the packet by using the link-layer address of the neighbor cache entry.

Figures 10-2 and 10-3 show the router forwarding process.

This entire process is repeated at each router in the path between the source and destination hosts.

IPv6 on the Destination Host

An IPv6 host uses the following algorithm when receiving an IPv6 packet:

1. Perform optional header error checks, such as ensuring that the Version field is set to 6 and that the source address is not the loopback address (::1) or a multicast address.

2. Verify whether the destination address in the IPv6 packet corresponds to an IPv6 address assigned to a local host interface.

    If the destination address is not assigned to a local host interface, silently discard the IPv6 packet.

3. Based on the Next Header field, process extension headers (if present) and verify that the protocol for the value of the Next Header field exists.

    If the protocol does not exist, send an ICMPv6 Parameter Problem-Unrecognized Next Header Type Encountered message back to the sender and discard the packet.

4. If the upper layer PDU is not a TCP segment or UDP message, pass the upper layer PDU to the appropriate protocol.

5. If the upper layer PDU is a TCP segment or UDP message, check the destination port.

    If no application exists for the UDP port number, send an ICMPv6 Destination Unreachable-Port Unreachable message back to

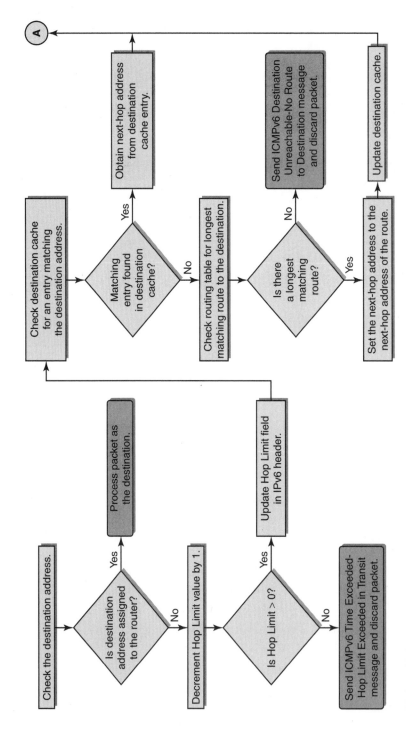

Figure 10-2. *Router forwarding process (part 1)*

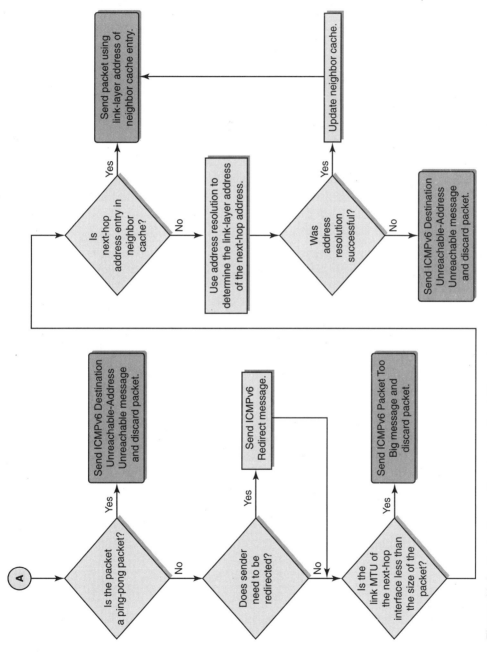

Figure 10-3. *Router forwarding process (part 2)*

the sender and discard the packet. If no application exists for the TCP port number, send a TCP Connection Reset segment back to the sender and discard the packet.

6. If an application exists for the UDP or TCP destination port, process the contents of the TCP segment or UDP message.

Figure 10-4 shows the receiving host process.

IPV6 ROUTING PROTOCOLS

The creation of an IPv6 network consists of multiple IPv6 subnets interconnected by IPv6 routers. To provide reachability to any arbitrary location on the IPv6 network, routes must exist on sending hosts and routers to forward the traffic to the desired destination. These routes can either be general routes, such as a default route that summarizes all locations, or specific routes, such as subnet routes that summarize all locations on a specific subnet.

Hosts typically use directly attached network routes to reach neighboring nodes and a default route to reach all other locations. Routers typically use specific routes to reach all locations within their site, and summary routes to reach other sites or the Internet. Although the configuration of hosts with directly attached or remote network routes and a default route is done automatically with a Router Advertisement message, configuration of routers is more complex. A router can have routes statically configured or dynamically configured through the use of routing protocols.

Static routing is based on routing table entries that are manually configured and do not change with changing network topology. A router with manually configured routing tables is known as a static router. A network administrator, with knowledge of the network topology, manually builds and updates the routing table, entering all routes in the routing table. Static routers can work well for small networks but do not scale well to large or dynamically changing networks due to their requirement for manual administration.

Static routers are not fault tolerant. The lifetime of a manually configured static route is infinite and, therefore, static routers do not sense and recover from downed routers or downed links.

A computer running the IPv6 protocol for the Windows .NET Server 2003 family or Windows XP can be configured as a static IPv6 router.

Overview of Dynamic Routing

Dynamic routing is the automatic updating of routing table entries for changes in network topology. A router with dynamically configured routing tables is

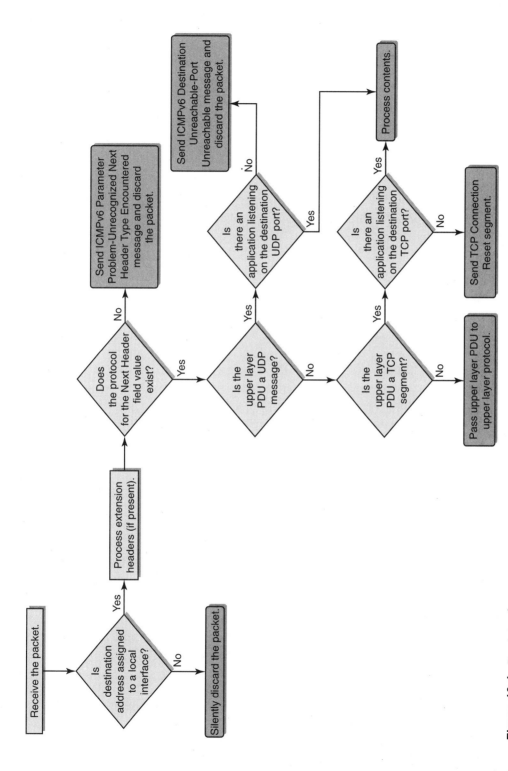

Figure 10-4. *Receiving host process*

known as a dynamic router. The routing tables of dynamic routers are built and maintained automatically through ongoing communication between routers. This communication is facilitated by a routing protocol, which employs a series of periodic or on-demand messages containing routing information that is exchanged between routers. Except for their initial configuration, typical dynamic routers require little ongoing maintenance, and therefore can scale to larger networks.

The ability to scale and recover from network faults makes dynamic routing the better choice for medium, large, and very large networks.

Dynamic routers use routing protocols to facilitate the ongoing communication and dynamic updating of routing tables. Routing protocols are used between routers and represent additional network traffic overhead on the network. This additional traffic can become an important factor in planning WAN link usage.

Some widely used routing protocols for IPv4 are Routing Information Protocol (RIP), Open Shortest Path First (OSPF), and Border Gateway Protocol (BGP).

An important element of a routing protocol implementation is its ability to sense and recover from network faults. How quickly it can recover is determined by the type of fault, how it is sensed, and how the routing information is propagated through the network. When all the routers on the network have the correct routing information in their routing tables, the network has converged. When convergence is achieved, the network is in a stable state and all routing occurs along optimal paths.

When a link or router fails, the network must reconfigure itself to reflect the new topology. Information in routing tables must be updated. Until the network reconverges, it is in an unstable state in which routing loops and black holes can occur. The time it takes for the network to reconverge is known as the convergence time. The convergence time varies based on the routing protocol and the type of failure (downed link or downed router).

Windows XP and the Windows .NET Server 2003 family do not include any IPv6 routing protocols.

Routing Protocol Technologies

Routing protocols are based either on a distance vector, link state, or path vector technology.

NOTE:
The following is a brief explanation of routing protocol technologies. For more details, see the *Internetworking Guide* volume of the *Microsoft Windows 2000 Server Resource Kit*.

Distance Vector

Distance vector routing protocols propagate routing information in the form of a network ID and its "distance" (hop count). Routers use distance vector-based routing protocols to periodically advertise the routes in their routing tables. Routing information exchanged between typical distance vector-based routers is unsynchronized and unacknowledged. The advantages of distance vector-based routing protocols include simplicity and ease of configuration. The disadvantages of distance vector-based routing protocols include relatively high network traffic, a long convergence time, and inability to scale to a large or very large network.

Link State

Routers using link state-based routing protocols exchange link state advertisements (LSAs) throughout the network to update routing tables. LSAs consist of a router's attached network prefixes and their assigned costs and are advertised upon startup and when changes in the network topology are detected. Link state updates are sent using unicast or multicast traffic rather than broadcasting. Link state routers build a database of link state advertisements and use the database to calculate the optimal routes to add to the routing table. Routing information exchanged between link state-based routers is synchronized and acknowledged.

The advantages of link state-based routing protocols are low network overhead, low convergence time, and the ability to scale to large and very large networks. The disadvantages of link state-based routing protocols are that they can be more complex and difficult to configure.

Path Vector

Routers use path vector–based routing protocols to exchange sequences of hop numbers, for example autonomous system numbers, indicating the path for a route. An autonomous system is a portion of the network under the same administrative authority. Autonomous systems are assigned a unique, autonomous system identifier. Routing information exchanged between path vector–based routers is synchronized and acknowledged. The advantages of path vector–based routing protocols are low network overhead, low convergence time, and the ability to scale to very large networks containing multiple autonomous systems. The disadvantages of path vector–based routing protocols are that they can be complex and difficult to configure.

Routing Protocols for IPv6

As of the writing of this book, the following routing protocols are defined for IPv6:

- RIPng for IPv6

- OSPF for IPv6

- Integrated Intermediate System-to-Intermediate System (IS-IS) for IPv6

- BGP-4

- Inter-Domain Routing Protocol version 2 (IDRPv2)

RIPng for IPv6

RIP Next Generation (RIPng) is a distance vector routing protocol for IPv6 that is defined in RFC 2080. RIPng for IPv6 is an adaptation of the RIPv2 protocol—defined in RFC 1723—to advertise IPv6 network prefixes. RIPng for IPv6 has a simple packet structure and uses UDP port 521 to periodically advertise its routes, respond to requests for routes, and asynchronously advertise route changes.

RIPng for IPv6 has a maximum distance of 15, where 15 is the accumulated cost (hop count). Locations that are a distance of 16 or further are considered unreachable. RIPng for IPv6 is a simple routing protocol with a periodic route-advertising mechanism designed for use in small- to medium-sized IPv6 networks. RIPng for IPv6 does not scale well to a large or very large IPv6 network.

RIPng for IPv6 Operation

When a RIPng for IPv6 router is initialized, it announces the appropriate routes in its routing table on all interfaces. The RIPng for IPv6 router also sends a General Request message on all interfaces. All neighboring routers send the contents of their routing tables in response; those responses build the initial routing table. Learned routes are given a 3-minute lifetime (by default) before being removed from the IPv6 routing table by RIPng for IPv6.

After initialization, the RIPng for IPv6 router periodically announces (every 30 seconds, by default) the appropriate routes in its routing table for each interface. The exact set of routes being announced depends on whether the RIPng for IPv6 router is implementing split horizon (where routes are not announced over the interfaces on which they were learned) or split horizon with poison reverse (where routes are announced as unreachable over the interfaces on which they were learned).

Fault tolerance for RIP networks is based on the timeout of RIPng for IPv6-learned routes. If a change occurs in the network topology, RIPng for IPv6 routers can send a triggered update—a routing update, sent immediately—rather than waiting for a scheduled announcement.

For a detailed explanation of RIPng for IPv6, see RFC 2080.

OSPF for IPv6

OSPF for IPv6 is a link state routing protocol defined in RFC 2740. It is designed to be run as a routing protocol for a single autonomous system. OSPF for IPv6 is an adaptation of the OSPF routing protocol version 2 for IPv4 defined in RFC 2328. The OSPF cost of each router link is a unitless number that the network administrator assigns, and it can include delay, bandwidth, and monetary cost factors. The accumulated cost between network segments in an OSPF network must be less than 65,535. OSPF messages are sent as an upper layer PDU using the next header value of 89.

OSPF for IPv6 has the following changes from OSPF version 2:

■ The structure of OSPF packets has been modified to remove dependencies on IPv4 addressing.

■ New LSAs are defined to carry IPv6 addresses and prefixes.

■ OSPF runs over each link, rather than each subnet.

■ The scope of the network for flooding LSAs is generalized.

■ The OSPF protocol no longer provides authentication. Instead, OSPF relies on the Authentication header (AH) and Encapsulating Security Payload (ESP) header and trailer.

OSPF for IPv6 Operation

Each router has an LSA that describes its current state. The LSA of each OSPF for IPv6 router is efficiently propagated throughout the OSPF network through logical relationships between neighboring routers called adjacencies. When the propagation of all current router LSAs is complete, the OSPF network has converged.

Based on the collection of OSPF LSAs—known as the link state database (LSDB)—OSPF calculates the lowest-cost path to each route, and those paths become OSPF routes in the IPv6 routing table. To reduce the size of the LSDB, OSPF allows the creation of areas. An OSPF area is a grouping of contiguous network segments. In all OSPF networks, there is at least one area called the backbone area. OSPF areas allow the summarization or aggregation of routing information at the boundaries of an OSPF area. A router at the boundary of an OSPF area is known as an area border router (ABR).

A detailed explanation of OSPF for IPv6 is beyond the scope of this book. For more information, see RFC 2740.

Integrated IS-IS for IPv6

Integrated IS-IS, also known as dual IS, is a link state routing protocol very similar to OSPF that is defined in International Standards Organization (ISO) document 10589. IS-IS supports both IPv4 and Connectionless Network Protocol (CLNP), the Network layer of the OSI protocol suite. IS-IS allows two levels of hierarchical scaling, whereas OSPF allows only one (areas). Integrated IS-IS for IPv6 is described in the Internet draft titled "Routing IPv6 with IS-IS."

A detailed explanation of Integrated IS-IS for IPv6 is beyond the scope of this book. For more information, see ISO 10589 and the Internet draft titled "Routing IPv6 with IS-IS."

BGP-4

Border Gateway Protocol version 4 (BGP-4) is a path vector routing protocol defined in RFC 1771. Unlike RIPng for IPv6 and OSPF for IPv6, which are used within an autonomous system, BGP-4 is designed to exchange information between autonomous systems. BGP-4 routing information is used to create a logical path tree, which describes all the connections between autonomous systems. The path tree information is then used to create loop-free routes in the routing tables of BGP-4 routers. BGP-4 messages are sent using TCP port 179. BGP-4 is the primary inter-domain protocol used to maintain routing tables on the IPv4 Internet.

BGP-4 has been defined to be independent of the address family for which routing information is being propagated. For IPv6, BGP-4 has been extended to support IPv6 address prefixes as described in RFCs 2545 and 2858. A detailed explanation of BGP-4 for IPv6 is beyond the scope of this book. For more information, see RFCs 1771, 2545, and 2858.

IDRPv2

Inter-Domain Routing Protocol (IDRP) is a path vector routing protocol defined in ISO document 10747. IDRP was originally created for CLNP. Like BGP-4, IDRP is designed to be used between autonomous systems, known as routing domains in IDRP.

The version of IDRP suitable for IPv6 is IDRP version 2 (IDRPv2). IDRPv2 is a better routing protocol for IPv6 than BGP-4 because, rather than using additional autonomous system identifiers (as are used on the IPv4 Internet and for BGP-4), routing domains in IDRP are identified by an IPv6 prefix. Additionally, routing domains can be grouped into routing domain confederations, also identified by prefix, to create an arbitrary hierarchical structure to summarize routing.

A detailed explanation of IDRPv2 is beyond the scope of this book. For more information, see ISO 10747.

STATIC ROUTING WITH THE IPV6 PROTOCOL FOR THE WINDOWS .NET SERVER 2003 FAMILY AND WINDOWS XP

The IPv6 protocol for the Windows .NET Server 2003 family and Windows XP supports static routing. You can configure a computer running Windows XP or a member of the Windows .NET Server 2003 family as a static IPv6 router by enabling forwarding on the computer's interfaces and then configuring it to advertise network prefixes to local hosts.

Figure 10-5 shows an example network using a simple static routing configuration consisting of three subnets, three host computers running Windows XP or a member of the Windows .NET Server 2003 family (Host A, Host B, and Host C), and two router computers running Windows XP or a member of the Windows .NET Server 2003 family (Router 1 and Router 2).

After the IPv6 protocol is installed on all computers on this example network, you must enable forwarding and advertising over the two network adapters of Router 1. Use the following command:

netsh interface ipv6 set interface *InterfaceName*|*InterfaceIndex* **forwarding=enabled advertise=enabled**

where *InterfaceName* is the name of the network connection in the Network Connections folder and *InterfaceIndex* is the interface index number from

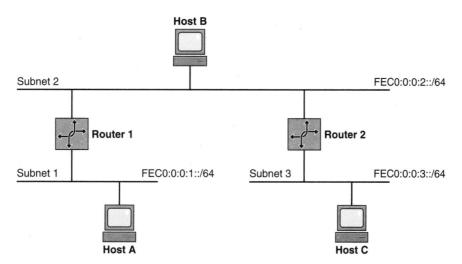

Figure 10-5. *Static routing with the IPv6 protocol for the Windows .NET Server family and Windows XP*

the display of the **netsh interface ipv6 show interface** command. You can use either the interface name or its index number.

For example, for Router 1, if the interface index of the network adapter connected to Subnet 1 is 4 and the interface index of the network adapter connected to Subnet 2 is 5, the commands would be:

netsh int ipv6 set int 4 forw=enabled adv=enabled
netsh int ipv6 set int 5 forw=enabled adv=enabled

NOTE:

Each netsh parameter can be abbreviated to its shortest unambiguous form.

After forwarding and advertising are enabled, the routers must be configured with the address prefixes for their attached subnets. For the IPv6 protocol for the Windows .NET Server 2003 family and Windows XP, this is done by adding routes to the router's routing table with instructions to advertise the route. Use the following command:

netsh interface ipv6 set route *Address/PrefixLength InterfaceName|*
InterfaceIndex **publish=yes**

where *Address* is the address portion of the prefix and *PrefixLength* is the prefix length portion of the prefix.

To publish a route (to include it in a router advertisement), you can specify **publish=yes**, which, in the absence of the **validlifetime** and **preferredlifetime** parameters, advertises the prefix with infinite preferred and valid lifetimes (in the initial release of Windows XP, these infinite lifetimes must be explicitly implemented by specifying **publish=immortal**).

For example, for Router 1 using the example interface indexes, the commands are:

netsh int ipv6 set rou fec0:0:0:1::/64 4 pub=yes
netsh int ipv6 set rou fec0:0:0:2::/64 5 pub=yes

The result of this configuration is the following:

- Router 1 sends Router Advertisement messages on Subnet 1 that contain a Prefix Information option to autoconfigure addresses for Subnet 1 (FEC0:0:0:1::/64), an MTU option for the link MTU of Subnet 1, and a Route Information option for the subnet prefix of Subnet 2 (FEC0:0:0:2::/64). By default, the MTU of the link is advertised.

- Router 1 sends Router Advertisement messages on Subnet 2 that contain a Prefix Information option to autoconfigure addresses for

Subnet 2 (FEC0:0:0:2::/64), an MTU option for the link MTU of Subnet 2, and a Route Information option for the subnet prefix of Subnet 1 (FEC0:0:0:1::/64).

When Host A receives the Router Advertisement message, it automatically configures a site-local address on its network adapter interface with the prefix FEC0:0:0:1::/64 and an EUI-64-derived interface identifier. It also adds a route for the locally attached Subnet 1 (FEC0:0:0:1::/64) and a route for Subnet 2 (FEC0:0:0:2::/64) with the next-hop address of the link-local address of Router 1's interface on Subnet 1 to its routing table.

When Host B receives the Router Advertisement message, it automatically configures a site-local address on its network adapter interface with the prefix FEC0:0:0:2::/64 and an EUI-64-derived interface identifier. It also adds a route for the locally attached Subnet 2 (FEC0:0:0:2::/64) and a route for Subnet 1 (FEC0:0:0:1::/64) with the next-hop address of the link-local address of Router 1's interface on Subnet 2 to its routing table.

Notice that in this configuration, Router 1 does not advertise itself as a default router (the Router Lifetime field in the Router Advertisement message is set to 0) and there is no default route in the routing tables of either Host A or Host B. A computer running the IPv6 protocol for the Windows .NET Server 2003 family or Windows XP will not advertise itself as a default router unless there is a default route that is configured to be published.

To continue this example configuration, the interface index of Router 2's network adapter connected to Subnet 2 is 4 and the interface index of Router 2's network adapter connected to Subnet 3 is 5. To provide connectivity between Subnet 2 and Subnet 3, the commands issued on Router 2 are:

netsh int ipv6 set int 4 forw=enabled adv=enabled

netsh int ipv6 set int 5 forw=enabled adv=enabled

netsh int ipv6 set rou fec0:0:0:2::/64 4 pub=yes

netsh int ipv6 set rou fec0:0:0:3::/64 5 pub=yes

The result of this configuration is the following:

- Router 2 sends Router Advertisement messages on Subnet 2 that contain a Prefix Information option to autoconfigure addresses for Subnet 2 (FEC0:0:0:2::/64), an MTU option for the link MTU of Subnet 2, and a Route Information option for the subnet prefix of Subnet 3 (FEC0:0:0:3::/64).

- Router 2 sends Router Advertisement messages on Subnet 3 that contain a Prefix Information option to autoconfigure addresses for

Subnet 3 (FEC0:0:0:3::/64), an MTU option for the link MTU of Subnet 3, and a Route Information option for the subnet prefix of Subnet 2 (FEC0:0:0:2::/64).

When Host B receives the Router Advertisement message from Router 2, it does not automatically configure a site-local address using the FEC0:0:0:2::/64 prefix, because a site-local address with that prefix already exists. Host B also adds a route for Subnet 3 (FEC0:0:0:3::/64) with the next-hop address of the link-local address of Router 2's interface on Subnet 2 to its routing table.

When Host C receives the Router Advertisement message, it automatically configures a site-local address on its network adapter interface with the prefix FEC0:0:0:3::/64 and an EUI-64-derived interface identifier. It also adds a route for the locally attached subnet (Subnet 3) (FEC0:0:0:3::/64) and a route for Subnet 2 (FEC0:0:0:2::/64) with the next-hop address of the link-local address of Router 2's interface on Subnet 3 to its routing table.

The result of this configuration is that, although Host B can communicate with both Host A and Host C, Host A and Host C cannot communicate because there are no routes on Host A to Subnet 3 and no routes on Host C to Subnet 1. There are two solutions to this problem:

1. Configure Router 1 to publish a route to Subnet 3 with the next-hop address of Router 2's link-local address on Subnet 2 and configure Router 2 to publish a route to Subnet 1 with the next-hop address of Router 1's link-local address on Subnet 2.

2. Configure Router 1 to publish a default route with the next-hop address of Router 2's link-local address on Subnet 2 and configure Router 2 to publish a default route with the next-hop address of Router 1's link-local address on Subnet 2.

In solution 1, Router 1 will advertise two Route Information options on Subnet 1—one for Subnet 2 and one for Subnet 3. Therefore, Host A will add two routes to its routing table—one for FEC0:0:0:2::/64 and a second for FEC0:0:0:3::/64. Router 1 will continue to advertise only one Route Information option (for Subnet 1) on Subnet 2. Similarly, Router 2 will advertise two Route Information options on Subnet 3—one for Subnet 1 and one for Subnet 2. Therefore, Host C will add two routes to its routing table—one for FEC0:0:0:1::/64 and a second for FEC0:0:0:2::/64. Router 2 will continue to advertise only one Route Information option (for Subnet 3) on Subnet 2. The result of this configuration is that all the hosts and all the routers have specific routes to all the subnets.

In solution 2, Router 1 will advertise itself as a default router with one Route Information option (for Subnet 2) on Subnet 1. Therefore, Host A will add two routes to its routing table—one for the default route ::/0 and one for FEC0:0:0:2::/64. Similarly, Router 2 will advertise itself as a default router with one Route Information option (for Subnet 2) on Subnet 3. Therefore, Host C will add two routes to its routing table—one for the default route ::/0 and one for FEC0:0:0:2::/64. The result of this configuration is that all the hosts and all the routers have a combination of specific and general routes to all the subnets, with the exception of Host B, which has only specific routes to all the subnets. The problem with solution 2 is that Router 1 and Router 2 have default routes pointing to each other. Any non-link-local traffic sent from Host A or Host C that does not match the prefixes FEC0:0:0:1::/64, FEC0:0:0:2::/64, and FEC0:0:0:3::/64 is sent in a routing loop between Router 1 and Router 2.

This network of three subnets and two routers can be extended to include more subnets and more routers; however, the administrative overhead to manage the configuration of the static routers does not scale. At some point, you may want to consider the use of an IPv6 routing protocol.

REFERENCES

RFC 1723 – "RIP Version 2"

RFC 1771 – "A Border Gateway Protocol 4 (BGP-4)"

RFC 2080 – "RIPng for IPv6"

RFC 2328 – "OSPF Version 2"

RFC 2545 – "Use of BGP-4 Multiprotocol Extensions for IPv6 Inter-Domain Routing"

RFC 2740 – "OSPF for IPv6"

RFC 2858 – "Multiprotocol Extensions for BGP-4"

Internet draft – "Mobility Support in IPv6"

Internet draft – "Routing IPv6 with IS-IS"

Internet draft – "Avoiding ping-pong packets on point-to-point links"

ISO 10589 – "Intermediate system to Intermediate system intra-domain routing information exchange protocol for use in conjunction with the protocol for providing the connectionless-mode Network Service"

ISO 10747 – "Protocol for exchange of inter-domain routing information among intermediate systems to support forwarding of ISO 8473 PDUs"

TESTING FOR UNDERSTANDING

To test your understanding of IPv6 routing, answer the following questions. See Appendix D to check your answers.

1. How does IPv6 determine the single route in the routing table to use when forwarding a packet?

2. Describe the conditions that would cause a router to send the following ICMPv6 error messages:

    ICMPv6 Packet Too Big

    ICMPv6 Destination Unreachable-Address Unreachable

    ICMPv6 Time Exceeded-Hop Limit Exceeded in Transit

    ICMPv6 Destination Unreachable-Port Unreachable

    ICMPv6 Destination Unreachable-No Route to Destination

    ICMPv6 Parameter Problem-Unrecognized IPv6 Option Encountered

3. A host running the IPv6 protocol for the Windows .NET Server 2003 family or Windows XP is configured with the IPv4 address of 10.98.116.47 and receives a Router Advertisement message from a router advertising itself as a default router with the link-local address of   FE80:: 2AA:FF:FE45:A431:2C5D, and containing a Prefix Information option to autoconfigure an address with the prefix FEC0:0:0:952A::/64 and a Route Information option with the prefix FEC0:0:0:952C::/64. Fill in the expected entries for the host in the following abbreviated routing table.

    ```
    Network Destination     Gateway
    -------------------     -------
    ```

4. What happens when a node running the IPv6 protocol for the Windows .NET Server 2003 family or Windows XP sends a packet and there is no matching route in the routing table? How is this different from the behavior of an IPv4 node?

5. Describe the difference between distance vector, link state, and path vector routing protocol technologies in terms of convergence time,

ability to scale, ease of deployment, and appropriate use (intranet vs. Internet).

6. Why is IDRPv2 a better choice than BGP-4 for the routing protocol to use on the IPv6 Internet?

7. A static router running the IPv6 protocol for the Windows .NET Server 2003 family or Windows XP is configured with the following commands.

> **netsh int ipv6 set int 4 forw=enabled adv=enabled**
>
> **netsh int ipv6 set int 5 forw=enabled adv=enabled**
>
> **netsh int ipv6 add rou FEC0:0:0:1A4C::/64 4 pub=yes**
>
> **netsh int ipv6 add rou FEC0:0:0:90B5::/64 5 pub=yes**

With just these commands being run on the static router, will a host on the subnet FEC0:0:0:90B5::/64 have a default route? Why or why not?

Chapter 11

Coexistence and Migration

At the end of this chapter, you should be able to:

■ List and describe the IPv4 to IPv6 transition criteria.

■ List and describe the different types of nodes.

■ List and describe the use of each type of compatibility address.

■ Describe the mechanisms for IPv6/IPv4 coexistence.

■ List and describe the types of tunneling configurations.

■ Describe configured and automatic tunneling.

■ Describe 6over4 in terms of its purpose, requirements, and addresses used when encapsulating.

■ Describe 6to4 in terms of its purpose, requirements, and addresses used when encapsulating.

■ Describe the features, functionality, and configuration of 6to4 support in Windows XP and the Windows .NET Server 2003 family.

■ Describe ISATAP in terms of its purpose, requirements, and addresses used when encapsulating.

■ Describe the purpose and configuration of PortProxy in Windows XP and the Windows .NET Server 2003 family.

■ List and describe the steps in migrating from IPv4 to IPv6.

COEXISTENCE AND MIGRATION OVERVIEW

Protocol transitions are not easy and the transition from IPv4 to IPv6 is no exception. Protocol transitions are typically deployed by installing and configuring the new protocol on all nodes within the network and verifying that all host and router operations work successfully. Although this might be easily managed in a small or medium-sized organization, the challenge of making a rapid protocol transition in a large organization is very difficult. Additionally, given the scope of the Internet, rapid protocol transition of the total environment becomes an impossible task.

The designers of IPv6 recognize that the transition from IPv4 to IPv6 will take years and that there might be organizations or nodes within organizations that will continue to use IPv4 indefinitely. Therefore, although migration is the long-term goal, equal consideration must be given to the interim coexistence of IPv4 and IPv6 nodes.

The designers of IPv6 in the original "The Recommendation for the IP Next Generation Protocol" specification (RFC 1752) defined the following transition criteria:

- Existing IPv4 hosts can be upgraded at any time, independent of the upgrade of other hosts or routers.

- New hosts, using only IPv6, can be added at any time, without dependencies on other hosts or routing infrastructure.

- Existing IPv4 hosts, with IPv6 installed, can continue to use their IPv4 addresses and do not need additional addresses.

- Little preparation is required to either upgrade existing IPv4 nodes to IPv6 or deploy new IPv6 nodes.

The inherent lack of dependencies between IPv4 and IPv6 hosts, IPv4 routing infrastructure, and IPv6 routing infrastructure requires a number of mechanisms that allow seamless coexistence.

Node Types

RFC 2893 defines the following node types:

- **IPv4-only node**
  An IPv4-only node implements only IPv4 (and is assigned only IPv4 addresses). This node does not support IPv6. Most hosts and routers installed today are IPv4-only nodes.

■ **IPv6-only node**

This node implements only IPv6 (and is assigned only IPv6 addresses). It is able to communicate with IPv6 nodes and applications only. Although this type of node is not common today, it may become more prevalent as smaller devices such as cellular phones and handheld computing devices include IPv6 stacks.

■ **IPv6/IPv4 node**

This node has an implementation of both IPv4 and IPv6. It is IPv6-enabled if it has an IPv6 interface configured.

■ **IPv4 node**

An IPv4 node implements IPv4 (it can send and receive IPv4 packets). It can be an IPv4-only node or an IPv6/IPv4 node.

■ **IPv6 node**

This node implements IPv6 (it can send and receive IPv6 packets). An IPv6 node can be an IPv6-only node or an IPv6/IPv4 node.

For coexistence to occur, the largest number of nodes (IPv4 or IPv6 nodes) can communicate using an IPv4 infrastructure, an IPv6 infrastructure, or an infrastructure that is a combination of IPv4 and IPv6. True migration is achieved when all IPv4 nodes are converted to IPv6-only nodes. However, for the foreseeable future, practical migration is achieved when as many IPv4-only nodes as possible are converted to IPv6/IPv4 nodes. IPv4-only nodes can communicate with IPv6-only nodes only when using an IPv4-to-IPv6 proxy or translation gateway. For more information about support for IPv4-to-IPv6 proxying using the IPv6 protocol for Windows XP and the Windows .NET Server 2003 family, see "PortProxy" in this chapter.

Compatibility Addresses

The following addresses are defined to aid in the coexistence of IPv4 and IPv6 nodes:

■ **IPv4-compatible addresses**

The IPv4-compatible address, 0:0:0:0:0:0:*w.x.y.z* or ::*w.x.y.z* (where *w.x.y.z* is the dotted decimal representation of a public IPv4 address), is used by IPv6/IPv4 nodes that are communicating with IPv6 over an IPv4 infrastructure. When the IPv4-compatible address is used as an IPv6 destination, the IPv6 traffic is automatically encapsulated with an IPv4 header and sent to the destination using the IPv4 infrastructure. The IPv6 protocol for Windows XP and the Windows .NET Server 2003 family supports the use of IPv4-compatible addresses but by default does not automatically configure them.

- **IPv4-mapped addresses**

  The IPv4-mapped address, 0:0:0:0:0:FFFF:*w.x.y.z* or ::FFFF:*w.x.y.z*, is used to represent an IPv4-only node to an IPv6 node. It is used only for internal representation. The IPv4-mapped address is never used as a source or destination address of an IPv6 packet. The IPv6 protocol for Windows XP and the Windows .NET Server 2003 family does not support the use of IPv4-mapped addresses. The IPv4-mapped address is used by some IPv6 implementations when acting as a translator between IPv4-only and IPv6-only nodes.

- **6over4 addresses**

  6over4 addresses are composed of a valid 64-bit unicast address prefix and the interface identifier ::*WWXX:YYZZ* (where *WWXX: YYZZ* is the colon hexadecimal representation of *w.x.y.z*, a unicast IPv4 address assigned to an interface). An example of a link-local 6over4 address based on the IPv4 address of 131.107.4.92 is FE80:: 836B:45C. When the automatic tunneling mechanism defined in RFC 2529 is used, 6over4 addresses are assigned to IPv6 nodes that are connected to an IPv4 multicast-enabled infrastructure. For more information, see "6over4" in this chapter.

- **6to4 addresses**

  6to4 addresses are based on the prefix 2002:*WWXX:YYZZ*::/48 (in which *WWXX:YYZZ* is the colon hexadecimal representation of *w.x.y.z,* a public IPv4 address). When the automatic tunneling mechanism defined in RFC 3056 is used, 6to4 address prefixes are used to create global address prefixes for sites and global addresses for IPv6 nodes within sites. For more information, see "6to4" in this chapter.

- **ISATAP addresses**

  ISATAP addresses are composed of a valid 64-bit unicast address prefix and the interface identifier ::0:5EFE:*w.x.y.z* (where *w.x.y.z* is a unicast IPv4 address assigned to an interface). An example of a link-local ISATAP address is FE80::5EFE:131.107.4.92. When the automatic tunneling mechanism defined in the Internet draft titled "Intra-Site Automatic Tunnel Addressing Protocol (ISATAP)" is used, addresses using ISATAP-derived interface identifiers are assigned to IPv6/IPv4 nodes. For more information, see "ISATAP" in this chapter.

NOTE:
Despite the similarity in names, 6over4 and 6to4 are very different coexistence technologies.

COEXISTENCE MECHANISMS

To coexist with an IPv4 infrastructure and to provide eventual migration to an IPv6-only infrastructure, the following mechanisms are used:

- Dual IP layer
- IPv6 over IPv4 tunneling
- DNS infrastructure

Dual IP Layer

The dual IP layer is an implementation of the TCP/IP suite of protocols that includes both an IPv4 Internet layer and an IPv6 Internet layer. This is the mechanism used by IPv6/IPv4 nodes so that communication with both IPv4 and IPv6 nodes can occur. A dual IP layer contains a single implementation of Host-to-Host layer protocols such as TCP and UDP. All upper layer protocols in a dual IP layer implementation can communicate over IPv4, IPv6, or IPv6 tunneled over IPv4.

Figure 11-1 shows a dual IP layer architecture.

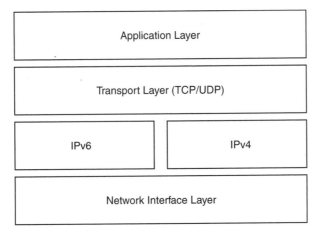

Figure 11-1. *A dual IP layer architecture*

The IPv6 protocol for Windows XP and the Windows .NET Server 2003 family is not a dual IP layer. The IPv6 protocol driver, Tcpip6.sys, contains a separate implementation of TCP and UDP and is sometimes referred to as a dual-stack implementation. Figure 11-2 shows the dual stack architecture for the IPv6 protocol for Windows XP and the Windows .NET Server 2003 family.

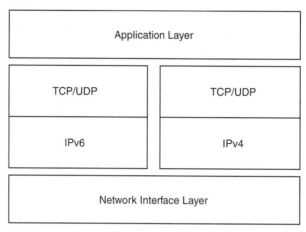

Figure 11-2. *The dual stack architecture for Windows XP and the Windows .NET Server 2003 family*

Although the IPv6 protocol for Windows XP and the Windows .NET Server 2003 family is not a dual IP layer, it functions in the same way as a dual IP layer in terms of providing functionality for coexistence and migration.

IPv6 over IPv4 Tunneling

IPv6 over IPv4 tunneling is the encapsulation of IPv6 packets with an IPv4 header so that IPv6 packets can be sent over an IPv4 infrastructure. Within the IPv4 header:

- The IPv4 Protocol field is set to 41 to indicate an encapsulated IPv6 packet.

- The Source and Destination fields are set to IPv4 addresses of the tunnel endpoints. The tunnel endpoints are either manually configured as part of the tunnel interface or are automatically derived from the sending interface, the next-hop address of the matching route, or the source and destination IPv6 addresses in the IPv6 header.

Figure 11-3 shows IPv6 over IPv4 tunneling.

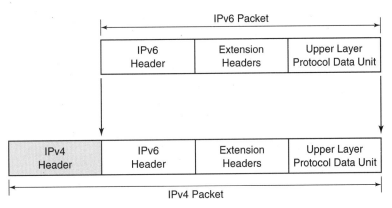

Figure 11-3. *IPv6 over IPv4 tunneling*

For IPv6 over IPv4 tunneling, the IPv6 path MTU for the destination is typically 20 less than the IPv4 path MTU for the destination. However, if the IPv4 path MTU is not stored for each tunnel, there are instances in which the IPv4 packet will need to be fragmented at an intermediate IPv4 router. In this case, an IPv6 over IPv4 tunneled packet must be sent with the Don't Fragment flag in the IPv4 header set to 0.

Network Monitor Capture

Here is an example of an ICMPv6 Echo Request message encapsulated with an IPv4 header as displayed by Network Monitor (capture 11_01 in the \NetworkMonitorCaptures folder on the companion CD-ROM):

```
+ Frame: Base frame properties
+ ETHERNET: ETYPE = 0x0800 : Protocol = IP:  DOD Internet Protocol
   IP: Protocol = IPv6 - Ipv6; Packet ID = 65372; Total IP Length =
  100; Options = No Options
        IP: Type of Service = Normal Service
        IP: Total Length = 100 (0x64)
        IP: Identification = 65372 (0xFF5C)
     +  IP: Fragmentation Summary = 0 (0x0)
        IP: Time to Live = 128 (0x80)
        IP: Protocol = IPv6 - IPv6
        IP: Checksum = 60987 (0XEE3B)
        IP: Source Address = 157.54.138.19
        IP: Destination Address = 157.60.136.82
   IP6: Proto = ICMP6; Len = 40
        IP6: Version = 6 (0x6)
```

```
        IP6: Traffic Class = 0 (0x0)
        IP6: Flow Label = 0 (0x0)
        IP6: Payload Length = 40 (0x28)
        IP6: Next Header = 58 (ICMP6)
        IP6: Hop Limit = 128 (0x80)
        IP6: Source Address = fe80::5efe:9d36:8a13
        IP6: Destination Address = fe80::5efe:9d3c:8852
        IP6: Payload: Number of data bytes remaining = 40 (0x0028)
    + ICMP6: Echo Request; ID = 0, Seq = 17
```

Notice that the Protocol field in the IP header indicates an IPv6 packet. In this example, link-local ISATAP addresses are used to tunnel IPv6 packets across an IPv4 infrastructure. For more information about link-local ISATAP addresses, see "ISATAP" in this chapter.

DNS Infrastructure

A DNS infrastructure is needed for successful coexistence because of the prevalent use of names (rather than addresses) to refer to network resources. Upgrading the DNS infrastructure consists of populating the DNS servers with AAAA and PTR records to support IPv6 name-to-address and address-to-name resolutions. After the addresses are obtained by using a DNS name query, the sending node must select which addresses are used for communication.

Address Records

The DNS infrastructure must contain the following resource records (populated either manually or dynamically) for the successful resolution of domain names to addresses:

- A records for IPv4-only and IPv6/IPv4 nodes
- AAAA records for IPv6-only and IPv6/IPv4 nodes

Pointer Records

The DNS infrastructure must contain the following resource records (populated either manually or dynamically) for the successful resolution of addresses to domain names (reverse queries):

- PTR records in the IN-ADDR.ARPA domain for IPv4-only and IPv6/IPv4 nodes
- PTR records in the IP6.INT domain for IPv6-only and IPv6/IPv4 nodes

Address Selection Rules

For name-to-address resolution, after the querying node obtains the set of addresses corresponding to the name, the node must determine the set of addresses to choose as source and destination for outbound packets.

This is not an issue in today's prevalent IPv4-only environment. However, in an environment in which IPv4 and IPv6 coexist, the set of addresses returned in a DNS query may contain multiple IPv4 and IPv6 addresses. The querying host is configured with at least one IPv4 address and (typically) multiple IPv6 addresses. Deciding which type of address (IPv4 vs. IPv6), and then the scope of the address (public vs. private for IPv4 and link-local vs. site-local vs. global vs. coexistence for IPv6), for both the source and the destination addresses is not an easy task.

Default address selection rules are currently under discussion and are described in the Internet draft titled "Default Address Selection for IPv6."

You can view the default address selection rules for the IPv6 protocol for Windows XP and the Windows .NET Server 2003 family by using the **netsh interface ipv6 show prefixpolicy** command to display the prefix policy table. You can modify the entries in the prefix policy table by using the **netsh interface ipv6 add|set|delete prefixpolicy** commands. By default, IPv6 addresses in DNS query responses are preferred over IPv4 addresses.

Tunneling Configurations

RFC 2893 defines the following tunneling configurations with which to tunnel IPv6 traffic between IPv6/IPv4 nodes over an IPv4 infrastructure:

- Router-to-router
- Host-to-router and router-to-host
- Host-to-host

NOTE:
IPv6 over IPv4 tunneling describes only an encapsulation of IPv6 packets with an IPv4 header so that IPv6 nodes are reachable across an IPv4 infrastructure. Unlike tunneling for PPTP and the Layer Two Tunneling Protocol (L2TP), there is no exchange of messages for tunnel setup, maintenance, or termination.

Router-to-Router

In the router-to-router tunneling configuration, two IP infrastructures—IPv4, IPv6, or mixed—are connected by two IPv6/IPv4 routers over an IPv4 infrastructure. The tunnel endpoints span a logical link in the path between the source and destination. The IPv6 over IPv4 tunnel between the two routers acts as a single hop. Routes within each IPv4 or IPv6 infrastructure point to the IPv6/IPv4 router on the edge. For each IPv6/IPv4 router, there is a tunnel interface representing the IPv6 over IPv4 tunnel and routes that use the tunnel interface.

Figure 11-4 shows router-to-router tunneling.

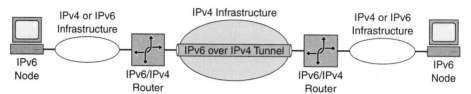

Figure 11-4. *Router-to-router tunneling*

Examples of this tunneling configuration are:

- An IPv6-only test lab that tunnels across an organization's IPv4 infrastructure to reach the IPv6 Internet.

- Two IPv6-only routing domains that tunnel across the IPv4 Internet.

- A 6to4 router that tunnels across the IPv4 Internet to reach another 6to4 router or a 6to4 relay router. For more information about 6to4, see "6to4" in this chapter.

Host-to-Router and Router-to-Host

In the host-to-router tunneling configuration, an IPv6/IPv4 node that resides within an IPv4 infrastructure creates an IPv6 over IPv4 tunnel to reach an IPv6/IPv4 router. The tunnel endpoints span the first segment of the path between the source and destination nodes. The IPv6 over IPv4 tunnel between the IPv6/IPv4 node and the IPv6/IPv4 router acts as a single hop.

On the IPv6/IPv4 node, a tunnel interface representing the IPv6 over IPv4 tunnel is created and a route (typically a default route) is added using the tunnel interface. The IPv6/IPv4 node tunnels the IPv6 packet based on the matching route, the tunnel interface, and the next-hop address of the IPv6/IPv4 router.

In the router-to-host tunneling configuration, an IPv6/IPv4 router creates an IPv6 over IPv4 tunnel across an IPv4 infrastructure to reach an IPv6/IPv4 node. The tunnel endpoints span the last segment of the path between the source and destination nodes. The IPv6 over IPv4 tunnel between the IPv6/IPv4 router and the IPv6/IPv4 node acts as a single hop.

On the IPv6/IPv4 router, a tunnel interface representing the IPv6 over IPv4 tunnel is created and a route (typically a subnet route) is added using the tunnel interface. The IPv6/IPv4 router tunnels the IPv6 packet based on the matching subnet route, the tunnel interface, and the destination address of the IPv6/IPv4 node.

Figure 11-5 shows host-to-router (for traffic traveling from Node A to Node B) and router-to-host (for traffic traveling from Node B to Node A) tunneling.

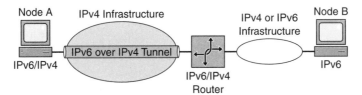

Figure 11-5. *Host-to-router and router-to-host tunneling*

Examples of host-to-router and router-to-host tunneling are:

■ An IPv6/IPv4 host that tunnels across an organization's IPv4 infrastructure to reach the IPv6 Internet (host-to-router tunneling).

■ An ISATAP host that tunnels across an IPv4 network to an ISATAP router to reach the IPv4 Internet, another IPv4 network, or an IPv6 network (host-to-router tunneling). For more information about ISATAP, see "ISATAP" in this chapter.

■ An ISATAP router that tunnels across an IPv4 network to reach an ISATAP host (router-to-host tunneling).

Host-to-Host

In the host-to-host tunneling configuration, an IPv6/IPv4 node that resides within an IPv4 infrastructure creates an IPv6 over IPv4 tunnel to reach another IPv6/IPv4 node that resides within the same IPv4 infrastructure. The tunnel endpoints span the entire path between the source and destination nodes. The IPv6 over IPv4 tunnel between the IPv6/IPv4 nodes acts as a single hop.

On each IPv6/IPv4 node, an interface representing the IPv6 over IPv4 tunnel is created. Routes might be present to indicate that the destination node is on the same logical subnet defined by the IPv4 infrastructure. Based on the sending interface, the optional route, and the destination address, the sending host tunnels the IPv6 traffic to the destination.

Figure 11-6 shows host-to-host tunneling.

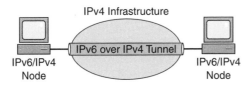

Figure 11-6. *Host-to-host tunneling*

Examples of this tunneling configuration are:

- IPv6/IPv4 hosts that use ISATAP addresses to tunnel across an organization's IPv4 infrastructure.

- IPv6/IPv4 hosts that use IPv4-compatible addresses to tunnel across an organization's IPv4 infrastructure.

Types of Tunnels

RFC 2893 defines the following types of tunnels:

- Configured
- Automatic

Configured Tunnels

A configured tunnel requires manual configuration of the tunnel endpoints. In a configured tunnel, the IPv4 addresses of tunnel endpoints are not encoded in the IPv6 source or destination addresses, nor in the next-hop address of the matching route.

Typically, router-to-router and host-to-router tunneling configurations are configured manually. The tunnel interface configuration, consisting of the IPv4 addresses of the tunnel endpoints, must be specified manually along with static routes that use the tunnel interface.

To manually create configured tunnels for the IPv6 protocol for Windows XP and the Windows .NET Server 2003 family, use the **netsh interface ipv6 add v6v4tunnel** command.

Automatic Tunnels

An automatic tunnel is a tunnel that does not require manual configuration. Tunnel endpoints are determined by the use of logical tunnel interfaces, routes, and source and destination IPv6 addresses.

As defined in RFC 2893, IPv6 Automatic Tunneling is the tunneling that occurs when IPv4-compatible addresses (::*w.x.y.z* where *w.x.y.z* is a public IPv4 address) are used. IPv6 Automatic Tunneling is a host-to-host tunnel between two IPv6/IPv4 hosts using IPv4-compatible addresses.

For example, Host A (with the public IPv4 address of 157.60.91.123 and corresponding IPv4-compatible address of ::157.60.91.123) sends traffic to Host B (with the IPv4 address of 131.107.210.49 and corresponding IPv4-compatible address of ::131.107.210.49). The addresses in the IPv6 and IPv4 headers are as listed in Table 11-1.

Table 11-1. An Example of IPv6 Automatic Tunneling Addresses

Field	Value
IPv6 Source Address	::157.60.91.123
IPv6 Destination Address	::131.107.210.49
IPv4 Source Address	157.60.91.123
IPv4 Destination Address	131.107.210.49

To test connectivity, use the ping command. For example, Host A would use the following command to ping Host B by using its IPv4-compatible address:

```
ping ::131.107.210.49
```

Because IPv4-compatible addresses are defined only for public IPv4 addresses and are not widely used, IPv4-compatible addresses for the IPv6 protocol for Windows XP and the Windows .NET Server 2003 family are disabled by default. Instead, link-local ISATAP addresses can be used to test connectivity of two IPv6/IPv4 nodes across an IPv4 infrastructure. For more information, see "ISATAP" in this chapter.

To enable IPv4-compatible addresses, use the **netsh interface ipv6 set state v4compat=enabled** command. When enabled for the IPv6 protocol for Windows XP and the Windows .NET Server 2003 family, communication to IPv4-compatible addresses is facilitated by a ::/96 route in the IPv6 routing table that uses the Automatic Tunneling Pseudo-Interface (interface index 2). This route indicates that all addresses with the first 96 bits set to 0 are forwarded to their destination addresses using the Automatic Tunneling Pseudo-Interface. The Automatic Tunneling Pseudo-Interface uses the last 32 bits in the source and destination IPv6 addresses (corresponding to the embedded IPv4 addresses) as the source and destination IPv4 addresses for the outgoing IPv4 packet.

NOTE:

In this book, the term "IPv6 Automatic Tunneling" refers to the use of IPv4-compatible addresses. The term "automatic tunneling" is tunneling that occurs without manual configuration, independent of the type of addressing being used.

6OVER4

6over4, also known as IPv4 multicast tunneling, is a host-to-host, host-to-router, and router-to-host automatic tunneling technology that is used to provide unicast and multicast IPv6 connectivity between IPv6 nodes across an IPv4 intranet. 6over4 is described in RFC 2529. 6over4 hosts use a valid 64-bit prefix for unicast addresses and the interface identifier ::*WWXX:YYZZ*, where *WWXX:YYZZ* is the colon hexadecimal representation of an IPv4 address (*w.x.y.z*) assigned to the host. By default, 6over4 hosts automatically configure the link-local address FE80::*WWXX:YYZZ* on each 6over4 interface.

6over4 treats an IPv4 infrastructure as a single link with multicast capabilities. This means that ND processes, such as address resolution and router discovery, work as they do over a physical link with multicast capabilities. To emulate a multicast-capable link, the IPv4 infrastructure must be IPv4 multicast-enabled. Figure 11-7 shows a 6over4 configuration.

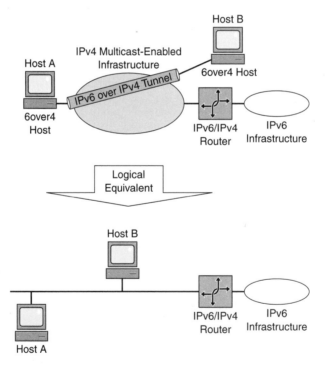

Figure 11-7. *A 6over4 configuration*

To facilitate IPv6 multicast communications over an IPv4 multicast-enabled infrastructure, RFC 2529 defines the following mapping to translate an IPv6 multicast address to an IPv4 multicast address:

239.192.[*second to last byte of IPv6 address*].[*last byte of IPv6 address*]

The following are example mappings for IPv6 multicast addresses:

■ FF02::1 (link-local scope all-nodes multicast address) is mapped to 239.192.0.1.

■ FF02::2 (link-local scope all-routers multicast address) is mapped to 239.192.0.2.

■ FF02::1:FF28:9C5A (example solicited-node multicast address) is mapped to 239.192.156.90.

When 6over4 is enabled, the IPv4 layer uses IGMP messages to inform local IPv4 routers of its interest in receiving IPv4 multicast traffic that is sent to the mapped IPv4 multicast addresses. 6over4-enabled hosts also register additional multicast MAC addresses with their network adapters that correspond to the mapped IPv4 multicast addresses. For example, for an Ethernet adapter:

■ The corresponding multicast MAC address for 239.192.0.1 is 01-00-5E-40-00-01.

■ The corresponding multicast MAC address for 239.192.0.2 is 01-00-5E-40-00-02.

■ The corresponding multicast MAC address for 239.192.156.90 is 01-00-5E-40-9C-5A.

Because the IPv4 infrastructure acts as a multicast-capable link, hosts can use Neighbor Solicitation and Neighbor Advertisement messages to resolve each other's link-layer addresses. The embedded IPv4 addresses in the interface identifier portion of 6over4 addresses are the tunnel endpoints. Hosts and routers can use Router Solicitation and Router Advertisement messages for router, prefix, and parameter discovery. To facilitate ND messages, RFC 2529 defines the format for the Source and Target Link-Layer Address options as shown in Figure 11-8.

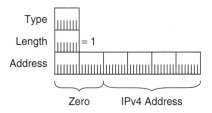

Figure 11-8. *Source and Target Link-Layer Address options for 6over4*

For example, when Host A (with the public IPv4 address of 157.60.91.123 and corresponding link-local 6over4 address of FE80::9D3C:5B7B) sends traffic to Host B (with the public IPv4 address of 131.107.210.49 and corresponding link-local 6over4 address of FE80::836B:D231), the addresses in the IPv6 and IPv4 headers are as listed in Table 11-2.

Table 11-2. EXAMPLE 6OVER4 ADDRESSES

Field	*Value*
IPv6 Source Address	FE80::9D3C:5B7B
IPv6 Destination Address	FE80::836B:D231
IPv4 Source Address	157.60.91.123
IPv4 Destination Address	131.107.210.49

The IPv6 protocol for Windows XP and the Windows .NET Server 2003 family supports 6over4, but it is disabled by default. To enable 6over4, use the **netsh interface ipv6 set state 6over4=enabled** command. This command creates a new 6over4 tunneling pseudo-interface for each IPv4 address assigned to the node. If router advertisements are received over a 6over4 tunneling interface (via the multicast mapping mechanism described earlier), appropriate addresses and routes are configured automatically. When you enable 6over4 with the **netsh interface ipv6 set state 6over4=enabled** command, it creates a 6over4 tunneling interface with a globally unique identifier (GUID)-based name. To create a 6over4 tunneling interface with a friendlier name, use the **netsh interface ipv6 add 6over4tunnel** command instead.

Communication to 6over4 addresses is facilitated by routes and 6over4 tunneling pseudo-interfaces. For example, a host has a 6over4 interface named "6over4 Tunneling Interface" with the interface index of 5. A router advertisement from a router with the 6over4 address of FE80::C0A8:1501 is received. The router advertisement is advertising the router as a default router and contains the auto-configuration prefix FEC0:0:0:21A8::/64. For this example, the host will have the following 6over4-related routes in the routing table:

```
Publish  Type      Met  Prefix               Idx  Gateway/Interface Name
-------  --------  ---  -------------------  ---  -----------------------
no       Autoconf    8  fec0:0:0:21a8::/64     5  6over4 Tunneling Interface
no       Autoconf  256  ::/0                    5  fe80::c0a8:1501
```

A packet addressed to a destination matching the prefix FEC0:0:0:21A8::/64 is sent to the next-hop address of the destination by using the 6over4 Tunneling Interface. The 6over4 Tunneling Interface uses address resolution for the destination address to determine the source and destination link-layer addresses (and corresponding IPv4 addresses) to use when sending the IPv4-encapsulated IPv6 packet.

A packet addressed to a destination matching the default route is sent to the next-hop address of FE80::C0A8:1501 using the 6over4 Tunneling Interface. The 6over4 Tunneling Interface uses address resolution for the next-hop address to determine the source and destination link-layer addresses (and corresponding IPv4 addresses) to use when sending the IPv4-encapsulated IPv6 packet.

To test connectivity using 6over4 addresses, use the ping command. In the example in Table 11-2, Host A would use the following command to ping Host B by using Host B's link-local 6over4 address:

```
ping FE80::836B:D231%5
```

Because the destination of the ping command is a link-local address, the *%ZoneID* portion of the command is used to specify the interface index of the interface from which traffic is sent. In this case, %5 specifies interface 5, which is the interface index assigned to the 6over4 tunneling interface in this example.

NOTE:

Because 6over4 requires an IPv4 multicast infrastructure to work properly, it is not widely used.

6TO4

6to4 is an address assignment and router-to-router automatic tunneling technology that is used to provide unicast IPv6 connectivity between IPv6 sites and hosts across the IPv4 Internet. 6to4 is described in RFC 3056. 6to4 uses the global address prefix:

$$2002:WWXX:YYZZ::/48$$

in which *WWXX:YYZZ* is the NLA ID portion of a global address and the colon hexadecimal representation of a public IPv4 address (*w.x.y.z*) assigned to a site. The full 6to4 address is:

$$2002:WWXX:YYZZ:[SLA\ ID]:[Interface\ ID]$$

RFC 3056 defines the following terms:

■ **6to4 host**

A 6to4 host is any IPv6 host that is configured with at least one 6to4 address (a global address with the 2002::/16 prefix). 6to4 hosts do not require manual configuration and they create 6to4 addresses by using standard address autoconfiguration mechanisms.

■ **6to4 router**

A 6to4 router is an IPv6/IPv4 router that supports the use of a 6to4 tunnel interface and is typically used to forward 6to4-addressed traffic between the 6to4 hosts within a site and other 6to4 routers or 6to4 relay routers on an IPv4 network, such as the Internet. 6to4 routers require additional processing logic for proper encapsulation and decapsulation and might require additional manual configuration.

■ **6to4 relay router**

A 6to4 relay router is an IPv6/IPv4 router that forwards 6to4-addressed traffic between 6to4 routers on the Internet and hosts on the IPv6 Internet.

Figure 11-9 shows 6to4 components.

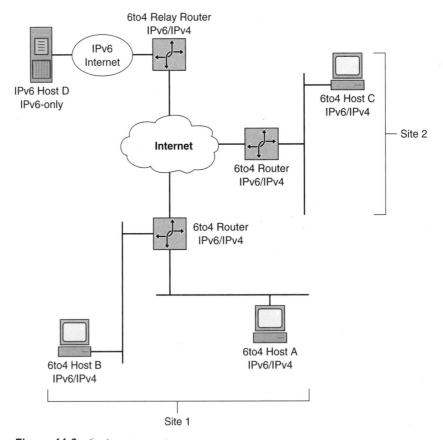

Figure 11-9. *6to4 components*

Within a site, local IPv6 routers advertise 2002:*WWXX*:*YYZZ*:[*SLA ID*]::/64 prefixes so that hosts can create an autoconfigured 6to4 address and 64-bit prefix routes are used to deliver traffic between 6to4 hosts within the site. Hosts on individual subnets are configured automatically with a 64-bit subnet route for direct delivery to neighbors and a default route with the next-hop address of the advertising router. All IPv6 traffic that does not match a 64-bit prefix used by one of the subnets within the site is forwarded to a 6to4 router on the site border.

The 6to4 router on the site border has a 2002::/16 route that is used to forward traffic to other 6to4 sites and a default route (::/0) that is used to forward traffic to a 6to4 relay router.

In the example network shown in Figure 11-9, Host A and Host B can communicate with each other because of a default route that uses the next-hop address of the 6to4 router in Site 1. When Host A communicates with Host C in another site, Host A sends the traffic as an IPv6 packet to the 6to4 router in Site 1. The 6to4 router in Site 1, using the 6to4 tunnel interface and the 2002::/16 route in its routing table, encapsulates the packet with an IPv4 header and tunnels it to the 6to4 router in Site 2. When the 6to4 router in Site 2 receives the tunneled packet, it removes the IPv4 header and, using the 64-bit prefix route in its routing table, forwards the IPv6 packet to Host C.

In this example, Host A (with the interface ID ID_A) resides on subnet 1 within Site 1, and uses the public IPv4 address of 157.60.91.123. Host C (with the interface ID ID_C) resides on subnet 2 within Site 2, and uses the public IPv4 address of 131.107.210.49. When the 6to4 router in Site 1 sends the IPv4-encapsulated IPv6 packet to the 6to4 router in Site 2, the addresses in the IPv6 and IPv4 headers are as listed in Table 11-3.

Table 11-3. EXAMPLE 6TO4 ADDRESSES

Field	*Value*
IPv6 Source Address	2002:9D3C:5B7B:1:[ID_A]
IPv6 Destination Address	2002:836B:D231:2:[ID_C]
IPv4 Source Address	157.60.91.123
IPv4 Destination Address	131.107.210.49

For a more detailed example of 6to4 traffic using ISATAP-derived interface identifiers, see "ISATAP" in this chapter.

When you use 6to4 hosts, an IPv6 routing infrastructure within a site, a 6to4 router at the site boundary, and a 6to4 relay router, the following types of communication are possible:

- A 6to4 host can communicate with another 6to4 host within the same site.

  This type of communication is available by using the IPv6 routing infrastructure, which provides reachability to all hosts within the site. In Figure 11-9, this is the communication between Host A and Host B.

- A 6to4 host can communicate with 6to4 hosts in other sites across the IPv4 Internet.

  This type of communication occurs when a 6to4 host forwards IPv6 traffic–that is destined to a 6to4 host in another site–to the local site 6to4 router. The local-site 6to4 router tunnels the IPv6 traffic to the 6to4 router at the destination site on the IPv4 Internet. The 6to4 router at the destination site removes the IPv4 header and forwards the IPv6 packet to the appropriate 6to4 host by using the IPv6 routing infrastructure of the destination site. In Figure 11-9, this is the communication between Host A and Host C.

- A 6to4 host can communicate with hosts on the IPv6 Internet.

  This type of communication occurs when a 6to4 host forwards IPv6 traffic–that is destined for an IPv6 Internet host–to the local-site 6to4 router. The local-site 6to4 router tunnels the IPv6 traffic to a 6to4 relay router that is connected to both the IPv4 Internet and the IPv6 Internet. The 6to4 relay router removes the IPv4 header and forwards the IPv6 packet to the appropriate IPv6 Internet host by using the IPv6 routing infrastructure of the IPv6 Internet. In Figure 11-9, this is the communication between Host A and Host D.

All of these types of communication use IPv6 traffic without the requirement of obtaining either a direct connection to the IPv6 Internet or an IPv6 global address prefix from an ISP.

NOTE:
Because 6to4 requires only a single IPv4 public address to obtain global IPv6 connectivity, it is likely to be widely used.

6to4 Support in Windows XP and the Windows .NET Server 2003 Family

Support for 6to4 hosts and 6to4 routers is provided by the IPv6 Helper service (known as the *6to4 service* in Windows XP) that is included with the IPv6 protocol for Windows XP and the Windows .NET Server 2003 family. If there is a public IPv4 address assigned to an interface on the host and a global prefix is not received in a router advertisement, the IPv6 Helper service:

■ Automatically configures 6to4 addresses on the 6to4 Tunneling Pseudo-Interface for all public IPv4 addresses that are assigned to interfaces on the computer.

■ Automatically creates a 2002::/16 route that forwards all 6to4 traffic with the 6to4 Tunneling Pseudo-Interface (interface index 3). All traffic forwarded by this host to 6to4 destinations is encapsulated with an IPv4 header.

■ Automatically performs a DNS query to obtain the IPv4 address of a 6to4 relay router on the Internet. You can also use the **netsh interface ipv6 6to4 set relay** command to specify the DNS name to query. If the query is successful, a default route is added by using the 6to4 Tunneling Pseudo-Interface and the next-hop address is set to the 6to4 address of the 6to4 relay router.

The results of the IPv6 Helper service autoconfiguration vary depending on the configuration of the host. Figure 11-10 shows how 6to4 is configured for different types of hosts running Windows XP or the Windows .NET Server 2003 family (except IPv6 Host D).

For a host that is assigned a private IPv4 address and receives a router advertisement for a global prefix, there are no 6to4 addresses assigned to the 6to4 Tunneling Pseudo-Interface. Addresses are autoconfigured based on the global prefix and both a 64-bit global prefix route and a default route being present in the routing table. This configuration corresponds to Host A, Host B, and Host C in Figure 11-10.

For a host that is assigned a public IPv4 address and does not receive a router advertisement for a global prefix, a 6to4 address of the form 2002:*WWXX:YYZZ*::*WWXX:YYZZ* is configured automatically on the 6to4 Tunneling Pseudo-Interface. A 2002::/16 route using the 6to4 Tunneling Pseudo-Interface is added and, if the DNS query for the 6to4 relay router is successful, a default route using the 6to4 Tunneling Pseudo-Interface and the next-hop address of the 6to4 address of the 6to4 relay router is added. This configuration corresponds to Host E in Figure 11-10, a host that is connected directly to the IPv4 Internet. In this case, the host is acting as its own site and its own 6to4 router.

The IPv6 Helper service can also enable a computer running Windows XP or the Windows .NET Server 2003 family to act as a 6to4 router by utilizing the configuration of the Internet Connection Sharing (ICS) feature. This configuration corresponds to the 6to4 routers in Site 1 and Site 2 in Figure 11-10.

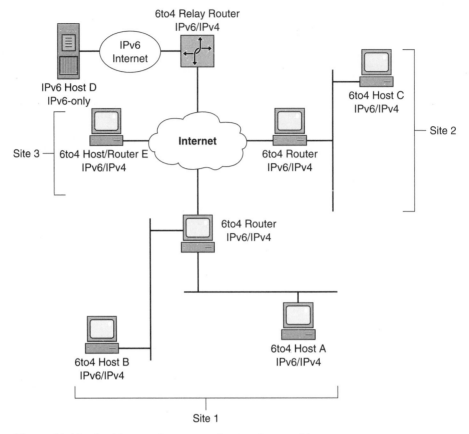

Figure 11-10. *6to4 for Windows XP or the Windows .NET Server family hosts*

If ICS is enabled on an interface that is assigned a public IPv4 address, the IPv6 Helper service:

■ Enables IPv6 forwarding on both the public and private interfaces.
The public interface is connected to the Internet. The private interface is connected to a single-subnet intranet and uses private IPv4 addresses from the 192.168.0.0/24 prefix.

■ Sends Router Advertisement messages on the private interface.
The router advertisements advertise the ICS computer as a default router and contain a global 6to4 address prefix that is based on the public IPv4 address assigned to the public interface. The SLA ID in the 6to4 address prefix is set to the interface index of the interface on which the advertisements are sent.

For example, for an ICS computer using the public IPv4 address of 131.107.23.89 and interface 5 as the interface index of the private interface, the advertised prefix would be 2002:836B:1759:5::/64. Private hosts receiving this router advertisement would create global addresses through normal address autoconfiguration and add a 2002:836B:1759:5::/64 route for the local subnet and a default route with a next-hop address of the link-local address of the ICS computer's private interface. Private hosts can communicate with each other on the same subnet by using the 2002:836B:1759:5::/64 route. For all other destinations to other 6to4 sites or the IPv6 Internet, the IPv6 packets are forwarded to the ICS computer by using the default route.

For traffic to other 6to4 sites, the ICS computer uses its 2002::/16 route and encapsulates the IPv6 traffic with an IPv4 header and sends it across the IPv4 Internet to another 6to4 router. For all other IPv6 traffic, the ICS computer uses its default route and encapsulates the IPv6 traffic with an IPv4 header and sends it across the IPv4 Internet to a 6to4 relay router.

To configure 6to4 parameters manually, use commands in the **netsh interface ipv6 6to4** context.

NOTE:

The IPv6 Helper service is not performing network address translation on the IPv6 packets being forwarded. However, ICS is providing network address translation services on IPv4 packets being forwarded to and from private hosts. The IPv6 Helper service uses the ICS configuration to determine the public IPv4 address and public interface.

ISATAP

ISATAP is an address assignment and host-to-host, host-to-router, and router-to-host automatic tunneling technology that is used to provide unicast IPv6 connectivity between IPv6 hosts across an IPv4 intranet. ISATAP is described in the Internet draft titled "Intra-Site Automatic Tunnel Addressing Protocol (ISATAP)." ISATAP hosts do not require any manual configuration and create ISATAP addresses by using standard address autoconfiguration mechanisms.

ISATAP can be used for communication between IPv6/IPv4 nodes on an IPv4 network. ISATAP addresses use the locally administered interface identifier ::0:5EFE:*w.x.y.z* where:

- The 0:5EFE portion is formed from the combination of an Organizational Unit Identifier (OUI) assigned by the Internet Assigned

Numbers Authority (IANA) (00-00-5E), and a type that indicates an embedded IPv4 address (FE).

■ The *w.x.y.z* portion is any unicast IPv4 address, which includes both public and private addresses.

The ISATAP interface identifier can be combined with any 64-bit prefix that is valid for IPv6 unicast addresses. This includes the link-local address prefix (FE80::/64), site-local prefixes, and global prefixes (including 6to4 prefixes).

Like IPv4-mapped addresses, 6over4 addresses, and 6to4 addresses, ISATAP addresses contain an embedded IPv4 address that can be used to determine either the source or destination IPv4 addresses within the IPv4 header when ISATAP-addressed IPv6 traffic is tunneled across an IPv4 network.

By default, the IPv6 protocol for Windows XP and the Windows .NET Server 2003 family automatically configures the link-local ISATAP address of FE80::5EFE:*w.x.y.z* on the Automatic Tunneling Pseudo-Interface (interface index 2) for each IPv4 address that is assigned to the node. These link-local ISATAP addresses allow two hosts to communicate over an IPv4 network by using each other's link-local ISATAP address.

For example, Host A is configured with the IPv4 address of 10.40.1.29 and Host B is configured with the IPv4 address of 192.168.41.30. When the IPv6 protocol for Windows XP or the Windows .NET Server 2003 family is started, Host A is automatically configured with the ISATAP address of FE80::5EFE:10.40.1.29 and Host B is automatically configured with the ISATAP address of FE80::5EFE:192.168.41.30. This configuration is shown in Figure 11-11.

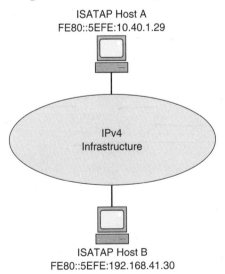

Figure 11-11. *An ISATAP configuration*

When Host A sends IPv6 traffic to Host B by using Host B's link-local ISATAP address, the source and destination addresses for the IPv6 and IPv4 headers are as listed in Table 11-4.

Table 11-4. **EXAMPLE LINK-LOCAL ISATAP ADDRESSES**

Field	*Value*
IPv6 Source Address	FE80::5EFE:10.40.1.29
IPv6 Destination Address	FE80::5EFE:192.168.41.30
IPv4 Source Address	10.40.1.29
IPv4 Destination Address	192.168.41.30

To test connectivity, use the ping command. For example, Host A would use the following command to ping Host B by using Host B's link-local ISATAP address:

```
ping FE80::5EFE:192.168.41.30%2
```

Because the destination of the ping command is a link-local address, the *%ZoneID* portion of the command is used to specify the interface index of the interface from which traffic is sent. In this case, %2 specifies interface 2, which is the interface index assigned to the Automatic Tunneling Pseudo-Interface on Host A. The Automatic Tunneling Pseudo-Interface uses the link-local ISATAP address assigned to the interface as a source, and uses the last 32 bits in the source and destination IPv6 addresses (corresponding to the embedded IPv4 addresses) as the source and destination IPv4 addresses.

Using an ISATAP Router

The use of link-local ISATAP addresses allows IPv6/IPv4 hosts on the same logical subnet (an IPv4 network) to communicate with each other, but not with other IPv6 addresses on other subnets. To communicate outside the logical subnet by using ISATAP-derived global or site-local addresses, IPv6 hosts using ISATAP addresses must tunnel their packets to an ISATAP router.

An ISATAP router is an IPv6 router that performs the following:

■ Forwards packets between ISATAP hosts on a logical subnet (an IPv4 network) and hosts on other subnets.

The other subnets can be other IPv4 networks (such as a portion of an organization network or the IPv4 Internet) or subnets in a native IPv6 routing domain (such as an organization's IPv6 network or the IPv6 Internet).

■ Acts as a default router for ISATAP hosts.

■ Advertises address prefixes to identify the logical subnet on which ISATAP hosts are located. ISATAP hosts use the advertised address prefixes to configure site-local and global ISATAP addresses.

When an ISATAP host receives a router advertisement from an ISATAP router, a default route (::/0) is added using the Automatic Tunneling Pseudo-Interface with the next-hop address set to the link-local ISATAP address that corresponds to the logical subnet interface of the ISATAP router. When packets destined to locations outside the logical subnet are sent, they are tunneled to the IPv4 address of the ISATAP router. The specific IPv4 address corresponds to the ISATAP router's interface on the logical subnet defined by the IPv4 network that contains the ISATAP router and the ISATAP host. The ISATAP router then forwards the IPv6 packet.

For the IPv6 protocol for Windows XP and the Windows .NET Server 2003 family, the configuration of the intranet IPv4 address of the ISATAP router is obtained through the following:

■ The successful resolution of the name ISATAP to an IPv4 address

■ The **netsh interface ipv6 isatap set router** command

Resolving the ISATAP Name

When the IPv6 protocol for the Windows .NET Server 2003 family starts, it attempts to resolve the name ISATAP to an IPv4 address by using normal TCP/IP name resolution techniques that include the following:

1. Checking the local host name.

2. Checking the Hosts file in the *SystemRoot*\system32\drivers\etc folder.

3. Using ISATAP to form a fully qualified domain name and sending a DNS name query. For example, if the Windows XP computer is a member of the example.microsoft.com domain (and example.microsoft.com is the only domain name in the search list), the computer sends a DNS query to resolve the name ISATAP.example.microsoft.com.

4. Converting the ISATAP name into the NetBIOS name "ISATAP <00>" and checking the NetBIOS name cache.

5. Sending a NetBIOS name query to a configured WINS server.

6. Sending NetBIOS broadcasts.

7. Checking the Lmhosts file in the *SystemRoot*\system32\drivers\etc folder.

To ensure that at least one of these attempts is successful, do one of the following:

- If the ISATAP router is a computer running a member of the Windows .NET Server 2003 family, name the computer ISATAP and it will automatically register the appropriate records in DNS and WINS.

- Manually create an ISATAP address (A) record in the appropriate domain in DNS. For example, for the example.microsoft.com domain, create an A record for ISATAP.example.microsoft.com.

- Manually create a static WINS record in WINS for the NetBIOS name "ISATAP <00>".

- Add the following entry to the Hosts file of the computers that need to resolve the name ISATAP:

  IPv4Address ISATAP

- Add the following entry to the Lmhosts file of the computers that need to resolve the name _ISATAP:

  IPv4Address _ISATAP

Resolving the _ISATAP Name for Windows XP

When the IPv6 protocol for Windows XP starts, it attempts to resolve the name "_ISATAP" rather than "ISATAP." To ensure that a computer running Windows XP can resolve the name ISATAP, you can do one of the following:

- Manually create a _ISATAP canonical name (CNAME) record in the appropriate domain in DNS. A CNAME record maps a name that is an alias to another name. For example, assuming that an A record already exists for the name ISATAP.example.microsoft.com, create a CNAME record that maps _ISATAP.example.microsoft.com to ISATAP. example.microsoft.com

- Manually create a static WINS record in WINS for the NetBIOS name "_ISATAP <00>".

- Add the following entry to the Hosts file of the computers running Windows XP:

  IPv4Address _ISATAP

- Add the following entry to the Lmhosts file of the computers running Windows XP:

  IPv4Address _ISATAP

NOTE

Windows XP with Service Pack 1 (SP1) attempts to resolve the name "ISATAP" to determine the IPv4 address of the ISATAP router. The methods described here are not needed if all your computers are running either a member of the Windows .NET Server 2003 family or Windows XP with SP1.

Using the netsh interface ipv6 isatap set router Command

Although the automatic resolution of the ISATAP name is the recommended method for configuring the IPv4 address of the ISATAP router, you can also use the **netsh interface ipv6 isatap set router** command for manual configuration. The syntax of this command is:

netsh interface ipv6 isatap set router *AddressorName*

in which *AddressorName* is either the IPv4 address of the ISATAP router's intranet interface or the name of the ISATAP router to resolve. For example, if the ISATAP router's IPv4 address is 192.168.39.1, the command is:

netsh interface ipv6 isatap set router 192.168.39.1

Regardless of how the IPv4 address of the ISATAP router is obtained, the host sends an IPv4-encapsulated Router Solicitation message to the ISATAP router. The ISATAP router responds with an IPv4-encapsulated unicast Router Advertisement message advertising itself as a default router and containing prefixes to use for autoconfiguration of ISATAP-based addresses.

Network Monitor Capture

Here is an example of the IPv4-encapsulated Router Solicitation message as displayed by Network Monitor (frame 1 of capture 11_02 in the \NetworkMonitorCaptures folder on the companion CD-ROM):

```
+ Frame: Base frame properties
+ ETHERNET: ETYPE = Internet IP (IPv4)
IP: Protocol = IPv6 - Ipv6; Packet ID = 114; Total IP Length = 68;
Options = No Options
        IP: Version = IPv4; Header Length = 20
        IP: Type of Service = Normal Service
        IP: Total Length = 68 (0x44)
        IP: Identification = 114 (0x72)
        IP: Fragmentation Summary = 0 (0x0)
        IP: Time to Live = 128 (0x80)
```

```
        IP: Protocol = IPv6 - IPv6
        IP: Checksum = 4324 (0x10E4)
        IP: Source Address = 157.60.136.217
        IP: Destination Address = 172.31.87.6
    IP6: Proto = ICMP6; Len = 8
        IP6: Version = 6 (0x6)
        IP6: Traffic Class = 0 (0x0)
        IP6: Flow Label = 0 (0x0)
        IP6: Payload Length = 8 (0x8)
        IP6: Next Header = 58 (ICMP6)
        IP6: Hop Limit = 255 (0xFF)
        IP6: Source Address = fe80::5efe:9d3c:88d9
        IP6: Destination Address = ff02::2
        IP6: Payload: Number of data bytes remaining = 8 (0x0008)
    ICMP6: Router Solicitation
        ICMP6: Type = 133 (Router Solicitation)
        ICMP6: Code = 0 (0x0)
        ICMP6: Checksum = 0xF822
        ICMP6: Reserved
```

Notice that the IPv4 address of the ISATAP router is 172.31.87.6. Also note the use of the link-local scope all-routers multicast address in the IPv6 header.

Here is an example of the IPv4-encapsulated Router Advertisement message as displayed by Network Monitor (in the \NetworkMonitorCaptures folder on the companion CD-ROM, frame 2 of capture 11_02):

```
+ Frame: Base frame properties
+ ETHERNET: ETYPE = Internet IP (IPv4)
    IP: Protocol = IPv6 - Ipv6; Packet ID = 34933; Total IP Length =
148; Options = No Options
        IP: Version = IPv4; Header Length = 20
        IP: Type of Service = Normal Service
        IP: Total Length = 148 (0x94)
        IP: Identification = 34933 (0x8875)
        IP: Fragmentation Summary = 0 (0x0)
        IP: Time to Live = 125 (0x7D)
        IP: Protocol = IPv6 - IPv6
        IP: Checksum = 35728 (0x8B90)
        IP: Source Address = 172.31.87.6
        IP: Destination Address = 157.60.136.217
```

```
IP6: Proto = ICMP6; Len = 88
    IP6: Version = 6 (0x6)
    IP6: Traffic Class = 0 (0x0)
    IP6: Flow Label = 0 (0x0)
    IP6: Payload Length = 88 (0x58)
    IP6: Next Header = 58 (ICMP6)
    IP6: Hop Limit = 255 (0xFF)
    IP6: Source Address = fe80::5efe:ac1f:5706
    IP6: Destination Address = fe80::5efe:9d3c:88d9
    IP6: Payload: Number of data bytes remaining = 88 (0x0058)
ICMP6: Router Advertisement
    ICMP6: Type = 134 (Router Advertisement)
    ICMP6: Code = 0 (0x0)
    ICMP6: Checksum = 0xE6CB
    ICMP6: Current Hop Limit = 0 (0x0)
    ICMP6: 0....... = Not managed address config
    ICMP6: .0...... = Not other stateful config
    ICMP6: Router Lifetime = 0 (0x0)
    ICMP6: Reachable Time = 0 (0x0)
    ICMP6: Retransmission Timer = 0 (0x0)
    ICMP6: MTU = 1280 (0x500)
        ICMP6: Type = 5 (0x5)
        ICMP6: Length = 1 (0x1)
        ICMP6: Reserved
        ICMP6: MTU = 1280 (0x500)
    ICMP6: Prefix = fec0:0:0:f28b::
        ICMP6: Type = 3 (0x3)
        ICMP6: Length = 4 (0x4)
        ICMP6: Prefix Length = 64 (0x40)
        ICMP6: 1....... = On-link determination allowed
        ICMP6: .1...... = Autonomous address configuration
        ICMP6: Valid Lifetime = 4294967295 (0xFFFFFFFF)
        ICMP6: Preferred Lifetime = 4294967295 (0xFFFFFFFF)
        ICMP6: Reserved
        ICMP6: Prefix = fec0:0:0:f28b::
    ICMP6: Prefix = 3ffe:2900:d005:f28b::
        ICMP6: Type = 3 (0x3)
        ICMP6: Length = 4 (0x4)
        ICMP6: Prefix Length = 64 (0x40)
        ICMP6: 1....... = On-link determination allowed
```

```
ICMP6: .1...... = Autonomous address configuration
ICMP6: Valid Lifetime = 4294967295 (0xFFFFFFFF)
ICMP6: Preferred Lifetime = 4294967295 (0xFFFFFFFF)
ICMP6: Reserved
ICMP6: Prefix = 3ffe:2900:d005:f28b::
```

Notice that the Router Advertisement message contains an MTU option setting the MTU over the tunnel interface to 1,280 and two Prefix Information options—one for the global prefix 3FFE:2900:D005:F28B::/64 and one for the site-local prefix FEC0:0:0:F28B::/64.

Upon receipt of this Router Advertisement message, a computer running Windows XP or the Windows .NET Server 2003 family and assigned the single IPv4 address 157.60.136.217 will:

- Autoconfigure the addresses of 3FFE:2900:D005:F28B:0:5EFE:157. 60.136.217 and FEC0::F28B:0:5EFE:157.60.136.217 on the Automatic Tunneling Pseudo-Interface.

   If the host had multiple IPv4 addresses assigned, the IPv4 address used in the ISATAP-derived interface ID would be that which is the best source to reach 172.31.87.6, the IPv4 address of the ISATAP router.

- Use DNS Dynamic Update to automatically register the addresses of 3FFE:2900:D005:F28B:0:5EFE:157.60.136.217 and FEC0::F28B:0: 5EFE:157.60.136.217 as AAAA records in DNS (provided that the host has already automatically registered the IPv4 address of 157.60.136.217).

Configuring the IPv6 Protocol for Windows XP and the Windows .NET Server 2003 Family as an ISATAP Router

A computer running the IPv6 protocol for Windows XP and the Windows .NET Server 2003 family can be configured as an ISATAP router. Assuming that the router is already configured to forward IPv6 traffic on its LAN interfaces and has a default route that is configured to be published, the additional commands that need to be issued on the router are:

netsh interface ipv6 set interface 2 forwarding=enabled advertise= enabled

netsh interface ipv6 set route *Address/PrefixLength* **2 publish=yes**

The first command enables forwarding and advertising on interface index 2, the interface index assigned to the Automatic Tunneling Pseudo-Interface. The Automatic Tunneling Pseudo-Interface is the interface on which Router Solicitation messages and traffic to be forwarded is received.

The second command enables the advertisement of a specific prefix (*Address/PrefixLength*) over the Automatic Tunneling Pseudo-Interface. Use this command one or multiple times to advertise as many prefixes as required. All the prefixes configured using this command are included in the Router Advertisement message sent back to the ISATAP host.

If the router is not named ISATAP or the name ISATAP is not resolved to the IPv4 address of the router's intranet interface, you also need to issue the following command on the router:

netsh interface ipv6 isatap set router *AddressorName*

in which *AddressorName* is either the IPv4 address of the router's intranet interface or the name of the router that resolves to the IPv4 address of the router's intranet interface.

For information about how to configure a computer running the IPv6 protocol for Windows XP and the Windows .NET Server 2003 family to forward IPv6 traffic on its LAN interfaces and advertise itself as a default router, see Chapter 10 "IPv6 Routing."

ISATAP and 6to4 Example

Figure 11-12 shows two ISATAP hosts using 6to4 prefixes that are communicating across the Internet even though each site is using the 192.168.0.0/16 private address space internally.

In this configuration:

■ ISATAP Host A automatically configures a link-local ISATAP address of FE80::5EFE:192.168.12.9 on its Automatic Tunneling Pseudo-Interface.

■ 6to4 Router A automatically configures the link-local ISATAP addresses of FE80::5EFE:192.168.204.1 and FE80::5EFE:157.54.0.1 on its Automatic Tunneling Pseudo-Interface.

■ 6to4 Router B automatically configures the link-local ISATAP addresses of FE80::5EFE:192.168.39.1 and FE80::5EFE:131.107.0.1 on its Automatic Tunneling Pseudo-Interface.

■ ISATAP Host B automatically configures a link-local ISATAP address of FE80::5EFE:192.168.141.30 on its Automatic Tunneling Pseudo-Interface.

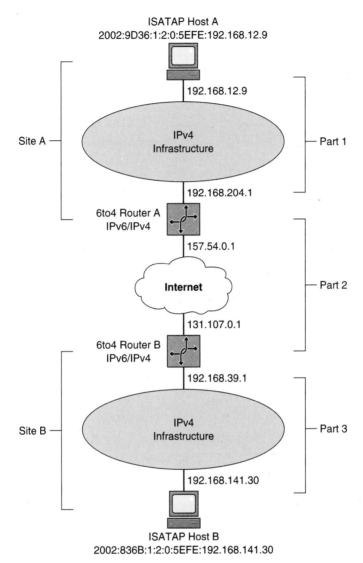

Figure 11-12. *Communication between ISATAP hosts in different 6to4 sites*

ISATAP Host A can reach 6to4 Router A and all other hosts within Site A by using link-local ISATAP addresses. However, ISATAP Host A cannot reach any addresses outside Site A. As a 6to4 router, 6to4 Router A constructs the global prefix 2002:9D36:1:5::/64 (9D36:1 is the colon hexadecimal notation for 157.54.0.1 and 5 is the interface index of 6to4 Router A's intranet interface) and advertises it using a router advertisement on its intranet interface. However,

ISATAP Host A is not on 6to4 Router A's intranet subnet and will never create a global address based on this 6to4 prefix.

To configure ISATAP Host A to receive the router advertisement from 6to4 Router A, the network administrator for Site A has configured 6to4 Router A as an ISATAP router and added an A record to Site A's DNS infrastructure so that the name ISATAP is resolved to the IPv4 address of 192.168.204.1. Upon startup, the IPv6 protocol on Host A resolves the ISATAP name and sends a Router Solicitation message to the addresses as listed in Table 11-5.

Table 11-5. ADDRESSES IN THE ROUTER SOLICITATION MESSAGE

Field	Value
IPv6 Source Address	FE80::5EFE:192.168.12.9
IPv6 Destination Address	FF02::2
IPv4 Source Address	192.168.12.9
IPv4 Destination Address	192.168.204.1

Upon receipt of the Router Solicitation message from ISATAP Host A, 6to4 Router A sends back a unicast Router Advertisement message advertising 6to4 Router A as a default router and with a Prefix Information option to automatically configure IPv6 addresses using the prefix 2002:9D36:1:2::/64 (9D36:1 is the colon hexadecimal notation for 157.54.0.1 and 2 is the interface index of 6to4 Router A's Automatic Tunneling Pseudo-Interface).

The Router Advertisement message is sent to the addresses as listed in Table 11-6.

Table 11-6. ADDRESSES IN THE ROUTER ADVERTISEMENT MESSAGE

Field	Value
IPv6 Source Address	FE80::5EFE:192.168.204.1
IPv6 Destination Address	FE80::5EFE:192.168.12.9
IPv4 Source Address	192.168.204.1
IPv4 Destination Address	192.168.12.9

Upon receipt of the Router Advertisement message, ISATAP Host A autoconfigures the address 2002:9D36:1:2:0:5EFE:192.168.12.9, a default route (::/0) using the Automatic Tunneling Pseudo-Interface (interface index 2) with the next-hop address of FE80::5EFE:192.168.204.1, and a 2002:9D36:1:2::/64 route using the Automatic Tunneling Pseudo-Interface.

Similarly, 6to4 Router B is configured as an ISATAP router and Site B has an appropriate A record in its DNS infrastructure so that ISATAP Host B autoconfigures the address 2002:836B:1:2:0:5EFE:192.168.141.30 (836B:1 is the colon hexadecimal notation for 131.107.0.1), a default route (::/0) using the Automatic Tunneling Pseudo-Interface (interface index 2) with the next-hop address of FE80::5EFE:192.168.39.1, and a 2002:836B:1:2::/64 route using the Automatic Tunneling Pseudo-Interface.

ISATAP Host A can now send a packet to ISATAP Host B. Let's examine the packet addressing in three parts (as shown in Figure 11-12) during its trip from ISATAP Host A to ISATAP Host B.

Part 1: From ISATAP Host A to 6to4 Router A

When ISATAP Host A sends the IPv6 packet, it sends it with the ::/0 route that uses the Automatic Tunneling Pseudo-Interface to the next-hop address of FE80::5EFE:192.168.204.1. By using this route, the next-hop address for this packet is set to the link-local ISATAP address of 6to4 Router A (FE80::5EFE: 192.168.204.1).

Using the Automatic Tunneling Pseudo-Interface, the packet is tunneled by using IPv4 from the IPv4 address assigned to its intranet interface (192.168.12.9) to the embedded IPv4 address in the ISATAP interface ID of the next-hop address (192.168.204.1). The resulting addresses are listed in Table 11-7.

Table 11-7. ADDRESSES IN PART 1

Field	Value
IPv6 Source Address	2002:9D36:1:2:0:5EFE:192.168.12.9
IPv6 Destination Address	2002:836B:1:2:0:5EFE:192.168.141.30
IPv4 Source Address	192.168.12.9
IPv4 Destination Address	192.168.204.1

Part 2: From 6to4 Router A to 6to4 Router B

6to4 Router A receives the IPv4 packet and removes the IPv4 header. When 6to4 Router A forwards the IPv6 packet, it forwards it with the 2002::/16 route that uses the 6to4 Tunneling Pseudo-Interface. By using this route, the next-hop address for this packet is set to the destination address (2002:836B:1:2:0:5EFE: 192.168.141.30).

Using the 6to4 Tunneling Pseudo-Interface, the packet is tunneled by using IPv4 from the IPv4 address assigned to its Internet interface (157.54.0.1) to the embedded IPv4 address in the 6to4 NLA ID of the next-hop address (131.107.0.1). The resulting addresses are listed in Table 11-8.

Table 11-8. ADDRESSES IN PART 2

Field	Value
IPv6 Source Address	2002:9D36:1:2:0:5EFE:192.168.12.9
IPv6 Destination Address	2002:836B:1:2:0:5EFE:192.168.141.30
IPv4 Source Address	157.54.0.1
IPv4 Destination Address	131.107.0.1

Part 3: From 6to4 Router B to ISATAP Host B

6to4 Router B receives the IPv4 packet and removes the IPv4 header. When 6to4 Router B forwards the IPv6 packet, it forwards it with the 2002:836B:1:2::/64 route that uses its Automatic Tunneling Pseudo-Interface. By using this route, the next-hop address for this packet is set to the destination address (2002:836B:1:2:0:5EFE:192.168.141.30).

Because the Automatic Tunneling Pseudo-Interface is used to forward the packet, the packet is tunneled by using IPv4 from the IPv4 address assigned to its intranet interface (192.168.39.1) to the embedded IPv4 address in the ISATAP interface ID of the next-hop IPv6 address (192.168.141.30). The resulting addresses are listed in Table 11-9.

Table 11-9. ADDRESSES IN PART 3

Field	Value
IPv6 Source Address	2002:9D36:1:2:0:5EFE:192.168.12.9
IPv6 Destination Address	2002:836B:1:2:0:5EFE:192.168.141.30
IPv4 Source Address	192.168.39.1
IPv4 Destination Address	192.168.141.30

PORTPROXY

To facilitate the communication between nodes or applications that cannot connect using a common Internet layer protocol (IPv4 or IPv6), the IPv6 protocol for Windows XP and the Windows .NET Server 2003 family provides PortProxy, a component that allows the proxying of the following traffic:

■ **IPv4 to IPv4**

Traffic to an IPv4 address is proxied to TCP traffic to another IPv4 address.

- **IPv4 to IPv6**

  Traffic to an IPv4 address is proxied to TCP traffic to an IPv6 address.

- **IPv6 to IPv6**

  Traffic to an IPv6 address is proxied to TCP traffic to another IPv6 address.

- **IPv6 to IPv4**

  Traffic to an IPv6 address is proxied to TCP traffic to an IPv4 address.

The most interesting and useful proxying for IPv6/IPv4 coexistence and migration is from IPv4 to IPv6 and from IPv6 to IPv4. For coexistence and migration, PortProxy enables the following scenarios:

- **An IPv4-only node can access an IPv6-only node.**

  In the IPv4 DNS infrastructure of the IPv4-only node, the name of the IPv6-only node resolves to an IPv4 address assigned to an interface of the PortProxy computer. (This might require manual configuration of an A record in the DNS.) The PortProxy computer is configured to proxy IPv4 to IPv6. All TCP traffic sent by the IPv4-only node is proxied in a manner similar to Internet proxy servers: the IPv4-only node establishes a TCP connection with the PortProxy computer and the PortProxy computer establishes a separate TCP connection with the IPv6-only node. The TCP connection data is transferred between the IPv4-only node and the IPv6-only node by PortProxy.

- **An IPv6-only node can access an IPv4-only node.**

  In the IPv6 DNS infrastructure of the IPv6-only node, the name of the IPv4-only node resolves to an IPv6 address assigned to an interface of the PortProxy computer. (This might require manual configuration of AAAA records in the DNS.) The PortProxy computer is configured to proxy IPv6 to IPv4. TCP traffic sent by the IPv6-only node to the PortProxy computer is proxied to the IPv4-only node.

- **An IPv6 node can access an IPv4-only service running on an IPv6/IPv4 node.**

  In the IPv6 DNS infrastructure of the IPv6-only node, the name of the IPv6/IPv4 node resolves to an IPv6 address assigned to an interface of the PortProxy computer. The PortProxy computer is configured to proxy from IPv6 to IPv4 on the PortProxy computer. TCP traffic sent by the IPv6 node to the PortProxy computer is

297

proxied to an IPv4-only service or application running on the PortProxy computer.

Notice that the default DNS behavior of the IIS server (an IPv6/IPv4 node) is to dynamically register both its IPv6 and IPv4 addresses in the DNS. The default behavior of a computer running Windows XP or a member of the Windows .NET Server 2003 family is to query the DNS for all record types, preferring the use of IPv6 addresses over IPv4 addresses. When the Web client is a computer running Windows XP or a member of the Windows .NET Server 2003 family, it attempts to connect using IPv6 first. With PortProxy properly configured on the IIS server, the first attempt to connect using an IPv6 address of the IIS server should be successful without manual configuration of DNS records.

To configure the PortProxy component, use the **netsh interface portproxy add | set | delete v4tov4 | v4tov6 | v6tov4 | v6tov6** commands. For example, the syntax for the **netsh interface portproxy add v6tov4** command is:

netsh interface portproxy add v6tov4
[**listenport=**]*LPortNumber* | *LPortName*
[[**connectaddress=**]*IPv4Address* | *IPv4HostName*]
[[**connectport=**]*CPortNumber* | *CPortName*]
[[**listenaddress=**]*IPv6Address* | *IPv6HostName*]

in which *LPortNumber* | *LPortName* is the TCP port number or service name on which PortProxy is listening, *IPv6Address* | *IPv6HostName* is the IPv6 address or host name on which PortProxy is listening (if unspecified, all IPv6 addresses assigned to the PortProxy computer are assumed), *CPortNumber* | *CPortName* is the TCP port number or service name that PortProxy attempts to connect to (if unspecified, the connect port is set to the same port as the listening port), and *IPv4Address* | *IPv4HostName* is the IPv4 address or host name that PortProxy attempts to connect to (if unspecified, the loopback address is assumed).

NOTE:

PortProxy works only for TCP traffic (at the time of this writing) and for application-layer protocols that do not embed address or port information inside the upper-layer PDU. Unlike NATs, there are no equivalents to NAT editors for PortProxy. An example of a protocol that will not work across a PortProxy computer is FTP, which embeds IPv4 addresses when using the FTP Port command.

MIGRATING TO IPV6

To be sure, the migration of IPv4 to IPv6 will be a long process and some details of migration have yet to be determined. As a general methodology, to migrate from IPv4 to IPv6 you must perform the following steps:

1. Upgrade your applications to be independent of any specific version of IP.

   Windows Sockets applications must be changed to use new application programming interfaces (APIs) so that name resolution and socket creation is independent of whether IPv4 or IPv6 is being used. For more information about Windows Sockets API changes, see Appendix B.

2. Update the DNS infrastructure to support IPv6 addresses and PTR records.

   The DNS infrastructure might need to be upgraded to support the new AAAA records (required) and PTR records in the IP6.INT reverse domain (optional).

3. Upgrade hosts to IPv6/IPv4 nodes.

   Hosts must be upgraded to use a dual IP layer or dual IP stack. DNS resolver support must also be added to process DNS query results that contain both IPv4 and IPv6 addresses

4. Upgrade routing infrastructure for native IPv6 routing.

   Routers must be upgraded to support native IPv6 routing and IPv6 routing protocols. For more information on IPv6 routing protocols, see Chapter 10, "IPv6 Routing."

5. Convert IPv6/IPv4 nodes to IPv6-only nodes.

   IPv6/IPv4 nodes can be upgraded to be IPv6-only nodes. This should be a long-term goal because it will take years for all current IPv4-only network devices to be upgraded to IPv6-only. For those IPv4-only nodes that cannot be upgraded to IPv6/IPv4 or IPv6-only, employ translation gateways or proxies as appropriate so that IPv4-only nodes can communicate with IPv6-only nodes.

REFERENCES

RFC 1752 – "The Recommendation for the IP Next Generation Protocol"

RFC 2529 – "Transmission of IPv6 over IPv4 Domains without Explicit Tunnels"

RFC 2893 – "Transition Mechanisms for IPv6 Hosts and Routers"

RFC 3056 – "Connection of IPv6 Domains via IPv4 Clouds"

Internet draft – "Intra-Site Automatic Tunnel Addressing Protocol (ISATAP)"

Internet draft – "Default Address Selection for IPv6"

TESTING FOR UNDERSTANDING

To test your understanding of IPv6/IPv4 coexistence and migration, answer the following questions. See Appendix D to check your answers.

1. Describe the difference between migration and coexistence.

2. Why do the criteria for the IPv4-to-IPv6 transition require no dependencies between IPv4 and IPv6 hosts, addresses, and routing infrastructure?

3. How does an IPv4-only host communicate with an IPv6-only host?

4. What is the difference between an IPv4-compatible address and an IPv4-mapped address?

5. Is the IPv6 protocol for Windows XP and the Windows .NET Server 2003 family a dual IP layer? Why or why not?

6. How are the source and destination addresses in the IPv4 header determined for IPv6 over IPv4 tunnel traffic?

7. Describe the components of the 6to4 address and how the address is mapped to an IPv4 address when forwarded across an IPv4 infrastructure by a 6to4 router using the 2002::/16 route.

8. What is the public IP address of the 6to4 router that is being used as a site border router for the ISATAP host with the address 2002:9D3C:2B5A:5:0:5EFE:131.107.24.103?

9. Describe how 6to4 and ISATAP can be used together.

10. For a 6over4 host using an Ethernet adapter, describe how the joining of an IPv6 multicast group on all interfaces creates two multicast entries in the table of interesting destination MAC addresses on the Ethernet adapter.

11. A common misconception is that ISPs must support native IPv6 routing in order to use IPv6. Describe why this is a misconception.

Chapter 12

IPv6 Mobility

At the end of this chapter, you should be able to:

- Describe how IPv6 mobility provides application transparency for communication to and from mobile nodes when they are away from home.

- List and describe the components of IPv6 mobility.

- List and describe the IPv6 mobility messages and options.

- Describe the information contained in the IPv6 mobility data structures.

- Describe the details of the communication between the mobile node and the correspondent node.

- Describe the details of the communication between the mobile node and the home agent.

- Describe the details of the following IPv6 mobility processes: attaching to the home link, moving from a home link to a foreign link, moving to a different foreign link, and returning home.

- Describe how IPv6 mobility changes the host sending and receiving algorithms.

NOTE:
The discussion of IPv6 mobility in this chapter is based on draft 13 of the Internet draft titled "Mobility Support in IPv6" (draft-ietf-mobileip-ipv6-13.txt in the \RFCs_and_Drafts folder on the companion CD-ROM).

IPv6 MOBILITY OVERVIEW

IPv6 mobility allows an IPv6 node to be mobile—to arbitrarily change its location on the IPv6 Internet—and still maintain existing connections. When an IPv6 node changes its location, it might also change its link. When an IPv6 node changes its link, its IPv6 address must also change in order to maintain reachability. There are mechanisms to allow for the change in addresses when moving to a different link, such as stateful and stateless address autoconfiguration for IPv6. However, these mechanisms ungracefully terminate all the existing connections of the mobile node that are using the address assigned when it was on the previous link.

The key benefit of IPv6 mobility is that, even though the mobile node is changing locations and addresses, the existing connections through which the mobile node is communicating are maintained. Connection maintenance for mobile nodes is not done by modifying connection-oriented protocols such as TCP, but by handling the change of addresses at the Internet layer. Transport-layer protocols are completely unaware that the address of the mobile node has changed. A connection is established with a specific address assigned to the mobile node and remains connected no matter how many times the mobile node changes its location and address.

IPv6 Mobility Components

IPv6 mobility consists of the following components, as shown in Figure 12-1.

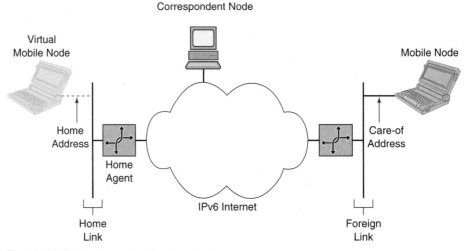

Figure 12-1. *Components of IPv6 mobility*

- Home link
  The home link is the link that is assigned the home subnet prefix. The mobile node uses the home subnet prefix to create a home address.

- Home address
  A home address is an address assigned to the mobile node when it is attached to the home link and through which the mobile node is

always reachable, regardless of its location on the IPv6 Internet. Packets addressed to addresses matching the home subnet prefix are delivered to the home link using normal IPv6 routing processes. If the mobile node is attached to the home link, IPv6 mobility processes are not used and communication occurs normally. If the mobile node is away from home (not attached to the home link), IPv6 mobility processes are used to either deliver or tunnel traffic addressed to the mobile node's home address to its current location on the IPv6 Internet. Because the mobile node is always assigned the home address, it always has a virtual connection to the home link. This relationship is shown in Figure 12-1 as the Virtual Mobile Node.

■ Home agent
The home agent is a router on the home link that maintains an awareness of the mobile nodes of its home link that are away from home and the addresses that they are currently using. If the mobile node is on the home link, the home agent acts as an IPv6 router, forwarding packets addressed to the mobile node. If the mobile node is away from home, the home agent tunnels data sent to the mobile node's home address to the mobile node's current location on the IPv6 Internet.

■ Mobile node
A mobile node is an IPv6 node that can change links, and therefore addresses, and maintain reachability using its home address. A mobile node has awareness of its home address and the global address of its current link address, and indicates its home address/ current link address mapping to the home agent and IPv6 nodes with which it is communicating.

■ Foreign link
A foreign link is a link that is not the mobile node's home link. A foreign link is assigned a foreign subnet prefix.

■ Care-of address
A care-of address is an address used by a mobile node while it is attached to a foreign link. The care-of address is a combination of the foreign subnet prefix and an interface ID determined by the mobile node. A mobile node can be assigned multiple care-of addresses; however, only one care-of address is registered as the primary care-of address with the mobile node's home agent. The association of a care-of address with a home address for a mobile node is known as a *binding*. Correspondent nodes and home agents keep information on bindings in a binding cache.

- Correspondent node
A correspondent node is an IPv6 node that is capable of communicating with a mobile node while it is away from home. A correspondent node can also be a mobile node.

NOTE:

The drawings in this chapter assume that the common IPv6 infrastructure is the IPv6 Internet. However, all of the IPv6 mobility components, messages, and processes also work if the IPv6 nodes are separated by an IPv4 infrastructure (such as the Internet) and are using a coexistence technology (such as 6to4) to achieve IPv6 connectivity.

To achieve Application layer transparency for the home address while the mobile node is assigned a care-of address, the following is used:

- When the mobile node sends data to a correspondent node, the packet is sent from the care-of address and includes the mobile node's home address in a Home Address option in a Destination Options extension header. When the correspondent node receives the packet, it logically replaces the source address of the packet (the care-of address) with the home address stored in the Home Address option. The Home Address option is described later in this chapter.

- When the correspondent node sends data to the mobile node, the packet is sent to the care-of address and includes a Routing extension header containing a single address, the mobile node's home address. When the mobile node receives the packet, it processes the Routing header and logically replaces the destination address of the packet (the care-of address) with the home address from the Routing header.

For IPv6 nodes, there are the following levels of correspondent node support:

- None
If an IPv6 node has no correspondent node support, then it will be unable to communicate with mobile nodes that are away from home. Packets sent by a mobile node that is away from home always contain a Destination Options header with the Home Address option. The Home Address option uses the Option Type of 201. For this option type, the two high-order bits are set to 11 (binary), which means that if the receiving host does not recognize the option, then

it sends back an ICMPv6 Parameter Problem-Unrecognized IPv6 Option Encountered message to the sender and discards the packet. Therefore, a node that has no correspondent node support does not recognize the Home Address option and never receives the packets sent by a mobile node that is away from home.

- Minimal
  An IPv6 node that has minimal correspondent node support recognizes the Home Address option in the Destination Options header of received packets. However, packets sent by the correspondent node to the mobile node that is away from home are always intercepted by the home agent, who then tunnels the packets to the mobile node. The result is inefficient communication for packets sent by the correspondent node to the mobile node.

- Full
  An IPv6 node that has full correspondent node support recognizes the Home Address and Binding Update options in the Destination Options header, sends the Binding Acknowledgement and Binding Request options as needed, includes a Routing header in packets sent to mobile nodes that are away from home, and maintains a binding cache that maps the home address to the care-of address of mobile nodes that are away from home. The Binding Update, Binding Acknowledgment, and Binding Request options are discussed later in this chapter.

The IPv6 protocol for Windows XP and the Windows .NET Server 2003 family supports full correspondent node functionality, with the exception of sending binding requests. The IPv6 protocol for Windows XP and the Windows .NET Server 2003 family does not support mobile node or home agent functionality.

IPV6 MOBILITY MESSAGES AND OPTIONS

The following options, messages, and modifications to existing messages are needed to facilitate the processes of IPv6 mobility.

Destination Options Header Options

The Destination Options extension header is used to contain the following IPv6 mobility-related options:

- Binding Update
- Binding Acknowledgement

■   Binding Request

■   Home Address

For information on the structure of these options, see Chapter 4, "The IPv6 Header."

Binding Update Option

The Binding update option is used by a mobile IPv6 node that is away from home to update another node with its new care-of address. The Binding Update option is an option used within the Destination Options extension header for the destination node and can be included in an existing packet sent to the destination or in a packet that contains just the Destination Options header. In this latter case, the Next Header field in the Destination Options header is set to 59, indicating no next header. A binding update is a packet that contains the Binding Update option. A binding update always contains the Home Address option (described later in this chapter).

The Binding Update option is used for the following:

■   To update the home agent with a new primary care-of address. This is known as a home registration binding update. The home agent uses the home address in the Home Address option and the source address of the packet to update its Home Address/Primary Care-of Address binding cache entry for the mobile node.

■   To update a correspondent node with which the mobile node is actively communicating with a new binding that maps the home address of the mobile node to its care-of address. The correspondent node uses the home address in the Home Address option and the source address of the packet to update its Home Address/Care-of Address binding cache entry for the mobile node.

The mobile node can use the Alternate Care-of Address sub-option in the Binding Update option to specify a care-of address that is different than the source address of the binding update.

Binding Acknowledgement Option

The Binding Acknowledgement option is used to acknowledge the receipt of a binding update whose Acknowledge (A) flag has been set, and to report errors in the binding update. The mobile node sets the A flag when it wants to receive confirmation that the Binding Update message was received. The Binding Acknowledgement option can be included in an existing packet sent to the destination, or in a packet that contains just the Destination Options header. In this latter case, the Next Header field in the Destination Options header is set to 59, indicating no next header. A binding acknowledgement is a packet that contains the Binding Acknowledgement option.

Included in the binding acknowledgement is an indication of how long the node will cache the binding. For home agents, this lifetime indicates how long the home agent will be in service as the home agent for the mobile node. To refresh the binding, either the mobile node sends a new binding update or the correspondent nodes and home agent send a request to update the binding.

The binding acknowledgement also includes an indication of how often the mobile node should send binding updates.

Binding Request Option

A Binding Request option is used to request the current binding from a mobile node. If a mobile node receives a binding request, it responds with a binding update. A correspondent node sends a binding request when the binding cache entry is in active use and the lifetime of the binding cache entry approaches expiration. A home agent sends a binding request when the lifetime of the binding cache entry approaches expiration.

The Binding Request option can be included in an existing packet sent to the destination or in a packet that contains just the Destination Options header. In this latter case, the Next Header field in the Destination Options header is set to 59, indicating no next header. A binding request is a packet that contains the Binding Request option.

Home Address Option

The Home Address option is used to indicate the home address of the mobile node. The Home Address option is included in any packet sent to correspondent nodes and home agents by a mobile node when it is away from home (with the exception of a tunneled Router Solicitation message sent to the home agent). When a mobile node sends a packet, the source address in the IPv6 header is set to the care-of address. If the source address in the IPv6 header is set to the home address, then the router on the foreign link might discard the packet because the source address does not match the prefix of the link on which the mobile node is located. To help minimize Internet attacks in which the source address of attack packets is spoofed with an address that is not assigned to the attacking computer, peripheral routers can implement ingress filtering and silently discard packets that do not have topologically correct source addresses. Ingress in this instance is defined relative to the Internet for packets entering the Internet, rather than packets entering an intranet from the Internet.

By using the care-of address as the source address in the packet (a topologically correct address on the foreign link), and including the Home Address destination option, the packet is forwarded by the router on the foreign link to its destination. When the packet is received at the destination, the correspondent node processes the Destination Options header, and before passing the payload to the upper layer protocol, logically replaces the source address of the packet with the address in the Home Address option. As far as the upper layer protocol is concerned, the packet was sent from the home address.

The Home Address option is also included with the binding update so that the home address for the binding is indicated to the receiving node.

ICMPv6 Messages

The following ICMPv6 messages are used by the mobile node for dynamic home agent address discovery:

- Home Agent Address Discovery Request
- Home Agent Address Discovery Reply

Dynamic home agent address discovery is a process through which the mobile node dynamically discovers the global address of the home agent on the home link. This process is needed only if the mobile node is not already configured with the address of its home agent or if the current home agent becomes unavailable.

Home Agent Address Discovery Request

The ICMPv6 Home Agent Address Discovery Request message is used by a mobile node to begin dynamic home agent address discovery. This message is sent to the Mobile IPv6 Home-Agents anycast address that is described in RFC 2526. The Mobile IPv6 Home-Agents anycast address is composed of the 64-bit home subnet prefix and the interface ID of ::FEFF:FFFF:FFFF:FFFE. All home agents are configured automatically with this anycast address. The home agent that is topologically closest to the mobile node receives the request message.

Figure 12-2 shows the structure of the ICMPv6 Home Agent Address Discovery Request message.

In the Home Agent Address Discovery Request message, the Type field is set to 150 and the Code field is set to 0. Following the Checksum field is a 16-bit Identifier field. The value of the Identifier field is chosen by the sending node and copied to the Identifier field of the Home Agent Address Discovery Reply message to match a reply with its request. Following the Identifier field is an 80-bit Reserved field that is set to 0 by the sender and a 128-bit Home Address field. The Home Address field contains the home address of the mobile node.

The Home Agent Address Discovery Request message is sent with the source address in the IPv6 header set to the mobile node's care-of address. The Home Address destination option is not included.

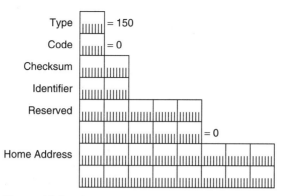

Figure 12-2. *The structure of ICMPv6 Home Agent Address Discovery Request message*

Home Agent Address Discovery Reply

The ICMPv6 Home Agent Address Discovery Reply message is used by a home agent to complete the dynamic home agent address discovery process by informing the mobile node of the addresses of the set of routers attached to the mobile node's home link that are capable of being a home agent.

Figure 12-3 shows the structure of the ICMPv6 Home Agent Address Discovery Reply message.

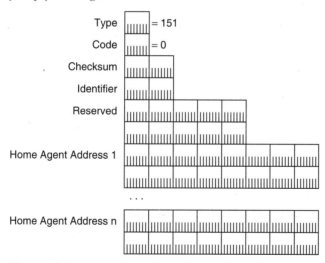

Figure 12-3. *The structure of the ICMPv6 Home Agent Address Discovery Reply message*

In the Home Agent Address Discovery Reply message, the Type field is set to 151 and the Code field is set to 0. Following the Checksum field is a 16-bit Identifier field. The value of the Identifier field is set to the same value as the Identifier field of the received Home Agent Address Discovery Request message.

Following the Identifier field is an 80-bit Reserved field that is set to 0 by the sender, and one or more 128-bit Home Agent Address fields. The Home Agent Address fields contain the global addresses of home agents on the home link in preference order (highest preference first).

The Home Agent Address Discovery Reply message is sent with the source address in the IPv6 header set to the global address of the answering home agent, and the destination address set to the mobile node's care-of address. A Routing extension header is not included.

Modifications to Neighbor Discovery Messages and Options

IPv6 mobility defines the following changes to ND messages and options:

- Modified Router Advertisement message
- Modified Prefix Information option
- New Advertisement Interval option
- New Home Agent Information option

For more information about the structure of these ND messages and options, see Chapter 6, "Neighbor Discovery."

Modifications to the Router Advertisement Message

IPv6 mobility defines an additional flag in the Router Advertisement message to help facilitate home agent discovery by the home agents and mobile nodes on a home link. The new flag, known as the Home Agent (H) flag, indicates whether the advertising router is capable of being a home agent. Each of the home agents on the home link set this flag when they send their router advertisements, and each home agent and mobile node receives each router advertisement. Therefore, each home agent and mobile node can compile the list of possible home agents.

Additionally, IPv6 mobility allows a router advertisement to be sent more frequently than every 3 seconds, as specified in RFC 2461. By sending router advertisements more frequently, IPv6 mobile nodes can use a newly received router advertisement to detect movement to a foreign link more quickly. Recommended values for the pseudo-periodic router advertisement process for routers that might provide connectivity for mobile IPv6 nodes are a minimum of 0.5 seconds and a maximum of 1.5 seconds.

Modified Prefix Information Option

To indicate the global address of the advertising router, IPv6 mobility defines an additional flag and a redefined use of the Prefix field in the Prefix Information option.

As per RFC 2461, which defines Neighbor Discovery, router advertisements are sent from the link-local address. However, the global address for a home agent must be indicated in the router advertisement it sends so that a list of home agents can be compiled by each home agent and mobile node. IPv6 mobility defines the Router Address (R) flag in the Prefix Information option. When set, the R flag indicates to the receiver that the Prefix field contains the global address of the advertising router. In the originally defined Prefix field, the high-order bits corresponding to the value of the Prefix Length field are set to the appropriate values for the advertised prefix and the bits beyond the indicated prefix length are set to 0. With this new definition, the Prefix Length field is advertised in the same way, except the Prefix field contains the entire 128-bit global address of the advertising router.

Advertisement Interval Option

The Advertisement Interval option is sent in Router Advertisement messages to specify how often the router sends unsolicited multicast router advertisements. A mobile node that receives a router advertisement with the Advertisement Interval option can use the advertisement interval to detect whether it has moved to another link.

The Advertisement Interval option contains a 32-bit field that indicates the maximum number of milliseconds between consecutive unsolicited multicast Router Advertisement messages sent by the router using the pseudo-periodic advertising scheme described in section 6.2.4 of RFC 2461.

Home Agent Information Option

The Home Agent Information option is sent in Router Advertisement messages sent by a home agent to specify the home agent's configuration. Included in the Home Agent Information option are the home agent preference (a number indicating a preference level for the advertising router to be a home agent) and the home agent lifetime (how long the home agent is acting as a home agent).

The home agents on a home link use the home agent preference values to order the list of home agents sent to the mobile node during home agent address discovery. The mobile nodes on a home link use the home agent preference values to select the home agent that has the highest preference value.

IPv6 MOBILITY DATA STRUCTURES

The following data structures are needed to facilitate the processes of IPv6 mobility:

- Binding cache
- Binding update list
- Home agents list

Binding Cache

The binding cache is a table maintained by each correspondent node and home agent and contains the current bindings for mobile nodes. Each binding cache entry contains the following information:

- The home address for the mobile node

- The care-of address for the mobile node

- The lifetime of the binding cache entry
  The lifetime is obtained from the Lifetime field of the last binding update that was received for this cache entry.

- A flag indicating whether the binding is a home registration
  This flag is set only for the binding cache entries on home agents.

- A flag indicating whether the mobile node for this binding cache entry should be advertised as a router
  If this flag is set, the home agent will advertise the mobile node as a router (by setting the Router flag) when proxying Neighbor Advertisement messages on behalf of the mobile node. This flag is valid only for home registration entries and set only for the binding cache entries on home agents.

- The value of the Prefix Length field of the last binding update that was received for this cache entry

- The maximum value of the Sequence Number field of the binding updates that have been received for this cache entry

- The time that the last binding request was sent

The actual implementation details for the binding cache are not specified, as long as the external behavior is consistent with the IPv6 mobility draft. For example, you could either maintain a separate binding cache or combine the binding cache with the destination cache. If you have a separate binding cache, you could either check it before you check the destination cache or have a pointer from the destination cache entry to the corresponding binding cache entry.

In any case, the information in the binding cache takes precedence over the information in the neighbor cache. For mobile destinations that are away from home, packets should be sent to the home address by way of the care-of address. If packets are sent directly to the home address while the mobile node is away from home, the home agent must intercept the packets and tunnel them to the mobile node, lowering the efficiency and performance of the communication between the correspondent node and the mobile node.

For the IPv6 protocol for Windows XP and the Windows .NET Server 2003 family, a separate binding cache is maintained. Each binding cache entry stores the home address, its current care-of address, and a pointer to the entry in the destination cache for the care-of address. A destination cache entry for a home address of a mobile node that is away from home has a pointer to an entry in the binding cache. The entry in the binding cache maps the home address to its care-of address and indicates the entry in the destination cache for the care-of address. The care-of address destination cache entry stores the next-hop address and interface for the care-of address. You can view the binding cache entries with the **netsh interface ipv6 show bindingcacheentries** command.

For more information about how a node sends a packet in an IPv6 mobility environment, see the "IPv6 Mobility Host Sending Algorithm" section in this chapter.

Binding Update List

The binding update list is maintained by a mobile node to record the most recent binding updates sent for the home agent and correspondent nodes. A binding update list entry contains:

- The address of the node to which the binding update was sent

- The home address for the binding update

- The care-of address sent in the last binding update

- The value of the Lifetime field in the binding update

- The remaining lifetime of the binding
  The initial value is the value of the Lifetime field in the binding update. When the lifetime expires, the entry is deleted from the binding update list.

- The maximum value of the Sequence Number field sent in previous binding updates

- The time that the last binding update was sent

- An indication of whether a retransmission is needed for binding updates sent with the Acknowledge (A) flag set and when the retransmission is to be sent

- A flag indicating that no future binding updates need to be sent
  This flag is set when the mobile node receives an ICMPv6 Parameter Problem-Unrecognized IPv6 Option Encountered message in response to a binding update.

Home Agents List

The home agents list is maintained by home agents and mobile nodes, and records information about each router from which a router advertisement was received on the home link with the Home Agent (H) flag set. Home agents maintain the home agents list so that they can send the list of home agents to a requesting mobile node away from home during home agent address discovery. Mobile nodes maintain the home agents list so that they can select a home agent.

A home agents list entry contains the following:

- The link-local address of the router on the link, obtained from the source address of the received Router Advertisement message

- The global address or addresses of the home agent, obtained from the Prefix field in the Prefix Information options in the Router Advertisement message with the Router Address (R) flag set

- The remaining lifetime of this entry
  The initial lifetime is obtained from either the Home Agent Lifetime field in the Home Agent Information option or the Router Lifetime field in the Router Advertisement message. When the lifetime expires, the entry is deleted from the home agents list.

- The preference for the home agent, obtained from the Home Agent Preference field in the Home Agent Information option
  If the router advertisement does not contain a Home Agent Information option, the preference is set to 0. Based on the definition of the Home Agent Preference field, 0 is a medium priority level. A mobile node uses the preference value to select the home agent. A home agent uses the preference value to order by preference value the list of home agents returned to a mobile node during home agent address discovery. When the mobile node receives the list of home agents, it chooses the first home agent in the list.

IPV6 MOBILITY COMMUNICATION

Before understanding the various processes used for IPv6 mobility, it is important to understand how packets containing mobility options and Application layer data are sent in a mobility-enabled environment. The following are the types of IPv6 mobility communication:

- Between a mobile node and a correspondent node

- Between a mobile node and a home agent

Communication Between a Mobile Node and a Correspondent Node

Communication between a mobile node and a correspondent node is one of the following:

- From the mobile node to the correspondent node
- From the correspondent node to the mobile node

From the Mobile Node to the Correspondent Node

The mobile node sends the correspondent node the following types of packets:

- Binding updates
- Data

Binding Updates

Binding updates sent from the mobile node to the correspondent node are shown in Figure 12-4.

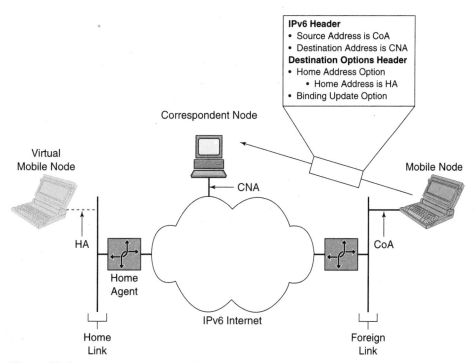

Figure 12-4. *Binding updates sent from the mobile node to the correspondent node*

The packet contains the following:

- IPv6 header

  In the IPv6 header, the source address is the care-of address of the mobile node (indicated by CoA in Figure 12-4) and the destination address is the correspondent node's address (indicated by CNA in Figure 12-4). By using the care-of address rather than the home address, ingress filtering by the foreign link router does not prevent the packet from being forwarded.

- Destination Options header

  The Destination Options extension header contains two options: the Home Address option and the Binding Update option. By including the Home Address option, the home address (indicated by HA in Figure 12-4) for the binding is indicated to the correspondent node.

The binding update can be sent either with data (an upper layer PDU) or in a separate packet. Figure 12-4 shows the binding update sent as a separate packet.

Version 13 of the IPv6 mobility draft (draft-ietf-mobileip-ipv6-13.txt in the \RFCs_and_Drafts folder on the companion CD-ROM) requires the use of an Authentication Header (AH) to provide sender authentication, data integrity, and replay protection for binding updates. Many implementations allow you to disable security for IPv6 mobility messages. If an AH is present, there are two different Destination Options headers: one before the AH and one after the AH. The first Destination Options header contains the Home Address option and the second Destination Options header contains the Binding Update option. This is not shown in Figure 12-4. If an AH is not present, both the Home Address and Binding Acknowledgement options are included in a single Destination Options header. This is shown in Figure 12-4.

If the correspondent node is also mobile, the destination address in the IPv6 header is set to the correspondent node's care-of address and the packet includes a Routing header with the correspondent node's home address. The Routing header is placed before the Destination Options header. If an AH is present, there are two different Destination Options headers: one before the AH and one after the AH. The first Destination Options header contains the Home Address option and the second Destination Options header contains the Binding Update option. In this case, the order of the extension headers is: Routing, Destination Options (w/Home Address option), AH, Destination Options (w/ Binding Update). If an AH is not present, both the Home Address and Binding Acknowledgement options are included in a single Destination Options header that is placed after the Routing header. This is not shown in Figure 12-4.

Data

When the mobile node is away from home, it can choose to either send data from its home address using mobility options, or its care-of address without using mobility options, based on the following:

■ For Transport layer connection data (such as TCP sessions) that is long-term and being sent to a correspondent node, the mobile node sends the data from its home address and includes the Home Address option.

■ For short-term communication that does not require a logical connection, such as the exchange of DNS Name Query and DNS Name Query Response messages for DNS name resolution, the mobile node can send data from its care-of address and not use a Home Address option. In this case, the mobile node is sending and receiving packets normally from its care-of address.

Packets containing Transport layer connection data sent from the mobile node to the correspondent node are shown in Figure 12-5.

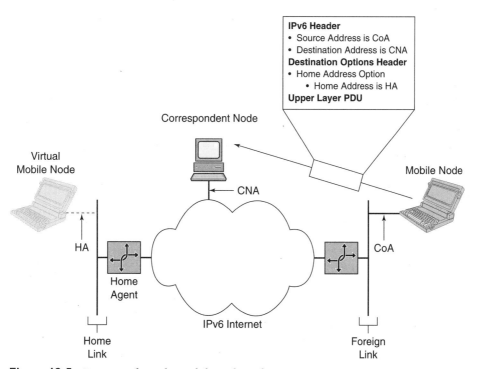

Figure 12-5. *Data sent from the mobile node to the correspondent node*

The packet contains the following:

■ IPv6 header
In the IPv6 header, the source address is the care-of address of the mobile node and the destination address is the correspondent node's address. By using the care-of address rather than the home address, ingress filtering by the foreign link router does not prevent the packet from being forwarded.

■ Destination Options header
In the Destination Options extension header, the Home Address option contains the home address of the mobile node. When the correspondent node processes the Home Address option, it indicates to upper layer protocols that the source address of the packet is the home address, rather than the care-of address.

■ Upper layer PDU
The upper layer PDU contains the Application layer data sent from the mobile node to the correspondent node. From the Application layer perspective, the data was addressed from the home address to the correspondent node address.

If the correspondent node is also mobile, the destination address in the IPv6 header is set to the correspondent node's care-of address and the packet includes a Routing header with the correspondent node's home address. The Routing header is placed before the Destination Options header. This is not shown in Figure 12-5.

From the Correspondent Node to the Mobile Node
The correspondent node sends the mobile node the following types of packets:

■ Binding maintenance

■ Data

Binding Maintenance
Binding maintenance packets sent from the correspondent node to the mobile node are either binding acknowledgments or binding requests and are shown in Figure 12-6.
The packets contain the following:

■ IPv6 header
In the IPv6 header, the source address is the correspondent node's address and the destination address is the mobile node's care-of address.

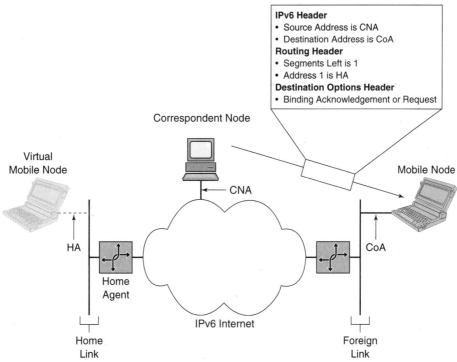

Figure 12-6. *Binding maintenance packets sent from the correspondent node to the mobile node*

- Routing header

  In the Routing extension header, the Routing Type field is set to 0, the Segments Left field is set to 1, and the Address 1 field (the final destination address of the packet) is set to the mobile node's home address. When the mobile node receives the packet, it processes the Routing header and notes that the next destination address (the address in the Address 1 field) is its own home address. The mobile node removes the Routing header and logically replaces the care-of address with the home address as the destination address in the IPv6 header. When the packet is passed to the upper layer protocol, it appears to have been addressed to the mobile node's home address.

- Destination Options header

  The Destination Options extension header contains either a Binding Acknowledgement option (if a received binding update had the Acknowledge [A] flag set) or a Binding Request option.

The binding acknowledgement or binding request can be sent either with data (an upper layer PDU) or in a separate packet. Figure 12-6 shows the binding acknowledgement or binding request sent as a separate packet.

The IPv6 mobility draft requires the use of an AH to provide data authentication, data integrity, and replay protection for binding acknowledgements. Many implementations allow you to disable security for IPv6 mobility messages. The AH is placed between the Routing header and the Destination Options header and is not shown in Figure 12-6.

If the correspondent node is also mobile, the source address in the IPv6 header is set to the correspondent node's care-of address and the packet includes the Home Address option containing the correspondent node's home address. If an AH is present, there are two different Destination Options headers: one before the AH and one after the AH. The first Destination Options header contains the Home Address option and the second Destination Options header contains the Binding Acknowledgement option. In this case, the order of the extension headers is: Routing, Destination Options (w/Home Address option), AH, Destination Options (w/Binding Acknowledgement). If an AH is not present, both the Home Address and Binding Acknowledgement options are included in a single Destination Options header that is placed after the Routing header. This is not shown in Figure 12-6.

Data with a Binding Cache Entry Present

The form of data packets sent from the correspondent node to mobile nodes depends on whether the correspondent node has a binding cache entry for the mobile node's home address. A packet containing an upper layer PDU sent from the correspondent node to the mobile node when a binding cache entry for the mobile node's care-of address is present is shown in Figure 12-7.

The packet contains the following:

- IPv6 header
  In the IPv6 header, the source address is the correspondent node's address and the destination address is the mobile node's care-of address. By using the care-of address rather than the home address, the packet is delivered to the mobile node's current location on the IPv6 Internet.

- Routing header
  In the Routing extension header, the Routing Type field is set to 0, the Segments Left field is set to 1, and the Address 1 field (the final destination address of the packet) is set to the mobile node's home address. When the mobile node receives the packet, it processes the Routing header and notes that the next destination address (the

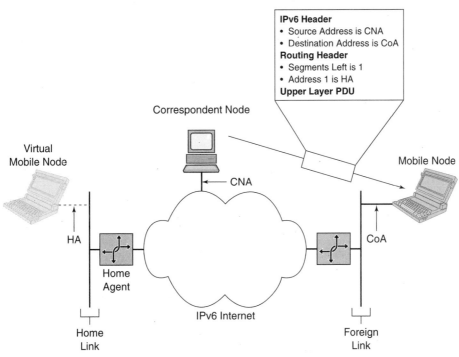

Figure 12-7. *Data sent from the correspondent node when a binding cache entry for the mobile node is present*

address in the Address 1 field) is its own home address. The mobile node removes the Routing header and logically replaces the care-of address with the home address as the destination address in the IPv6 header. When the packet is passed to the upper layer protocol, it appears to have been addressed to the mobile node's home address.

■ Upper layer PDU
The upper layer PDU contains the Application layer data sent from the correspondent node to the mobile node. From the Application layer perspective, the data was addressed from the correspondent node address to the home address.

If the correspondent node is also mobile, the source address in the IPv6 header is set to the correspondent node's care-of address and the packet includes a Destination Options header with the Home Address option containing the correspondent node's home address. The Destination Options header is placed after the Routing header. This is not shown in Figure 12-7.

Data with a Binding Cache Entry Not Present

A packet containing an upper layer PDU sent from the correspondent node to the mobile node when a binding cache entry for the mobile node is not present is shown in Figure 12-8.

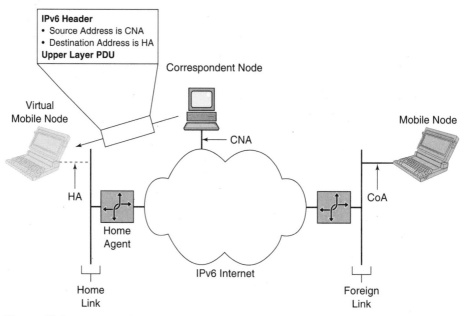

Figure 12-8. *Data sent from the correspondent node when a binding cache entry for the mobile node is not present*

The packet contains the following:

- IPv6 header
  In the IPv6 header, the source address is the correspondent node address and the destination address is the mobile node's home address. Because a binding cache entry does not exist, the correspondent node sends the packet as if the mobile node were physically attached to the home link.

- Upper layer PDU
  The upper layer PDU contains the Application layer data sent from the correspondent node to the mobile node.

  While addressed to the mobile node's home address (represented by the Virtual Mobile Node in Figure 12-8), the home agent, which has a binding cache entry for the mobile node, intercepts the packet and forwards it to the mobile node by encapsulating the

IPv6 packet with an IPv6 header. This is known as IPv6-over-IPv6 tunneling. For more information, see the "Communication Between a Mobile Node and Its Home Agent" section in this chapter.

If the correspondent node is also mobile, the source address in the IPv6 header is set to the correspondent node's care-of address and the packet includes a Destination Options header with the Home Address option containing the correspondent node's home address. The Destination Options header is placed after the IPv6 header. This is not shown in Figure 12-8.

Communication Between a Mobile Node and Its Home Agent

Communication between a mobile node and a home agent is one of the following:

- From the mobile node to its home agent
- From the home agent to the mobile node

From the Mobile Node to its Home Agent

The mobile node sends the home agent the following types of packets:

- Binding update
- ICMPv6 Home Agent Address Discovery Request message

Binding Update

Binding updates sent from the mobile node to the home agent are shown in Figure 12-9.

The binding update contains the following:

- IPv6 header
  In the IPv6 header, the source address is the mobile node's care-of address and the destination address is the home agent's address (indicated by HAA in Figure 12-9). By using the care-of address rather than the home address, ingress filtering by the foreign link router does not prevent the packet from being forwarded.

- Destination Options header
  The Destination Options extension header contains two options: the Home Address option and the Binding Update option.
  The Home Address option contains the home address of the mobile node. By including the Home Address option, the home address for the binding is indicated to the home agent.

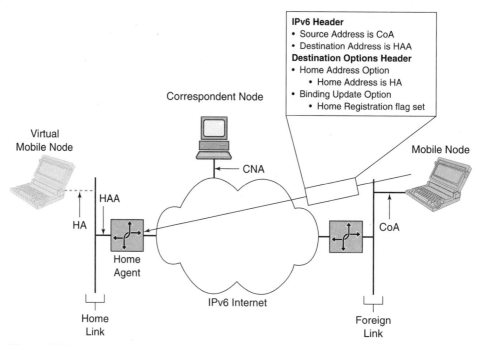

Figure 12-9. *Binding updates sent from the mobile node to the home agent*

In the Binding Update option, the Home Registration (H) flag is set, indicating that the sender is requesting that the receiver be the home agent for the mobile node. The Acknowledge (A) flag is also set to request a binding acknowledgement from the home agent.

If security for binding updates is enabled and an AH is present, there are two different Destination Options headers: one before the AH and one after the AH. The first Destination Options header contains the Home Address option and the second Destination Options header contains the Binding Update option. This is not shown in Figure 12-9.

ICMPv6 Home Agent Address Discovery Request Message

When the mobile node sends an ICMPv6 Home Agent Address Discovery Request message, it has the form shown in Figure 12-10.

■ IPv6 header
In the IPv6 header, the source address is the care-of address of the mobile node and the destination address is the Mobile IPv6 Home-Agents anycast address corresponding to the home link prefix.

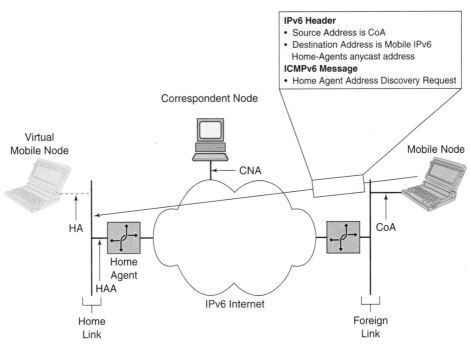

IPv6 Header
- Source Address is CoA
- Destination Address is Mobile IPv6
  Home-Agents anycast address

ICMPv6 Message
- Home Agent Address Discovery Request

Figure 12-10. *ICMPv6 Home Agent Address Discovery Request message sent from the mobile node*

◼ ICMPv6 Home Agent Address Discovery Request message
The ICMPv6 Home Agent Address Discovery Request message is used by the mobile node to query the home link for a list of home agents. For more information, see the "ICMPv6 Messages" section in this chapter.

From the Home Agent to the Mobile Node

Communication from the home agent to the mobile node takes the following forms:

◼ Binding maintenance

◼ ICMPv6 Home Agent Address Discovery Reply message

◼ Tunneled data

Binding Maintenance

Binding maintenance packets sent from the home agent to the mobile node are either binding acknowledgments or binding requests and are shown in Figure 12-11.

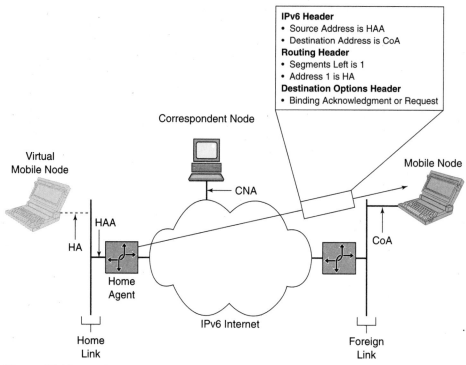

IPv6 Header
- Source Address is HAA
- Destination Address is CoA

Routing Header
- Segments Left is 1
- Address 1 is HA

Destination Options Header
- Binding Acknowledgment or Request

Figure 12-11. *Binding maintenance packets sent from the home agent to the mobile node*

The packet contains the following:

- IPv6 header
  In the IPv6 header, the source address is the home agent's address and the destination address is the mobile node's care-of address.

- Routing header
  In the Routing extension header, the Routing Type field is set to 0, the Segments Left field is set to 1, and the Address 1 field (the final destination address of the packet) is set to the mobile node's home address. When the mobile node receives the packet, it processes the Routing header and notes that the next destination address (the address in the Address 1 field) is its own home address. The mobile node removes the Routing header and logically replaces the care-of address with the home address as the destination in the IPv6 header.

- Destination Options header
  The Destination Options extension header contains either a Binding Acknowledgement option (if a received binding update had the Acknowledge [A] flag set) or a Binding Request option.

If security for binding updates is enabled, an AH is present between the Routing header and the Destination Options header for the binding acknowledgement. This is not shown in Figure 12-11.

ICMPv6 Home Agent Address Discovery Reply Message

When the home agent sends an ICMPv6 Home Agent Address Discovery Reply message, it has the form shown in Figure 12-12.

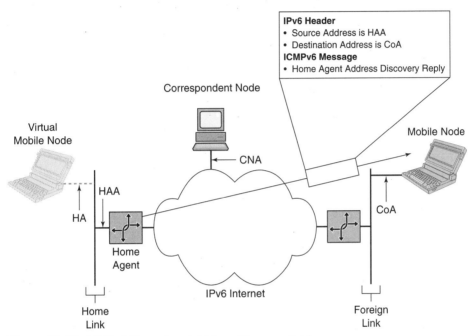

IPv6 Header
• Source Address is HAA
• Destination Address is CoA
ICMPv6 Message
• Home Agent Address Discovery Reply

Figure 12-12. *ICMPv6 Home Agent Address Discovery Reply message sent from the home agent*

■ IPv6 header
In the IPv6 header, the source address is the home agent's address and the destination address is the mobile node's care-of address.

■ ICMPv6 Home Agent Address Discovery Reply message
The ICMPv6 Home Agent Address Discovery Reply message contains the list of home agents on the home link in order of preference. For more information, see the "ICMPv6 Messages" section in this chapter.

Tunneled Packet

When the home agent intercepts a packet sent directly to a mobile node's home address when the mobile node is away from home, it forwards the packet to the mobile node by using the form shown in Figure 12-13.

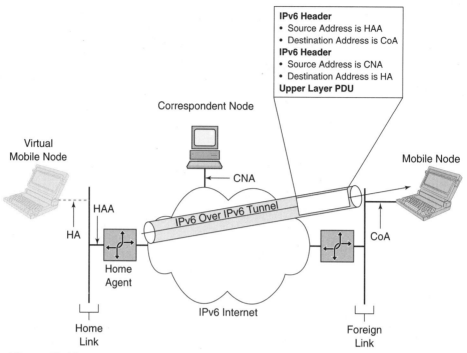

Figure 12-13. *Intercepted packet tunneled to a mobile node by its home agent*

- IPv6 header (outer)
  In the outer IPv6 header, the source address is the home agent's address and the destination address is the mobile node's care-of address.

- IPv6 header (inner)
  In the inner IPv6 header, the source address is the correspondent node's address and the destination address is the mobile node's home address.

- Upper layer PDU
  The upper layer PDU contains the Application layer data sent from the correspondent node to the mobile node at its home address. From the Application layer perspective, the data was addressed from the correspondent node address to the home address.

Notice that this packet is the original packet sent by the correspondent node that did not have a binding cache entry for the mobile node with an additional IPv6 header addressed from the home agent's address to the mobile node's care-of address. The original packet is described in the "Data with a Binding Cache Entry Not Present" section of this chapter.

IPV6 MOBILITY PROCESSES

IPv6 mobility provides a method for a mobile node to determine it is on its home link as well as providing message exchanges for the following processes:

- Moving from the home link to a foreign link

- Moving from a foreign link to another foreign link

- Returning home

Additionally, the sending host and receiving host processes are modified to include special processing for mobility support.

> **NOTE:**
> The following discussion assumes that the correspondent node supports full correspondent node functionality and is not a mobile node that is away from home.

Attaching to the Home Link

The method used by a mobile node to determine that it is attached to the home link is not defined in the IPv6 mobility draft. Once an IPv6 mobile node determines that it is connected to its home link, it can store the home subnet prefix, home address, and the global address of its home agent. The following methods for configuring home link parameters are based on implementations in development or existence at the time of the writing of this book:

- Manual configuration
  In the simplest case, the home subnet prefix, home address, and the global address of the home agent are manually configured, typically through a keyboard-based command, and are permanent until manually changed. These implementations do not support the dynamic discovery of home agents or changes in the home subnet prefix.

- Pseudo-automatic configuration
  For pseudo-automatic configuration, when an IPv6 node is attached to a link, the user has the option (typically through a button in the user interface of the operating system) to indicate to the IPv6 protocol that the node is now connected to the home link. Based on this indication, the IPv6 protocol stores the home subnet prefix and home address and listens for additional router advertisements containing the Home Agent (H) flag. The home agent is the router advertising itself with home agent capabilities and has the highest

preference level. Once determined, the IPv6 protocol stores the address of the home agent. These implementations may or may not support the dynamic discovery of home agents or changes in the home subnet prefix.

■ Automatic configuration
With automatic configuration, the IPv6 node is always listening for router advertisements that have the H flag set. Based on additional protocol or operating system parameters, the IPv6 node determines that it is potentially on its home link. Next, it chooses the most preferred home agent and attempts to establish a security relationship with it. If the security relationship with the home agent fails, the IPv6 node concludes it is not on its home link. If the security relationship succeeds, the IPv6 node is on its home link and stores its home subnet prefix, its home address, and the address of its home agent. These implementations may or may not support the dynamic discovery of home agents or changes in the home subnet prefix.

Moving From the Home Link to a Foreign Link

When the mobile node is at home, it autoconfigures its home address through the receipt of a router advertisement, and communication with other nodes occurs normally without the use of IPv6 mobility functionality.

Attaching to the Foreign Link

When the mobile node attaches to the foreign link, it must perform the following functions:

■ Receive a new care-of address.

■ Discover the home agent on the home link (if needed).

■ Register the primary care-of address with the home agent on the home link.

When the mobile node attaches to the foreign link, the following occurs:

1. The mobile node sends a multicast Router Solicitation message on the foreign link. The mobile node might send a router solicitation either because the link layer indicated a media change or because the node received a router advertisement that contained a new prefix. Depending on the IPv6 mobility implementation, the mobile node sends a router solicitation either from its link-local address (assuming that the link-local address of the mobile node is most likely

unique on the foreign link) or from the unspecified address (::) (assuming that the link-local address of the mobile node might not be unique on the foreign link).

2. All routers on the foreign link reply with a Router Advertisement message. Depending on the source address of the Router Solicitation message, the reply is either unicast (because the router solicitation was sent from a link-local address) or multicast (because the router solicitation was sent from the unspecified address). Figure 12-14 shows the router advertisement being unicast to the mobile node.

    From the receipt of the Router Advertisement message(s), the mobile node determines that it has connected to a foreign link because the router advertisements contain new address prefixes. The mobile node forms care-of addresses from the advertised prefixes, verifies their uniqueness by using duplicate address detection, and joins the corresponding solicited node multicast groups (not shown in Figure 12-14).

3. If the mobile node is already configured with the address of its home agent, go to step 5. If not, to discover the home agent on the mobile node's home link, the mobile node sends an ICMPv6 Home Agent Address Discovery Request message to the Mobile IPv6 Home-Agents anycast address formed from the home subnet prefix.

    Depending on the implementation, mobile nodes might not maintain a list of home agents while connected to the home link. To automatically discover the home agents on the home link, it is sufficient for the mobile node to learn its home subnet prefix. When the mobile node leaves its home link and moves to the first foreign link, it sends an ICMPv6 Home Agent Address Discovery Request message to the Mobile IPv6 Home-Agents anycast address formed from the home subnet prefix.

4. A home agent on the home link that is using the Mobile IPv6 Home-Agents anycast address corresponding to the home subnet prefix and is topologically closest to the mobile node receives the Home Agent Address Discovery Request message. Next, it sends back an ICMPv6 Home Agent Address Discovery Reply message containing the entries in the home agent's home agent list in preference order.

    Upon receipt of the ICMPv6 Home Agent Address Discovery Reply message, the mobile node selects the first home agent in the list as its home agent.

5. To register the primary care-of address with the home agent, the mobile node sends the home agent a binding update. In the binding

update, the Home Registration (H) and Acknowledge (A) flags are set.

6. The home agent receives the binding update and updates its binding cache. To intercept packets destined for the mobile node's home address while the mobile node is away from home, the home agent performs proxy Neighbor Discovery for the mobile node by answering neighbor solicitations on behalf of the mobile node. Depending on the implementation, the home agent might send an unsolicited multicast Neighbor Advertisement message as if it were the mobile node immediately or respond only to multicast neighbor solicitations for the mobile node's home address.

    In the first case, to ensure that the nodes on the home link are updated with the new link-layer address of the home agent's interface on the home link, the home agent sends an unsolicited multicast Neighbor Advertisement message to the link-local scope all-nodes multicast address (FF02::1) with the Override (O) flag set. Additionally, the home agent joins the multicast group for the solicited node multicast address corresponding to the mobile node's home address, and registers interest in receiving link-layer multicast frames to the multicast MAC address corresponding to the solicited node multicast address. This is shown in Figure 12-14.

    In the second case, the home agent does not send an unsolicited multicast Neighbor Advertisement message. However, the home agent does join the multicast group for the solicited node multicast address corresponding to the mobile node's home address, and registers interest in receiving link-layer multicast frames to the multicast MAC address corresponding to the solicited node multicast address. If a node on the home link was communicating with the mobile node while it was at home, neighbor unreachability detection would eventually cause the home node to send three unicast neighbor solicitations (while in the PROBE state) and then send a multicast neighbor solicitation. The multicast neighbor solicitation is then answered by the home agent on behalf of the mobile node. This is not shown in Figure 12-14.

7. Because the binding update had the A flag set, the home agent responds with a binding acknowledgement.

    This process is shown in Figure 12-14.

    Notice that the mobile node does not send a binding update to all the nodes with which the mobile node was communicating when connected to the home link (as there are no entries in the binding update list). Rather, the

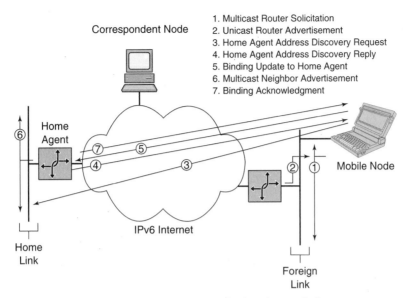

Correspondent Node

1. Multicast Router Solicitation
2. Unicast Router Advertisement
3. Home Agent Address Discovery Request
4. Home Agent Address Discovery Reply
5. Binding Update to Home Agent
6. Multicast Neighbor Advertisement
7. Binding Acknowledgment

Figure 12-14. *Mobile node attaching to the first foreign link*

mobile node relies on the receipt of tunneled traffic from the home agent to send binding updates to correspondent nodes.

Mobile Node Initiates a New TCP Connection with a New Correspondent Node

When a mobile node that is away from home initiates a new TCP connection with a correspondent node, the following occurs:

1. The mobile node sends a TCP SYN (synchronize) segment containing the Destination Options header and the Home Address and Binding Update options to the correspondent node.

2. The correspondent node receives the TCP SYN segment and processes the Home Address and Binding Update options. The correspondent node updates its binding cache and sends the TCP SYN-ACK (synchronize-acknowledgement) segment that includes a Routing header with the mobile node's home address and, if requested, a binding acknowledgment.

3. Upon receipt of the TCP SYN-ACK from the correspondent node, the mobile node sends a TCP ACK (acknowledge) segment that contains the Home Address option to the correspondent node.

This process is shown in Figure 12-15.

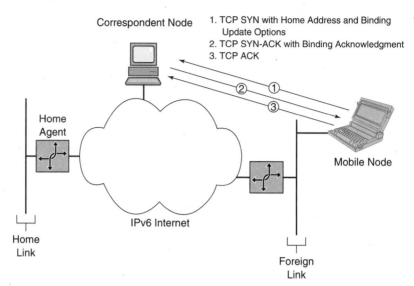

Figure 12-15. *A mobile node initiating a new TCP connection with a new correspondent node*

If the mobile node is resuming communication using an existing TCP connection, then the same process described here is done for the first three TCP segments exchanged over the resumed TCP connection.

After this process is complete, data between the correspondent node and the mobile node is sent as follows:

■ Data from the mobile node is sent from the mobile node's care-of address to the correspondent node's address and includes the Home Address option in the Destination Options header.

■ Data from the correspondent node is sent to the mobile node's care-of address and includes a Routing header containing the mobile node's home address.

NOTE:

If the mobile node is multihomed, it is possible for the mobile node to register different care-of addresses with different correspondent nodes. Which care-of address is chosen depends on the source address selection algorithm. The mobile node will choose the care-of address that is matched in scope and topologically closest to the correspondent node.

Mobile Node Initiates Non-TCP-based Communication with a New Correspondent Node

When a mobile node that is away from home either resumes or initiates communication with a correspondent node that does not use a TCP connection (such as ICMPv6 or an Application layer protocol that uses UDP), the following occurs:

1. The mobile node sends the initial message to the correspondent node containing the Destination Options header with the Home Address option.

2. The correspondent node receives the initial message and processes the Home Address option. Because a binding does not yet exist for the mobile node, the correspondent node sends the response message to the home address.

3. Because the home agent has a binding for the mobile node and is acting as an ND proxy for the mobile node, it intercepts the response message sent to the mobile node's home address and tunnels it to the mobile node at the mobile node's care-of address.

4. Upon receipt of the tunneled response message from the home agent, the mobile node queues a binding update to the correspondent node. Whether the binding update is sent as a separate packet or is included as part of upper layer data depends on the implementation. For this example, the binding update is included in the next message sent to the correspondent node.

5. Upon receipt of the next message with the binding update, the correspondent node updates its binding cache and sends back, if requested, a binding acknowledgment that includes a Routing header with the mobile node's home address.

This process is shown in Figure 12-16.

After this process is complete, data between the correspondent node and the mobile node is sent as follows:

- Data from the mobile node is sent from the mobile node's care-of address to the correspondent node's address and includes the Home Address option in the Destination Options header.

- Data from the correspondent node is sent to the mobile node's care-of address and includes a Routing header containing the mobile node's home address.

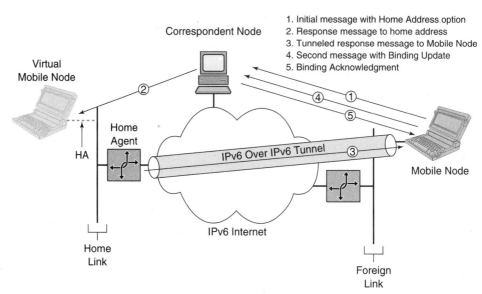

Figure 12-16. *A mobile node initiating non-TCP-based communication with a new correspondent node*

A New Correspondent Node Communicates with a Mobile Node

When a new correspondent node either resumes communication or initiates communication with a mobile node using the mobile node's home address and the mobile node is away from home, the following occurs (example assumes a new TCP connection):

1. The new correspondent node sends a TCP SYN segment to the mobile node's home address. The packet is delivered by the routers of the IPv6 Internet to a router connected to the mobile node's home link.

2. Because the home agent has a binding for the mobile node and is acting as its ND proxy, it intercepts the TCP SYN segment sent to the mobile node's home address and tunnels it to the mobile node's care-of address.

3. Upon receipt of the tunneled TCP SYN segment from the home agent, the mobile node adds an entry for the correspondent node to its binding update list and sends a TCP SYN-ACK with a Destination Options header that contains the Home Address and Binding Update options.

4. Upon receipt of the TCP SYN-ACK segment with the binding update, the correspondent node updates its binding cache and sends back a TCP ACK segment that includes a Routing header with the mobile

node's home address and, if requested, a binding acknowledgement in the Destination Options header.

This process is shown in Figure 12-17.

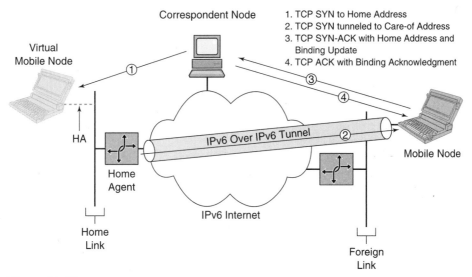

Figure 12-17. *A new correspondent node communicating with a mobile node*

After this process is complete, data between the correspondent node and the mobile node is sent as follows:

- Data from the mobile node is sent from the care-of address to the correspondent node's address and includes the Home Address option in the Destination Options header.

- Data from the correspondent node is sent to the mobile node's care-of address and includes a Routing header containing the mobile node's home address.

This same process is performed if the correspondent node removes the binding for the mobile node from its binding cache.

A Node on the Home Link Communicates with the Mobile Node

When a node on the home link either resumes or initiates communication with a mobile node using the mobile node's home address and the mobile node is away from home, the following occurs (example assumes a new TCP connection):

1. The node on the home link sends a multicast Neighbor Solicitation message to the solicited node multicast address corresponding to the mobile node's home address.

2. The home agent is acting as an ND proxy for the mobile node. It has registered the solicited node multicast address corresponding to the mobile node's home address as a multicast address to which the home agent is listening. The home agent receives the neighbor solicitation and sends a unicast neighbor advertisement containing the home agent's link-layer address in the Target Link-Layer Address option.

3. The node on the home link sends the TCP SYN segment to the home agent with the mobile node's home address as the destination IPv6 address and the home agent's link-layer address as the destination link-layer address.

4. Because the IPv6 packet is addressed to the home address of the mobile node, the home agent tunnels the TCP SYN segment to the mobile node's care-of address.

5. Upon receipt of the tunneled TCP SYN segment from the home agent, the mobile node adds an entry for the node on the home link to its binding update list and sends a TCP SYN-ACK with a Destination Options header that contains the Home Address and Binding Update options.

6. Upon receipt of the TCP SYN-ACK segment with the binding update, the node on the home link updates its binding cache and sends a TCP ACK segment that includes a Routing header with the mobile node's home address and, if requested, a binding acknowledgement in the Destination Options header.

This process is shown in Figure 12-18.

This same process of intercepting a packet for the mobile node (steps 1 through 3) is used when a packet addressed to the mobile node's home address is delivered to the home link by a router that is not the mobile node's home agent.

Mobile Node Obtains a New Home Address

The home address of the mobile node was initially obtained through the receipt of a router advertisement while the mobile node was connected to the home link, and the stateless address might have a finite lifetime. Because the mobile node is away from home, it does not receive the pseudo-periodic multicast router advertisements sent by the routers on the home link. To refresh a home address that is approaching the end of its valid lifetime or receive a new home address, the following process is used:

1. The mobile node sends an IPv6-tunneled Router Solicitation message to its home agent. The inner IPv6 header is addressed from the mobile node's home address to the home agent's address. The outer

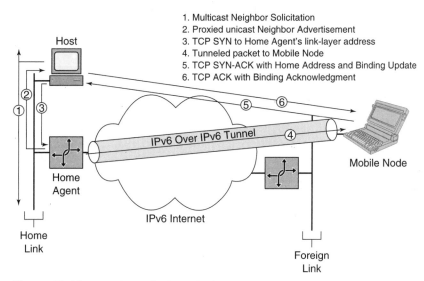

1. Multicast Neighbor Solicitation
2. Proxied unicast Neighbor Advertisement
3. TCP SYN to Home Agent's link-layer address
4. Tunneled packet to Mobile Node
5. TCP SYN-ACK with Home Address and Binding Update
6. TCP ACK with Binding Acknowledgment

Figure 12-18. *A node on the home link communicating with the mobile node*

IPv6 header is addressed from the mobile node's care-of address to the home agent's address.

2. Upon receipt of the tunneled router solicitation, the home agent responds with a unicast Router Advertisement message that is sent from the home agent's address to the mobile node's care-of address and includes a Routing header with the mobile node's home address.

Upon receipt of the router advertisement, the mobile node examines the Prefix Information option(s) and does the following:

- If there is no change in the home subnet prefix and therefore no change in the home address, then the mobile node refreshes the valid and preferred lifetimes of the stateless home address.

- If there is a change in the home subnet prefix, then the mobile node autoconfigures a new home address and sends binding updates for all the entries of its binding update list (the home agent and all correspondent nodes).

Moving from a Foreign Link to Another Foreign Link

When the mobile node attaches to a new foreign link after being attached to another foreign link, it must perform the following functions:

- Receive a new care-of address.

■ Register the new care-of address with the home agent on the home link.

■ Send binding updates to all correspondent nodes.

NOTE:

The IPv6 mobility draft also describes the registration of the new care-of address with a router that has home agent capabilities on the previous foreign link to establish forwarding of packets sent to an outdated care-of address. This is not widely supported and is not described in this chapter.

When the mobile node attaches to the new foreign link, the following occurs:

1. The mobile node sends a multicast Router Solicitation message on the new foreign link. Depending on the IPv6 mobility implementation, the mobile node sends a router solicitation either from its link-local address (assuming that the link-local address of the mobile node is most likely unique on the new foreign link) or from the unspecified address (::) (assuming that the link-local address of the mobile node might not be unique on the new foreign link).

2. All routers on the new foreign link reply with a Router Advertisement message. Depending on the source address of the Router Solicitation message, the reply is either unicast (because the router solicitation was sent from a link-local address) or multicast (because the router solicitation was sent from the unspecified address). Figure 12-19 shows the router advertisement being unicast to the mobile node.

   From the receipt of the Router Advertisement message(s), the mobile node forms care-of address(es), verifies their uniqueness by using duplicate address detection, and joins the corresponding solicited node multicast groups (not shown in Figure 12-19).

3. To register the new primary care-of address with the home agent, the mobile node sends the home agent a binding update. In the binding update, the Home Registration (H) and Acknowledge (A) flags are set.

4. For each correspondent node in the mobile node's binding update list, the mobile node sends a binding update.

   The mobile node does not have to immediately send a binding update. Because the binding update is carried in the Destination

Options header, the mobile node can delay the sending of the binding update to the correspondent node so that it is sent with the next packet. However, a delay in sending the binding update to correspondent nodes can result in data loss when packets sent by the correspondent node are delivered to the previous foreign link.

5. Upon the receipt of the binding update, the home agent updates its binding cache, and responds with a binding acknowledgement.

   Upon receipt of the binding update, each correspondent node updates its binding cache and, if requested by the mobile node, sends a binding acknowledgment.

This process is shown in Figure 12-19.

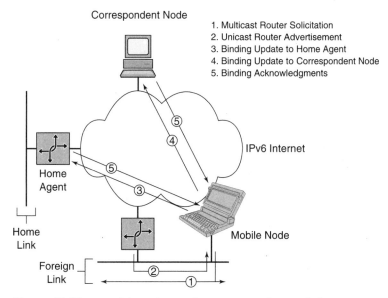

Figure 12-19. *A mobile node attaching to a new foreign link*

If the binding update sent by the mobile node to a correspondent node is dropped from the network, the correspondent node continues to send packets to the mobile node's previous care-of address based on the contents of its now outdated binding cache entry. The packets are forwarded to the previous foreign link and the router on the previous foreign link attempts to deliver them. If the previous foreign link router still considers the mobile node reachable on the previous foreign link, packets are forwarded to the mobile node's link layer address. Because the mobile node is no longer attached to the previous foreign link, the packets are dropped.

The methods for correcting this error condition are the following:

- The mobile node, after not receiving a binding acknowledgment from the correspondent node, retransmits a binding update. The retransmitted binding update is received by the correspondent node and its binding cache is updated with the mobile node's new care-of address.

- The previous foreign link router uses neighbor unreachability detection to determine that the mobile node is no longer attached to the previous foreign link. For a point-to-point link such as a wireless connection, the unreachability of the mobile node is indicated immediately by the lack of a wireless signal from the mobile node. For a broadcast link such as an Ethernet segment, the entry in the previous foreign link router's neighbor cache goes through the REACHABLE, STALE, DELAY, and PROBE states as described in Chapter 6, "Neighbor Discovery." After the neighbor cache entry for the mobile node is removed, attempts to deliver to the mobile node's previous care-of address are unsuccessful and the previous foreign link router will send an ICMPv6 Destination Unreachable-Address Unreachable message to the correspondent node. Upon receiving this message, the correspondent node will remove the entry for the mobile node from its binding cache and communication resumes as described in the "A New Correspondent Node Communicates with a Mobile Node" section of this chapter.

- All binding cache entries have a finite lifetime as determined by the Lifetime field of the last received binding update. After the lifetime expires, the binding cache entry is removed and communication resumes as described in the "A New Correspondent Node Communicates with a Mobile Node" section of this chapter.

Returning Home

When the mobile node attaches to its home link after being away from home, it must perform the following functions:

- Send a binding update to the home agent to delete the binding for the mobile node.

- Inform home link nodes that the correct link-layer address for the home address is now the mobile node's link-layer address.

- Send binding updates to all correspondent nodes to delete the bindings for the mobile node.

These functions are shown in Figure 12-20.

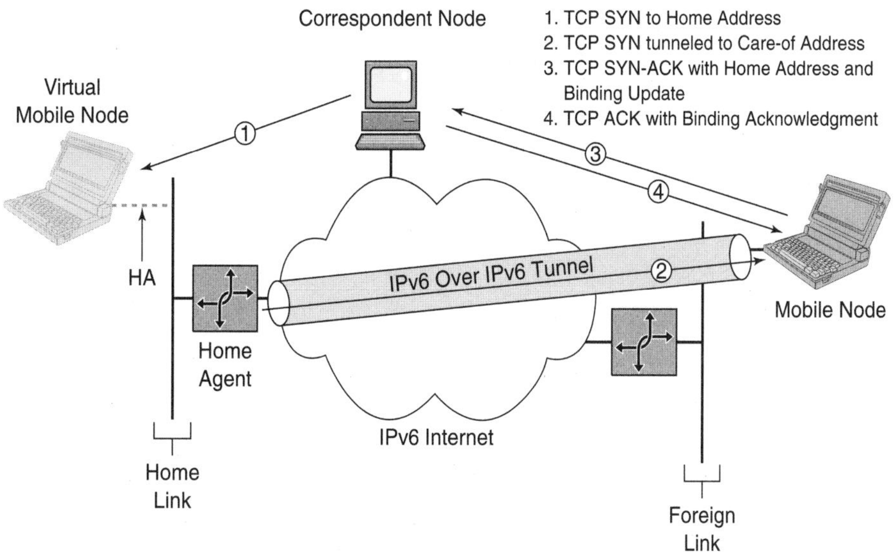

Figure 12-20. *A mobile node returning home*

When the mobile node returns home (reattaches to its home link), the following occurs:

1. The mobile node sends a multicast Router Solicitation message on the home link. The mobile node might send a router solicitation either because the link layer indicated a media change or because the node received a router advertisement that contained a new prefix. Depending on the IPv6 mobility implementation, the mobile node sends a router solicitation either from its link-local address (assuming that the link-local address of the mobile node is most likely unique on the home link) or from the unspecified address (::) (assuming that the link-local address of the mobile node might not be unique on the home link).

2. All routers on the home link reply with a Router Advertisement message. Depending on the source address of the Router Solicitation message, the reply is either unicast (because the router solicitation was sent from a link-local address) or multicast (because the router solicitation was sent from the unspecified address). Figure 12-20 shows the router advertisement being unicast to the mobile node.

    Because the router advertisement contains an address prefix that matches its home address prefix, the mobile node determines that it is attached to its home link. Depending on the IPv6 mobility implementation, the mobile node may or may not perform duplicate address detection for its home address because the home agent is acting as an ND proxy for the mobile node and defending the use of the mobile node's home address. If the mobile node does perform duplicate address detection, it must ignore the neighbor advertisement reply sent from the home agent.

3.   To remove the binding cache entry from the home agent, the mobile node sends the home agent a binding update with the care-of address set to the mobile node's home address and with the Home Registration (H) and Acknowledge (A) flags set.

If multiple router advertisements are received, the mobile node can determine which router is its home agent from the router advertisement with the Prefix Information option that contains the home agent's global address in the Prefix field.

The mobile node determines the home agent's link-layer address from the Link-Layer Address field in the Source Link-Layer Address option in the router advertisement sent by the home agent. If the Source Link-Layer Address option is not included, then the mobile node can determine the link-layer address of the home agent using address resolution, because the global address of the home agent is known.

4.   For each correspondent node in the mobile node's binding update list, the mobile node sends a binding update to the correspondent node with the care-of address set to the mobile node's home address.

5.   Upon receipt of the binding update, the home agent removes the entry for the mobile node from its binding cache, stops defending the use of the mobile node's home address on the home link, and responds with a binding acknowledgement. This is shown in Figure 12-20. Additionally, the home agent removes itself from the multicast group for the solicited node multicast address corresponding to the mobile node's home address and stops listening for link-layer multicast frames addressed to the multicast MAC address corresponding to the solicited node multicast address.

Upon receipt of the binding update, the correspondent nodes remove the entry for the mobile node in their binding cache and, if requested by the mobile node, send a binding acknowledgment.

6.   After receiving the binding acknowledgement from the home agent, the mobile node must inform nodes on the home link that the

link-layer address for the home address has changed to the link-layer address of the mobile node. It sends an unsolicited multicast Neighbor Advertisement message to the link-local scope all-nodes multicast address (FF02::1) with the Override (O) flag set.

The sending of the unsolicited multicast Neighbor Advertisement message is not required. If it is not sent, nodes on the home link that were communicating with the mobile node while it was away from home might still have an entry in their neighbor cache that contains the mobile node's home address and the link-layer address of the home agent. This is a redirect situation, in which a node is sending a packet to a router when the destination is on-link. When the home node sends a packet to the mobile node by using the link-layer address of the home agent, the home agent forwards the packet to the mobile node and sends a Redirect message containing the Target Link-Layer Address option to update the neighbor cache of the home node.

The mobile node also joins the multicast group for the solicited node multicast address corresponding to the mobile node's home address, and registers interest in receiving link-layer multicast frames to the multicast MAC address corresponding to the solicited node multicast address.

IPv6 Mobility Host Sending Algorithm

The IPv6 host sending algorithm is described in Chapter 6, "Neighbor Discovery." However, the discussion in Chapter 6 does not include full IPv6 mobility functionality. An IPv6 mobile node can be both a mobile node and correspondent node at the same time. Therefore, the host sending algorithm for an IPv6 mobility node must take into account the following:

■   If the sending host is away from home
     If so, the sending host must set the source address of the IPv6 header to the sending host's care-of address and include the Destination Options header with the Home Address option set to the sending host's home address.

■   If the destination node is away from home
     If so, the sending host must set the destination address of the IPv6 header to the destination node's care-of address and include a Routing header with the Address 1 field set to the destination node's home address.

An IPv6 mobility host uses the following algorithm when sending a unicast or anycast packet to an arbitrary destination:

1. Check the destination cache for an entry matching the destination address.

2. If an entry matching the destination address is not found in the destination cache, go to step 7.

3. If an entry matching the destination address is found in the destination cache, check for a pointer to an entry in the binding cache. This pointer will be present if the destination is a mobile node away from home.

4. If there is a pointer to an entry in the binding cache, the sending host sets the destination address in the IPv6 header to the destination node's care-of address and inserts a Routing header that includes the destination node's home address in the Address 1 field. The binding cache entry for the home address contains a pointer to the destination cache entry for the care-of address, from which the sending host obtains the next-hop address and interface for the care-of address.

5. If there is a no pointer to an entry in the binding cache, then the sending host obtains the next-hop address and interface from the destination cache entry.

6. If the sending host is a mobile node away from home, it sets the source address in the IPv6 header to the sending host's care-of address and inserts a Destination Options header that includes the Home Address option containing the sending host's home address. Go to step 10.

7. Check the local IPv6 routing table for the longest matching route that has the lowest metric to the destination address. If there are multiple longest matching routes with the lowest metric, IPv6 chooses a route to use.

8. Based on the chosen route, determine the next-hop interface and address used for forwarding the packet.

   If no route is found, IPv6 assumes that the destination is directly reachable. The next-hop address is set to the destination address and an interface is chosen.

9. Update the destination cache.

10. Check the neighbor cache for an entry matching the next-hop address.

11. If an entry matching the next-hop address is found in the neighbor cache, obtain the link-layer address.

12. If an entry matching the next-hop address is not found in the neighbor cache, use address resolution to obtain the link-layer address for the next-hop address.

    If address resolution is not successful, indicate an error.

13. Send the packet by using the link-layer address of the neighbor cache entry.

    Figure 12-21 shows the IPv6 mobility host sending process.

IPv6 Mobility Host Receiving Algorithm

The IPv6 host receiving algorithm is described in Chapter 10, "IPv6 Routing." However, the discussion in Chapter 10 does not include full IPv6 mobility functionality. An IPv6 mobile node can be both a mobile node and correspondent node at the same time. Therefore, the host receiving algorithm for an IPv6 mobility node must take into account the following:

- If the receiving node is away from home
  If so, the receiving node processes the Routing header in the IPv6 packet and logically sets the destination address of the IPv6 header to the value of the Address 1 field in the Routing header.

- If the sending host is away from home
  If so, the receiving node processes the Destination Options header and logically sets the source address of the IPv6 packet to the home address contained in the Home Address option.

Additionally, a receiving IPv6 mobility host must recognize a packet tunneled from its home agent in order to determine when to send a binding update to a new correspondent node.

An IPv6 mobility host uses the following algorithm when receiving a unicast or anycast packet from an arbitrary source:

1. Verify whether the destination address in the IPv6 packet corresponds to an IPv6 address assigned to a local host interface.

   If the destination address is not assigned to a local host interface, silently discard the IPv6 packet.

2. Check to see if there is a Routing header present. If so, process the Routing header and set the destination address of the IPv6 packet to the value of the last address field in the Routing header. For

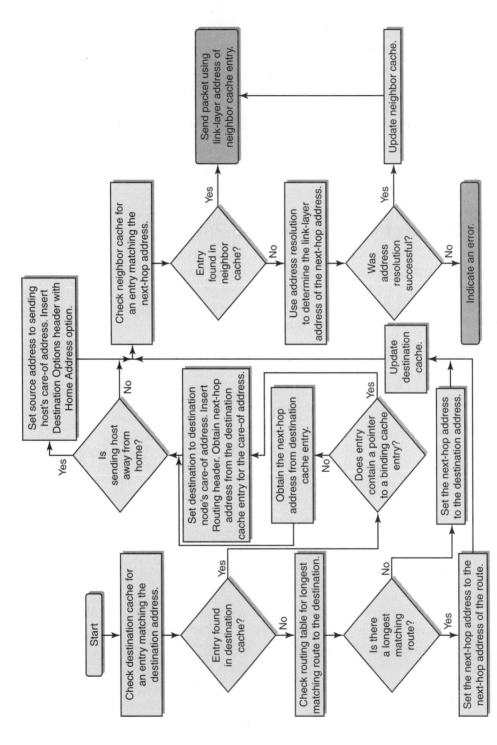

Figure 12-21. *The IPv6 mobility host sending process*

packets sent from correspondent nodes, the last address field is the Address 1 field, which contains the mobile node's home address.

Although all IPv6 hosts must support the processing of a Routing header, this was not described in Chapter 10 to keep the discussion of the host receiving algorithm as simple as possible. Because a mobility-based Routing header is placed in the packet when the destination mobile node is away from home, it is explicitly described here.

3. Check to see if the packet was tunneled from the home agent. In the outer IPv6 header, the destination address is set to the receiving node's care-of address, the source address is set to the home agent's address, and the protocol field is set to 41. If so, strip the outer header, set the destination and source addresses of the packet to the addresses in the inner IPv6 header, and queue a binding update to the source address in the inner IPv6 header. The binding update is sent either as a separate packet or is sent with response data to the new correspondent node.

   For data sent to an IPv6 mobile node when it is away from home, an incoming IPv6 packet will either be tunneled from the home agent or sent with a Routing header containing the home address.

   Although all IPv6 hosts must support the processing of IPv6 tunneled packets, this was not described in Chapter 10 to keep the discussion of the host receiving algorithm as simple as possible. Because IPv6 packets are tunneled by a home agent when the destination mobile node is away from home, it is explicitly described here.

4. Check to see if there is a Destination Options header with a Home Address option. If so, logically set the source address of the IPv6 packet to the home address in the Home Address option.

5. Based on the Next Header field, process extension headers (if present) and pass the upper layer PDU to the appropriate upper-layer protocol.

   If the protocol does not exist, send an ICMPv6 Parameter Problem-Unrecognized Next Header Type Encountered message back to the sender and discard the packet.

6. If the upper layer PDU is not a TCP segment or UDP message, pass the upper layer PDU to the appropriate protocol.

7. If the upper layer PDU is a TCP segment or UDP message, check the destination port.

If no application exists for the UDP port number, send an ICMPv6 Destination Unreachable-Port Unreachable message back to the sender and discard the packet. If no application exists for the TCP port number, send a TCP Connection Reset segment back to the sender and discard the packet.

8. If an application exists for the UDP or TCP destination port, process the contents of the TCP segment or UDP message.

Figure 12-22 shows the IPv6 mobility host receiving process.

REFERENCES

RFC 2461 – "Neighbor Discovery for IP Version 6 (IPv6)"

RFC 2526 – "Reserved IPv6 Subnet Anycast Addresses"

Internet draft – "Mobility Support in IPv6" (version 13)

TESTING FOR UNDERSTANDING

To test your understanding of IPv6 mobility, answer the following questions. See Appendix D to check your answers.

1. How does a mobile node determine its home subnet prefix, home address, and the address of its home agent?

2. When does a home agent or correspondent node send a binding request?

3. How does a home agent compile a list of home agents on the home link and then convey that information to the mobile node while it is away from home?

4. How does the mobile node determine when it has attached to a new link?

5. What kinds of packets are sent between the home agent and the mobile node?

6. What kinds of packets are sent between the correspondent node and the mobile node?

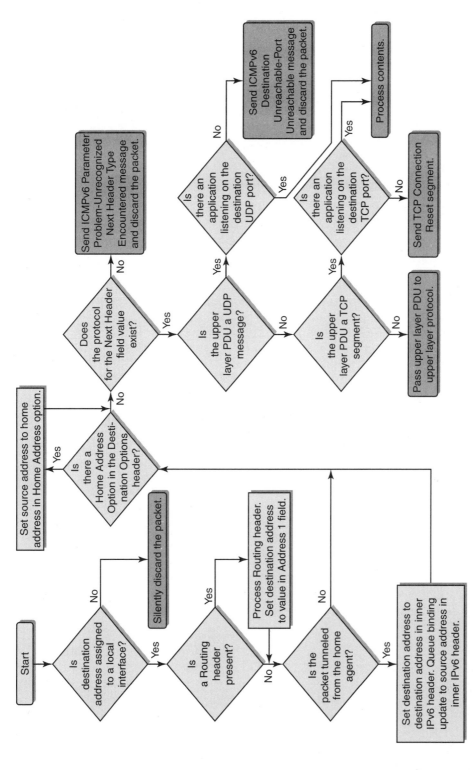

Figure 12-22. *The IPv6 mobility host receiving process*

7. What kinds of packets are sent between the correspondent node and the home agent?

8. Describe the addressing in the IPv6 header, and the sequence of IPv6 extension headers and their contents, for a packet sent by a mobile node that is away from home to another mobile node that is away from home for which a binding cache entry is present.

9. When does the mobile node send a binding update to the home agent? When does the mobile node send a binding update to the correspondent node?

10. How does a mobile node determine when it has returned home?

11. How does the mobile node avoid duplicate address conflicts when it returns home?

Appendix A

Link-Layer Support for IPv6

This appendix describes the link-layer encapsulation for IPv6 packets for common LAN and WAN technologies and how IPv6 packets are encapsulated when sent across an IPv4 infrastructure.

BASIC STRUCTURE OF IPV6 PACKETS

On LAN and WAN media, IPv6 packets exist as link-layer frames. Figure A-1 shows the basic structure of IPv6 packets sent over LAN and WAN media.

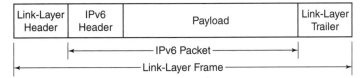

Figure A-1. *Basic structure of IPv6 packets sent on LAN and WAN media*

The structure of IPv6 packets sent on LAN and WAN media consists of:

- **A link-layer header and trailer**
  The encapsulation placed on the IPv6 packet at the link layer is composed of a link-layer header and trailer.

- **An IPv6 header**
  This is the new IPv6 header. For more information, see Chapter 4, "The IPv6 Header."

- **Payload**
  The payload of the IPv6 packet includes zero or more IPv6 extension headers and the upper layer PDU. For more information, see Chapter 4, "The IPv6 Header."

LAN MEDIA

To successfully troubleshoot IPv6 problems on a LAN, it is important to understand LAN encapsulations. LAN technologies encompass desktop technologies such as Ethernet, Token Ring, and FDDI. In some technologies (such as Ethernet), multiple encapsulations may exist. In each of these technologies, the IPv6 packet needs to be delimited, addressed, and identified as an IPv6 packet.

Current RFCs exist for sending IPv6 packets over the following LAN media:

- Ethernet (RFC 2464)

- Token Ring (RFC 2470)

- FDDI (RFC 2467)

- ARCnet (RFC 2497)

NOTE:

ARCnet is not discussed in this appendix. For more information about ARCnet encapsulation of IPv6 packets, see RFC 2497.

The IPv6 protocol for the Windows .NET Server 2003 family and Windows XP supports only the sending and receiving of IPv6 packets over FDDI interfaces and any LAN interface that registers itself with the Network Device Interface Specification (NDIS) layer as an 802.3 media type. This media type includes Ethernet, IEEE 802.11 wireless, phone line, power line, and other technologies.

Ethernet: Ethernet II

When sent over an Ethernet network, IPv6 packets use either Ethernet II or IEEE 802.3 Sub-Network Access Protocol (SNAP) encapsulation. IPv6 encapsulation for Ethernet links is described in RFC 2464. Figure A-2 shows Ethernet II encapsulation of IPv6 packets.

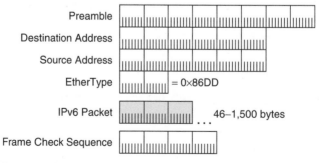

Figure A-2. *Ethernet II encapsulation of IPv6 packets*

The fields in the Ethernet header and trailer are:

- **Preamble**
  The Preamble field is used to synchronize the receiver and indicate the start of the Ethernet frame. The size of this field is 64 bits.

- **Destination Address**
  The Destination Address field contains the MAC address of the destination Ethernet node. The size of this field is 48 bits.

- **Source Address**
  The Source Address field contains the MAC address of the sending Ethernet node. The size of this field is 48 bits.

- **EtherType**
  The EtherType field indicates the upper layer protocol of the Ethernet payload. The size of this field is 16 bits. The EtherType field is set to 0x86DD for IPv6 packets. In contrast, the EtherType field is set to 0x800 for IPv4 packets.

- **Frame Check Sequence**
  The value of this field is a checksum that is used to check for bit-level errors in the Ethernet frame. The checksum value is computed by the sending Ethernet node and verified by the receiving Ethernet node. The size of this field is 32 bits.

IPv6 packets sent using Ethernet II encapsulation have a maximum size of 1,500 bytes and a minimum size of 46 bytes. IPv6 packets under 46 bytes in length are padded to 46 bytes to preserve the Ethernet minimum frame size of 64 bytes (not including the Preamble field).

Network Monitor Capture

Here is an example of Ethernet II encapsulation as displayed by Network Monitor (capture AppA_01 in the \NetworkMonitorCaptures folder on the companion CD-ROM):

```
+ Frame: Base frame properties
  ETHERNET: ETYPE = IPv6
     ETHERNET: Destination address : 3333FF52F9D8
        ETHERNET: .......1 = Group address
        ETHERNET: ......1. = Locally administered address
     ETHERNET: Source address : 00B0D0234733
        ETHERNET: ......0. = Universally administered address
```

```
ETHERNET: Frame Length : 86 (0x0056)
ETHERNET: Ethernet Type : 0x86DD
ETHERNET: Ethernet Data: Number of data bytes remaining =
                         72 (0x0048)
+ IP6: Hop Opts; Proto = ICMP6; Len = 24
+ ICMP6: Group Membership Report
```

Notice that Network Monitor does not display the Preamble and Frame Check Sequence fields.

Ethernet: IEEE 802.3 SNAP

The IEEE 802.3 SNAP encapsulation uses a SNAP header to encapsulate the IPv6 packet so that it can be sent on an IEEE 802.3-compliant network. IEEE 802.3 SNAP encapsulation consists of an IEEE 802.3 header, an IEEE 802.2 Logical Link Control (LLC) header, a SNAP header, and an IEEE 802.3 trailer. Figure A-3 shows Ethernet IEEE 802.3 SNAP encapsulation of IPv6 packets.

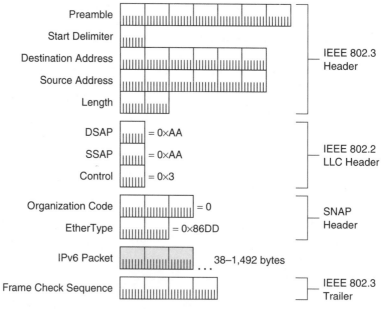

Figure A-3. *Ethernet IEEE 802.3 SNAP encapsulation of IPv6 packets*

The fields in the IEEE 802.3 SNAP encapsulation are:

■ **Preamble**
The Preamble field is used to synchronize the receiver. The size of this field is 56 bits.

■ **Start Delimiter**

The Start Delimiter field indicates the start of the Ethernet frame. The size of this field is 8 bits.

■ **Destination Address**

The Destination Address field contains the MAC address of the destination Ethernet node. The size of this field is 48 bits.

■ **Source Address**

The Source Address field contains the MAC address of the sending Ethernet node. The size of this field is 48 bits.

■ **Length**

The Length field specifies the number of bytes in the IEEE 802.3 payload. This includes the IEEE 802.2 header and the SNAP header. The size of this field is 16 bits.

■ **Destination Service Access Point (DSAP)**

The DSAP field indicates the upper layer protocol of the payload for the destination. For SNAP-encapsulated payloads, the DSAP is set to the defined value of 0xAA. The size of this field is 8 bits.

■ **Source Service Access Point (SSAP)**

The SSAP field indicates the upper layer protocol of the payload for the sender. For SNAP-encapsulated payloads, the SSAP is set to the defined value of 0xAA. The size of this field is 8 bits.

■ **Control**

For SNAP-encapsulated payloads, the Control field is set to the defined value of 0x3, indicating that the 802.2 frame is an unnumbered frame. The size of this field is 8 bits.

■ **Organization Code**

The Organization Code field indicates the ID of the organization that defines the values in the two-byte field that follows the Organization Code field. For SNAP encapsulation, the Organization Code field is set to 0, indicating the IETF, who administers the values of the EtherType field. The size of this field is 24 bits.

■ **EtherType**

The EtherType field indicates the upper layer protocol of the payload. The size of this field is 16 bits. The EtherType field is set to 0x86DD for IPv6 packets.

■ **Frame Check Sequence**

The value of this field is a checksum that is used to check for bit-level errors in the Ethernet frame. The checksum value is computed by the sending Ethernet node and verified by the receiving Ethernet node. The size of this field is 32 bits.

IPv6 packets sent using an IEEE 802.3 SNAP frame have a maximum size of 1,492 bytes and a minimum size of 38 bytes. IPv6 packets under 38 bytes in length are padded to 38 bytes to preserve the Ethernet minimum frame size of 64 bytes (not including the Preamble and Start Delimiter fields).

Token Ring: IEEE 802.5 SNAP

When sent over a Token Ring network, IPv6 packets use the IEEE 802.5 SNAP encapsulation. IPv6 encapsulation for Token Ring links is described in RFC 2470. Figure A-4 shows IEEE 802.5 SNAP encapsulation of IPv6 packets.

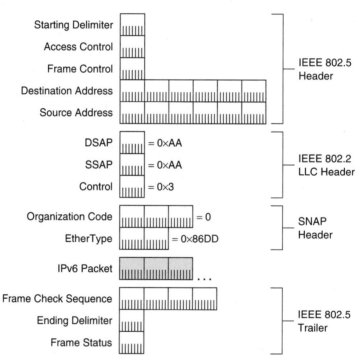

Figure A-4. *IEEE 802.5 SNAP encapsulation of IPv6 packets*

The fields in the Token Ring encapsulation are:

■ **Starting Delimiter**
The Starting Delimiter field indicates the start of the Token Ring frame. The size of this field is 8 bits.

■ **Access Control**

The Access Control field indicates the frame type (token or data frame), the frame's priority, the frame's reservation level, and whether the frame has passed the ring monitor station. The size of this field is 8 bits.

■ **Frame Control**

The Frame Control field indicates whether the frame is a data frame or a Token Ring management frame and if a Token Ring management frame, the specific type. The size of this field is 8 bits.

■ **Destination Address**

The Destination Address field contains the MAC address of the destination Token Ring node. The size of this field is 48 bits.

■ **Source Address**

The Source Address field contains the MAC address of the sending Token Ring node. The size of this field is 48 bits.

■ **DSAP**

The DSAP field indicates the upper layer protocol of the payload for the destination. For SNAP-encapsulated payloads, the DSAP is set to the defined value of 0xAA. The size of this field is 8 bits.

■ **SSAP**

The SSAP field indicates the upper layer protocol of the payload for the sender. For SNAP-encapsulated payloads, the SSAP is set to the defined value of 0xAA. The size of this field is 8 bits.

■ **Control**

For SNAP-encapsulated payloads, the Control field is set to the defined value of 0x3, indicating that the 802.2 frame is an unnumbered frame. The size of this field is 8 bits.

■ **Organization Code**

The Organization Code field indicates the ID of the organization that defines the values in the two-byte field that follows the Organization Code field. For SNAP encapsulation, the Organization Code field is set to 0, indicating the IETF, who administers the values of the EtherType field. The size of this field is 24 bits.

■ **EtherType**

The EtherType field indicates the upper layer protocol of the payload. The size of this field is 16 bits. The EtherType field is set to 0x86DD for IPv6 packets.

■ **Frame Check Sequence**

The value of this field is a checksum that is used to check for bit-level errors in the Token Ring frame. The checksum value is computed by the sending Token Ring node and verified by the receiving Token Ring node. The size of this field is 32 bits.

■ **Ending Delimiter**

The Ending Delimiter field indicates the end of the Token Ring frame. The size of this field is 8 bits.

■ **Frame Status**

The Frame Status field indicates whether or not the destination address was recognized and whether or not the frame was copied. The size of this field is 8 bits.

IPv6 packets sent using Token Ring have a variety of MTUs depending on the maximum amount of time that a token ring node can hold the token, which can vary based on the data rate and the number of nodes on the ring. For more information, see RFC 2470.

FDDI

FDDI also uses the SNAP encapsulation. IPv6 encapsulation for FDDI links is described in RFC 2467. Figure A-5 shows FDDI encapsulation of IPv6 packets. The fields in the FDDI encapsulation are:

■ **Preamble**

The Preamble field is used to synchronize the receiver. The size of this field is 16 bits.

■ **Starting Delimiter**

The Starting Delimiter field indicates the start of the FDDI frame. The size of this field is 8 bits.

■ **Frame Control**

The Frame Control field indicates the frame class, the size of the source and destination addresses, and the frame type (token or data frame). The size of this field is 8 bits.

■ **Destination Address**

The Destination Address field contains the MAC address of the destination FDDI node. The size of this field is 48 bits.

■ **Source Address**

The Source Address field contains the MAC address of the sending FDDI node. The size of this field is 48 bits.

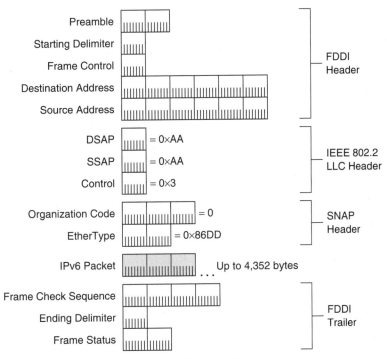

Figure A-5. *FDDI encapsulation of IPv6 packets*

- **DSAP**

  The DSAP field indicates the upper layer protocol of the payload for the destination. For SNAP-encapsulated payloads, the DSAP is set to the defined value of 0xAA. The size of this field is 8 bits.

- **SSAP**

  The SSAP field indicates the upper layer protocol of the payload for the sender. For SNAP-encapsulated payloads, the SSAP is set to the defined value of 0xAA. The size of this field is 8 bits.

- **Control**

  For SNAP-encapsulated payloads, the Control field is set to the defined value of 0x3, indicating that the 802.2 frame is an unnumbered frame. The size of this field is 8 bits.

- **Organization Code**

  The Organization Code field indicates the ID of the organization that defines the values in the two-byte field that follows the Organization Code field. For SNAP encapsulation, the Organization Code field is set to 0, indicating the IETF, who administers the values of the EtherType field. The size of this field is 24 bits.

■ **EtherType**

The EtherType field indicates the upper layer protocol of the payload. The size of this field is 16 bits. The EtherType field is set to 0x86DD for IPv6 packets.

■ **Frame Check Sequence**

The value of this field is a checksum that is used to check for bit-level errors in the FDDI frame. The checksum value is computed by the sending FDDI node and verified by the receiving FDDI node. The size of this field is 32 bits.

■ **Ending Delimiter**

The Ending Delimiter field indicates the end of the FDDI frame. The size of this field is 8 bits.

■ **Frame Status**

The Frame Status field indicates whether or not the destination address was recognized, whether or not the frame was copied, and whether or not the Frame Check Sequence field is valid. The size of this field is 16 bits.

FDDI allows an MTU of 4,352 bytes for IPv6 packets. The IPv6 MTU is derived from the 4,500 byte maximum payload for FDDI, less 22 bytes for FDDI MAC overhead, 8 bytes for the SNAP header, and 118 bytes that are reserved for future MAC header uses. All IPv6 packets are transmitted as asynchronous LLC frames using unrestricted tokens.

WAN MEDIA

To successfully troubleshoot IPv6 problems in a wide area network, it is important to understand WAN encapsulations. WAN technologies encompass point-to-point technologies (for example, analog phone lines, Integrated Services Digital Network (ISDN), T-Carrier, and Switched-56) and packet switched technologies (for example, X.25, Frame Relay, and ATM). In each of these technologies, the packet needs to be delimited, addressed, and identified as an IPv6 packet.

Current RFCs exist for sending IPv6 packets over the following WAN media:

■ PPP (RFC 2472)

■ X.25 (RFC 1356)

■ Frame Relay (RFC 2590)

■ ATM (RFC 2492)

The IPv6 protocol for the Windows .NET Server 2003 family and Windows XP does not support the sending and receiving of IPv6 packets over any WAN media. However, IPv6 packets encapsulated with an IPv4 header can be sent over any WAN media that supports IPv4 packets.

PPP

PPP, described in RFC 1661, is a standardized serial line encapsulation method that can be used over asynchronous serial lines, such as analog phone lines, and synchronous serial lines, such as T-Carrier, ISDN, or Synchronous Optical Network (SONET). PPP is a family of protocols that describe:

- A multi-protocol encapsulation method.

- A Link Control Protocol (LCP) for establishing, configuring, and testing the data-link connection.

- A family of Network Control Protocols (NCPs) for establishing and configuring different network-layer protocols. RFC 2472 describes the IPv6 Control Protocol (IPv6CP), which is the NCP for configuring the IPv6 protocol over a PPP link.

Only the encapsulation method is described here.

PPP encapsulation uses a variant of the ISO High Level Data Link Control (HDLC) protocol as described in RFC 1662. IPv6 encapsulation for PPP links is described in RFC 2472. Figure A-6 shows PPP encapsulation of IPv6 packets.

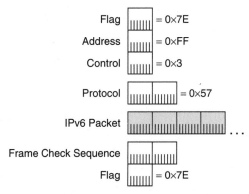

Figure A-6. *PPP with HDLC framing encapsulation of IPv6 packets*

The fields in the PPP header and trailer are:

- **Flag**

  The Flag field indicates the start and end of a PPP frame and is set to 0x7E. In consecutive PPP frames, only a single Flag character is used to mark both the end of a PPP frame and the beginning of the next PPP frame. The size of this field is 8 bits.

- **Address**

  The Address field is used in HDLC environments to address the frame to a destination node. On a point-to-point link, the destination node does not need to be addressed. Therefore, for PPP, the Address field is set to 0xFF, which is the broadcast address. The size of this field is 8 bits. Typically, the use of this field is suppressed.

- **Control**

  The Control field is used in HDLC environments for data-link layer sequencing and acknowledgments. For PPP, the Control field is set to 0x3 to indicate an unnumbered information (UI) frame. The size of this field is 8 bits. Typically, the use of this field is suppressed.

- **Protocol**

  The Protocol field identifies the protocol of the PPP payload. The Protocol field is set to 0x57 to indicate an IPv6 packet. In contrast, the Protocol field is set to 0x21 to indicate an IPv4 packet. The size of this field is 16 bits. Although defined as a 16-bit field, typically the Protocol field size is compressed to 8 bits.

- **Frame Check Sequence**

  The Frame Check Sequence field stores a checksum value that is used to check for bit-level errors in the PPP frame. The size of this field is 16 bits.

The MTU for a PPP connection (called the MRU, or Maximum Receive Unit) is negotiated by using LCP. The default MRU is 1,500 octets. If negotiated lower, a PPP host must still have the ability to receive 1,500-octet frames in the case of link synchronization failure.

NOTE:

The IPv6 protocol for the Windows .NET Server 2003 family and Windows XP does not support RFC 2472. Because PPP is not supported, IPv6 packets over PPTP and L2TP links are also not supported. However, IPv6 traffic can be sent over a PPP link if it is encapsulated with an IPv4 header using the coexistence technologies described in Chapter 11, "Coexistence and Migration."

X.25

X.25 was developed in the 1970s to provide dumb terminals with WAN connectivity across public data networks (PDNs). However, because of its flexibility and reliability, X.25 has emerged as an international standard for sending data across PDNs.

X.25 is a connection-oriented interface to a packet switched network (PSN) and provides error checking with guaranteed delivery of packets over the PSN by using either switched virtual circuits (SVCs) or permanent virtual circuits (PVCs). Because of its reliability and guaranteed delivery, X.25 works effectively for applications that require reliable transmission.

A router can connect via a Packet Assembler/Disassembler (PAD) to the X.25 network. The PAD is responsible for breaking down messages into packets and addressing them appropriately. The connection between the router and the PAD, the operations at the PAD, and the connection from the PAD to the carrier office is defined by the X.28, X.3, and X.29 specifications.

The X.25 specification maps to layers 1 through 3 of the OSI model. However, the X.25 specification was developed before the OSI model, so layer names are slightly different. The Physical layer is called X.21 and specifies the electrical and physical interface. The Data Link Layer is the Link Access Procedure-Balanced (LAPB) protocol, which takes care of frame composition, flow control, and error checking at the Link Access layer. The Packet layer corresponds to the Network layer and is responsible for the set up and addressing of the virtual circuit.

When IPv6 packets are encapsulated for transmission on X.25 networks, they are wrapped with two sets of headers that correspond to the X.25 Network and Data Link layers. The X.25 Network layer uses the Packet Layer Protocol (PLP). The X.25 Data Link layer uses LAPB, which is the same HDLC format as PPP.

Figure A-7 shows X.25 encapsulation of IPv6 packets.

The fields in the PLP header are:

- **General Format Indicator**
  The General Format Indicator (GFI) indicates X.25 control information. The size of this field is 4 bits.

- **Logical Channel Number**
  The Logical Channel Number (LCN) field indicates the virtual circuit over which the packet is sent. When an X.25 virtual circuit is created, an X.25 LCN is assigned to that virtual circuit so that data can be addressed to the proper destination. The size of this field is 12 bits, allowing a maximum of 4,095 simultaneous connections (LCN 0 is used for X.25 signaling).

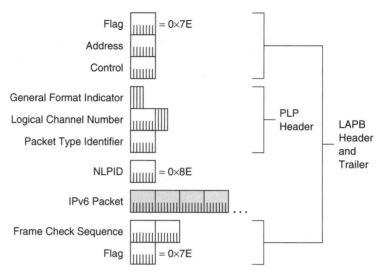

Figure A-7. *X.25 encapsulation of IPv6 packets*

- **Packet Type Identifier**

    The Packet Type Identifier field indicates the type of X.25 packet (X.25 signaling messages vs. X.25 user data). The size of this field is 8 bits.

    The fields in the LAPB header and trailer are:

- **Flag**

    The Flag field indicates the start and end of the X.25 frame and is fixed at 0x7E. The size of this field is 8 bits.

- **Address**

    The Address field is used to specify X.25 commands and responses. The size of this field is 8 bits.

- **Control**

    The Control field is used to indicate sequencing and acknowledgments for reliable data transfer. The size of this field is 8 bits.

- **Frame Check Sequence**

    The value of this field is a checksum used to check for bit-level errors in the LAPB frame. The size of this field is 16 bits.

    To identify the X.25 payload being encapsulated, X.25 packets use the Network Layer Protocol Identifier (NLPID) field. The size of this field is 8 bits.

For IPv6 packets, the NLPID is set to 0x8E. For IPv4 packets, the NLPID is set to 0xCC.

IPv6 packets sent over X.25 links have a default MTU size of 1,280 bytes, unless negotiated higher by the sender and receiver. Most X.25 networks have a maximum X.25 packet size of 256 or 512 bytes. In this case, X.25 fragmentation is used to send the 1,280-byte IPv6 packets across the X.25 network.

Frame Relay

Frame Relay was originally conceived as a protocol for use over ISDN interfaces. Because Frame Relay could be applied outside the realm of ISDN, it was developed as an independent protocol. Frame Relay is a Data Link layer protocol that is much faster than X.25 because it is more streamlined and does not provide error correction and flow control.

Within the Frame Relay PDN, Frame Relay switching implements statistical multiplexing instead of time division multiplexing. With statistical multiplexing, circuits can be used from devices that are not currently using their allocated circuits. This makes real-time networks that are "bursty" in nature ideal candidates for Frame Relay.

The Local Management Interface (LMI) manages the link. LMI is responsible for establishing a link and monitoring PVCs. Because modern digital links are less susceptible to errors, Frame Relay employs only a checksum to detect a corrupted frame and does not include an error correction mechanism. Frame Relay also relies on upper protocols for flow control over the link.

IPv6 packets sent over a Frame Relay network are encapsulated in a header and trailer that are also derived from the ISO HDLC protocol and has a similar structure to the PPP encapsulation. IPv6 packet behavior and encapsulation for Frame Relay links is described in RFCs 2491 and 2590. Figure A-8 shows Frame Relay encapsulation of IPv6 packets.

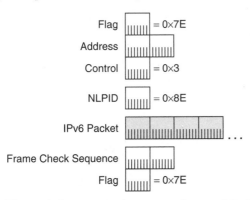

Figure A-8. *Frame Relay encapsulation of IPv6 packets*

The fields in the Frame Relay header and trailer are:

■ **Flag**
The Flag field indicates the start and end of the Frame Relay frame and is fixed at 0x7E. The size of this field is 8 bits.

■ **Address**
The Address field contains both the Data Link Connection Identifier (DLCI) that identifies the virtual circuit over which the frame is sent and congestion flags. Frame Relay standards allow for an Address field of variable size, but most implementations use a size of 16 bits.

■ **Control**
The Control field is set to 0x3 to indicate a UI frame. The size of this field is 8 bits.

■ **Frame Check Sequence**
The Frame Check Sequence (FCS) field stores a checksum value that is used to check for bit-level errors in the Frame Relay frame. The size of this field is 16 bits.

Like X.25, Frame Relay uses the NLPID field to identify the encapsulated payload. For IPv6 packets, the NLPID is set to 0x8E. For IPv4 packets, the NLPID is set to 0xCC.

MTUs for Frame Relay links vary according to the Frame Relay provider. As specified in RFC 2590, Frame Relay links have a maximum frame size of at least 1,600 bytes. Therefore, the default IPv6 MTU for Frame Relay links that use a 16-bit Address field is 1,592.

ATM: Null Encapsulation

ATM technology is based on the development of Broadband Integrated Services Digital Network (B-ISDN) for the high-speed transfer of voice, video, and data through PDNs. ATM is a connection-oriented non-guaranteed delivery service. ATM scales very well to LANs and WANs and can be used in a private network as well as a public data network.

ATM is different from Frame Relay in that, instead of sending messages that have frames of variable size, all messages are segmented and sent as equally sized cells. Each cell consists of a 5-byte header and a 48-byte payload. By making all messages the same size, switching is optimized and the need to buffer messages of varying sizes is eliminated. With these improvements, ATM is capable of reaching speeds from 64 kilobits per seconds (Kbps) to 9.6 gigabits per second (Gbps), depending upon the underlying physical layer.

Because it is an asynchronous mechanism, ATM differs from synchronous transfer mode methods, in which time-division multiplexing (TDM) techniques are employed to pre-assign devices to time slots. TDM is inefficient relative to ATM because with TDM the station can transmit only at a specified time, even though all the other time slots are empty. With ATM, a station can send cells whenever necessary.

Relative to IPv6, ATM functions as a link layer. ATM itself has its own set of layers that define:

- How ATM cells are sent over several different physical mediums, such as SONET and Digital Service (DS)-3.

- How connections are established and cells are passed through the ATM network.

- How the data of higher level protocols, such as IPv4 and IPv6, are segmented and reassembled using 48-byte segments suitable for transmission over an ATM network. This layer is known as the ATM Adaptation layer.

IPv6 packets sent over an ATM network have an MTU of 9,180 bytes and are encapsulated by using ATM Adaptation Layer 5 (AAL5). AAL5 encapsulation consists of an AAL5 trailer added to the end of the IPv6 packet. The resulting data block (called the AAL5 PDU) is then segmented into 48-byte segments that become the payloads for 53-byte ATM cells.

IPv6 encapsulation for ATM links is described in RFC 2492. Figure A-9 shows ATM null encapsulation of IPv6 packets.

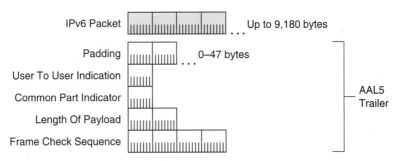

Figure A-9. *ATM null encapsulation of IPv6 packets*

The fields in the AAL5 trailer are:

- **Padding**
  The Padding field is added to the IPv6 packet so that the AAL5 PDU is an integral number of 48-byte segments. The size of this field varies from 0 to 47 bytes.

- **User to User Indication**

    The User to User Indication field is used to transfer information between AAL5 nodes. The size of this field is 8 bits.

- **Common Part Indicator**

    The Common Part Indicator field is used for alignment purposes so that the unpadded portion of the AAL5 trailer is on an 8-byte boundary. The size of this field is 8 bits.

- **Length of Payload**

    The Length of Payload field specifies the length in bytes of the IPv6 packet so that the receiver can discard the Padding field. The size of this field is 16 bits.

- **Frame Check Sequence**

    The Frame Check Sequence field stores a checksum value that is used to check for bit-level errors in the AAL5 PDU. The size of this field is 32 bits. AAL5 uses the same CRC-32 algorithm as 802.x networks such as Ethernet and Token Ring.

Before being sent on the ATM network, the AAL5 PDU is segmented by the ATM Segmentation and Reassembly (SAR) sublayer into 48-byte units. These units become the ATM payloads for a stream of ATM cells. When the last 48-byte segment is sent, a bit in the Payload Type field of the ATM header is set to 1 to indicate the last cell in the AAL5 PDU.

When the last cell is received, the receiver uses the Frame Check Sequence field to check the validity of the bits in the AAL5 PDU. The receiver then uses the Length of Payload field to discard any padding. The AAL5 trailer is stripped and the originally transmitted IPv6 packet is then passed to the IPv6 protocol for processing. If a single ATM cell for the AAL5 PDU is dropped from the network, the entire IPv6 packet must be resent.

ATM: SNAP Encapsulation

The ATM null encapsulation can be used when only the IPv6 protocol is operating over a given ATM virtual circuit. Multiple protocols operating over the same ATM virtual circuit require a protocol identifier so that the receiver can determine the protocol being sent and pass the resulting data to the appropriate protocol parsing or routing routine. This capability is especially important for multiprotocol routers.

To add a protocol identifier to the AAL5 PDU, an IEEE 802.x SNAP header is added. It contains the EtherType (set to 0x86DD) that identifies the payload as an IPv6 packet. As part of the virtual channel connection (VCC) negotiation process between two ATM endpoints, an agreement is reached on whether a single protocol is to be used (in which case the SNAP header is not required) or multiple protocols are to be used (in which case a SNAP header is required).

Figure A-10 shows ATM SNAP encapsulation of IPv6 packets.

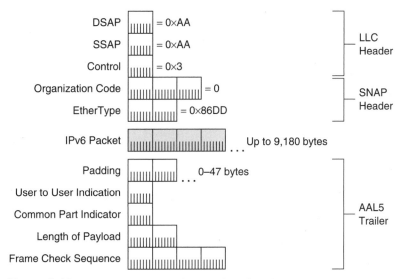

Figure A-10. *ATM SNAP encapsulation of IPv6 packets*

IPV6 OVER IPV4

IPv6 over IPv4 tunneling is the encapsulation of IPv6 packets with an IPv4 header so that IPv6 packets can be sent over an IPv4 infrastructure. Figure A-11 shows IPv4 encapsulation of IPv6 packets.

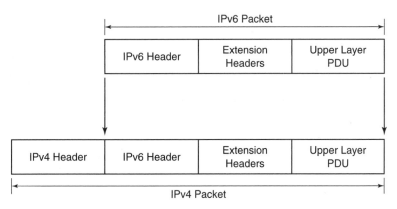

IP Protocol field set to 41 (IPv6 packet)

Figure A-11. *IPv4 encapsulation of IPv6 packets*

Within the IPv4 header:

■ The IPv4 Protocol field is set to 41 to indicate an encapsulated IPv6 packet.

■ The Source and Destination fields are set to the IPv4 addresses of the tunnel endpoints. The tunnel endpoints are either manually configured as part of the tunnel interface or are determined from the IPv4 address of the sending interface and the next-hop address of the destination address in the IPv6 header.

For IPv6 over IPv4 tunneling, the IPv6 path MTU for the destination is typically 20 less than the IPv4 path MTU for the destination (to a minimum of 1,280 bytes between the tunnel endpoints). However, if the IPv4 path MTU is not stored for each tunnel, there are instances in which the IPv4 packet will need to be fragmented at an intermediate router. In this case, the IPv6 over IPv4 tunneled packet must be sent with the Don't Fragment flag in the IPv4 header set to 0.

REFERENCES

RFC 1356 – "Multiprotocol Interconnect on X.25 and ISDN in the Packet Mode"

RFC 1661 – "The Point to Point Protocol (PPP)"

RFC 1662 – "PPP in HDLC-like Framing"

RFC 2464 – "Transmission of IPv6 Packets over Ethernet Networks"

RFC 2467 – "Transmission of IPv6 Packets over FDDI Networks"

RFC 2470 – "Transmission of IPv6 Packets over Token Ring Networks"

RFC 2472 – "IP Version 6 over PPP"

RFC 2491 – "IPv6 over Non-Broadcast Multiple Access (NBMA) Networks"

RFC 2492 – "IPv6 over ATM Networks"

RFC 2497 – "Transmission of IPv6 Packets over ARCnet Networks"

RFC 2590 – "Transmission of IPv6 Packets over Frame Relay Networks Specification"

Appendix B

Windows Sockets Changes for IPv6

This appendix includes information on changes that have been made to the Windows Sockets API to support IPv6 applications. The following topics are discussed:

- Added constants
- Address data structures
- Wildcard addresses
- Core sockets functions
- Name-to-address translation
- Address-to-name translation
- Address conversion functions
- Socket options
- New macros
- Unsupported APIs

Examples of how and when to utilize these changes in an application are discussed. Additional details can be found on the Microsoft Developer Network web site at http://msdn.microsoft.com.

ADDED CONSTANTS

A new address family name for IPv6 is required so that the address structure can be correctly identified and parsed. Similarly, a new protocol family name (with the same value as the address family name) must be defined so that a socket is created using the appropriate protocol. The address family name and protocol family name constants for IPv6 are:

- AF_INET6
- PF_INET6

ADDRESS DATA STRUCTURES

The term *sockets* defines a protocol-specific data structure that holds elements of a socket address. For IPv4, this structure is *sockaddr_in*. Sockets also defines a protocol-independent structure (*sockaddr*) for the protocol-specific structures to be cast into. The identifying field (the address family) in the protocol-specific structure overlays the family field in the generic structure. Because IPv6 addresses are different than IPv4 addresses, a new protocol-specific structure for IPv6 is required.

The data structures *sockaddr* and *sockaddr_in* are the same size which could lead one into making incorrect assumptions about the size of their related address structures. The IPv6 address structure, *sockaddr_in6*, is larger by necessity. For example, the *sockaddr* structure cannot be used to allocate storage for *sockaddr_in6*. This is discussed in more detail below.

in6_addr

```
struct in6_addr {
    union {
        u_char Byte[16];
        ushort Word[8];
        } u;
};
```

The socket address structure contains information above and beyond the address for the socket. One portion of the structure, however, must be the address. In IPv4's address structure, this address is contained in *in_addr*. A larger structure, *in6_addr,* has been defined to hold the larger IPv6 address.

sockaddr_in6

In addition to the larger address size, there are other members that must be represented in the socket address structure for IPv6. Although the IPv4 *sockaddr_in* structure has unused space, it is not enough to contain this additional information. The *sockaddr_in6* structure is used to contain an IPv6 address.

```
struct sockaddr_in6 {
    sa_family_t     sin6_family;
    in_port_t       sin6_port;
    uint32_t        sin6_flowinfo;
    struct in6_addr sin6_addr;
    uint32_t        sin6_scope_id;
};
```

In addition to the family, port, and address information, this structure contains sin6_flowinfo and sin6_scope_id members. *sin6_flowinfo* is intended to contain the traffic class and flow label from and for the IPv6 header. *sin6_flowinfo* is not supported in Windows XP and the Windows .NET Server 2003 family. *sin6_scope_id* contains the scope ID, which is used to identify a set of interfaces that are appropriate for the address carried in the address field.

sockaddr_storage

As mentioned earlier, *sockaddr* and *sockaddr_in6* have different sizes. Because of this, *struct sockaddr* cannot be used to allocate storage and then be cast to a *sockaddr_in6* pointer. If static allocation of storage for *sockaddr_in6* (or even *sockaddr_in*) structures is needed, *struct sockaddr_storage* should be used. Here is an example:

```
struct sockaddr_storage newaddr;
...
msgsock = accept(listen_socket,(struct sockaddr*)&newaddr, &newaddrlen);
```

In addition to being large enough to accommodate all known protocol-specific socket address structures (including *sockaddr_in6*), *sockaddr_storage* is aligned at an appropriate boundary so that protocol-specific socket address data-structure pointers can be cast to it, enabling it to access fields without experiencing alignment problems.

WILDCARD ADDRESSES

To allow the protocol implementation to choose the source address for a connection or datagram with IPv4, a constant of INADDR_ANY (the wildcard address) is used as the address in the bind( ) call.

The IPv6 address type (*in6_addr*) is a structure. A constant cannot be used in an assignment for this variable, but can be used to initialize the structure. Thus, we end up with two possible ways to provide the wildcard address.

The global variable, in6addr_any, can be used in an assignment. For example:

```
sin6.sin6_addr = in6addr_any;
```

Or the constant, IN6ADDR_ANY_INIT, can be used to initialize the address structure (at declaration time only). For example:

```
struct in6_addr anyaddr = IN6ADDR_ANY_INIT;
```

in6addr_loopback and IN6ADDR_LOOPBACK_INIT

Similarly, the INADDR_LOOPBACK constant is used in IPv4 connect( ), send( ), and sendmsg( ) calls to communicate with services that reside on the local node. For IPv6 loopback, a global variable (*in6addr_loopback*) is used for assignment and a constant (IN6ADDR_LOOPBACK_INIT) is used for initialization at declaration time.

NOTE:

The IPv4 INADDR_*XXX* constants were defined in host-byte order. The IPv6 equivalents are defined in network-byte order.

CORE SOCKETS FUNCTIONS

An address is passed in core Sockets functions as an opaque address pointer and length. Because of this, changes need not be made to these core Sockets functions for IPv6. The application developer needs simply to supply the appropriate IPv6 address structure and family constants.

Sockets functions that pass addresses are the following:

- bind( )
- connect( )
- sendmsg( )
- sendto( )

Sockets functions that return addresses are the following:

- accept( )
- recvfrom( )
- recvmsg( )
- getpeername( )
- getsockname( )

NAME-TO-ADDRESS TRANSLATION

To resolve a host name to one or more IP addresses in IPv4, the application might use gethostbyname( ). This API does not allow the caller to specify anything about the types of addresses wanted and the structure contains only enough space to store an IPv4 address. To address these issues, a new API named getaddrinfo() is introduced with IPv6. This API is protocol-independent and can be used for both IPv4 and IPv6 name-to-address resolutions. The return from this call is in the form of *addrinfo* structures that can subsequently be used to both open and use a socket.

The function prototype for getaddrinfo() is the following:

```
int getaddrinfo(
    IN const char FAR *nodename,
    IN const char FAR *servname,
    IN const struct addrinfo FAR *hints,
    OUT struct addrinfo FAR *FAR *res
    );
struct addrinfo {
    int ai_flags;
    int ai_family;
    int ai_socktype;
    int ai_protocol;
    size_t ai_addrlen;
    char *ai_canonname;
    struct sockaddr *ai_addr;
struct addrinfo *ai_next;
};
```

As arguments, either a node name or service name (or both) are provided. The node name can (optionally) be a numeric address string and the service name can (optionally) be a decimal port number. An *addrinfo* structure can be provided (optionally) to provide hints for the type of socket that the caller supports. The *addrinfo* structure pointed to by this hints parameter can specify a preferred socket type, family and protocol, and the following flags:

- AI_PASSIVE

  This flag indicates that the caller plans to use the returned address structure in a bind() call when set, or a connect() call when not set. Setting the node name to NULL has additional meaning depending on this flag. If the node name in the hints is NULL, and this flag is set, the returned addresses will be wildcard addresses. If the node name in the hints is NULL, and this flag is not set, the returned addresses will be loopback addresses.

- AI_CANONNAME
  The AI_CANONNAME flag indicates (when set) that the first *addrinfo* structure returned should contain a null-terminated string that contains the canonical name of the node name in the ai_canonname member.

- AI_NUMERICHOST
  This flag indicates that the nodename in the call is a numeric address string.

- AI_V4MAPPED
  If the address family specified is AF_INET6, the caller will accept IPv4-mapped IPv6 addresses. The IPv6 protocol for Windows XP and the Windows .NET Server 2003 family does not support the use of IPv4-mapped addresses.

- AI_ALL
  Used with the AI_V4MAPPED flag to indicate that the caller would like all addresses, both true IPv6 addresses and IPv4-mapped IPv6 addresses. The address family specified must be AF_INET6. The IPv6 protocol for Windows XP and the Windows .NET Server 2003 family does not support the use of this flag.

- AI_ADDRCONFIG
  The AI_ADDRCONFIG flag controls whether the query requests AAAA DNS records or A records, based on the locally configured source addresses. AAAA records will be queried only if the node has at least one IPv6 source address. A records will be queried only if the node has at least one IPv4 source address.

A pointer to a linked list of *addrinfo* structures is returned. The order of the addresses is in decreasing order of desirability.

The *addrinfo* structures (and structures contained as members within those structures) are dynamically allocated and must be released by calling freeaddrinfo( ) with a pointer to the linked list of *addrinfo* structures.

The function prototype for freeaddrinfo( ) is the following:

```
void freeaddrinfo(
  struct addrinfo FAR *ai
);
```

ADDRESS-TO-NAME TRANSLATION

A reverse lookup can be performed by using another new Sockets function, getnameinfo( ). To use this API, a socket address structure is provided. The function prototype for getnameinfo( ) is the following:

```
int getnameinfo(
    IN const struct sockaddr FAR *sa,
    IN socklen_t salen,
    OUT char FAR *host,
    IN size_t hostlen,
    OUT char FAR *serv,
    IN size_t servlen,
    IN int flags
    );
```

It contains the address and port in question. This can be either an IPv4 or IPv6 socket address structure because the length is also provided.

Additionally, buffers are provided to receive the node name and service name associated with that address, and the flags field can be used to change the default behavior of the API. The lengths of these buffers are provided in the call, and constants are defined (NI_MAXHOST, NI_MAXSERV) to aid the application in allocating buffers of the maximum size required.

The flags adjust the behavior as follows:

- NI_NOFQDN
  Setting the NI_NOFQDN flag results in returning only the node name (not the fully qualified domain name, or FQDN) for local hosts.

- NI_NUMERICHOST
  Setting this flag results in returning the numeric form of the host's address instead of its name.

- NI_NAMEREQD
  Setting the NI_NAMEREQD flag results in returning an error if the name cannot be located.

- NI_NUMERICSERV
  Setting NI_NUMERICSERV results in returning the numeric port number instead of the service name.

- NI_DGRAM
  Setting this flag specifies that the service is a datagram service, causing a search for a UDP service (instead of a TCP service).

Using getaddrinfo

Here is an example of a client application using getaddrinfo( ) to connect to a specific server:

```
{/* Client Side...*/}
if (getaddrinfo(service_name, port, NULL, &ai) != 0) {/* Error Handling */}

conn_socket = socket(ai->ai_family, ai->ai_socktype,ai->ai_protocol);
if (conn_socket <0 ) {/* Error Handling */}

if (connect(conn_socket,ai->ai_addr,ai->ai_addrlen) == SOCKET_ERROR)
{/* Error Handling */}

freeaddrinfo(ai);
```

For an example of an application that checks each address returned, see the white paper titled "Adding IPv6 Capability to Windows Sockets Applications" in the \White_Papers folder on the companion CD-ROM.

Here is an example of the corresponding server application using getaddrinfo( ) to resolve the address information for the socket creation and bind calls:

```
{/* Server Side... */}
hints.ai_family = AF_INET6;
hints.ai_socktype = SOCK_STREAM;
hints.ai_flags = AI_NUMERICHOST | AI_PASSIVE;

retval = getaddrinfo(interface, port, &hints, &ai);
if (retval != 0) {/* Error Handling */}

listen_socket = socket(ai->ai_family, ai->ai_socktype, ai->ai_protocol);
if (listen_socket == INVALID_SOCKET){/* Error Handling */}

if (bind(listen_socket,ai->ai_addr,ai->ai_addrlen )== SOCKET_ERROR)
{/* Error Handling */}

freeaddrinfo(ai);
```

The interface parameter in this call could be NULL, or could be set to a numeric string.

ADDRESS CONVERSION FUNCTIONS

The inet_addr() and inet_ntoa() functions are provided to convert IPv4 addresses between binary and text formats. The IETF defined the similar functions, inet_pton() and inet_ntop(), to convert both IPv4 and IPv6 addresses. These functions contain an additional address family argument to make them protocol-independent.

Because getaddrinfo() and getnameinfo() provide the same functionality, the IETF is in the process of deprecating the inet_pton() and the inet_ntop() functions. As a result, the IPv6 protocol for Windows XP and the Windows .NET Server 2003 family does not support the inet_pton() and the inet_ntop() functions.

SOCKET OPTIONS

A new socket option level, IPPROTO_IPV6, has been defined for IPv6-specific socket options. Although an application can send multicast UDP packets by specifying a multicast address in sendto(), most of the new socket options currently defined for IPv6 are intended to adjust multicast behavior. New socket options are the following:

- IPV6_MULTICAST_IF
  This option sets the default interface to use for outgoing multicast traffic to the interface indicated by the index specified in the argument (0 indicates that the system chooses the interface).

- IPV6_MULTICAST_HOPS
  This option sets the hop limit for outgoing multicast packets based on the argument. Valid values are either 0 to 255 inclusive or –1 (to use the system default).

- IPV6_MULTICAST_LOOP
  This option controls whether outgoing multicast packets addressed to a group, of which the interface is a member, is looped back.

For reception of multicast traffic, new options are defined to join and leave multicast groups. These options take an argument of an *ipv6_mreq* structure:

```
struct ipv6_mreq {
    struct in6_addr ipv6mr_multiaddr;
    unsigned int ipv6mr_interface;
};
```

This structure contains the multicast address of the group to be joined or left, and an interface index to use for this join or leave.

New multicast socket options are:

■ IPV6_JOIN_GROUP
This option is used to join the specified multicast group on the interface indicated (0 indicates that the system chooses the interface).

■ IPV6_LEAVE_GROUP
The IPV6_LEAVE_GROUP option is used to leave the specified group on the interface indicated.

In addition, another socket option, IPV6_UNICAST_HOPS, is defined to control the hop limit for outgoing unicast packets.

NEW MACROS

The additions to Windows Sockets that support IPv6 include the following set of macros to test addresses and determine whether they are special IPv6 addresses:

■ IN6_IS_ADDR_UNSPECIFIED

■ IN6_IS_ADDR_LOOPBACK

■ IN6_IS_ADDR_MULTICAST

■ IN6_IS_ADDR_LINKLOCAL

■ IN6_IS_ADDR_SITELOCAL

■ IN6_IS_ADDR_V4MAPPED

■ IN6_IS_ADDR_V4COMPAT

■ IN6_IS_ADDR_MC_NODELOCAL

■ IN6_IS_ADDR_MC_LINKLOCAL

■ IN6_IS_ADDR_MC_SITELOCAL

■ IN6_IS_ADDR_MC_ORGLOCAL

■ IN6_IS_ADDR_MC_GLOBAL

The first seven macros return a true value if the address is of the specified type. The last five test the scope of a multicast address, returning a true value if the address is a multicast address of the specified scope and a false value if the address is either not a multicast address or is not of the specified scope.

The IN6_IS_ADDR_V4MAPPED macro can be use to determine whether the destination address for a socket is an IPv4 node. IPv4-mapped addresses are not supported by the IPv6 protocol for Windows XP and the Windows .NET Server 2003 family.

UNSUPPORTED APIS

The following are APIs that are currently specified in RFC 2553 or RFC 2292 that the IPv6 protocol for Windows XP and the Windows .NET Server 2003 family does not support:

- The APIs getipnodebyname(), getipnodebyaddr(), inet_pton(), and inet_ntop() are being deprecated by the IETF. They are redundant, as the functionality they provide is available with getaddrinfo() and getnameinfo().

- There is a set of name/interface index conversion functions that are not supported, but might be supported in future versions of Windows.

- The IETF is in the process of revising the advanced API specification (RFC 2292). The revised RFC will include a discussion of programming raw sockets and access to various options for IPv6 packets.

REFERENCES

RFC 2553 – "Basic Socket Interface Extensions for IPv6"

RFC 2292 – "Advanced Sockets API for IPv6"

Appendix C

IPv6 RFC Index

This appendix contains tables of the most relevant IPv6 RFCs and Internet drafts for the IPv6 protocol for Windows XP and the Windows .NET Server 2003 family current at the time of publication of this book, arranged by function. All of these RFCs and Internet drafts are provided on the companion CD-ROM.

General

Table C-1. IPv6 GENERAL RFCs AND INTERNET DRAFTS

RFC #	Category	Title
1752	Standards Track	The Recommendation for the IP Next Generation Protocol
1924	Informational	A Compact Representation of IPv6 Addresses
2851	Standards Track	Textual Conventions for Internet Network Addresses
	Internet draft	The Case for IPv6

Addressing

Table C-2. IPv6 ADDRESSING RFCs AND INTERNET DRAFTS

RFC #	Category	Title
1881	Informational	IPv6 Address Allocation Management
1887	Informational	An Architecture for IPv6 Unicast Address Allocation
1888	Experimental	OSI NSAPs and IPv6
2373	Standards Track	IP Version 6 Addressing Architecture
	Internet draft	IP Version 6 Addressing Architecture

continued

Table C-2 *continued*

RFC #	Category	Title
2374	Standards Track	An IPv6 Aggregatable Global Unicast Address Format
2375	Informational	IPv6 Multicast Address Assignments
2450	Informational	Proposed TLA and NLA Assignment Rules
2471	Experimental	IPv6 Testing Address Allocation
2526	Standards Track	Reserved IPv6 Subnet Anycast Addresses
2921	Informational	6BONE pTLA and pNLA Formats (pTLA)
2928	Informational	Initial IPv6 Sub-TLA ID Assignments
3041	Standards Track	Privacy Extensions for Stateless Address Autoconfiguration in IPv6
	Internet draft	Site prefixes in Neighbor Discovery
	Internet draft	Dynamic Host Configuration Protocol for IPv6 (DHCPv6)
	Internet draft	A flexible method for managing the assignment of bits of an IPv6 address block

Applications

Table C-3. **IPv6 Applications RFCs and Internet Drafts**

RFC #	Category	Title
1886	Standards Track	DNS Extensions to support IP version 6
2428	Standards Track	FTP Extensions for IPv6 and NATs
2732	Standards Track	Format for Literal IPv6 Addresses in URL's
2874	Standards Track	DNS Extensions to Support IPv6 Address Aggregation and Renumbering
	Internet draft	IPv6 Node Information Queries

Sockets API

Table C-4. **IPv6 SOCKETS API RFCs AND INTERNET DRAFTS**

RFC #	Category	Title
2292	Informational	Advanced Sockets API for IPv6
	Internet draft	Advanced Sockets API for IPv6
2553	Informational	Basic Socket Interface Extensions for IPv6
	Internet draft	An Extension of Format for IPv6 Scoped Addresses

Transport Layer

Table C-5. **IPv6 TRANSPORT LAYER RFCs AND INTERNET DRAFTS**

RFC #	Category	Title
2452	Standards Track	IP Version 6 Management Information Base for the Transmission Control Protocol
2454	Standards Track	IP Version 6 Management Information Base for the User Datagram Protocol
	Internet draft	The UDP Lite Protocol

Network Layer

Table C-6. **IPv6 NETWORK LAYER RFCs AND INTERNET DRAFTS**

RFC #	Category	Title
1809	Informational	Using the Flow Label Field in IPv6
1981	Standards Track	Path MTU Discovery for IP version 6
2460	Standards Track	Internet Protocol, Version 6 (IPv6) Specification
2461	Standards Track	Neighbor Discovery for IP Version 6 (IPv6)

continued

Table C-6 *continued*

RFC #	Category	Title
2462	Standards Track	IPv6 Stateless Address Autoconfiguration
2463	Standards Track	Internet Control Message Protocol (ICMPv6) for the Internet Protocol Version 6 (IPv6) Specification
	Internet draft	Internet Control Message Protocol (ICMPv6) for the Internet Protocol Version 6 (IPv6)
2465	Standards Track	Management Information Base for IP Version 6: Textual Conventions and General Group
2466	Standards Track	Management Information Base for IP Version 6: ICMPv6 Group
2474	Standards Track	Definition of the Differentiated Services Field (DS Field) in the IPv4 and IPv6 Headers
2675	Standards Track	IPv6 Jumbograms
2710	Standards Track	Multicast Listener Discovery (MLD) for IPv6
2711	Standards Track	IPv6 Router Alert Option
2767	Informational	Dual Stack Hosts using the "Bump-In-the-Stack" Technique (BIS)
3019	Standards Track	IP Version 6 Management Information Base for the Multicast Listener Discovery Protocol
3122	Standards Track	Extensions to IPv6 Neighbor Discovery for Inverse Discovery Specification
	Internet draft	Mobility Support in IPv6
	Internet draft	Default Address Selection for IPv6

Network Layer Security

Table C-7. **IPv6 NETWORK LAYER SECURITY RFCs AND INTERNET DRAFTS**

RFC #	Category	Title
1828	Standards Track	IP Authentication using Keyed MD5
1829	Standards Track	The ESP DES-CBC Transform
2401	Standards Track	Security Architecture for the Internet Protocol
2402	Standards Track	IP Authentication Header
2403	Standards Track	The Use of HMAC-MD5-96 within ESP and AH
2404	Standards Track	The Use of HMAC-SHA-1-96 within ESP and AH
2406	Standards Track	IP Encapsulating Security Payload (ESP)

Link Layer

Table C-8. **IPv6 LINK LAYER RFCs AND INTERNET DRAFTS**

RFC #	Category	Title
2464	Standards Track	Transmission of IPv6 Packets over Ethernet Networks
2467	Standards Track	Transmission of IPv6 Packets over FDDI Networks
2470	Standards Track	Transmission of IPv6 Packets over Token Ring Networks
2472	Standards Track	IP Version 6 over PPP
2473	Standards Track	Generic Packet Tunneling in IPv6 Specification
2491	Standards Track	IPv6 over Non-Broadcast Multiple Access (NBMA) networks

continued

Table C-8 *continued*

RFC #	Category	Title
2492	Standards Track	IPv6 over ATM Networks
2497	Standards Track	Transmission of IPv6 Packets over ARCnet Networks
2507	Standards Track	IP Header Compression
2508	Standards Track	Compressing IP/UDP/RTP Headers for Low-Speed Serial Links
2509	Standards Track	IP Header Compression over PPP
2590	Standards Track	Transmission of IPv6 Packets over Frame Relay Networks Specification
3146	Standards Track	Transmission of IPv6 Packets over IEEE 1394 Networks

Routing

Table C-9. IPv6 ROUTING RFCs AND INTERNET DRAFTS

RFC #	Category	Title
2080	Standards Track	RIPng for IPv6
2185	Informational	Routing Aspects of IPv6 Transition
2283	Standards Track	Multiprotocol Extensions for BGP-4
2545	Standards Track	Use of BGP-4 Multiprotocol Extensions for IPv6 Inter-Domain Routing
2740	Standards Track	OSPF for IPv6
2772	Informational	6Bone Backbone Routing Guidelines
2894	Standards Track	Router Renumbering for IPv6

Coexistence and Migration

Table C-10. IPv6 COEXISTENCE AND MIGRATION RFCs AND INTERNET DRAFTS

RFC #	Category	Title
2529	Standards Track	Transmission of IPv6 over IPv4 Domains without Explicit Tunnels
2893	Standards Track	Transition Mechanisms for IPv6 Hosts and Routers
3053	Informational	IPv6 Tunnel Broker
3056	Standards Track	Connection of IPv6 Domains via IPv4 Clouds
	Internet draft	Intra-Site Automatic Tunnel Addressing Protocol (ISATAP)

For the latest list of RFCs and Internet drafts describing IPv6, see the IETF IPv6 Working Group at http://www.ietf.org/html.charters/ipv6-charter.html. For the latest list of RFCs and Internet drafts describing IPv6/IPv4 transition, see the IETF Next Generation Transition Working Group at http://www.ietf.org/html.charters/ngtrans-charter.html. For additional RFCs, see the IEFT Request for Comments Web page at http://www.ietf.org/rfc.html.

Appendix D

Testing for Understanding Answers

This appendix contains the answers to the "Testing for Understanding" sections of Chapters 1 through 12.

CHAPTER 1: INTRODUCTION TO IPV6

1. What are the problems with IPv4 on today's Internet?

Some of the problems are:

- It has a rapidly depleting public address space.

- There are large routing tables for Internet backbone routers.

- Its configuration could be simpler.

- Security at the IP level should be required so that applications can count on standardized Internet layer security services.

- IPv4 has limited support for QoS delivery.

2. How does IPv6 solve these problems?

128-bit address length allows for a large public address space.

Better address aggregation results in small routing tables for Internet backbone routers.

IPv6 provides automatic configuration (even without DHCP).

Security (IPSec) is an implementation requirement.

Better support for QoS delivery using the Traffic Class and Flow Label fields.

3. How does IPv6 provide better QoS support?

IPv6 uses a combination of the Traffic Class field (to define a specific type of service) and the Flow Label field (which identifies that the packet requires special handling, even when the payload is encrypted).

4. Describe at least three ways in which IPv6 is more efficient than IPv4.

IPv6 addresses are hierarchical and summarizable, leading to smaller routing tables.

The IPv6 address space removes the need for NATs, making end-to-end communication faster because no translation is needed.

The IPv6 header is designed for minimal overhead and optimal processing at intermediate routers.

IPv6 Neighbor Discovery (ND) replaces broadcast-based ARP with unicast and multicast ND messages. Common neighbor operations such as address resolution involve very few nodes.

IPv6 hosts are self-configuring and do not require a DHCP server to discover addresses and other configuration information. Host startup times are reduced.

5. Explain how NATs prevent peer-to-peer applications from working properly.

Because each peer behind a NAT is represented by two addresses (a public address and a private address), peers cannot connect without manually configuring the NAT or relay address information about each other without making the peer-to-peer application NAT-aware.

6. What are the key benefits of deploying IPv6 now?

You will be able to take advantage of a much larger address space.

You can get IPv6 address space in areas of the world that have very few available public IPv4 addresses.

It would restore true end-to-end communication without intermediate translation. Peer-to-peer applications can now connect without compensating for one or more NATs between peers.

IPv6 forwarding is more efficient and is address-scope aware.

CHAPTER 2: IPV6 PROTOCOL FOR THE WINDOWS .NET SERVER 2003 FAMILY

1. List and describe the features of the IPv6 protocol that allow for IPv4 and IPv6 coexistence.

6to4 allows automatic tunneling and unicast IPv6 connectivity between IPv6/IPv4 hosts across the IPv4 Internet.

ISATAP allows IPv6/IPv4 nodes within an IPv4 infrastructure of a site to use unicast IPv6 to communicate with each other and with nodes on an IPv6-enabled network, either within the site or the IPv6 Internet.

6over4 allows IPv6/IPv4 nodes to communicate using IPv6 unicast or multicast over an IPv4 multicast-enabled infrastructure with each other and with nodes on an IPv6-enabled network, either within the site or the IPv6 Internet.

PortProxy functions as a TCP proxy to facilitate the communication between nodes or applications that cannot connect using a common Internet layer protocol (IPv4 or IPv6).

2. How do you configure the IPv6 protocol for the Windows .NET Server 2003 family after it has been installed?

   For most hosts, no configuration is required because stateless address autoconfiguration automatically configures addresses, routes, and other settings. To manually configure the IPv6 protocol for the Windows .NET Server 2003 family, use the **netsh interface ipv6** commands.

3. Under what circumstances will a Windows .NET Server IPv6 router advertise itself as a default router?

   A Windows .NET Server IPv6 router advertises itself as a default router if it has a default route that is configured to be published.

4. List and describe the types of network communication in which both the client and server components are IPv6-enabled in the Windows .NET Server 2003 family.

   HTTP: Both Internet Explorer and IIS are IPv6-enabled.

   CIFS/SMB: Both the file- and printer-sharing client (the Workstation service) and server (the Server service) are IPv6-enabled.

5. List the two ways to install the IPv6 protocol for the Windows .NET Server 2003 family.

   1. As a protocol for a LAN connection in the Network Connections folder.
   2. By using the **netsh interface ipv6 install** command.

6. List how the common TCP/IP utilities have been enhanced to support IPv6 in the Windows .NET Server 2003 family.

Ipconfig.exe now displays both IPv4 and IPv6 configurations.

Route.exe now displays both IPv4 and IPv6 routing tables.

Ping.exe now uses both ICMPv4 Echo and ICMPv6 Echo Request messages and supports additional options for IPv6.

Tracert.exe now uses both ICMPv4 Echo and ICMPv6 Echo Request messages and supports additional options for IPv6.

Pathping.exe now uses both ICMPv4 Echo and ICMPv6 Echo Request messages and supports additional options for IPv6.

Netstat.exe now displays the IPv6 routing table and information about the IPv6, ICMPv6, TCP over IPv6, and UDP over IPv6 protocols.

CHAPTER 3: IPV6 ADDRESSING

1. Why is the IPv6 address length 128 bits?

   The IPv6 address length is 128 bits so that it can be divided into hierarchical routing domains that reflect the topology of the modern-day Internet. The use of 128 bits, 64 bits for the subnet ID and 64 bits for the interface ID, allows for multiple levels of hierarchy and flexibility in designing hierarchical addressing and routing between the backbone of the IPv6 Internet and the individual subnets within an organization's site.

2. Define the Format Prefixes (FPs) for commonly used unicast addresses.

   Global: 001

   Link-local: 1111 1110 10

   Site-local: 1111 1110 11

3. Express FEC0:0000:0000:0001:02AA:0000:0000:0007A more efficiently.

   FEC0::1:2AA:0:0:7A or FEC0:0:0:1:2AA::7A. By convention, when there are multiple equal-length blocks of zeros that can be compressed, the left-most block is compressed.

4. How many bits are expressed by "::" in the addresses 3341::1:2AA:9FF:FE56:24DC and FF02::2?

   In 3341::1:2AA:9FF:FE56:24DC, :: expresses 32 bits ((8 - 6) × 16).

   In FF02::2, :: expresses 96 bits ((8 - 2) × 16).

5. Describe the difference between unicast, multicast, and anycast addresses in terms of a host sending packets to zero or more interfaces.

A sending host uses a unicast address to send packets to a single interface (within the scope of the unicast address).

A sending host uses a multicast address to send packets to zero or more interfaces belonging to the multicast group (within the scope of the multicast address).

A sending host uses an anycast address to send packets to a single nearest interface belonging to the set of interfaces using the anycast address (within the scope of the anycast address).

6. Why are no broadcast addresses defined for IPv6?

All IPv4 broadcast addresses are replaced with IPv6 multicast addresses.

7. Define the structure, including field sizes, of the aggregatable global unicast address.

TLA ID – Top-Level Aggregation Identifier. The size of this field is 13 bits. The TLA ID identifies the highest level in the routing hierarchy. TLA IDs are administered by IANA and allocated to local Internet registries that, in turn, allocate individual TLA IDs to large, long haul ISPs.

Res – Eight bits that are reserved for future use in expanding the size of either the TLA ID or the NLA ID.

NLA ID – Next-Level Aggregation Identifier. The size of this field is 24 bits. The NLA ID allows an ISP to create multiple levels of addressing hierarchy within its network to both organize addressing and routing for downstream ISPs and identify organization sites.

SLA ID – Site-Level Aggregation Identifier. The SLA ID is used by an individual organization to identify subnets within its site. The size of this field is 16 bits.

Interface ID – Indicates the interface on a specific subnet. The size of this field is 64 bits.

8. Define the scope for each of the different types of typically used unicast addresses.

Global: The IPv6 Internet

Site-local: A site, an organization network or portion of an organization's network that has a defined geographical location (such as an office, an office complex, or a campus)

Link-local: A single link

9. Explain how global and site-local addressing can share the same subnetting infrastructure within an organization.

The global address and site-local address share the same structure beyond the first 48 bits of the address. In global addresses, the SLA ID field identifies the subnet within an organization. For site-local addresses, the Subnet ID field performs the same function. Because of this, you can create a subnetting infrastructure that is used for both site-local and global unicast addresses.

10. Define the structure, including field sizes, of the multicast address.

Flags – Indicates flags set on the multicast address. The size of this field is 4 bits.

Scope – Indicates the scope of the IPv6 network for which the multicast traffic is intended to be delivered. The size of this field is 4 bits.

Group ID – Identifies the multicast group and is unique within the scope. The size of this field is 112 bits. RFC 2373 recommends setting the 80 high-order bits to zero and using only the low-order 32 bits for the group ID.

11. Why does RFC 2373 recommend using only the last 32 bits of the IPv6 multicast address for the multicast group ID?

The last 32 bits of an IPv6 multicast address map to the last 32 bits of an Ethernet multicast MAC address. By using only the last 32 bits of the IPv6 multicast address as the group ID, there is a one-to-one correlation between a multicast group ID and an Ethernet multicast MAC address.

12. Explain how the solicited-node multicast address acts as a pseudo-unicast address.

Because the last 24 bits of the solicited-node multicast address either is based on the manufacturer ID portion of an IEEE 802 address or is randomly derived, the chances of two nodes on the same link having the same solicited-node multicast address is small. Therefore, because there is typically only one listener on a subnet for a given solicited-node multicast address, it is almost like using a unicast address.

13. How do routers know the nearest location of an anycast group member?

Routers within the routing domain of the anycast address have host routes that provide information on the location of the nearest anycast group member. Routers outside the routing domain of the anycast address have a summary route that provides information on the location of the routing domain of the anycast address.

14. Perform a 4-bit subnetting on the site-local prefix FEC0:0:0:3D80::/57.

The result is the following subnetted network prefixes:

1 - FEC0:0:0:3D80::/61	2 - FEC0:0:0:3D88::/61
3 - FEC0:0:0:3D90::/61	4 - FEC0:0:0:3D98::/61
5 - FEC0:0:0:3DA0::/61	6 - FEC0:0:0:3DA8::/61
7 - FEC0:0:0:3DB0::/61	8 - FEC0:0:0:3DB8::/61
9 - FEC0:0:0:3DC0::/61	10 - FEC0:0:0:3DC8::/61
11 - FEC0:0:0:3DD0::/61	12 - FEC0:0:0:3DD8::/61
13 - FEC0:0:0:3DE0::/61	14 - FEC0:0:0:3DE8::/61
15 - FEC0:0:0:3DF0::/61	16 - FEC0:0:0:3DF8::/61

15. What is the IPv6 interface identifier for the universally administered, unicast IEEE 802 address of 0C-1C-09-A8-F9-CE? What is the corresponding link-local address? What is the corresponding solicited-node multicast address?

::E1C:9FF:FEA8:F9CE

FE80::E1C:9FF:FEA8:F9CE

FF02::1:FFA8:F9CE

16. What is the IPv6 interface identifier for the locally administered, unicast EUI-64 address of 02-00-00-00-00-00-00-09? What is the corresponding link-local address?

::9

FE80::9

17. What is the site-local scope multicast address corresponding to the Ethernet multicast MAC address of 33-33-00-0A-4F-11?

Assuming the RFC 2373 recommendation of using the last 32-bits of the multicast address as the multicast group ID, either FF05::A:4F11 (Transient flag set to 0) or FF15::A:4F11 (Transient flag set to 1).

18. For each type of address, identify how the address begins in colon hexadecimal notation.

Type of Address	*Begins with ...*
Link-local unicast address	FE80
Site-local unicast address	FEC0
Global address	2 or 3
Multicast address	FF

continued

continued

Type of Address	Begins with...
Link-local scope multicast address	FF02 or FF12
Site-local scope multicast address	FF05 or FF15
Solicited-node multicast address	FF02::1:FF
IPv4-compatible address	::
IPv4-mapped address	::FFFF
6to4 address	2002:

CHAPTER 4: THE IPV6 HEADER

1. Why does the IPv6 header not include a checksum?

In IPv6, the link layer performs bit-level error detection for the entire IPv6 packet.

2. What is the IPv6 equivalent to the IHL field in the IPv4 header?

There is no equivalent. The IPv6 header is always a fixed size of 40 bytes.

3. How does the combination of the Traffic Class and Flow Label fields provide better support for QoS traffic?

The Traffic Class field is equivalent to the IPv4 Type of Service field. The Flow Label field allows the flow—the series of packets between a source and destination with a non-zero flow label—to be identified by intermediate routers for non-default QoS handling without relying on upper-layer protocol stream identifiers such as TCP or UDP ports (which may be encrypted with ESP).

4. Which extension headers are fragmentable and why? Which extension headers are not fragmentable and why?

Fragmentable:
Authentication header - Needed only by final destination
ESP header and trailer - Needed only by final destination
Destination Options header (for final destination) - Needed only by final destination

Not fragmentable:
Hop-by-Hop Options header - Needed by every intermediate router
Destination Options header (for intermediate destinations) - Might be needed by intermediate destinations
Routing header - Might be needed by intermediate destinations
Fragment header - Not present prior to fragmentation

5. Describe a situation that results in an IPv6 packet that contains a Fragment header in which the Fragment Offset field is set to 0 and the More Fragments flag is not set.

    IPv6 packets sent to IPv4 destinations that undergo IPv6-to-IPv4 header translation may receive a path MTU update of less than 1,280. In this case, the sending host sends IPv6 packets with a Fragment header and a smaller payload size of 1,272 bytes. In the Fragment header, the Fragment Offset field is set to 0 and the More Fragments flag is not set. The Fragment header is included so that the IPv6-to-IPv4 translator can use the Identification field in the Fragment header to perform IPv4 fragmentation to reach the IPv4 destination.

6. Describe how the new upper-layer checksum calculation affects transport layer protocols such as TCP and UDP.

    TCP and UDP implementations must be updated to perform the checksum calculation that includes the new IPv6 pseudo-header when sending or receiving data over IPv6.

7. If the minimum MTU for IPv6 packets is 1,280 bytes, then how are 1,280-byte packets sent on a link that supports only 512-byte frames?

    The link layer must provide a fragmentation and reassembly scheme that is transparent to IPv6.

CHAPTER 5: ICMPv6

1. How do you distinguish ICMPv6 error messages from ICMPv6 informational messages?

    The value of the Type field for error messages is in the range 0 to 127. (The high-order bit is set to 0.) The value of the Type field for informational messages is in the range 128 to 255. (The high-order bit is set to 1.)

2. Which fields of the Echo Request message are echoed in the Echo Reply message?

    Identifier, Sequence Number, Data

3. For a maximum-sized IPv6 packet with a Fragment extension header sent on an Ethernet link, how many bytes of the original payload are returned in an ICMPv6 Destination Unreachable message?

    1,184 bytes (1,280 - 40 byte IPv6 header - 8 byte ICMPv6 header - 40 byte IPv6 header - 8 byte Fragment header)

4. How can you tell whether a returned packet was discarded by a firewall that is enforcing network policy or a router that could not resolve the link-layer address of the destination?

If the Code field in the ICMPv6 Destination Unreachable message is set to 1, the packet was discarded by a firewall that is enforcing network policy. If the Code field is set to 3, a router could not resolve the link-layer address of the destination.

5. Why is the MTU field in the ICMPv6 Packet Too Big message 4 bytes long when the Next Hop MTU field in the ICMPv4 Destination Unreachable-Fragmentation Needed and DF Set message is only 2 bytes long?

The maximum IPv4 packet size is 65,535 bytes, a number that can be expressed with 16 bits. To support IPv6 jumbograms, 32 bits are needed to express the MTU of the link.

6. Why isn't the ICMPv6 Parameter Problem-Unrecognized Option message sent when the 2 high-order bits of an option's Option Type field are set to either 00 (binary) or 01 (binary)?

If the 2 high-order bits in the Option Type field are set to 00, the option is ignored. If the 2 high-order bits in the Option Type field are set to 01, the packet is silently discarded.

7. Based on the IPv6 design requirement to minimize processing at IPv6 routers, why is there no equivalent to the ICMPv4 Source Quench message in IPv6?

A Source Quench message is sent to inform a sending host to lower its transmission rate when the router is congested. To minimize the processing of the router, the router should devote its processing and resources to clearing the congestion, and not creating and sending Source Quench packets.

CHAPTER 6: NEIGHBOR DISCOVERY

1. List the IPv4 facilities that are replaced by the IPv6 ND protocol.

ARP, Gratuitous ARP, ICMP Router Discovery, Redirect

2. List the capabilities of the IPv6 ND protocol that are not present in IPv4.

Neighbor unreachability detection; ability to advertise changes in link-layer addresses and the node's role on the network; ability to advertise configuration parameters, address prefixes, and routes.

3. List the five different ND messages and the options that can be included with them.

Router Solicitation: Source Link-Layer Address option

Router Advertisement: Source Link-Layer Address, Prefix Information, MTU, Advertisement Interval, Home Agent Information, Route Information options

Neighbor Solicitation: Source Link-Layer Address option

Neighbor Advertisement: Target Link-Layer Address option

Redirect: Redirected Header, Target Link-Layer Address options

4. Describe the interpretation of the Length field in ND options.

The Length field is the number of 8-byte blocks in the entire Neighbor Discovery option.

5. What is the value of the Length field for a maximum-sized Redirected Header option (assuming no IPv6 extension headers are present)?

[1280 - 40 (IPv6 header) - 40 (ICMPv6 Redirect message header)]/8 = 150

6. Describe how you would use the MTU option to provide seamless connectivity between Ethernet nodes and ATM nodes on a transparently bridged link.

Set the MTU option on the router to advertise a 1,500-byte link MTU so that the ATM nodes do not send 9,180-byte IPv6 packets.

7. Why is the Source Link-Layer Address option not included in the Neighbor Solicitation message sent during duplicate address detection?

It is not included because the reply must be multicast to all nodes on the link, rather than unicast to the sender of the Neighbor Solicitation message.

8. Describe the configuration parameters and their corresponding fields sent in the Router Advertisement message (not including options). Describe the configuration parameters and their corresponding fields sent in the Prefix Information option.

Router Advertisement message:

- Default value of the Hop Limit field: Current Hop Limit

- Whether to use a stateful address configuration protocol to obtain addresses or other configuration information: Managed Address Configuration flag, Other Stateful Configuration flag

- Whether the advertising router is capable of acting as a home agent: Home Agent flag

- The default router preference level of the advertising router: Default Router Preference

- Whether the advertising router is a default router, and for how long: Router Lifetime

- The value of the reachable time for neighbor unreachability detection: Reachable Time

- The time interval between successive Neighbor Solicitation messages: Retransmission Timer

Prefix Information option:

- The prefix: Prefix Length, Prefix

- Whether the advertised prefix is on-link: On-link flag

- Whether to create a stateless address based on the prefix: Autonomous flag

- Whether the Prefix field contains the address of the home agent: Router Address flag

- Whether to update the site prefix table with a site prefix: Site Prefix flag, Site Prefix Length

- The valid lifetime of the stateless address: Valid Lifetime

- The preferred lifetime of the stateless address: Preferred Lifetime

9. Under what circumstances is an unsolicited Neighbor Advertisement message sent?

   An unsolicited Neighbor Advertisement message is sent in response to a duplicate address detection Neighbor Solicitation and when either the link-layer address or the role of the node changes.

10. What are the differences in address resolution and duplicate address detection node behavior for anycast addresses?

    In Neighbor Advertisement messages, the Override flag is always set to 0. Duplicate address detection is not performed for anycast addresses.

11. Why is the response to a duplicate address detection sent as multicast? Who sends the response, the offending or defending node?

    The response is multicast because the sender of the Neighbor Solicitation message cannot receive unicast packets at the duplicated IPv6 address. The defending node always sends the response.

12. Why is the value of the Hop Limit field set to 255 for all ND messages?

To prevent ND-based attacks from being launched from off-link nodes. The Hop Limit field for all traffic of an off-link node is always less than 255.

13. Describe the purpose of each of the host data structures described in RFC 2461.

■ Destination cache: maps a destination address to a next-hop address and stores the PMTU to the destination

■ Neighbor cache: maps a next-hop address to a link-layer address and stores the state of the entry for neighbor unreachability detection

■ Prefix list: stores all the on-link prefixes

■ Default router list: stores all the routers that advertised themselves as default routers

14. What field in the Redirect message contains the next-hop address of the better router to use for packets addressed to a specific destination? Describe how the contents of that field are used to update the conceptual host data structures for subsequent data sent to the destination.

The Target Address field. The Target Address field updates the Next-hop Address field of the destination cache entry corresponding to the Destination Address field on the host that receives the Redirect message.

15. Under what circumstances does a router send a Router Advertisement?

Pseudo-periodically and in response to a Router Solicitation message.

16. For Host A and Host B on the same link, why is the exchange of a Neighbor Solicitation message (sent by Host A to Host B) and a Neighbor Advertisement message (sent by Host B to Host A) not considered by Host B as proof that Host A is reachable?

Host B receives no confirmation that Host A received and processed the Neighbor Advertisement sent by Host B.

17. What is the next-hop address of a destination set to for a host that does not have a prefix matching the destination address or a default router?

It is set to the destination address of the IPv6 packet. The destination is considered to be on-link.

CHAPTER 7: MULTICAST LISTENER DISCOVERY

1. Why is the IPv6 Router Alert Option used in the Hop-by-Hop Options header for MLD messages?

The IPv6 Router Alert option is used to ensure that routers process MLD messages that are sent to multicast addresses on which the router is not listening.

2. Which addresses are used as the source address in MLD messages?

The Source Address field is set to the link-local address of the interface on which the message is being sent. If a Multicast Listener Report message is for a solicited-node multicast address corresponding to a unicast address for which duplicate address detection has not completed successfully, the source address is set to the unspecified address (::).

3. How do you distinguish a general query from a multicast-address-specific query in the Multicast Listener Query message?

In the general query, the Destination Address field in the IPv6 header is set to the link-local scope all-nodes multicast address (FF02::1) and the Multicast Address field in the MLD message is set to the unspecified address (::). In the multicast-address-specific query, the Destination Address field in the IPv6 header and the Multicast Address field in the MLD message are set to the specific address being queried.

4. For which multicast addresses are Multicast Listener Report messages never sent?

The link-local scope all-nodes multicast address (FF02::1)

5. In which MLD message is the value of the Maximum Response Delay field significant?

Multicast Listener Query (both general and multicast-address-specific)

6. Describe the use of the Multicast Address field for each MLD message.

- Multicast Listener Query: Requests reporting for all multicast addresses (except FF02::1) or for a specified multicast address

- Multicast Listener Report: Reports group membership for the specified multicast address

- Multicast Listener Done: Reports that there might not be any more members on the subnet for the specified multicast address

CHAPTER 8: ADDRESS AUTOCONFIGURATION

1. List and describe the states of an IPv6 autoconfigured address.

    ■   Tentative: The address is in the process of being verified as unique

    ■   Valid: The address can be used for sending and receiving unicast traffic

        ❑   Preferred: The address is valid and it can be used for unlimited communication

        ❑   Deprecated: The address is valid but its use is discouraged for new communication

    ■   Invalid: The address can no longer be used to send or receive unicast traffic

2. What is the formula for calculating the amount of time an autoconfigured address remains in the deprecated state?

    Valid Lifetime - Preferred Lifetime

3. How does a router obtain addresses other than link-local addresses?

    It obtains them through manual configuration.

4. According to RFC 2462, what addresses are autoconfigured for LAN interfaces on hosts when duplicate address detection for the EUI-64-derived link-local address fails? What is the behavior for the IPv6 protocol for the Windows .NET Server 2003 family and Windows XP?

    None.

    If the EUI-64-derived link-local address is a duplicate, the IPv6 protocol for the Windows .NET Server 2003 family and Windows XP can continue with the receipt of a multicast Router Advertisement message containing site-local or global prefixes and automatically configure site-local or global addresses based on the EUI-64-derived interface ID or a temporary global address with a randomly-derived interface ID.

5. A host computer is running Windows .NET Standard Server and is assigned the IPv4 address 172.30.90.65 on its single LAN interface. IPv6 on this computer starts up and receives a Router Advertisement message on its LAN interface that contains both a site-local prefix (FEC0:0:0:29D8::/64) and a global prefix (3FFE:FFFF:A3:29D8::/64). List and describe the autoconfigured addresses for all interfaces on this host.

LAN interface: FE80::[EUI-64 interface ID], FEC0::29D8:[EUI-64 interface ID], 3FFE:FFFF:A3:29D8:[EUI-64 interface ID], 3FFE:FFFF:A3:29D8:[random interface ID]

Automatic Tunneling Pseudo-Interface: FE80::5EFE:172.30.90.65
Loopback Interface: ::1, FE80::1

CHAPTER 9: IPV6 AND NAME RESOLUTION

1. Why is the RFC 1886-defined DNS record for IPv6 name resolution named the "AAAA" record?

   It is named the "AAAA" record because 128-bit IPv6 addresses are four times longer than 32-bit IPv4 addresses, which use a host (A) record.

2. What is the benefit to using the Windows .NET Server 2003 family DNS Server service over the Windows 2000 DNS Server service when manually configuring AAAA records?

   With the Windows .NET Server 2003 family DNS Server service, you can type the IPv6 address as a single string and use double-colons to compress a block of zeros.

3. A host computer is running Windows .NET Standard Server and is assigned the IPv4 address 172.30.90.65 on its single LAN interface. IPv6 on this computer starts up and receives a Router Advertisement message on its Automatic Tunneling Pseudo-Interface that contains both a site-local prefix (FEC0:0:0:C140::/64) and a global prefix (3FFE:FFFF:A3:C140::/64). List the IPv6 addresses for the AAAA records registered with DNS by this host.

   FEC0::C140:0:5EFE:172.30.90.65, 3FFE:FFFF:A3:C140::5EFE:172.30.90.65

4. Describe the importance of address selection rules for a node running both IPv4 and IPv6 that is using a DNS infrastructure containing both A and AAAA records.

   Address selection rules decide which type of address (IPv4 vs. IPv6) and the scope of the address (public vs. private for IPv4 and link-local vs. site-local vs. global vs. coexistence for IPv6), for both the source and the destination addresses for subsequent communication.

CHAPTER 10: IPV6 ROUTING

1. How does IPv6 determine the single route in the routing table to use when forwarding a packet?

   Based on the list of matching routes, the route that has the largest prefix length is chosen. If there are multiple longest matching routes, the router uses the lowest metric to select the best route. If there are multiple longest matching routes with the lowest metric, IPv6 can choose which routing table entry to use.

2. Describe the conditions that would cause a router to send the following ICMPv6 error messages:

   ICMPv6 Packet Too Big

   The IPv6 MTU of the forwarding interface is lower than the size of the IPv6 packet being forwarded.

   ICMPv6 Destination Unreachable-Address Unreachable

   The neighboring destination node does not respond to Neighbor Solicitation messages being sent to resolve its link-layer address. Or, the packet is a ping-pong packet (a packet being sent to a destination address that does not exist on a point-to-point link).

   ICMPv6 Time Exceeded-Hop Limit Exceeded in Transit

   The Hop Limit field for a packet is less than 1 after decrementing it.

   ICMPv6 Destination Unreachable-Port Unreachable

   There is no application on the router listening on the UDP destination port (for packets sent to an address assigned to a router interface).

   ICMPv6 Destination Unreachable-No Route to Destination

   There is no matching route in the IPv6 routing table.

   ICMPv6 Parameter Problem-Unrecognized IPv6 Option Encountered

   The router processed an unrecognized option within a Hop-by-Hop Options or Destination Options (for intermediate destinations) extension header and the two high-order bits of the Option Type field were set to either 10 or 11.

3. A host running the IPv6 protocol for the Windows .NET Server 2003 family or Windows XP is configured with the IPv4 address of 10.98.116.47 and receives a Router Advertisement message from a router advertising itself as a default router with the link-local address of FE80:: 2AA:FF:FE45:A431:2C5D, and containing a Prefix Information option to

autoconfigure an address with the prefix FEC0:0:0:952A::/64 and a Route Information option with the prefix FEC0:0:0:952C::/64. Fill in the expected entries for the host in the following abbreviated routing table.

```
Network Destination       Gateway

----------------------    -------------

::/0                      FE80::2AA:FF:FE45:A431:2C5D

FEC0:0:0:952A::/64        On-link

FEC0:0:0:952C::/64        FE80::2AA:FF:FE45:A431:2C5D
```

4. What happens when a node running the IPv6 protocol for the Windows .NET Server 2003 family or Windows XP sends a packet and there is no matching route in the routing table? How is this different from the behavior of an IPv4 node?

    The IPv6 node assumes that the destination is on-link (a neighbor) and attempts to send the packet. If a sending IPv4 node does not find a matching route in the IPv4 routing table, it indicates an internal forwarding error and does not attempt to send the packet.

5. Describe the difference between distance vector, link state, and path vector routing protocol technologies in terms of convergence time, ability to scale, ease of deployment, and appropriate use (intranet vs. Internet).

    ■   Distance vector: high convergence time, does not scale to large or very large networks, very easy to deploy, appropriate for use within a small intranet

    ■   Link state: low convergence time, scales to large networks, more difficult to deploy, appropriate for use within an intranet consisting of a single autonomous system

    ■   Path vector: low convergence time, scales to very large networks, difficult to deploy, appropriate for use between autonomous systems on the Internet

6. Why is IDRPv2 a better choice than BGP-4 for the routing protocol to use on the IPv6 Internet?

    IDRPv2 does not use a separate autonomous system identifier. IDRPv2 uses IPv6 prefixes to identify an AS or a routing domain confederation.

7. A static router running the IPv6 protocol for the Windows .NET Server 2003 family or Windows XP is configured with the following commands.

netsh int ipv6 set int 4 forw=enabled adv=enabled
netsh int ipv6 set int 5 forw=enabled adv=enabled
netsh int ipv6 add rou FEC0:0:0:1A4C::/64 4 pub=yes
netsh int ipv6 add rou FEC0:0:0:90B5::/64 5 pub=yes

With just these commands being run on the static router, will a host on the subnet FEC0:0:0:90B5::/64 have a default route? Why or why not?

No. In order for a static router running the IPv6 protocol for the Windows .NET Server 2003 family or Windows XP to advertise itself as a default router, it must have a default route that is configured to be published. For example, the command:

netsh int ipv6 add rou ::/0 6 FE80::2AA:FF:FE19:9B84 pub=yes

would add a publishable default route.

CHAPTER 11: COEXISTENCE AND MIGRATION

1. Describe the difference between migration and coexistence.

   Migration is the equipping and configuration of all nodes to replace one protocol (IPv4) with another (IPv6). Coexistence is the allowance of both types of protocols to maintain connectivity; an advantage while migration is occurring.

2. Why do the criteria for the IPv4-to-IPv6 transition require no dependencies between IPv4 and IPv6 hosts, addresses, and routing infrastructure?

   To allow for the maximum amount of flexibility for organizations and the Internet to migrate from IPv4 to IPv6 when needed, without compromising existing connectivity.

3. How does an IPv4-only host communicate with an IPv6-only host?

   It communicates by using an Application or Transport layer gateway or proxy that translates or proxies IPv4 traffic to IPv6 traffic, and vice versa. The PortProxy component of the IPv6 protocol for the Windows .NET Server 2003 family is an example of a Transport layer proxy.

4. What is the difference between an IPv4-compatible address and an IPv4-mapped address?

   An IPv4-compatible address is used to automatically tunnel IPv6 traffic across an IPv4 infrastructure. An IPv4-mapped address is used by an IPv6 implementation to internally represent IPv4-only hosts and IPv4 addresses.

5. Is the IPv6 protocol for Windows XP and the Windows .NET Server 2003 family a dual IP layer? Why or why not?

No. The IPv6 protocol for Windows XP and the Windows .NET Server 2003 family includes a separate implementation of TCP and UDP and is known as a dual stack implementation.

6. How are the source and destination addresses in the IPv4 header determined for IPv6 over IPv4 tunnel traffic?

For configured tunneling, the source and destination IPv4 addresses are determined from the manually configured tunnel endpoints.

For automatic tunneling, the source address is determined from the IPv4 address assigned to the interface that is forwarding the packets. The destination IPv4 address is derived from the next-hop address for the packet.

7. Describe the components of the 6to4 address and how the address is mapped to an IPv4 address when forwarded across an IPv4 infrastructure by a 6to4 router using the 2002::/16 route.

6to4 addresses have the following form:

2002:*WWXX*:*YYZZ*:[*SLA ID*]:[*Interface ID*]

in which *WWXX*:*YYZZ* is the NLA ID portion of a global address and the colon hexadecimal representation of a public IPv4 address (*w.x.y.z*) assigned to a site. The *SLA ID* and *Interface ID* are the same as defined for global addresses.

When a 6to4 router forwards an IPv6 packet with a 6to4 destination address using the 2002::/16 route, it encapsulates the IPv6 packet with an IPv4 header. In the IPv4 header, the source address is the IPv4 address of the sending interface and the destination address is the IPv4 address *w.x.y.z*.

8. What is the public IP address of the 6to4 router that is being used as a site border router for the ISATAP host with the address 2002:9D3C:2B5A:5:0:5EFE:131.107.24.103?

157.60.43.90

9. Describe how 6to4 and ISATAP can be used together.

6to4 is used to create a global address space based on an IPv4 public address (6to4 provides the first 64 bits of an IPv6 address). ISATAP is used to create interface identifiers based on assigned IPv4 addresses (ISATAP provides the last 64 bits of an IPv6 address). By combining 6to4 and ISATAP, you can use IPv6 to communicate across multiple IPv4 infrastructures.

10. For a 6over4 host using an Ethernet adapter, describe how the joining of an IPv6 multicast group on all interfaces creates two multicast entries in the table of interesting destination MAC addresses on the Ethernet adapter.

    When the host joins an IPv6 multicast group on a LAN interface, the IPv6 multicast address is mapped to an Ethernet multicast MAC address beginning with 33-33. This multicast address is added to the table of interesting destination MAC addresses on the Ethernet adapter.

    Because the host is a 6over4 host, the IPv6 multicast address is mapped to an IPv4 multicast address. When the host joins an IPv4 multicast group on a LAN interface, the IPv4 multicast address is mapped to an Ethernet multicast MAC address beginning with 01-00-5E. This multicast address is added to the table of interesting destination MAC addresses on the Ethernet adapter.

11. A common misconception is that ISPs must support native IPv6 routing in order to use IPv6. Describe why this is a misconception.

    By using 6to4, the ISP does not have to support native IPv6 routing. The ISP has to provide only IPv4 routing and the allocation of a single public IPv4 address to each customer.

Chapter 12: IPv6 Mobility

1. How does a mobile node determine its home subnet prefix, home address, and the address of its home agent?

   Manual configuration - The home subnet prefix, home address, and the address of the home agent are manually configured, typically through a keyboard-based command, and are permanent until manually changed.

   Pseudo-automatic configuration - The user has the option (typically through a button in the user interface of the operating system) to indicate to the IPv6 protocol that the node is now connected to the home link. Based on this indication, the IPv6 protocol stores the home subnet link prefix and home address and listens for additional router advertisements containing the Home Agent (H) flag.

Automatic configuration - The IPv6 node is always listening for router advertisements with the H flag set. Based on additional protocol or operating system parameters and the establishment of a security relationship with the home agent, the IPv6 node determines that it is on its home link.

2. When does a home agent or correspondent node send a binding request?

When the binding cache entry for the mobile node is about to expire.

3. How does a home agent compile a list of home agents on the home link and then convey that information to the mobile node while it is away from home?

The home agent compiles the list of home agents from received Router Advertisement messages with the H flag set. The list of home agents is conveyed to the mobile node through the ICMPv6 Home Agent Address Discovery process.

4. How does the mobile node determine when it has attached to a new link?

The link layer indicated a media change or because the node received a router advertisement that contains a new prefix.

5. What kinds of packets are sent between the home agent and the mobile node?

The mobile node sends the home agent the following types of packets:

- Binding update
- ICMPv6 Home Agent Address Discovery Request message

The home agent sends the mobile node the following types of packets:

- Binding maintenance (binding requests and binding acknowledgments)
- ICMPv6 Home Agent Address Discovery Reply message
- Tunneled data

6. What kinds of packets are sent between the correspondent node and the mobile node?

The mobile node sends the correspondent node the following types of packets:

- Binding updates

- Data (with the Home Address option in the Destination Options header)

The correspondent node sends the mobile node the following types of packets:

- Binding maintenance (binding requests or binding acknowledgments)

- Data (with the Routing header)

7. What kinds of packets are sent between the correspondent node and the home agent?

Although there are no packets sent directly between the correspondent node and the home agent, the home agent intercepts packets sent by the correspondent node to the mobile node's home address and tunnels them to the mobile node's care-of address.

8. Describe the addressing in the IPv6 header, and the sequence of IPv6 extension headers and their contents for a packet sent by a mobile node that is away from home to another mobile node that is away from home for which a binding cache entry is present.

In the IPv6 header, the source address is set to the sending node's care-of address and the destination address is set to the destination node's care-of address.

The Routing extension header contains the destination node's home address.

The Home Address option in the Destination Options header contains the source node's home address.

9. When does the mobile node send a binding update to the home agent? When does the mobile node send a binding update to the correspondent node?

The mobile node sends a binding update to the home agent when it attaches to its first foreign link, changes to a new foreign link, returns home, or in response to a binding request.

The mobile node sends a binding update to a correspondent node when it receives a packet from the correspondent node that was tunneled from the home agent, changes care-of addresses and the correspondent node is in its binding update list, or in response to a binding request.

10. How does a mobile node determine when it has returned home?

A mobile node determines it has returned home when it receives a router advertisement that contains its home prefix.

11. How does the mobile node avoid duplicate address conflicts when it returns home?

It does not perform duplicate address detection for its address. Instead, the mobile node informs the home agent that it has returned to the home link. After receiving a binding acknowledgment from the home agent, the mobile node then sends an unsolicited multicast Neighbor Advertisement message to the link-local scope all-nodes multicast address (FF02::1) with the Override (O) flag set to inform local hosts of the correct link-layer address for the mobile node's home address.

Appendix E

Setting Up an IPv6 Test Lab

This appendix provides information about how you can use five computers to create a test lab to configure and test the IPv6 protocol for Windows XP and the Windows .NET Server 2003 family. These instructions are designed to guide you through a set of tasks, exposing you to the IPv6 protocol and its associated functionality. Beyond the set of tasks, these instructions allow you to create a functioning IPv6 configuration. You can use this configuration to learn about and experiment with IPv6 features and functionality, and to aid in developing applications for IPv6 or modifying existing IPv4 applications to work over both IPv4 and IPv6.

SETTING UP THE INFRASTRUCTURE

The infrastructure for the IPv6 test lab network consists of five computers performing the following services:

■   A computer running Windows .NET Standard Server that is used as a DNS server. This computer is named DNS1.

■   A computer running Windows XP that is used as a client. This computer is named CLIENT1.

■   A computer running Windows XP that is used as a router. This computer is named ROUTER1.

■   A computer running Windows XP that is used as a router. This computer is named ROUTER2.

■   A computer running Windows XP that is used as a client. This computer is named CLIENT2.

Figure E-1 shows the configuration of the IPv6 test lab.
There are three network segments:

■   A network segment known as Subnet 1 that uses the private IP network ID of 10.0.1.0/24 and site-local subnet ID of FEC0:0:0:1::/64

■   A network segment known as Subnet 2 that uses the private IP network ID of 10.0.2.0/24 and site-local subnet ID of FEC0:0:0:2::/64

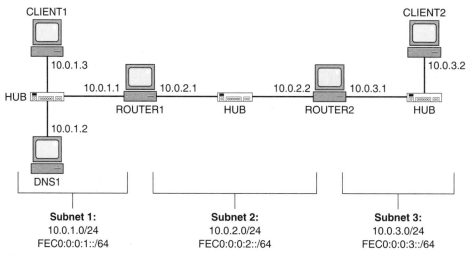

Figure E-1. *The configuration of the IPv6 test lab*

- A network segment known as Subnet 3 that uses the private IP network ID of 10.0.3.0/24 and site-local subnet ID of FEC0:0:0:3::/64

All computers on each subnet are connected to a separate common hub or Layer 2 switch. The two router computers, ROUTER1 and ROUTER2, have two network adapters installed.

For the IPv4 configuration, each computer is configured manually with the appropriate IP address, subnet mask, default gateway, and DNS server IP address. DHCP and WINS servers are not used. For the IPv6 configuration, link-local addresses are used initially.

The following sections describe how each of the computers in the test lab is configured. To reconstruct this test lab, please configure the computers in the order presented.

NOTE:

The following instructions are for configuring an IPv6 test lab using a minimum number of computers. Individual computers are needed to separate the services provided on the network and to clearly show the desired functionality. You can use any member of the Windows .NET Server family for DNS1 and any version of Windows XP or Windows .NET Server for the other computers. This configuration is neither designed to reflect best practices nor is it designed to reflect a desired or recommended configuration for a production network. The configuration, including addresses and all other configuration parameters, is designed to work on a separate test lab network.

DNS1

DNS1 is a computer running Windows .NET Standard Server. It is providing DNS Server services for the testlab.microsoft.com DNS domain. To configure DNS1 for this service, perform the following steps:

1. Install Windows .NET Standard Server as a stand-alone server. Set the Administrator password.

2. After restarting, log on as Administrator.

3. Configure the TCP/IP protocol with the IP address of 10.0.1.2, the subnet mask of 255.255.255.0, and the default gateway of 10.0.1.1.

4. Install the DNS Server service.

5. Create a forward lookup zone named "testlab.microsoft.com" as a primary zone that allows dynamic updates.

6. Install the IPv6 protocol.

> **NOTE:**
> The domain name testlab.microsoft.com is used here for example purposes only. You can use any domain name in your test lab configuration.

CLIENT1

CLIENT1 is a computer running Windows XP that is being used as a client. To configure CLIENT1 as a client computer, perform the following steps:

1. On CLIENT1, install Windows XP as a workgroup computer. Set the Administrator password.

2. After restarting, log on as Administrator.

3. Configure the TCP/IP protocol with the IP address of 10.0.1.3, the subnet mask of 255.255.255.0, a default gateway of 10.0.1.1, and the DNS server IP address of 10.0.1.2. Configure DNS properties so that the connection-specific suffix for the LAN connection is "testlab.microsoft.com" and specify to use the connection's DNS suffix in DNS registration.

4. Install the IPv6 protocol.

ROUTER1

ROUTER1 is a computer running Windows XP that is being used as a router between Subnet 1 and Subnet 2. To configure ROUTER1 as a router, perform the following steps:

1. On ROUTER1, install Windows XP as a workgroup computer. Set the Administrator password.

2. After restarting, log on as Administrator.

3. Install the IPv6 protocol.

4. In Control Panel-Network Connections, rename the LAN connection connected to Subnet 1 to "Subnet 1 Connection" and rename the LAN connection connected to Subnet 2 to "Subnet 2 Connection."

5. For Subnet 1 Connection, configure the TCP/IP protocol with the IP address of 10.0.1.1, the subnet mask of 255.255.255.0, and the DNS server IP address of 10.0.1.2. Configure DNS properties so that the connection-specific suffix for the connection is "testlab.microsoft.com" and specify to use the connection's DNS suffix in DNS registration.

6. For Subnet 2 Connection, configure the TCP/IP protocol with the IP address of 10.0.2.1, the subnet mask of 255.255.255.0, and a default gateway of 10.0.2.2. Configure DNS properties so that the connection-specific suffix for the connection is "testlab.microsoft.com" and specify to use the connection's DNS suffix in DNS registration.

7. Run the registry editor (Regedit.exe) and set HKEY_LOCAL_MACHINE\SYSTEM\CurrentControlSet\Services\Tcpip\Parameters\IPEnableRouter to 1. This enables IPv4 routing between Subnet 1 and Subnet 2.

8. Restart ROUTER1.

ROUTER2

ROUTER2 is a computer running Windows XP that is being used as a router between Subnet 2 and Subnet 3. To configure ROUTER2 as a router, perform the following steps:

1. On ROUTER2, install Windows XP as a workgroup computer. Set the Administrator password.

2. After restarting, log on as Administrator.

3. Install the IPv6 protocol.

4. In Control Panel-Network Connections, rename the LAN connection connected to Subnet 2 to "Subnet 2 Connection" and rename the LAN connection connected to Subnet 3 to "Subnet 3 Connection."

5. For Subnet 2 Connection, configure the TCP/IP protocol with the IP address of 10.0.2.2, the subnet mask of 255.255.255.0, a default gateway of 10.0.2.1, and the DNS server IP address of 10.0.1.2. Configure DNS properties so that the connection-specific suffix for the connection is "testlab.microsoft.com" and specify to use the connection's DNS suffix in DNS registration.

6. For Subnet 3 Connection, configure the TCP/IP protocol with the IP address of 10.0.3.1, and the subnet mask of 255.255.255.0. Configure DNS properties so that the connection-specific suffix for the connection is "testlab.microsoft.com" and specify to use the connection's DNS suffix in DNS registration.

7. Run the registry editor (Regedit.exe) and set HKEY_LOCAL_MACHINE\SYSTEM\CurrentControlSet\Services\Tcpip\Parameters\IPEnableRouter to 1. This enables IPv4 routing between Subnet 2 and Subnet 3.

8. Restart ROUTER2.

CLIENT2

CLIENT2 is a computer running Windows XP that is being used as a client. To configure CLIENT2 as a client computer, perform the following steps:

1. On CLIENT2, install Windows XP as a workgroup computer. Set the Administrator password.

2. After restarting, log on as Administrator.

3. Configure the TCP/IP protocol with the IP address of 10.0.3.2, the subnet mask of 255.255.255.0, a default gateway of 10.0.3.1, and the DNS server IP address of 10.0.1.2. Configure DNS properties so that the connection-specific suffix for the connection is "testlab.microsoft.com" and specify to use the connection's DNS suffix in DNS registration.

4. Verify the integrity of the IPv4 routing infrastructure with the following command:

   ping 10.0.1.3

   This tests whether or not IPv4 packets can be forwarded between CLIENT2 on Subnet 3 and CLIENT1 on Subnet 1.

5. Install the IPv6 protocol.

IPv6 Test Lab Tasks

The following tasks are designed to take you through the common IPv6 configurations by using the test lab infrastructure:

- Link-local ping
- Creating an IPv6 static routing infrastructure
- Using name resolution
- Using IPSec
- Using temporary addresses

Link-Local Ping

To ping a node using link-local addresses and view the entries created in the neighbor and destination caches, complete the following steps:

1. On ROUTER1, type the **netsh interface ipv6 show address** command to obtain the link-local address of the interface named Subnet 1 Connection.

2. On CLIENT1, type the **netsh interface ipv6 show address** command to obtain the link-local address and interface index of the interface named Local Area Connection.

3. On CLIENT1, type the following command to ping the link-local address of ROUTER1's interface on Subnet 1:

   ping *ROUTER1LinkLocalAddress%InterfaceIdentifier*

   For example, if the link-local address of ROUTER1's interface on Subnet 1 is FE80::2AA:FF:FE9D:10C5, and the interface index for the Local Area Connection interface on CLIENT1 is 3, the command is:

   ping FE80::2AA:FF:FE9D:10C5%3

4. On CLIENT1, type the **netsh interface ipv6 show neighbors** command to view the entry in the CLIENT1 neighbor cache for ROUTER1. You should see an entry for ROUTER1's link-local address.

5. On CLIENT1, type the **netsh interface ipv6 show destinationcache** command to view the entry in the CLIENT1 destination cache for ROUTER1.

6. On CLIENT1, type the **netsh interface ipv6 show routes** command to view the entries in the CLIENT1 routing table.

Creating an IPv6 Static Routing Infrastructure

To configure a static routing infrastructure so that all test lab nodes are reachable using IPv6 traffic, complete the following steps:

1. On ROUTER1, type the **netsh interface ipv6 show address** command to obtain the link-local addresses and interface index numbers of interfaces named Subnet 1 Connection and Subnet 2 Connection.

2. On ROUTER1, type the following commands:

   netsh interface ipv6 set interface *Subnet1InterfaceIndex* **forwarding=enabled advertise=enabled**

   netsh interface ipv6 set interface *Subnet2InterfaceIndex* **forwarding=enabled advertise=enabled**

   netsh interface ipv6 add route FEC0:0:0:1::/64 *Subnet1InterfaceIndex* **publish=yes**

   netsh interface ipv6 add route FEC0:0:0:2::/64 *Subnet2InterfaceIndex* **publish=yes**

   netsh interface ipv6 add route ::/0 *Subnet2InterfaceIndex/ ROUTER2AddressOnSubnet2* **publish=yes**

   in which:

   - ■ *Subnet1InterfaceIndex* is the interface index of ROUTER1's Subnet 1 Connection.

   - ■ *Subnet2InterfaceIndex* is the interface index of the ROUTER1's Subnet 2 Connection.

   - ■ *ROUTER2AddressOnSubnet2* is the link-local address assigned to ROUTER2's Subnet 2 Connection.

   For example, if ROUTER1's Subnet 1 Connection interface index is 4 and Subnet 2 Connection interface index is 5, and the link-local address of the ROUTER2's Subnet 2 Connection interface is FE80::2AA:FF:FE87:4D5C, the commands should be typed as follows:

   netsh int ipv6 set int 4 forw=enabled adv=enabled

   netsh int ipv6 set int 5 forw=enabled adv=enabled

   netsh int ipv6 add rou FEC0:0:0:1::/64 4 pub=yes

   netsh int ipv6 add rou FEC0:0:0:2::/64 5 pub=yes

   netsh int ipv6 add rou ::/0 5 FE80::2AA:FF:FE87:4D5C pub=yes

3. On ROUTER2, type the **netsh interface ipv6 show address** command to obtain the link-local addresses and interface index numbers of the Subnet 2 and Subnet 3 interfaces.

4. On ROUTER2, type the following commands:

   netsh interface ipv6 set interface *Subnet2InterfaceIndex* **forwarding=enabled advertise=enabled**

   netsh interface ipv6 set interface *Subnet3InterfaceIndex* **forwarding=enabled advertise=enabled**

   netsh interface ipv6 add route FEC0:0:0:2::/64 *Subnet2InterfaceIndex* **publish=yes**

   netsh interface ipv6 add route FEC0:0:0:3::/64 *Subnet3InterfaceIndex* **publish=yes**

   netsh interface ipv6 add route ::/0 *Subnet2InterfaceIndex/ ROUTER1AddressOnSubnet2* **publish=yes**

   For example, if the Subnet 2 interface index is 4, the Subnet 3 interface index is 5, and the link-local address of the ROUTER1 Subnet 2 interface is FE80::2AA:FF:FE9A:203F, the commands should be typed as follows:

   netsh int ipv6 set int 4 forw=enabled adv=enabled

   netsh int ipv6 set int 5 forw=enabled adv=enabled

   netsh int ipv6 add rou FEC0:0:0:2::/64 4 pub=yes

   netsh int ipv6 add rou FEC0:0:0:3::/64 5 pub=yes

   netsh int ipv6 add rou ::/0 4 FE80::2AA:FF:FE9A:203F pub=yes

5. On CLIENT1, type the **netsh interface ipv6 show address** command to view a new address on the LAN interface that is based on the site-local prefix of FEC0:0:0:1::/64.

6. On CLIENT1, type the **netsh interface ipv6 show routes** command to view new routes for FEC0:0:0:1::/64, FEC0:0:0:2::/64, and ::/0.

7. On CLIENT2, type the **netsh interface ipv6 show address** command to view a new address on the LAN interface that is based on the site-local prefix of FEC0:0:0:3::/64.

8. On CLIENT2, type the **netsh interface ipv6 show routes** command to view new routes for FEC0:0:0:2::/64, FEC0:0:0:3::/64, and ::/0.

9. On CLIENT1, type the following ping command to ping CLIENT2's site-local address:

    ping *CLIENT2SiteLocalAddress*

    On CLIENT1, type the following tracert command with the **-d** option to trace the route between CLIENT1 and CLIENT2:

    tracert -d *CLIENT2SiteLocalAddress*

    In the tracert display, you can view the address of the Subnet 1 Connection for ROUTER1 and the address of the Subnet 2 Connection for ROUTER2.

10. On ROUTER1, type the following commands:

    netsh interface ipv6 show neighbors

    to view the entries in the ROUTER1 neighbor cache for CLIENT1 and ROUTER2.

    netsh interface ipv6 show destinationcache

    to view the entries in the ROUTER1 destination cache for CLIENT1 and ROUTER2.

    As described in Chapter 10 "IPv6 Routing," the IPv6 protocol for the Windows .NET Server 2003 family and Windows XP advertises off-link prefixes using the Route Information option in Router Advertisement messages. These prefixes become routes in the routing table of the receiving host.

Using Name Resolution

To configure DNS and the local Hosts file to resolve names to IPv6 addresses, complete the following steps:

1. On DNS1, use the DNS snap-in to view the A and AAAA records in the testlab.microsoft.com forward lookup zone that were dynamically registered by the computers in the test lab. Verify that an AAAA, or "quad A," record for CLIENT2 exists.

2. If an AAAA record for CLIENT2 does not exist, create an AAAA resource record for CLIENT2 with the DNS name client2.testlab. microsoft.com for its site-local IPv6 address using the IPv6 Host resource record type.

    For example, if CLIENT2's site-local address is FEC0::3:260:8FF:FE52: F9D8, the AAAA resource record is configured as follows:

    Host: **client2**

    IP version 6 host address: **FEC0:0:0:3:260:8FF:FE52:F9D8**

3. On CLIENT1, type the following command:

   ping client2.testlab.microsoft.com

   The name client2.testlab.microsoft.com is resolved to its site-local address by sending a DNS query to DNS1.

4. On CLIENT2, create the following entry in the Hosts file (located in the *SystemRoot*\System32\Drivers\Etc folder):

   ```
   Client1SiteLocalAddress     cl1
   ```

   For example, if CLIENT1's site-local address is FEC0::1:260:8FF:FE2A:15F2, the entry in the Hosts file is:

   ```
   fec0::1:260:8ff:fe2a:15f2     cl1
   ```

5. On CLIENT2, type the following command:

   ping cl1

   The name cl1 is resolved to its site-local address by using the local Hosts file.

Using IPSec

To use IPSec between two computers running the IPv6 protocol for the Windows .NET Server 2003 family and Windows XP, complete the following steps:

1. On CLIENT1, create blank security association (.sad) and security policy (.spd) files by using the **ipsec6 s** command. For example, the command **ipsec6 s test** creates two files that have blank entries for manually configuring security associations (Test.sad) and security policies (Test.spd).

2. On CLIENT1, edit the .spd file, adding a security policy that secures all traffic between CLIENT1 and CLIENT2.

   Table E-1 shows the security policy entry that is added to the .spd file before the first entry (the first entry in Test.spd is not modified):

Table E-1. THE SECURITY POLICY ENTRY FOR TRAFFIC TO AND FROM CLIENT2

.spd File Field Name	*Value*
Policy	2
RemoteIPAddr	- *Client2SiteLocalAddress*
LocalIPAddr	- *

continued

Table E-1 *continued*

.spd File Field Name	Value
Protocol	- *
RemotePort	- *
LocalPort	- *
IPSecProtocol	AH
IPSecMode	TRANSPORT
RemoteGWIPAddr	*
SABundleIndex	NONE
Direction	BIDIRECT
Action	APPLY
InterfaceIndex	0

Type a semicolon at the end of the entry configuring this security policy. Policy entries must be placed in decreasing numerical order.

3. On CLIENT1, edit the .sad file, adding SA entries to secure all traffic between CLIENT1 and CLIENT2. Two security associations must be created, one for traffic to CLIENT2 and one for traffic from CLIENT2.

    Table E-2 shows the first SA entry that is added to the .sad file (for traffic to CLIENT2):

Table E-2. THE SECURITY ASSOCIATION ENTRY FOR TRAFFIC TO CLIENT2

.sad File Field Name	Value
SAEntry	2
SPI	3001
SADestIPAddr	*Client2SiteLocalAddress*
DestIPAddr	POLICY
SrcIPAddr	POLICY
Protocol	POLICY
DestPort	POLICY
SrcPort	POLICY
AuthAlg	HMAC-MD5
KeyFile	*KeyFileName*
Direction	OUTBOUND
SecPolicyIndex	2

Type a semicolon at the end of the entry configuring this SA. For the KeyFile column, *KeyFileName* is the file name of a file that contains the IPSec key. This file is created in Step 4.

The following table shows the second SA entry that is added to the .sad file (for traffic from CLIENT2):

Table E-3. THE SECURITY ASSOCIATION ENTRY FOR TRAFFIC FROM CLIENT2

.sad File Field Name	Value
SAEntry	1
SPI	3000
SADestIPAddr	*Client2SiteLocalAddress*
DestIPAddr	POLICY
SrcIPAddr	POLICY
Protocol	POLICY
DestPort	POLICY
SrcPort	POLICY
AuthAlg	HMAC-MD5
KeyFile	*KeyFileName*
Direction	INBOUND
SecPolicyIndex	2

Type a semicolon at the end of the entry configuring this SA. SA entries must be placed in decreasing numerical order.

4. On CLIENT1, create a file that contains data used to create and validate the Message Digest 5 (MD5) keyed hash on each IPSec-protected packet that is exchanged with CLIENT2. For example, create the file Test.key with the contents "This is a test." and no extra characters, spaces, or lines.

   The IPv6 protocol for the Windows .NET Server 2003 family and Windows XP supports only manually configured keys for quick mode SAs (also known as IPSec or Phase II SAs), because main mode negotiation using IKE is not performed. Manual keys are configured by creating files that contain either the text or binary data of the manual key. In this example, the same key for the SAs is used in both directions. You can use different keys for inbound and outbound SAs by creating different key files and referencing them with the KeyFile field in the .sad file.

5. On CLIENT2, use the **ipsec6 s** command to create blank security association (.sad) and security policy (.spd) files. For example, the **ipsec6 s test** command creates two files that have blank entries for manually configuring security associations (Test.sad) and security policies (Test.spd). In this example, the same file names for the .sad and .spd files are used on CLIENT2. You can choose to use different file names on each host.

6. On CLIENT2, edit the .spd file, adding a security policy that secures all traffic between CLIENT2 and CLIENT1.

    Table E-4 shows the security policy entry that is added to the .spd file before the first entry (The first entry in Test.spd is not modified.):

Table E-4. THE SECURITY POLICY ENTRY FOR TRAFFIC TO AND FROM CLIENT1

.spd File Field Name	Value
Policy	2
RemoteIPAddr	- *Client1SiteLocalAddress*
LocalIPAddr	- *
Protocol	- *
RemotePort	- *
LocalPort	- *
IPSecProtocol	AH
IPSecMode	TRANSPORT
RemoteGWIPAddr	*
SABundleIndex	NONE
Direction	BIDIRECT
Action	APPLY
InterfaceIndex	0

Type a semicolon at the end of the entry configuring this security policy. Policy entries must be placed in decreasing numerical order.

7. On CLIENT2, edit the .sad file, adding SA entries to secure all traffic between CLIENT2 and CLIENT1. Two security associations must be created: one for traffic to CLIENT1 and one for traffic from CLIENT1.

Table E-5 shows the first SA entry that is added to the .sad file (for traffic to CLIENT1):

Table E-5. THE SECURITY ASSOCIATION ENTRY FOR TRAFFIC TO CLIENT1

.sad File Field Name	*Value*
SAEntry	2
SPI	3000
SADestIPAddr	*Client1SiteLocalAddress*
DestIPAddr	POLICY
SrcIPAddr	POLICY
Protocol	POLICY
DestPort	POLICY
SrcPort	POLICY
AuthAlg	HMAC-MD5
KeyFile	*KeyFileName*
Direction	OUTBOUND
SecPolicyIndex	2

Type a semicolon at the end of the entry configuring this SA. For the KeyFile column, *KeyFileName* is the name of a file that contains the IPSec key. This file is created in Step 8.

The following table shows the second SA entry that is added to the .sad file (for traffic from CLIENT1):

Table E-6. THE SECURITY ASSOCIATION ENTRY FOR TRAFFIC FROM CLIENT1

.sad File Field Name	*Value*
SAEntry	1
SPI	3001
SADestIPAddr	*Client1SiteLocalAddress*
DestIPAddr	POLICY
SrcIPAddr	POLICY
Protocol	POLICY

continued

Table E-6 *continued*

.sad File Field Name	Value
DestPort	POLICY
SrcPort	POLICY
AuthAlg	HMAC-MD5
KeyFile	*KeyFileName*
Direction	INBOUND
SecPolicyIndex	2

Type a semicolon at the end of the entry configuring this SA. SA entries must be placed in decreasing numerical order.

8. On CLIENT2, create a file that contains data used to create and validate the Message Digest 5 (MD5) keyed hash on each IPSec-protected packet that is exchanged with CLIENT1. This must be the same data that is configured for the key file on CLIENT1. For example, create the file Test.key with the contents "This is a test." and no extra characters, spaces, or lines.

9. On CLIENT1, use the **ipsec6 l** command to add the configured security policies and SAs from the .spd and .sad files. For example, the **ipsec6 l test** command is run on CLIENT1 to load the Test.spd and Test.sad files stored on CLIENT1.

10. On CLIENT2, use the **ipsec6 l** command to add the configured security policies and SAs from the .spd and .sad files. For example, the **ipsec6 l test** command is run on CLIENT2 to load the Test.spd and Test.sad files stored on CLIENT2.

11. On CLIENT2, use the **ping** command to ping CLIENT1.

    If you use Network Monitor to capture the traffic, you should see the exchange of ICMPv6 Echo Request and Echo Reply messages, with an Authentication header (AH) between the IPv6 header and the ICMPv6 header.

12. On CLIENT1 and CLIENT2, type the following command lines:

    ipsec6 d sp 2

    ipsec6 d sa 1

    ipsec6 d sa 2

Using Temporary Addresses

To view the configuration temporary addresses (also known as anonymous addresses) for global address prefixes, complete the following steps:

1. On ROUTER1, type the following command:

    netsh int ipv6 add rou 3FFE:FFFF:0:1::/64 *Subnet1InterfaceIndex* **pub=yes**

    in which *Subnet1InterfaceIndex* is the interface index of ROUTER1's Subnet 1 Connection.

    For example, if ROUTER1's Subnet 1 Connection interface index is 4, the command is:

    netsh int ipv6 add rou 3FFE:FFFF:0:1::/64 4 pub=yes

2. On CLIENT1, type the **netsh interface ipv6 show address** command to view new addresses on the interface named Local Area Connection that is based on the global prefix of 3FFE:FFFF:0:1::/64.

    There should be two addresses that are based on the 3FFE:FFFF:0:1::/64 prefix. One address uses an interface identifier that is based on the EUI-64 address of the interface. The other address is a temporary address for which the interface identifier is derived randomly.

Appendix F

IPv6 Reference Tables

This appendix contains a series of summary reference tables for IPv6.

Table F-1. DEFINED VALUES FOR THE SCOPE FIELD FOR IPv6 MULTICAST ADDRESSES

Scope Field Value	Scope
0	Reserved
1	Node-local scope
2	Link-local scope
5	Site-local scope
8	Organization-local scope
E	Global scope
F	Reserved

Table F-2. TYPICAL VALUES OF THE NEXT HEADER FIELD IN THE IPv6 HEADER

Value (Decimal)	Header
0	Hop-by-Hop Options header
6	TCP
17	UDP
41	Encapsulated IPv6 header
43	Routing header
44	Fragment header
50	Encapsulating Security Payload header
51	Authentication header
58	ICMPv6
59	No next header
60	Destination Options header

Table F-3. OPTION TYPES FOR HOP-BY-HOP OPTIONS AND DESTINATION OPTIONS HEADERS

Option Type	*Option and Where It Is Used*	*Alignment Requirement*
0	Pad1 option: Hop-by-Hop and Destination Options headers	None
1	PadN option: Hop-by-Hop and Destination Options headers	None
194 (0xC2)	Jumbo Payload option: Hop-by-Hop Options header	$4n + 2$
5	Router Alert option: Hop-by-Hop Options header	$2n + 0$
198 (0xC6)	Binding Update option: Destination Options header	$4n + 2$
7	Binding Acknowledgement option: Destination Options header	$4n + 3$
8	Binding Request option: Destination Options header	None
201 (0xC9)	Home Address option: Destination Options header	$8n + 6$

Table F-4. IPv6 MTUs FOR COMMON LAN AND WAN TECHNOLOGIES

LAN or WAN Technology	*IPv6 MTU*
Ethernet (Ethernet II encapsulation)	1,500
Ethernet (IEEE 802.3 SubNetwork Access Protocol [SNAP] encapsulation)	1,492
Token Ring	Varies
FDDI	4,352
Attached Resource Computer Network (ARCNet)	9,072
PPP	1,500
X.25	1,280
Frame Relay	1,592
Asynchronous Transfer Mode (ATM) (Null or SNAP encapsulation)	9,180

Table F-5. **ICMPv6 Messages**

ICMPv6 Type	*Message*	*Chapter for Details*
1	Destination Unreachable	5
2	Packet Too Big	5
3	Time Exceeded	5
4	Parameter Problem	5
128	Echo Request	5
129	Echo Reply	5
130	Multicast Listener Query	7
131	Multicast Listener Report	7
132	Multicast Listener Done	7
133	Router Solicitation	6
134	Router Advertisement	6
135	Neighbor Solicitation	6
136	Neighbor Advertisement	6
137	Redirect	6
150	Home Agent Address Discovery Request	12
151	Home Agent Address Discovery Reply	12

Table F-6. **ICMPv6 Destination Unreachable Messages**

Code Field Value	*Description*
0 - No Route to Destination	No route matching the destination was found in the routing table.
1 - Communication with Destination Administratively Prohibited	The communication with the destination is prohibited by administrative policy. This is typically sent when the packet is discarded by a firewall.
2 - Beyond Scope of Source Address	The destination is beyond the scope of the source address. A router sends this when the packet is forwarded by using an interface that is not within the scoped zone of the source address. This message is defined in the Internet draft titled "IPv6 Scoped Address Architecture."

continued

Table F-6 *continued*

Code Field Value	Description
3 - Address Unreachable	The destination address is unreachable. This is typically sent because of an inability to resolve the destination's link-layer address.
4 - Port Unreachable	The destination port was unreachable. This is typically sent when an IPv6 packet containing a UDP message arrived at the destination but there were no applications listening on the destination UDP port.

Table F-7. **ICMPv6 Parameter Problem Messages**

Code Field Value	Description
0 - Erroneous Header Field Encountered	An error in a field within the IPv6 header or an extension header was encountered.
1 - Unrecognized Next Header Type Encountered	An unrecognized Next Header field value was encountered. This is equivalent to the ICMPv4 Destination Unreachable-Protocol Unreachable message.
2 - Unrecognized IPv6 Option Encountered	An unrecognized IPv6 option was encountered.

Table F-8. **IPv6 Neighbor Discovery Option Types**

Type	Option Name	Source Document
1	Source Link-Layer Address	RFC 2461
2	Target Link-Layer Address	RFC 2461
3	Prefix Information	RFC 2461
4	Redirected Header	RFC 2461
5	MTU	RFC 2461
7	Advertisement Interval	"Mobility Support in IPv6" draft
8	Home Agent Information	"Mobility Support in IPv6" draft
9	Route Information	"Default Router Preferences and More-Specific Routes" draft

Table F-9. NEIGHBOR DISCOVERY MESSAGES AND THE OPTIONS THAT MIGHT BE INCLUDED

ND Message	*ND Options That Might Be Included*
Router Solicitation	Source Link-Layer Address option: Used to inform the router of the link-layer address of the host for the unicast Router Advertisement response.
Router Advertisement	Source Link-Layer Address option: Used to inform the receiving host(s) of the link-layer address of the router.
	Prefix Information option(s): Used to inform the receiving host(s) of on-link prefixes and whether to autoconfigure stateless addresses.
	MTU option: Used to inform the receiving host(s) of the IPv6 MTU of the link.
	Advertisement Interval option: Used to inform the receiving host how often the router (the home agent) is sending unsolicited multicast router advertisements.
	Home Agent Information option: Used to advertise the home agent's preference and lifetime.
	Route Information option(s): Used to inform the receiving host(s) of specific routes to add to a local routing table.
Neighbor Solicitation	Source Link-Layer Address option: Used to inform the receiving node of the link-layer address of the sender.
Neighbor Advertisement	Target Link-Layer Address option: Used to inform the receiving node(s) of the link-layer address corresponding to the Target Address field.
Redirect	Redirected Header option: Used to include all or a portion of the packet that was redirected.
	Target Link-Layer Address option: Used to inform the receiving node(s) of the link-layer address corresponding to the Target Address field.

Glossary

_ISATAP name: See ISATAP name.

.NET Framework: The programming model of the .NET platform for building, deploying, and running Extensible Markup Language (XML) Web services and applications.

6over4: An IPv6 coexistence technology that is used to provide IPv6 unicast and multicast connectivity across a multicast-enabled IPv4 infrastructure by treating the IPv4 network as a logical multicast link.

6over4 address: An address of the type [*64-bit prefix*]:0:0:*WWXX:YYZZ*, where *WWXX:YYZZ* is the colon hexadecimal representation of *w.x.y.z* (a public or private IPv4 address), which is used to represent a host for the 6over4 coexistence technology.

6to4: An IPv6 coexistence technology that is used to provide unicast IPv6 connectivity between IPv6 sites and hosts across the IPv4 Internet. 6to4 uses a public IPv4 address to construct a global IPv6 address prefix.

6to4 address: An address of the type 2002:*WWXX:YYZZ*:[*SLA ID*]:[*Interface ID*], where *WWXX:YYZZ* is the colon hexadecimal representation of *w.x.y.z* (a public IPv4 address), which is used to represent a node for the 6to4 coexistence technology.

6to4 host: An IPv6 host that is configured with at least one 6to4 address (a global address with the 2002::/16 prefix). 6to4 hosts do not require manual configuration and create 6to4 addresses by using standard address autoconfiguration mechanisms.

6to4 router: An IPv6/IPv4 router that supports the use of a 6to4 tunnel interface and is typically used to forward 6to4-addressed traffic between the 6to4 hosts within a site and other 6to4 routers or 6to4 relay routers on the IPv4 Internet.

6to4 relay router: An IPv6/IPv4 router that forwards 6to4-addressed traffic between 6to4 routers on the Internet and hosts on the IPv6 Internet.

A

AAAA record: The Domain Name System resource record type that is used to resolve a fully qualified domain name to an IPv6 address.

AAL5:   See ATM Adaptation Layer 5.

AH: See Authentication header.

address: An identifier that is assigned at the IPv6 layer to an interface or set of interfaces and can be used as the source or destination of IPv6 packets.

address autoconfiguration: The process of automatically configuring IPv6 addresses on an interface. See also stateless address autoconfiguration and stateful address autoconfiguration.

address resolution: The process of resolving the link-layer address for a next-hop IP address on a link.

address selection rules: The address selection logic that is needed to decide which pair of addresses to use for communication.

aggregatable global unicast address: Also known as global addresses, aggregatable global unicast addresses are identified by the Format Prefix of 001 (2000::/3). IPv6 global addresses are equivalent to public IPv4 addresses and are globally routable and reachable on the IPv6 portion of the Internet.

anonymous address: See temporary address.

anycast address: An address assigned from the unicast address space that identifies multiple interfaces and is used for one-to-one-of-many delivery. With the appropriate routing topology, packets addressed to an anycast address are delivered to a single interface—the nearest interface that is identified by the address.

APIPA: See Automatic Private IP Addressing.

Asynchronous Transfer Mode: A cell-based packet-switching technology that supports both isochronous (time-dependent) and non-isochronous data types.

ATM: See Asynchronous Transfer Mode.

ATM Adaptation Layer 5:   The ATM adaptation layer designed for LAN traffic and used to encapsulate IPv6 packets when they are sent across an ATM link.

Authentication header: An IPv6 extension header that provides data origin authentication, data integrity, and anti-replay services for the entire IPv6 packet, excluding changeable fields in the IPv6 header and extension headers.

Automatic Private IP Addressing: The automatic configuration of an IPv4 address in the 169.254.0.0/16 range and the subnet mask of 255.255.0.0 when an interface is configured for automatic configuration and a Dynamic Host Configuration Protocol (DHCP) server is not available.

automatic tunnel: An IPv6 over IPv4 tunnel in which the tunnel endpoints are determined by the use of logical tunnel interfaces, routes, and source and destination IPv6 addresses.

AutoNet: See Automatic Private IP Addressing.

B

binding acknowledgement: A message that contains the Binding Acknowledgement option in the Destination Options header. A binding acknowledgement is used in IPv6 mobility by correspondent nodes and home agents to confirm that a binding update was received and to indicate error conditions, if any.

binding cache: A table maintained by a correspondent node that maps the home address of mobile nodes that are away from home to their current care-of address.

binding request: A message that contains the Binding Request option in the Destination Options header. A binding request is used in IPv6 mobility by correspondent nodes and home agents to request a binding update from a mobile node that is away from home.

binding update: A message that contains the Binding Update option in the Destination Options header. A binding update is used in IPv6 mobility by a mobile node to update the binding cache entries of correspondent nodes and home agents for its current home address and care-of address.

binding update list: A list maintained by a mobile node that is away from home to record the most recent binding updates sent for the home agent and correspondent nodes.

C

care-of address: A global address used by a mobile node while it is connected to a foreign link.

CNA: See correspondent node address.

CoA: See care-of address.

coexistence: For IPv6, the use of technologies such as 6to4, ISATAP, and 6over4 to allow IPv6/IPv4 nodes to communicate while hosts and the routing infrastructure are being upgraded to support IPv6 or are being migrated from IPv4 to IPv6.

colon hexadecimal notation: The notation used to express IPv6 addresses. The 128-bit address is divided into 8 16-bit blocks. Each block is expressed as a hexadecimal number and adjacent blocks are delimited with colons. Within each block, leading zeros are suppressed. An example of an IPv6 unicast address in colon hexadecimal notation is 3FFE:FFFF:2A1D:48C:2AA:3CFF:FE21:81F9.

compatibility addresses: IPv6 addresses that are used when sending IPv6 traffic over an IPv4 infrastructure. Examples of compatibility addresses are IPv4-compatible addresses, 6to4 addresses, and ISATAP addresses.

configured tunnel: An IPv6 over IPv4 tunnel in which the tunnel endpoints are determined by manual configuration.

correspondent node: A node that is capable of communicating with a mobile node when it is away from home.

correspondent node address: The global address assigned to a correspondent node when it is communicating with a mobile node that is away from home.

critical router loop: The set of instructions that must be executed by a router to forward a packet.

D

DAD: See duplicate address detection.

default route: The route with the prefix ::/0. The default route matches all destinations and is the route used to determine the next-hop address if there are no other matching routes.

default router list: A list maintained by a host that lists all of the routers from which a router advertisement was received with the Router Lifetime field set to a nonzero value.

defending node: The node that is assigned a valid address set to a duplicate address being detected.

DELAY state: The state of the neighbor cache entry after it was in the STALE state and a packet is sent. The DELAY state is used to wait for an upper layer protocol to provide an indication that the neighbor is still reachable.

deprecated state: The state of an autoconfigured address in which the address is valid but its use is discouraged for new communication.

destination cache: A table maintained by IPv6 nodes that maps a destination address to a next-hop address and stores the path MTU.

Destination Options header: An IPv6 extension header that contains packet delivery parameters for either intermediate destinations or the final destination.

DHCP: See Dynamic Host Configuration Protocol.

distance vector: A routing protocol technology that propagates routing information in the form of a network ID and its "distance" (hop count).

DNS: See Domain Name System.

Domain Name System: A hierarchical namespace and protocol used for storing and querying name and address information.

double colon: The practice of compressing a single contiguous series of zero blocks of an IPv6 address to "::". For example, the multicast address FF02:0:0:0:0:0:0:2 is expressed as FF02::2. If there are two series of zero blocks of the same highest length, then by convention the left-most block is expressed as "::".

dual IP layer: The architecture of an IPv6/IPv4 node in which a single implementation of Transport layer protocols such as TCP and UDP operate over separate implementations of IPv4 and IPv6.

dual stack architecture: The architecture of an IPv6/IPv4 node that consists of two separate protocol stacks, one for IPv4 and one for IPv6, and each stack has its own implementation of the Transport layer protocols (TCP and UDP).

duplicate address detection: The process of using a Neighbor Solicitation message to confirm that a tentative address is not already assigned to an interface on the link.

Dynamic Host Configuration Protocol: A stateful address configuration protocol that provides an address and other configuration parameters.

E

Encapsulating Security Payload: An IPv6 extension header and trailer that provides data origin authentication, data integrity, data confidentiality, and anti-replay services for the payload encapsulated by the Encapsulating Security Payload header and trailer.

ESP: See Encapsulating Security Payload.

EUI: See Extended Unique Identifier.

EUI-64 address: A 64-bit link-layer address that is used as a basis for an IPv6 interface identifier.

Extended Unique Identifier: Link-layer addresses defined by the Institute of Electrical and Electronic Engineers (IEEE).

extension headers: Headers placed between the IPv6 header and the upper layer protocol data unit that provide IPv6 with additional capabilities.

F

FDDI: See Fiber Distributed Data Interface.

Fiber Distributed Data Interface: A desktop and backbone LAN technology specified by ANSI that uses token passing media access control, optical fiber, and operates at the bit rate of 100 Mbps.

flow: A series of packets exchanged between a source and a destination that requires special handling by intermediate IPv6 routers, as identified by the source and destination addresses and a non-zero value of the Flow Label field in the IPv6 header.

foreign link: A link that is not the mobile node's home link. A foreign link is identified by a foreign link prefix.

foreign link prefix: The global address prefix assigned to a foreign link and is used by a mobile node to obtain a care-of address.

Format Prefix: The high-order bits and their fixed values that define a type of IPv6 address.

FP: See Format Prefix.

fragment: A portion of an original IPv6 payload sent by a host. Fragments contain a Fragment header.

Fragment header: An IPv6 extension header that contains reassembly information for use by the receiving node.

fragmentation: The process of dividing an IPv6 payload into fragments by the sending host so that all the fragments are appropriately sized for the path MTU to the destination.

Frame Relay: A virtual circuit-based WAN technology designed to forward LAN data.

G

gateway: An IPv4 term for a router. IPv6 does not use the term "gateway" for a router.

global address: See aggregatable global unicast address.

Group ID: The last 112 bits or the last 32 bits (as per the recommendation of RFC 2373) of an IPv6 multicast address, which identifies the multicast group.

H

HA: See home address.

HAA: See home agent address.

home address: An address assigned to the mobile node when it is attached to the home link and through which the mobile node is always reachable, regardless of its location on the IPv6 Internet.

home agent: A router on the home link that maintains an awareness of the mobile nodes of its home link that are away from home and the care-of addresses that they are currently using. If the mobile node is on the home link, the home agent acts as an IPv6 router, forwarding packets addressed to the mobile node. If the mobile node is away from home, the home agent tunnels data sent to the mobile node's home address to the mobile node's current location on the IPv6 Internet.

home agent address: The global address of the home agent's interface on the home link.

Home Agent Address Discovery: An IPv6 mobility process in which a mobile node that is away from home discovers the list of home agents on its home link.

home agents list: A table maintained by home agents that contains the list of routers on the home link that can act as a home agent.

home link: The link that is assigned the home subnet prefix. The mobile node uses the home subnet prefix to create a home address.

Hop-by-Hop Options header: An IPv6 extension header that contains options that must be processed by every intermediate router and the destination.

host: A node that cannot forward IPv6 packets not explicitly addressed to itself (a nonrouter). A host is typically the source and a destination of IPv6 traffic, and silently discards traffic received that is not explicitly addressed to itself.

host group: The set of nodes listening for multicast traffic on a specific multicast address.

host route: A route to a specific IPv6 address. Host routes allow routing to occur on a per-IPv6 address basis. For host routes, the route prefix is a specific IPv6 address with a 128-bit prefix length.

Hosts file: A text file that is used to store name–to-address mappings. For computers running Windows XP or the Windows .NET Server 2003 family, the Hosts file is stored in the *SystemRoot*\System32\Drivers\Etc folder.

host-to-host tunneling: IPv6 over IPv4 tunneling where the tunnel endpoints are two hosts. For example, an IPv6/IPv4 node that resides within an IPv4 infrastructure creates an IPv6 over IPv4 tunnel to reach another host that resides within the same IPv4 infrastructure.

host-to-router tunneling: IPv6 over IPv4 tunneling where the tunnel begins at a sending host and ends at an IPv6/IPv4 router. For example, an IPv6/IPv4 node that resides within an IPv4 infrastructure creates an IPv6 over IPv4 tunnel to reach an IPv6/IPv4 router.

I

ICMPv6:   See Internet Control Message Protocol for IPv6.

IEEE 802 address: A 48-bit link-layer address defined by the IEEE. Ethernet, Token Ring, and FDDI network adapters use IEEE 802 addresses.

IEEE 802.3 SNAP encapsulation: The encapsulation used when IPv6 packets are sent over an IEEE 802.3-compliant Ethernet link.

IEEE 802.5 SNAP encapsulation: The encapsulation used when IPv6 packets are sent over a Token Ring link.

IEEE EUI-64 address: See EUI-64 address.

INCOMPLETE state: The state of a neighbor cache entry in which a neighbor solicitation has been sent and no response has been received.

interface: The representation of a physical or logical attachment of a node to a link. An example of a physical interface is a network adapter. An example of a logical interface is a tunnel interface that is used to send IPv6 packets across an IPv4 network by encapsulating the IPv6 packet inside an IPv4 header.

interface ID: The last 64 bits of an IPv6 unicast or anycast address.

Internet Control Message Protocol for IPv6:   A protocol that provides error messages for IPv6 packet routing and delivery and informational messages for diagnostics, Neighbor Discovery, Multicast Listener Discovery, and IPv6 mobility.

Internet Protocol Helper: An API that assists in the administration of the network configuration of the local computer. You can use Internet Protocol Helper (IP Helper) to programmatically retrieve information about the network configuration of the local computer, and to modify that configuration. IP Helper also provides notification mechanisms to ensure that an application is notified when certain aspects of the network configuration change on the local computer.

Internet Protocol security: A framework of open standards for ensuring private, secure communications at the Internet layer, through the use of cryptographic security services. IPSec supports network-level peer authentication, data origin authentication, data integrity, data confidentiality (encryption), and replay protection.

Intra-site Automatic Tunneling Addressing Protocol: A coexistence technology that is used to provide unicast IPv6 connectivity between IPv6 hosts across an

IPv4 intranet. ISATAP derives an interface ID based on the IPv4 address (public or private) assigned to a host. The ISATAP-derived interface ID is used for automatic tunneling across an IPv4 infrastructure.

invalid state: The state of an autoconfigured address in which it can no longer be used to send or receive unicast traffic. An address enters the invalid state after the valid lifetime expires.

IP Helper: See Internet Protocol Helper.

IP6.INT: The DNS domain created for IPv6 reverse queries. Also called pointer queries, reverse queries determine a host name based on the address.

IPSec: See Internet Protocol security.

IPv4 multicast tunneling: See 6over4.

IPv4 node: A node that implements IPv4. It can send and receive IPv4 packets. It can be an IPv4-only node or an IPv6/IPv4 node.

IPv4-compatible address: An address of the form $0:0:0:0:0:0:w.x.y.z$ or $::w.x.y.z$, in which $w.x.y.z$ is the dotted decimal representation of a public IPv4 address. For example, ::131.107.89.42 is an IPv4-compatible address. IPv4-compatible addresses are used for IPv6 Automatic Tunneling.

IPv4-mapped address: An address of the form $0:0:0:0:0:FFFF:w.x.y.z$ or ::FFFF:w.x.y.z, in which w.x.y.z is an IPv4 address. IPv4-mapped addresses are used to represent an IPv4-only node to an IPv6 node.

IPv4-only node: A node that implements only IPv4 (and is assigned only IPv4 addresses). This node does not support IPv6. Most hosts and routers installed today are IPv4-only nodes.

IPv6 Automatic Tunneling: The automatic tunneling performed when using IPv4-compatible addresses.

IPv6 host address record: See AAAA record.

IPv6 in IPv4:   See IPv6 over IPv4 tunneling.

IPv6 mobility: A set of messages and processes that allow an IPv6 node to arbitrarily change its location on the IPv6 Internet and still maintain existing connections.

IPv6 MTU: The maximum-sized IP packet that can be sent on a link.

IPv6 node: A node that implements IPv6. (It can send and receive IPv6 packets.) An IPv6 node can be an IPv6-only node or an IPv6/IPv4 node.

IPv6 over IPv4 tunneling: The encapsulation of IPv6 packets with an IPv4 header so that IPv6 traffic can be sent across an IPv4 infrastructure. In the IPv4 header, the Protocol field is set to 41.

IPv6 route table: See IPv6 routing table.

IPv6 routing table: The set of routes used to determine the next-hop address and interface for IPv6 traffic sent by a host or forwarded by a router.

IPv6/IPv4 node: A node that has an implementation of both IPv4 and IPv6.

IPv6-only node: A node that implements only IPv6 (and is assigned only IPv6 addresses). It is able to communicate with IPv6 nodes and applications only.

ISATAP: See Inter-site Automatic Tunneling Addressing Protocol.

ISATAP address: An address of the type [*64-bit prefix*]:0:5EFE:*w.x.y.z*, where *w.x.y.z* is a public or private IPv4 address, that is assigned to an ISATAP host.

ISATAP host: A host that is assigned an ISATAP address.

ISATAP name: The name that is resolved by computers running Windows XP with Service Pack 1 or a member of the Windows .NET Server 2003 family to automatically discover the IPv4 address of the ISATAP router. Computers running Windows XP attempt to resolve the name "_ISATAP."

ISATAP router: An IPv6/IPv4 router that responds to tunneled router solicitations from ISATAP hosts and forwards traffic between ISATAP hosts and nodes on another IPv6 subnet or network.

J

join latency: The time between when a new member of a multicast group on a subnet that does not contain any group members sends a Multicast Listener Report message and when multicast packets for that multicast group are sent on the subnet.

jumbogram: An IPv6 packet that has a payload larger than 65,535 bytes. Jumbograms are indicated by setting the Payload Length field in the IPv6 header to 0 and including a Jumbo Payload option in the Hop-by-Hop Options header.

Jumbo Payload option: An option in the Hop-by-Hop Options header that indicates the size of a jumbogram.

L

LAN segment: A portion of a link consisting of a single medium that is bounded by bridges or Layer 2 switches.

leave latency: The time between when the last member of the multicast group on a subnet sends a Multicast Listener Done message and when multicast packets for that multicast group are no longer sent on the subnet.

link: One or more LAN segments bounded by routers.

link MTU: The maximum transmission unit (MTU)—the number of bytes in the largest IPv6 packet—that can be sent on a link. Because the maximum frame size includes the link-layer medium headers and trailers, the link MTU is not the same as the maximum frame size of the link. The link MTU is the same as the maximum payload size of the link-layer technology.

link state: A routing protocol technology that exchanges routing information consisting of a router's attached network prefixes and their assigned costs. Link state information is advertised upon startup and when changes in the network topology are detected.

link-local address: A local-use address identified by the FP of 1111 1110 10 (FE80::/10), whose scope is the local link. Nodes use link-local addresses to communicate with neighboring nodes on the same link. Link-local addresses are equivalent to Automatic Private IP Addressing (APIPA) IPv4 addresses.

local-use address: An IPv6 unicast address that is not reachable on the IPv6 Internet. Local-use addresses include link-local and site-local addresses.

longest matching route: The algorithm used by the route determination process to select the routes in the routing table that most closely match the destination address of the packet being sent or forwarded.

loopback address: The IPv6 address of ::1 that is assigned to the loopback interface.

loopback interface: An internal interface created so that a node can send packets to itself.

M

MAC: See media access control, MAC address.

MAC address: The link-layer address for typical LAN technologies such as Ethernet, Token Ring, and FDDI. Also known as the physical address, the hardware address, or the network adapter address.

maximum transmission unit: The largest protocol data unit that can be sent. Maximum transmission units are defined at the link layer (maximum frame sizes) and at the Internet layer (maximum IPv6 packet sizes).

media access control: An IEEE-defined sub-layer of the ISO Data Link layer, whose responsibilities include framing and managing access to the media.

migration: For IPv6, the conversion of all IPv4-only nodes to IPv6-only nodes.

MLD: See Multicast Listener Discovery.

mobile IP: See IPv6 mobility.

mobile node: An IPv6 node that can change links, and therefore addresses, and maintain reachability using its home address. A mobile node has awareness of its home address and care-of address, and indicates its home address/care-of address mapping to the home agent and IPv6 nodes with which it is communicating.

MTU: See maximum transmission unit.

multicast address: An address that identifies zero or multiple interfaces and is used for one-to-many delivery. With the appropriate multicast routing topology, packets addressed to a multicast address are delivered to all interfaces identified by the address.

multicast group: The set of hosts listening on a specific multicast address.

Multicast Listener Discovery: A set of three ICMPv6 messages used by hosts and routers to manage multicast group membership on a subnet.

N

name resolution: The process of resolving a name to an address. For IPv6, name resolution resolves a host name or fully qualified domain name (FQDN) to an IPv6 address.

NAT: See Network Address Translator.

NBMA: See non-broadcast multiple access link.

ND: See Neighbor Discovery.

neighbor: A node connected to the same link.

neighbor cache: A cache maintained by every IPv6 node that stores the on-link IP address of a neighbor, its corresponding link-layer address, and an indication of the neighbor's reachability state. The neighbor cache is equivalent to the ARP cache in IPv4.

Neighbor Discovery: A set of ICMPv6 messages and processes that determine relationships between neighboring nodes. Neighbor Discovery replaces ARP, ICMP router discovery, and the ICMP Redirect message used in IPv4. ND also provides neighbor unreachability detection.

Neighbor Discovery options: Options in Neighbor Discovery messages that indicate link-layer addresses, prefix information, MTU, redirect, routes, and IPv6 mobility configuration information.

neighbor unreachability detection: The Neighbor Discovery process that determines whether the IPv6 layer of a neighbor is no longer receiving packets. The reachability state of each neighbor with which a node is communicating is stored in the node's neighbor cache.

network: Two or more subnets connected by routers. Another term for network is internetwork.

Network Address Translator: An IPv4 router that translates addresses and ports when forwarding packets between a privately addressed network and the Internet.

network prefix: The portion of an address that is fixed and used to determine the subnet ID, the route, or the address range.

network segment: See subnet.

next-hop determination: The process of determining the next-hop address and interface for sending or forwarding a packet based on the contents of the routing table.

Next-Level Aggregation Identifier: A 24-bit field in the aggregatable global unicast address that allows ISPs to create multiple levels of addressing hierarchy within their networks to both organize addressing and routing for downstream ISPs and identify organization sites.

NLA ID: See Next-Level Aggregation Identifier.

NO ENTRY EXISTS state: The state of a neighbor cache entry before it is added to the neighbor cache.

node: For IPv6, any device that runs an implementation of IPv6, which includes both routers and hosts.

non-broadcast multiple access link: A link-layer technology that supports a link with more than two nodes, but with no facility to broadcast a single packet to multiple locations. For example, X.25, Frame Relay, and ATM are NBMA network types.

NUD: See neighbor unreachability detection.

O

offending node: The node that is performing duplicate address detection for an address that is already in use on the subnet.

P

packet: The protocol data unit (PDU) that exists at the Internet layer. For IPv6, a packet is composed of an IPv6 header and a payload.

parameter discovery: A Neighbor Discovery process that enables hosts to discover configuration parameters, including the link MTU and the default hop limit for outgoing packets.

path MTU: The maximum-sized IPv6 packet that can be sent without using host fragmentation between a source and destination over a path in an IPv6 network. The path MTU is the smallest link MTU of all the links in the path.

Path MTU Discovery: The use of the ICMPv6 Packet Too Big message to discover the highest IPv6 MTU for all links between two hosts.

path vector: A routing protocol technology that exchanges sequences of hop information indicating the path for a route. For example, BGP-4 exchanges sequences of autonomous system numbers. An autonomous system is a portion of the network under the same administrative authority.

PDU: See protocol data unit.

PMTU: See path MTU.

Point-to-Point Protocol: A standardized point-to-point network encapsulation method that provides frame delimitation, protocol identification, and bit-level integrity services.

pointer records: See PTR records.

PortProxy: A component of IPv6 for the Windows .NET Server 2003 family that enables TCP proxying to facilitate the communication between nodes or applications that cannot connect using a common Internet layer protocol (IPv4 or IPv6).

PPP: See Point-to-Point Protocol.

preferred lifetime: The amount of time in which a unicast address configured through stateless address autoconfiguration remains in the preferred state. The preferred lifetime is indicated by the Preferred Lifetime field in the Prefix Information option in a Router Advertisement message.

preferred state: The state of an autoconfigured address for which the address is valid, its uniqueness has been verified, and it can be used for unlimited communications.

prefix: See network prefix.

prefix discovery: A Neighbor Discovery process by which hosts discover the network prefixes for local link destinations and for stateless address configuration.

prefix length notation: The practice of expressing network prefixes as *address/prefix-length,* in which *prefix-length* is the number of high-order bits in the address that are fixed.

prefix list: A list of link-prefixes maintained by each host. Each entry in the prefix list defines a range of IP addresses for destinations that are directly reachable (neighbors).

PROBE state: The state of a neighbor cache entry that was in the STALE and DELAY states for which reachability confirmation is in progress.

protocol data unit: The entity that exists at any layer of a layered network architecture. The protocol data unit of layer n becomes the payload of layer n-1 (a lower layer).

pseudo-header: A temporary header constructed for the purposes of calculating a checksum to associate the IPv6 header with its payload. For IPv6, a new pseudo-header format is used for the ICMPv6, TCP, and UDP checksum calculations.

pseudo-periodic: Occurring at intervals for which the interval between successive events is not constant. For example, router advertisements sent by IPv6 routers occur pseudo-periodically; the next interval for advertising is chosen randomly between a maximum and minimum value.

PTR records: DNS resource records that resolve an address to a name.

Q

quad-A record: See AAAA record.

R

rate limiting: The practice of sending messages based on a timer or a percentage of bandwidth, rather than for each message that encounters the same error. For example, ICMPv6 error messages are rate limited.

REACHABLE state: The state of an entry in the neighbor cache for which reachability has been confirmed by receipt of a solicited unicast Neighbor Advertisement message.

reassembly: The process of reconstructing the original payload from a series of fragments.

redirect: The Neighbor Discovery process of informing a host of a better first-hop IPv6 address to reach a destination.

Remote Procedure Call: An API that is used for creating distributed client/server programs. The RPC run-time stubs and libraries manage most of the details relating to network protocols and communication. RPC functions are used to forward application function calls to a remote system across the network.

route cache: See destination cache.

route determination process: The process of determining which single route in the routing table to use for forwarding a packet.

route table: See IPv6 routing table.

router: A node that can forward packets not explicitly addressed to itself. On an IPv6 network, a router also typically advertises its presence and host configuration information.

router advertisement: A Neighbor Discovery message sent by a router either pseudo-periodically or in response to a Router Solicitation message. Router advertisements typically contain at least one Prefix Information option, from which hosts create stateless autoconfigured unicast IPv6 addresses.

router discovery: A Neighbor Discovery process in which a host discovers the local routers on an attached link.

router-to-host tunneling: IPv6 over IPv4 tunneling in which the tunnel begins at a forwarding router and ends at an IPv6/IPv4 host. For example, an IPv6/IPv4 router creates an IPv6 over IPv4 tunnel to reach an IPv6/IPv4 host that resides within an IPv4 infrastructure.

router-to-router tunneling: IPv6 over IPv4 tunneling in which the tunnel begins at a forwarding router and ends at an IPv6/IPv4 router. For example, an IPv6/IPv4 router on the edge of an IPv6 network creates an IPv6 over IPv4 tunnel to reach another IPv6/IPv4 router.

Routing header: An IPv6 extension header that is used to perform source routing over an IPv6 network. A source route is a list of intermediate destinations for the packet to travel to on its path to the final destination.

routing loop: A condition on a network in which traffic is forwarded in a loop, never reaching its destination.

routing protocols: A series of periodic or on-demand messages containing routing information that is exchanged between dynamic routers.

routing table: See IPv6 routing table.

RPC: See Remote Procedure Call.

S

scope: For IPv6 addresses, the scope is the region of the network over which the traffic is intended to propagate.

scope ID: See *zone ID*.

SLA ID: See Site-Level Aggregation Identifier.

Site-Level Aggregation Identifier: A 16-bit field within the aggregatable global unicast address that is used by an individual organization to identify subnets within its site.

site-local address: A local-use address identified by the FP of 1111 1110 11 (FEC0::/10). The scope of a site-local address is the site. Site-local addresses are equivalent to the IPv4 private address space. Site-local addresses are not reachable from other sites, and routers must not forward site-local traffic outside the site.

site prefix: Typically, a 48-bit prefix that is used to indicate all the addresses in the site. Site prefixes are stored in a local site prefix table, which is used to confine traffic to the site.

solicited-node address: A multicast address used by nodes for the address resolution process. The solicited-node address is constructed from the prefix FF02::1:FF00:0/104 and the last 24 bits of a unicast IPv6 address. The solicited-node address acts as a pseudo-unicast address for very efficient address resolution on IPv6 links.

STALE state: The state of a neighbor cache entry for which the reachable time (the duration since the last reachability confirmation was received) has elapsed. The neighbor cache entry goes into the STALE state after the value (milliseconds) in the Reachable Time field in the Router Advertisement message (or a host default value) elapses and remains in this state until a packet is sent to the neighbor.

stateful address autoconfiguration: The use of a stateful address configuration protocol, such as DHCPv6, to configure IPv6 addresses and configuration parameters.

stateless address autoconfiguration: The use of Neighbor Discovery Router Advertisement messages to configure IPv6 addresses and configuration parameters.

static routing: The use of manually configured routes in the routing tables of routers.

subnet: For IPv6, one or more links that use the same 64-bit IPv6 address prefix. Another term for subnet is network segment.

subnet route: For IPv6, a route with a 64-bit prefix that indicates a specific IPv6 subnet.

subnet-router anycast address: The anycast address [*64-bit prefix*]:: that is assigned to router interfaces.

T

temporary address: An address that uses a randomly derived temporary interface ID. Temporary addresses change over time, making it more difficult to track someone's Internet usage based on their IPv6 address.

tentative address: A unicast address whose uniqueness has not yet been verified.

tentative state: The state of an autoconfigured address in which uniqueness has not yet been verified.

TLA ID: See Top-Level Aggregation Identifier.

Top-Level Aggregation Identifier: A 13-bit field in the aggregatable global unicast address that is allocated by IANA to local Internet registries that, in turn, allocate individual TLA IDs to large, long-haul ISPs.

U

unicast address: An address that identifies a single interface within the scope of the type of address and is used for one-to-one delivery. The scope of an address is the region of the IPv6 network over which the address is unique. With the appropriate unicast routing topology, packets addressed to a unicast address are delivered to a single interface.

unspecified address: The address 0:0:0:0:0:0:0:0 (or ::) that is used to indicate the absence of an address. It is equivalent to the IPv4 unspecified address of 0.0.0.0. The unspecified address is typically used as a source address for packets attempting to verify the uniqueness of a tentative address.

upper-layer checksum: The checksum calculation performed by ICMPv6, TCP, and UDP that incorporates the new IPv6 pseudo-header.

upper-layer protocol: A protocol above IPv6 that uses IPv6 as its transport. Examples include ICMPv6 and Transport layer protocols such as TCP and UDP (but not Application layer protocols such as FTP and DNS, which use TCP and UDP as their transport).

V

valid lifetime: The amount of time in which a unicast address configured through stateless address autoconfiguration remains in the valid state, which includes both the preferred and deprecated states. The valid lifetime is indicated by the Valid Lifetime field in the Prefix Information option sent in a Router Advertisement message.

valid state: The state of an autoconfigured address for which the address can be used for sending and receiving unicast traffic. The valid state includes both the preferred and deprecated states.

virtual mobile node: A node that represents the logical connection of a mobile node that is away from home to its home link. Because the mobile node that is away from home is always assigned its home address, it always has a virtual connection to the home link.

W

Win32 Internet Extensions: An API used for creating an Internet client application. An Internet client application is a program that accesses information from a network data source (server) by using Internet protocols such as FTP or HTTP.

Windows Sockets: A Windows API based on Berkeley Sockets that applications use to access the network services of TCP/IP, IPv6, and other protocols.

WinInet: See Win32 Internet Extensions.

WinSock: See Windows Sockets.

X

X.25:   A virtual circuit-based packet switching WAN technology originally designed in the 1970s to provide a reliable, connection-oriented service for LAN traffic.

Z

zone ID: An integer that specifies the zone of the destination for IPv6 traffic. In the Ping, Tracert, and Pathping commands, the syntax for specifying a zone ID is *IPv6Address%ZoneID*. Unless manually configured otherwise, the *ZoneID* value for link-local addresses is equal to the interface index. For site-local addresses, *ZoneID* is equal to the site number. If multiple sites are not being used, a zone ID for site-local addresses is not required. The *ZoneID* parameter is not needed when the destination is a global address.

Index

Index

JOSEPH DAVIES

Joseph Davies is a Microsoft Corporation employee working as a Program Manager for Content Development on the Networking and Communications team in the Windows .NET Server product group. He has been a technical writer and instructor of TCP/IP and networking technology topics for ten years. He wrote Windows 2000, Windows XP, and Windows .NET Server product documentation and Resource Kit chapters about TCP/IP, routing, remote access, virtual private networking, Internet Authentication Server (IAS), IPsec, and IPv6. Recently, he has written numerous white papers about IEEE 802.11 wireless deployment, IPv6, and Windows XP home networking; Joseph is the author for the monthly TechNet "Cable Guy" column (http://www.microsoft.com/technet). He is co-author of *Microsoft Windows 2000 TCP/IP Protocols and Services Technical Reference* and *Microsoft Windows .NET Server Family TCP/IP Protocols and Services Technical Reference*, both published by Microsoft Press. Joseph has a Bachelor's degree in Engineering Physics and is a Microsoft Certified Systems Engineer (MCSE), Microsoft Certified Trainer (MCT), and Master Certified NetWare Engineer (MCNE).

The manuscript for this book was prepared using Microsoft Word 2000. Pages were composed by Interactive Composition Corporation using Adobe PageMaker 6.5 for Windows, with text in Garamond and display type in Helvetica Black. Composed pages were delivered to the printer as electronic prepress files.

Cover Graphic Designer
Metholologie, Inc.

Cover Photographer
Creative Biz

Interior Graphic Designer
James D. Kramer

Copy Editor
Cathy Albano

Indexer
Lucie Haskins

HAND DRILL

Most of the hand tools in use today have changed little since the Middle Ages, the only major improvement being the use of steel instead of iron for cutting edges. One essential hand tool is the **hand drill,** often used to bore small holes—from ¼ inch down to $^1\!/_{16}$ inch or smaller—in wood, wallboard, and metal. A good hand drill has a three-jawed chuck, a cast-iron frame, and two rather than one pinion gears—the smaller gears that drive the big gear attached to the drill handle. A well-constructed hand drill runs smoothly and quietly.

At Microsoft Press, we use tools to illustrate our books for software developers and IT professionals. Tools very simply and powerfully symbolize human inventiveness. They're a metaphor for people extending their capabilities, precision, and reach. From simple calipers and pliers to digital micrometers and lasers, these stylized illustrations give each book a visual identity, and a personality to the series. With tools and knowledge, there's no limit to creativity and innovation. Our tagline says it all: *the tools you need to put technology to work.*

Get a **Free**
e-mail newsletter, updates,
special offers, links to related books,
and more when you

register on line!

Register your Microsoft Press® title on our Web site and you'll get a FREE subscription to our e-mail newsletter, *Microsoft Press Book Connections.* You'll find out about newly released and upcoming books and learning tools, online events, software downloads, special offers and coupons for Microsoft Press customers, and information about major Microsoft® product releases. You can also read useful additional information about all the titles we publish, such as detailed book descriptions, tables of contents and indexes, sample chapters, links to related books and book series, author biographies, and reviews by other customers.

Registration is easy. Just visit this Web page and fill in your information:

http://www.microsoft.com/mspress/register

Microsoft

MICROSOFT LICENSE AGREEMENT

Understanding IPv6 Companion CD

IMPORTANT—READ CAREFULLY: This Microsoft End-User License Agreement ("EULA") is a legal agreement between you (either an individual or an entity) and Microsoft Corporation for the Microsoft product identified above, which includes computer software and may include associated media, printed materials, and "online" or electronic documentation ("SOFTWARE PRODUCT"). Any component included within the SOFTWARE PRODUCT that is accompanied by a separate End-User License Agreement shall be governed by such agreement and not the terms set forth below. By installing, copying, or otherwise using the SOFTWARE PRODUCT, you agree to be bound by the terms of this EULA. If you do not agree to the terms of this EULA, you are not authorized to install, copy, or otherwise use the SOFTWARE PRODUCT; you may, however, return the SOFTWARE PRODUCT, along with all printed materials and other items that form a part of the Microsoft product that includes the SOFTWARE PRODUCT, to the place you obtained them for a full refund.

SOFTWARE PRODUCT LICENSE

The SOFTWARE PRODUCT is protected by United States copyright laws and international copyright treaties, as well as other intellectual property laws and treaties. The SOFTWARE PRODUCT is licensed, not sold.

1. **GRANT OF LICENSE.** This EULA grants you the following rights:

   a. **Software Product.** You may install and use one copy of the SOFTWARE PRODUCT on a single computer. The primary user of the computer on which the SOFTWARE PRODUCT is installed may make a second copy for his or her exclusive use on a portable computer.

   b. **Storage/Network Use.** You may also store or install a copy of the SOFTWARE PRODUCT on a storage device, such as a network server, used only to install or run the SOFTWARE PRODUCT on your other computers over an internal network; however, you must acquire and dedicate a license for each separate computer on which the SOFTWARE PRODUCT is installed or run from the storage device. A license for the SOFTWARE PRODUCT may not be shared or used concurrently on different computers.

   c. **License Pak.** If you have acquired this EULA in a Microsoft License Pak, you may make the number of additional copies of the computer software portion of the SOFTWARE PRODUCT authorized on the printed copy of this EULA, and you may use each copy in the manner specified above. You are also entitled to make a corresponding number of secondary copies for portable computer use as specified above.

   d. **Sample Code.** Solely with respect to portions, if any, of the SOFTWARE PRODUCT that are identified within the SOFTWARE PRODUCT as sample code (the "SAMPLE CODE"):

      i. **Use and Modification.** Microsoft grants you the right to use and modify the source code version of the SAMPLE CODE, *provided* you comply with subsection (d)(iii) below. You may not distribute the SAMPLE CODE, or any modified version of the SAMPLE CODE, in source code form.

      ii. **Redistributable Files.** Provided you comply with subsection (d)(iii) below, Microsoft grants you a nonexclusive, royalty-free right to reproduce and distribute the object code version of the SAMPLE CODE and of any modified SAMPLE CODE, other than SAMPLE CODE, or any modified version thereof, designated as not redistributable in the Readme file that forms a part of the SOFTWARE PRODUCT (the "Non-Redistributable Sample Code"). All SAMPLE CODE other than the Non-Redistributable Sample Code is collectively referred to as the "REDISTRIBUTABLES."

      iii. **Redistribution Requirements.** If you redistribute the REDISTRIBUTABLES, you agree to: (i) distribute the REDISTRIBUTABLES in object code form only in conjunction with and as a part of your software application product; (ii) not use Microsoft's name, logo, or trademarks to market your software application product; (iii) include a valid copyright notice on your software application product; (iv) indemnify, hold harmless, and defend Microsoft from and against any claims or lawsuits, including attorney's fees, that arise or result from the use or distribution of your software application product; and (v) not permit further distribution of the REDISTRIBUTABLES by your end user. Contact Microsoft for the applicable royalties due and other licensing terms for all other uses and/or distribution of the REDISTRIBUTABLES.

2. **DESCRIPTION OF OTHER RIGHTS AND LIMITATIONS.**

   - **Limitations on Reverse Engineering, Decompilation, and Disassembly.** You may not reverse engineer, decompile, or disassemble the SOFTWARE PRODUCT, except and only to the extent that such activity is expressly permitted by applicable law notwithstanding this limitation.

   - **Separation of Components.** The SOFTWARE PRODUCT is licensed as a single product. Its component parts may not be separated for use on more than one computer.

   - **Rental.** You may not rent, lease, or lend the SOFTWARE PRODUCT.

- **Support Services.** Microsoft may, but is not obligated to, provide you with support services related to the SOFTWARE PRODUCT ("Support Services"). Use of Support Services is governed by the Microsoft policies and programs described in the user manual, in "online" documentation, and/or in other Microsoft-provided materials. Any supplemental software code provided to you as part of the Support Services shall be considered part of the SOFTWARE PRODUCT and subject to the terms and conditions of this EULA. With respect to technical information you provide to Microsoft as part of the Support Services, Microsoft may use such information for its business purposes, including for product support and development. Microsoft will not utilize such technical information in a form that personally identifies you.

- **Software Transfer.** You may permanently transfer all of your rights under this EULA, provided you retain no copies, you transfer all of the SOFTWARE PRODUCT (including all component parts, the media and printed materials, any upgrades, this EULA, and, if applicable, the Certificate of Authenticity), **and** the recipient agrees to the terms of this EULA.

- **Termination.** Without prejudice to any other rights, Microsoft may terminate this EULA if you fail to comply with the terms and conditions of this EULA. In such event, you must destroy all copies of the SOFTWARE PRODUCT and all of its component parts.

3. COPYRIGHT. All title and copyrights in and to the SOFTWARE PRODUCT (including but not limited to any images, photographs, animations, video, audio, music, text, SAMPLE CODE, REDISTRIBUTABLES, and "applets" incorporated into the SOFTWARE PRODUCT) and any copies of the SOFTWARE PRODUCT are owned by Microsoft or its suppliers. The SOFTWARE PRODUCT is protected by copyright laws and international treaty provisions. Therefore, you must treat the SOFTWARE PRODUCT like any other copyrighted material **except** that you may install the SOFTWARE PRODUCT on a single computer provided you keep the original solely for backup or archival purposes. You may not copy the printed materials accompanying the SOFTWARE PRODUCT.

4. U.S. GOVERNMENT RESTRICTED RIGHTS. The SOFTWARE PRODUCT and documentation are provided with RESTRICTED RIGHTS. Use, duplication, or disclosure by the Government is subject to restrictions as set forth in subparagraph (c)(1)(ii) of the Rights in Technical Data and Computer Software clause at DFARS 252.227-7013 or subparagraphs (c)(1) and (2) of the Commercial Computer Software—Restricted Rights at 48 CFR 52.227-19, as applicable. Manufacturer is Microsoft Corporation/One Microsoft Way/Redmond, WA 98052-6399.

5. EXPORT RESTRICTIONS. You agree that you will not export or re-export the SOFTWARE PRODUCT, any part thereof, or any process or service that is the direct product of the SOFTWARE PRODUCT (the foregoing collectively referred to as the "Restricted Components"), to any country, person, entity, or end user subject to U.S. export restrictions. You specifically agree not to export or re-export any of the Restricted Components (i) to any country to which the U.S. has embargoed or restricted the export of goods or services, which currently include, but are not necessarily limited to, Cuba, Iran, Iraq, Libya, North Korea, Sudan, and Syria, or to any national of any such country, wherever located, who intends to transmit or transport the Restricted Components back to such country; (ii) to any end user who you know or have reason to know will utilize the Restricted Components in the design, development, or production of nuclear, chemical, or biological weapons; or (iii) to any end user who has been prohibited from participating in U.S. export transactions by any federal agency of the U.S. government. You warrant and represent that neither the BXA nor any other U.S. federal agency has suspended, revoked, or denied your export privileges.

DISCLAIMER OF WARRANTY

NO WARRANTIES OR CONDITIONS. MICROSOFT EXPRESSLY DISCLAIMS ANY WARRANTY OR CONDITION FOR THE SOFTWARE PRODUCT. THE SOFTWARE PRODUCT AND ANY RELATED DOCUMENTATION ARE PROVIDED "AS IS" WITHOUT WARRANTY OR CONDITION OF ANY KIND, EITHER EXPRESS OR IMPLIED, INCLUDING, WITHOUT LIMITATION, THE IMPLIED WARRANTIES OF MERCHANTABILITY, FITNESS FOR A PARTICULAR PURPOSE, OR NONINFRINGEMENT. THE ENTIRE RISK ARISING OUT OF USE OR PERFORMANCE OF THE SOFTWARE PRODUCT REMAINS WITH YOU.

LIMITATION OF LIABILITY. TO THE MAXIMUM EXTENT PERMITTED BY APPLICABLE LAW, IN NO EVENT SHALL MICROSOFT OR ITS SUPPLIERS BE LIABLE FOR ANY SPECIAL, INCIDENTAL, INDIRECT, OR CONSEQUENTIAL DAMAGES WHATSOEVER (INCLUDING, WITHOUT LIMITATION, DAMAGES FOR LOSS OF BUSINESS PROFITS, BUSINESS INTERRUPTION, LOSS OF BUSINESS INFORMATION, OR ANY OTHER PECUNIARY LOSS) ARISING OUT OF THE USE OF OR INABILITY TO USE THE SOFTWARE PRODUCT OR THE PROVISION OF OR FAILURE TO PROVIDE SUPPORT SERVICES, EVEN IF MICROSOFT HAS BEEN ADVISED OF THE POSSIBILITY OF SUCH DAMAGES. IN ANY CASE, MICROSOFT'S ENTIRE LIABILITY UNDER ANY PROVISION OF THIS EULA SHALL BE LIMITED TO THE GREATER OF THE AMOUNT ACTUALLY PAID BY YOU FOR THE SOFTWARE PRODUCT OR US$5.00; PROVIDED, HOWEVER, IF YOU HAVE ENTERED INTO A MICROSOFT SUPPORT SERVICES AGREEMENT, MICROSOFT'S ENTIRE LIABILITY REGARDING SUPPORT SERVICES SHALL BE GOVERNED BY THE TERMS OF THAT AGREEMENT. BECAUSE SOME STATES AND JURISDICTIONS DO NOT ALLOW THE EXCLUSION OR LIMITATION OF LIABILITY, THE ABOVE LIMITATION MAY NOT APPLY TO YOU.

MISCELLANEOUS

This EULA is governed by the laws of the State of Washington USA, except and only to the extent that applicable law mandates governing law of a different jurisdiction.

Should you have any questions concerning this EULA, or if you desire to contact Microsoft for any reason, please contact the Microsoft subsidiary serving your country, or write: Microsoft Sales Information Center/One Microsoft Way/Redmond, WA 98052-6399.

System Requirements

The companion CD consists of a number of folders, each containing unique files and programs intended to augment the book. Some folders have specific requirements, which are identified in the Readme files on the companion CD.

To view the eBook form of this book, you need any system that is capable of running Microsoft Internet Explorer version 5.01 or later. Microsoft Internet Explorer 6 is included on the CD.

To view the capture files (*.cap), you must have a version of Microsoft Network Monitor that is provided with Microsoft Systems Management Server 2.0 or the Windows .NET Server 2003 family.

The basic requirements of processor speed, memory size, hard disk space, display color-depth and resolution, and pointing device are determined by the version of Microsoft Windows you use to process the contents of the CD.

The CD-ROM drive should be 4X or faster. A faster drive is recommended if you intend to access the files and programs from the CD rather than copying them to a hard disk. Copying the CD contents to a hard disk and installing both the Microsoft Word Viewer program and the PowerPoint Viewer program will require approximately 65 MB of hard disk space.

There are no audio or video files on the CD; therefore, there are no requirements for sound cards.